Praise for *The Homeschooling Book of Answers*

"I can't imagine a more helpful book on homeschooling—a happy marriage of the realistic with the idealistic, the passionate with the practical. Until our schools are not just reformed but truly transformed, every parent should consider this alternative."

—George Leonard, author of *Education and Ecstasy* and *Mastery*

"If you plan to homeschool, make sure you read this book. Your child's education depends on it."

—Senator Vince Illuzzi

"*The Homeschoo* 　　　　　　　　　　　　　for homeschoolers or a 　　　　　　　　　　　　n's education. This book is a 　　　　　　　　　　　t their children learn—at hon 　　　　　　　　　　ts that have a difficult time 　　　　　　　　　　　　**per columnist**

"Delightfully 　　　　　　　　　　　　and critically *needed* work c 　　　　　　　　　　　oroughness. I can only app 　　　　　　　　　　　**arce, author of** *Magical Child*

LINDA DOBSON

THE

Homeschooling Book of Answers

The 88 Most Important Questions Answered by
Homeschooling's Most Respected Voices

PRIMA PUBLISHING

© 1998 by Linda Dobson

Photograph of Katharine Houk by Sandy McNay; photograph of Donna Nichols-White by Jill Sabella; photograph of Rebeccca Kochenderfer by Sirlin Photography; photograph of Janie Levine Hellyer by S. Vento; and photograph of Pat Montgomery by Terri Wheeler.

Products mentioned in this book are trademarks of their respective companies.

PRIMA PUBLISHING and colophon are registered trademarks of Prima Communications, Inc.

Library of Congress Cataloging-in-Publication Data

The homeschooling book of answers: the 88 most important questions answered by homeschooling's most respected voices / [compiled by] Linda Dobson.
    p.   cm.
  Includes index.
  ISBN 0–7615–1377–9
  1. Home schooling—United States—Miscellanea.   I. Dobson, Linda.
  LC40.H668 1998   98–18595
  371.04'2—dc21   CIP

  99 00 01 BB 10 9 8 7 6 5 4
Printed in the United States of America

How to Order
Single copies may be ordered from Prima Publishing, P.O. Box 1260BK, Rocklin, CA 95677; telephone (916) 632-4400. Quantity discounts are also available. On your letterhead, include information concerning the intended use of the books and the number of books you wish to purchase.

Visit us online at www.primapublishing.com

To the Memory of Grandma Lind,
who took the time to share the world
with a wide-eyed little girl

CONTENTS

1

Now That Homeschooling Is Legal and Safe . . .   3

2

Homeschool May Be Cheaper Than You Think   27

3

Can Homeschooling Fit *Your* Life Situation?   45

4

Rest in Peace, Fears About Socialization   79

5

"Educationese" You Can Understand   101

6

Okay, the Kids Are Home—*Now* What?   117

7

It's Effective! Assessing Your Child's Growth   171

8

You Mean I Don't Need to Know Algebra?! The Teen Years   185

9

Kids Say the Darnedest Things—About Homeschooling 209

10

The Home in Homeschool 229

11

Personally Speaking   245

12

Lifeboats: Final Inspiration   261

ACKNOWLEDGMENTS

Writing a book would always be twice as difficult without the continual support and encouragement given me by my cousin, Louise Pohlman, the big sister I never had. Over the years she has not just buoyed my spirit, but shared enough outlandish public school stories to keep me informed, laughing—and glad I'm homeschooling. Love you, "Weesie!"

Once again, my husband and at-home children, Adam and Erika, tolerated well the many times I was physically present but mentally absent, absorbed in the task of getting just the right words into the computer. Thanks for the little things you did to free up "just a few more minutes!" at the keyboard.

In a project involving as many people as this book has, there are countless more folks behind the scenes, like husbands and wives and children whose lives with the contributors inspire them, and whose support gives them time and opportunity to write. There are people like Mary E. Shannon who acted as e-mail go-between for Michelle Barone and me before Michelle got herself "wired," and Christine Webb who kindly became a contact person when I needed to get a message to her son, contributor Adam Grimm. Joan Harriss shared her specialized knowledge to help Rebecca Kochenderfer answer the question about sports, and Pat Lines and Laura Derrick kindly contributed the results of their research as appendices that make this book all the more valuable to its readers. There were still more writers who, upon learning of this project, volunteered their time and effort but, sadly, we were allotted a finite number of page to fill. Heartfelt appreciation to all. Your benevolent contributions were necessary pieces that helped make this book whole.

Many thanks, also, to the folks at Prima Publishing, from editors to legal staff, from Ben, wise enough to see the need for this book, to the sales staff who will make sure families have an opportunity to learn more about homeschooling through their work.

There remain only the contributors . . . and how to find the words to share with you how very much your support of this book has meant to me. Over the years as I've met most of you I've been touched by the depth of your understanding, the fire of your enthusiasm, and the warmth of your spirits. I still feel as if I know the few of you I haven't met in person from the way you sprinkle your writing with the same qualities.

We saw. We believed. We did it, gang! (And they say gathering homeschoolers is like trying to herd cats!) You shared the vision. You gave of yourselves—yet again—to the ideal of educational freedom we believe from the deepest parts of our Selves can serve this world's children well. And you did it all with joy in your hearts and smiles in your writing voices.

I've always thought a person fortunate if she discovers just a few kindred spirits while traveling through life. I have found *dozens*, and know life is that much sweeter because we call each other friend.

In as many ways as there are to "homeschool," I thank you.

INTRODUCTION

Another letter arrived today:

> Last September I was agonizing over the decision of whether or not to remove my two grade-school age children from public school. After reading your book, *The Art of Education*, I was inspired to give it a try. We've been homeschooling (unschooling, actually!) for almost four months and we all love it. I've seen great changes in my kids already—more creativity, curiosity, less stress. I . . . look at a lot of things differently now, including how we're socialized by institutions. I have a feeling this is just the beginning of a very interesting journey! Thank you so much for your inspiration and information. It changed our lives.

This sentiment is echoing across our nation and, increasingly, around the world: *Homeschooling changed our lives.*

It seems to give a lot of credit to what nonpractitioners see as merely an odd educational choice. Could it be there's something more to it than that?

Looking at homeschooling as an odd educational choice, or even as a valid educational choice, for that matter, places it in a very narrow context. This narrow context is unfortunate because it abruptly ends just where homeschooling begins. Considering homeschooling this way is like looking at someone's finger as it points toward a beautiful sunset. You will better understand the letter writer's enthusiasm when you look past the finger at this: *Homeschooling is a grassroots educational alternative that originates with the seed of parental love and commitment and blossoms into a lush garden of personal empowerment for child and parent.*

Herein lies the secret of the success of homeschooling as a national movement *and* the personal success of homeschoolers. The life-changing personal empowerment that results is still a secret after all these years, even though home education gets lots of media coverage. It's still a secret, even though just about everybody knows someone who homeschools these days. But it won't be a secret after you read this book.

To read *The Homeschooling Book of Answers* is to realize you can't separate homeschooling from the person practicing it. Homeschooling moves beyond a way to learn toward a way to live. This way of living necessitates well thought out, free choices within the framework of complete responsibility. There likely is nothing else you could do with your family that can so profoundly impact who you and your children become.

Since you can't separate homeschooling from the person doing it, this book gives you just that—more than four dozen people whose lives have been forever touched by this act. *The Homeschooling Book of Answers* reaps a bountiful harvest of personal empowerment. Collected for your easy reference is wisdom from parents with *over 400 years of homeschooling experience*. The dozen young contributors add *more than another 100 years' experience*. Additional contributors who have not practiced homeschooling themselves, but who have spent decades researching, writing, and speaking about it, lend their respected voices as well.

Be forewarned. These are voices that frankly express strong opinions. You won't agree with everyone; some may even make you grit your teeth. Hopefully, they'll all help you *think*— about what we as a society call education and what we do to our children in the name of that education. Hopefully, they'll all help you *feel*—what education can really be and what it's like to experience the promise of educational freedom fulfilled.

Who Should Read *The Homeschooling Book of Answers?*

Both the questions and respondents for *The Homeschooling Book of Answers* were carefully chosen to provide you with candid, informative, and entertaining answers to important questions about homeschooling. The questions cover the wide-ranging interests of those who repeatedly ask them. This book will be most helpful to:

- Parents who are considering or new to homeschooling
- Current homeschoolers looking for the ideas and inspiration usually found at homeschooling conferences
- Teachers, school board members, and school administrators
- Reporters, journalists, and political commentators
- Educational and social researchers
- Local, county, state, and national legislators

How to Use *The Homeschooling Book of Answers*

Please read the biographies first. Remember, you can't separate homeschooling from the person doing it. Get to know the people; that's what this book is all about. You'll discover they're very much like your neighbors, your friends, and your favorite aunt, just a lot more knowledgeable about how children learn, since they chose to accept complete responsibility for it. Before you read an answer, refer back to the biographies to see who wrote it. (Of course, if you have a photographic memory, you can skip this step.) Additionally, all contributors who listed contact information within their biographies are willing to be contacted for the legitimate needs of reporters, journalists, researchers, legislators, and so on.

Note the chapter titles. The titles reflect the broad topic areas into which the questions are divided. This way you can easily locate the topic you're most interested in at any particular reading. A quick scan of the questions within that topic in the table of contents will lead you to your particular question.

I hope you'll read *all* the answers to each question. This way you'll have a much broader understanding of the answer, and also begin to understand how many people—geographically, economically, politically, culturally, and religiously diverse—all came to similar conclusions while walking what are oftentimes very dissimilar paths.

The homeschooling books mentioned or recommended throughout this book are all included in appendix A so you may easily find the titles in your bookstore or library.

Sit back, put up your feet, and relax! While the education of our nation's youth is an important, serious issue, let these homeschoolers show you how to have your education and enjoy it, too!

The Bright Idea, or How *The Homeschooling Book of Answers* Came to Be

At the time I was in consultation with Prima Publishing acquisition editor Jamie Miller, I was in the midst of a summer spent speaking and giving workshops at homeschooling conferences. I met new friends and caught up with business and personal relationships with old friends, all of whom are some of the most interesting, educationally well-informed people I know. And I realized it was the collective energy and knowledge of all these people that made working at these conferences the enlightening, exciting, and personally rewarding experience it was. That's when it hit: The Bright Idea.

Not everyone can get to these conferences, I thought. Certainly those who are merely *considering* the idea of home education don't necessarily spend time to even search out a conference. Those with a professional interest in homeschooling often find themselves attending enough out of town conferences and events without adding more. Yet these are some of the people with the most important, most urgent questions about homeschooling, and the ones this collective energy and knowledge would most benefit.

So I proposed to Jamie The Bright Idea: a book of the most important and frequently asked questions about homeschooling answered by a few dozen or so of the most dedicated, most practiced, most knowledgeable, most commonsensical voices on homeschooling. Soon, the same mind that got The Bright Idea began spinning with the practical aspects of such a project. Did I just tell an editor I could get three dozen people, three dozen extremely active, busy people, to contribute to a book—without having asked any of them beforehand?

I told my husband what happened. "You must be crazy," he said.

"They'll do it," I said. "I just *know* they will." As I waited for acceptance of the idea, one day I hoped the publisher would like it and the next I hoped he would hate it and I wouldn't have to put what I *knew* to the ultimate test. I mean, what if most of them said no?

"It's a go," Jamie told me by phone. The publisher liked the idea, was excited about it, in fact.

Gulp.

Time to finalize the list of potential contributors. Time to create an invitation to contributors. Time to formulate the list of perfect questions. Time to decide which questions should go to whom. Time to send The Bright Idea out into the homeschooling community and see if it had wings.

I snail-mailed a few invitations, faxed one, and e-mailed the rest. I held my breath. The day is etched in my heart and mind forever.

Within an hour I nervously opened a return e-mail message which read, "I'm honored. Of course I will help in any way I can. Thank you for asking. Good luck! Rebecca (Kochenderfer)."

Two hours after sending the fax, I read the reply: "Hi, Linda. OK. Where are the questions; I'm not *here* very often! Love, John [Gatto]." I had actually found John, a favorite of the talk circuit, at home in his New York City apartment.

Lillian Jones wrote from California a couple of hours later: "This is so exciting—a dream come true! There are lots of good books around, but I can't point people to just one with certainty that they're going to 'get it.' This sounds like the closest thing to that dream book! . . .

So yes, yes—please deal me in. Wonderful idea! Thank you!"

The next few days were delightful as acceptances reached my computer via cyberspace. I could picture Deb Shell at the computer in her Vermont home responding, "This is such a timely project—so much of what you've said rings true; what's been nagging me since the [Growing Without Schooling] conference in August is the feeling that many long-time homeschoolers have accrued so much experience, yet there hasn't been an easily accessible means of communicating what we know. I embrace this project—yes, I would love to participate. Best regards, Deb." Two of Deb's daughters ultimately became contributors, too!

Did I forget to mention I asked these folks to contribute as the holiday season rapidly approached—and that I only gave them one month to complete their work?

"You can count me in!" wrote Janie Levine Hellyer from far-away Washington state. "Of course you just HAD to choose the busiest time of the year! Seriously, bring on the questions, and I'll clear some time on my calendar to work on them." My eyes—again—swelled with tears of gratitude.

"OK. You're on!" came the answer from Michigan's Clonlara School e-mail address. "But I give you fair warning that you will have to nudge me at least once, and possibly twice before I complete it. If you're game, I am. Pat (Montgomery)" But Pat surprised herself and me by meeting the deadline, just like *almost* all the other contributors. (Don't worry, gang, I'm not going to reveal any names here!)

Still others were sentimental about the project, like Katharine Houk. "The new book project sounds exciting," she wrote, "and I would be very happy to be part of it. Now that we are coming out at the other end of homeschooling, it would be an excellent time for synthesis and reflection on what this grand adventure has been about."

And then there was Donna Nichols-White. Not wanting any of the recipients to miss my e-mail message, I "shouted" the subject in all capital letters, in the fashion of the junk e-mail so many receive. "Good thing I noticed your screen name was ldobson," she wrote. "I thought you were selling girlie mags or something. I almost deleted your e-mail. I most definitely am willing to contribute to this book. It sounds great!" You'll soon be as glad as I was that Donna saved her invitation from a quick trip to the trash.

The responses from "the gang" were everything I'd hoped they would be—

and more. As acceptances piled up, the scope of what we as a team were about to attempt began to sink in, and yet again I wondered if I'd bitten off more than I could chew. I made and hung huge wall charts containing both the questions and contributors' names to ensure even distribution. I stuck dozens of index cards containing chapters and questions on the wall and constantly shuffled them around in search of the perfect order. Soon my makeshift office looked like a command post for . . . homeschool wisdom. After I gave the question distribution a tenth or twelfth "final" review, I scattered the questions across the United States and Canada.

You now hold the results in your hand: 500 collective years—half a millennium—of thoughts, observations, philosophies, tips, and personal stories that can lead you to the personal empowerment of homeschooling.

Thanks to this personal empowerment, growing numbers of children are today living and learning in the real world, donating time to community volunteer organizations, getting wooed by college admissions officers, and learning to get along with, enjoy, and appreciate people of all ages. The contributors have discovered that children growing free of the educational institution sprout up and learn naturally, following schedules suited to their unique interests and abilities.

Homeschooling brought learning, family life, values, and ideals of freedom into sharp focus for all of us. It allowed us to create this "dream" book. And, yes, homeschooling changed our lives. We hope this book and homeschooling can change yours, too.

CONTRIBUTOR BIOGRAPHIES

MICHELLE BARONE is a single homeschooling parent to two children and has been homeschooling for twelve years. She is a credentialed teacher in California. She is also a licensed marriage, family, and child counselor, and has a private counseling practice specializing in attachment-style parenting, alternative education, and personal growth issues. She also facilitates parent support and education groups. She is currently writing a book and lecturing on the topic of homeschooling as healing.

Phone: (818) 951-7744
E-mail: mebarone@earthlink.net

CHRIS CARDIFF, a homeschooling father of three girls, has over twelve years experience. He is the founding president of the California Homeschool Network and the former executive director of the Separation of School and State Alliance. With his two eldest daughters, he edits *AWL News,* the monthly newsletter of All Ways Learning of San Jose, California. A homeschooling crusader by night, during the day he's a mild-mannered director of engineering at Netscape Communications Corporation.

California Homeschool Network
Phone: (800) 327-5339
E-mail: tifchris@aol.com
Web site:
http://people.netscape.com/ccardiff

CAFI COHEN homeschooled her two children for eight years, from about ages ten to eighteen. She writes the "Older Kids" column for *Home Education Magazine,* cohosts the Web-based Kaleidoscapes Homeschooling Bulletin Boards, and presents workshops at homeschooling conferences across the nation. She wrote *And What About College? How Homeschooling Leads to Admissions to the Best Colleges and Universities.* Her Web site addresses the challenges of homeschooling teenagers. She and her husband live on California's central coast.

160 Cornerstone Lane
Arroyo Grande, CA 93420
Phone: (805) 473-4963
E-mail: cafi@worldnet.att.net
Web site:
http://www.concentric.net/~ctcohen

DAVID COLFAX is a fourth-term at-large trustee of his county's board of education, and until recently hosted a weekly public radio public affairs program. A former professor of sociology, he has served as a social research and forensic consultant to public and private, local, state, and national agencies such as the National Institutes of Health and the U.S. Department of Education. With his wife, Micki, he coauthored *Homeschooling for Excellence* and *Hard Times in Paradise.*

Colfax Associates
246 Redwood Ridge Road
Boonville, CA 95415
E-mail: dcolfax@pacific.net

For book information:
Mountain House Press
Box 353
Philo, CA 95466

MICKI COLFAX is a graduate of Penn State who attended the London School of Economics. She has taught in the United States, Canada, and England, and has served as director of field operations for many educational survey research projects. Micki and David are proud grandparents of Bailey, frequently speak at educational conferences, and together survived an onslaught of media attention when the first of their three sons was homeschooled into Harvard in the early 1980s. Their fourth son is currently a student in Sacramento.

(See David Colfax for contact information.)

ADAM DOBSON, fourteen, lives in the Adirondack mountains of New York and has been homeschooled his entire life. He enjoys music, sports, outdoor activities, computers, and his apprenticeships. He has won a Grammy, an Emmy, an Oscar, a Pulitzer, and a Nobel Peace Prize. He is also a spy for the American government. (He just needs a few years for reality to catch up.)

LINDA DOBSON is the author of *The Art of Education* (Holt Associates) and the forthcoming *Complete Book of Home Education: A Parent's Guide to Education the Natural Way* (Element Books); she has been *Home Education Magazine* news editor since 1992. She has learned at home with three children since 1985, cofounded a local support group, and written dozens of articles, including one of the first on homeschooling to appear in a national magazine: *Good Housekeeping*. Linda is a popular conference speaker and workshop presenter. She currently sits on the board of trustees of Saranac Lake Free Library, is an election inspector, a notary public, and a die-hard Beatles fan.

PO Box 85
Rainbow Lake, NY 12976
Phone/Fax: (518) 327-5245
E-mail: ldobson@aldus.northnet.org
Web site:
http://www.geocities.com/Athens/
Olympus/4196

KIRBY DODD, eleven, has never been to school, but nobody can tell without asking. His reading primers were *Nintendo Players' Guides* and *Nintendo Power Magazine,* and he has an orange belt in karate from the local Shorin Ryu dojo. He is named after his grandfather, not a Nintendo character or a vacuum cleaner (honest).

MARTY DODD (was at the time of this writing) an eight-year-old, ice-hockey-playing, unschooled kid in Albuquerque, New Mexico. He has an older brother and a younger sister. He wears his hair short to bald, sings funny songs, makes up characters and draws them. Marty's specialty is putting things together without the directions, a manly art that drives moms crazy (especially when the little men are good at it).

SANDRA DODD lives in Albuquerque, New Mexico, with her husband, Keith, and their three children, Kirby, Marty, and Holly, who have never been to school. Kirby was born in 1986, and Sandra's responses were made when he would have been in sixth grade (had he attended school). Sandra has a degree in English, and taught junior high school for six years. For fun she writes, plays music, and sings, and amazes her kids with things and ideas. Sandra edits *Home Education Magazine*'s "Online Newsletter."

2905 Tahiti Court, NE
Albuquerque, NM 87110
Phone: (505) 299-2476
E-mail: SANDRADODD@aol.com

SUSAN EVANS and her family, including four children (Luke, born in 1977; Jesse, in 1979; Margaret, in 1982; and Kathryn, in 1986), live in southeastern Michigan. She has volunteered over the years for several family centered organizations: counseling breastfeeding mothers in La Leche League, planning homeschooling conferences for Clonlara School, coordinating the office for the National Homeschool Association, leading workshops at the Family Empowerment Institute's retreats, and representing Holt Associates at midwestern homeschooling conferences.

E-mail: SAMagill@aol.com

JOHN TAYLOR GATTO was a public school teacher in New York for thirty-five years, including five at the university level. He was named New York State Teacher of the Year twice and New York City Teacher of the Year three times by various organizations. He has spoken at NASA, the White House, United Technologies, Omega Institute, and for over 500 other organizations in forty-nine states and seven foreign countries. He is the author of *Dumbing Us Down*, *The Exhausted School*, and *The Empty Child* (forthcoming), and is listed in *Who's Who*.

The Odysseus Group
295 E. 8th Street
New York, NY 10009
Phone: (212) 529-9327
Fax: (212) 721-6124 (Rarely able to respond to personal correspondence)

NANCY AND BILLY GREER met and became friends while attending colleges near each other. A crucial kiss in front of the library marked a turning point in the relationship and a shared passion for books that led to marriage in 1982. Involvement in homeschooling began in 1988 with the birth of their son. "In trying to decide if we should start saving for a private school education or rely on public education, we visited several schools and read about many educational philosophies. No one program offered everything we were interested in, and we saw that parental involvement seemed the most important factor in learning success. Homeschooling allowed us to tailor a program that suited our family and maximized parental involvement." In 1992 Nancy and Billy and two other people started North County Home Educators, a Maryland support group open to anyone interested in home learning. They created the Family Unschoolers Network in 1994, which offers support via *F.U.N. News,* a quarterly newsletter, and discounted books through F.U.N. Books.

> Family Unschoolers Network
> 1688 Belhaven Woods Court
> Pasadena, MD 21122-3727
> Fax/Voice Mail: (410) 360-7330
> E-mail: FUN@IQCweb.com
> Web site:
> http://www.IQCweb.com/fun

MARY GRIFFITH is the author of *The Unschooling Handbook: How to Make the World Your Classroom* and *The Homeschooling Handbook: From Preschool to High School, a Parent's Guide,* both from Prima Publishing. She is past editor of *California HomeSchooler* and a longtime activist with the Homeschool Association of California. For the past ten years, she's spent the bulk of her nonwriting time unschooling with her two daughters.

> 5098 Foothills Boulevard, Suite 3-398
> Roseville, CA 95678
> E-mail: mgriff@ns.net
> Web site: http://www.ns.net/~mgriff

ADAM GRIMM was named Oregon's only homeschooled National Merit Scholar in 1997. Adam earned a perfect 800 on the verbal portion of both his PSAT and SAT exams. Primarily an unschooler, as a teenager Adam chose to plot his own educational course, which included lots of exploring, travel, reading, video watching, lectures, museum visits, games, computer work, and some community college classes. He was also awarded a Type 1 Air Force ROTC scholarship, which he is using to study electrical engineering and computer science at

Rensselaer Polytechnic Institute (RPI) in New York, and a room and board scholarship from RPI.

> E-mail: grimma@rpi.edu

MARK AND HELEN HEGENER are the parents of five children, John, twenty-three; Jim, twenty-one; Jody Ellen, eighteen; Christopher, sixteen; and Michael, twelve. All of their children have always been homeschooled. The Hegener family has published *Home Education Magazine* since 1983, and they have appeared as featured speakers at homeschooling conferences across the nation. They lived in Washington until 1997, when they moved their entire family, their publishing business, and their several horses to Alaska.

> *Home Education Magazine*
> PO Box 1587
> Palmer, AK 99645
> Phone: (907) 746-1336
> Fax: (907) 746-1335
> E-mail: HomeEdMag@aol.com
> Web site: www.home-ed-press.com

SHARI HENRY and her husband, Tim Jones, live in Huntsville, Alabama. They have always homeschooled their three children—TJ, twelve; Bekah, nine; and Phoebe, five. Shari is a columnist and senior editor for *Homeschooling Today* magazine, and otherwise likes to read, cook, 'blade, bike, and laugh with her family.

> E-mail: ShariHenry@aol.com

DORIS HOHENSEE is the mother of six children, ages five to seventeen, who learn at home. When the New Hampshire legislature enacted a home education law in 1990, she found it necessary to become politically active while openly refusing to comply with the demands of the new law. In 1993, she started discussing politics on the Internet to try to hold back the tide of regulatory homeschooling laws.

15 Swart Terrace
Nashua, NH 03060
Phone: (603) 881-8323
E-mail: doris@mainstream.net

MICHAEL HOHENSEE was born in 1980. He is a science and engineering enthusiast who also fences epée. He acquired anarchistic attitudes primarily from the works of L. Neil Smith and Robert Heinlein. Since the age of four, he has been homeschooled, unschooled, high schooled ("briefly, thank heaven"), and college schooled, in that order. He prefers unschooling to homeschooling, and college to high school. Next fall he hopes to attend a university with like-minded technogeeks. He resides in Nashua, New Hampshire, with five younger siblings and nine pet cockatiels.

15 Swart Terrace
Nashua, NH 03060
Phone: (603) 881-8323
E-mail: michael@mainstream.net

KATHARINE HOUK, homeschooling since 1983, brings people together in groups, learning centers, and educational events. She believes that by learning together, we can each become spirited inventors of our lives. She is cofounder/director of the Alliance for Parental Involvement in Education (AllPIE), works as an artist in Chatham, New York, and is currently attending divinity school. Katharine's husband, Seth Rockmuller, and their children—Tahra, twenty-eight; Ben, nineteen; and Emily, sixteen—have been a vital part of her life and work.

Alliance for Parental Involvement in
   Education
PO Box 59
East Chatham, NY 12060-0059
Phone/Fax: (518) 392-6900
E-mail: allpie@taconic.net
Web site: http://www.croton.com/allpie

THERESA HYLAND, thirteen, has been homeschooling for three years. Her interests include history, music, science, world cultures, and anything Scottish. She enjoys belonging to the official *Star Wars* fan club. She is a member of the Johns Hopkins University Center for Talented Youth and received an academic award. Theresa plans to be a historian, with main interests in the Civil War and historical American music. She lives in Lake Clear, New York, where she produces *Mountain Whispers,* a subscription-based newsletter for homeschoolers.

LINDSEY JOHNSON, sixteen, has been unschooled her whole life. ("My parents discovered John Holt when I was three.") She has three brothers and two sisters who are also unschooled. Lindsey is writing a book about the dangers of compulsory education, a result of her new-found interest in why our current educational system is failing us. She plans to continue writing, pursue an acting career, and carry her autodidactic lifestyle as she gets older.

E-mail: TsalagiEye@aol.com

LILLIAN JONES earned a degree in anthropology, trained to be an elementary teacher, substituted in schools, but never felt comfortable with what she found there. She feels from firsthand experience that teaching credentials (and college degrees) are highly overrated as measures of competence in the real world. Along with her other interests, she is a homeschool advocate and a volunteer with the HomeSchool Association of California. She and her husband, Ed, have a teenage son, Ethan.

E-mail: wrensong@monitor.net

TJ JONES, twelve, has been homeschooling all his life and plans to stay home through high school. He enjoys all types of sports, especially hockey (ice and roller) and competitive swimming.

LARRY AND SUSAN KASEMAN have been learning through homeschooling with their four children since 1979. They are very active in the Wisconsin Parents Association, a statewide inclusive grassroots homeschooling organization of which Larry is executive director. They are the authors of *Taking Charge Through Homeschooling: Personal and Political Empowerment* and columnists for *Home Education Magazine*. Together they hike, sing, garden, work with families, and spend time with their children.

MEGAN KASEMAN, sixteen, is delighted to be making her debut as a published writer. She's been homeschooling forever and acting for eight years. Her favorite roles include Ophelia in *Hamlet*, title roles in *Othello* and *Romeo and Juliet* (Romeo), and

Rebecca Gibbs in *Our Town*. Other activities include singing, listening to music, spending time with her family and her cat, Katza. She dedicates her writing to Richard and Anne with a heart full of thanks and love.

REBECCA KOCHENDERFER is editor and publisher of "The Education Source," an Internet newsletter with 150,000 readers. Recent features include Internet reviews and educational information on science, math, distance learning, and alternative education. In addition to her newsletter, Rebecca is currently writing a book on alternative education. She has a master of arts degree in education, and over ten years teaching experience in the United States, Japan, Germany, and the Caribbean. Although her children are young (seven and under), she feels as if she has been homeschooling them since they were born.

The Education Source
3751 Bolsa Court
Sacramento, CA 95864
Phone: (916) 488-6589
E-mail: editor@edusource.com
Web site: http://www.edusource.com

JANIE LEVINE HELLYER has been active in the homeschool community for many years and is a frequent guest speaker at conferences and conventions across the country. She is the editor and publisher of *Family Learning Exchange Online* (FLExOnline), an electronic homeschooling magazine, and hosts several popular Internet chats for homeschool parents. She has developed and teaches a course on homeschooling at

Evergreen State College in Olympia, Washington, and is the mother of three homeschoolers, ages fifteen to twenty-seven.

> Family Learning Exchange
> PO Box 5629
> Lacey, WA 98509-5629
> Phone: (360) 491-5193
> E-mail: Editor@flexonline.org
> Web site: http://www.flexonline.org

PATRICIA LINES has been writing on homeschooling for over twenty years, tracking the movement practically from its infancy. She is the proud mom of a twenty-four-year-old computer genius who was never formally homeschooled, but who learned quite a lot on his own outside of school. She is currently on sabbatical from her position with the National Institute on Student Achievement, Curriculum and Assessment, and is writing a dissertation for Catholic University of America on the idea of education as a private affair, as articulated by thinkers from John Locke to the Antifederalists. She is also a senior fellow at Discovery Institute in Seattle.

> Discovery Institute
> 1402 Third Avenue
> Seattle, WA 98101
> Phone: (206) 292-0401
>
> After October 1998:
> 916 Maryland Avenue, NE
> Washington, D.C. 20002
> Phone: (202) 543-3370

MARY H. MCCARTHY and family have been homeschooling since 1981, after hearing John Holt speak. They live in New Jersey, where Mary occasionally writes for *Home Education Magazine* when she isn't searching the house for her sanity.

> 231 North Avenue W. #183
> Westfield, NJ 07090
> E-mail: HSLRAnj@home.com

DR. PAT MONTGOMERY is an energetic, indefatigable advocate for home-based educators and the mother of two adult "children." In 1967, she started an innovative private day school for her children in Ann Arbor, Michigan. They taught her a great deal about the natural development of children, and she's been sharing it with anyone who will listen ever since. She extended the philosophy and practices of her school to home educators the world over through the Clonlara School Home-Based Education Program, founded in 1979.

DR. RAYMOND MOORE is an author, researcher, former city school superintendent, and college, university, and consortium head: Chicago, Johns Hopkins, Stanford, Tulane, and Wisconsin. He is noted for upgrading and making colleges and universities debt-free. While graduate research and programs officer for the U.S. Department of Education, he wrote books and articles pioneering interinstitutional cooperation in higher education. He is also internationally known for creative work-study plans at all educational levels here and abroad, and international research on school entrance age. Moore is considered by many to be the "grandfather" of modern homeschooling, America's largest successful education movement.

The Moore Foundation
Box 1
Camas, WA 98607
Phone: (360) 835-5500
Fax: (360) 835-5392
E-mail: moorefnd@pacifier.com
Web site: www.casslink.com/
    moorefoundation

DOROTHY MOORE is an internationally known author, consultant, editor, and child specialist in curricula, reading, and remedial education, and a university teacher honored by school systems, colleges, and universities. She is also the founding head of a medical school cerebral palsy center. Known by many as "grandmother" of the modern homeschool movement, which she has been involved in since 1944. She is the co-author of the scholarship-winning Moore Formula, a customized low-cost, low-stress, readiness-oriented plan for achievement, behavior, and sociability through a study-work-service balance.

See Raymond Moore.

DONNA NICHOLS-WHITE is the mother of three homeschoolers, the owner and publisher of *The Drinking Gourd Multicultural Home Education Magazine, The Catalog for Independent Learning,* a public speaker, and a writer. She is a contributing author to several books, including *500 Great Books by Women: A Reader's Guide, Freedom Challenge: African-American Homeschoolers,* and *Deschooling Our Lives.* Her book, *Brainwash Your Own,* will be distributed in July 1998.

The Drinking Gourd
PO Box 2557
Redmond, WA 98073
Phone: (206) 836-0336
Fax: (206) 868-1371
E-mail: TDrnkngGrd@aol.com
Web site: www.thedrinkinggourd.com

NANCY PLENT was a school hater who married another school hater. They traded horror stories for years and were determined to find a way out for their son. John Holt and GWS (Growing Without Schooling) came along at just the right time. "I got caught up in the movement. For the last twenty years I have been publishing a New Jersey newsletter, doing seminars, writing 'unschool' curriculum, and am currently working on a book about famous homeschoolers."

Unschoolers Network
2 Smith Street
Farmingdale, NJ 07727
Phone: (732) 938-2473

WENDY PRIESNITZ is a Canadian homeschooling pioneer. With her husband, Rolf, she helped their two daughters Heidi, twenty-five, and Melanie, twenty-four, learn at home when it was almost unheard of in Canada. In 1979, she founded the Canadian Alliance of Home Schoolers, which provides guidance, support, and information to families across Canada. She continues to share her experience and long-term perspective through workshops, speeches, articles and books, research, and consulting to individuals and governments. Among the eight books she has written is *School Free,* a Canadian bestseller about home-based education. As owner of The Alternate Press, a twenty-two-year-old periodical and book publishing company, Wendy edits *Natural Life,* a newsmagazine focusing on personal and grassroots efforts that integrate economic, political, and social issues. She is an established investigative journalist, writes a weekly small business newspaper column, hosts a daily radio program, and is featured in *Who's Who of Canadian Women.*

Natural Life
RR 1
St. George, Ontario N0E 1N0
Canada
Phone: (519) 448-4001
Fax: (519) 448-4411
E-mail: natural@life.ca
Web site: http://www.life.ca/wendy

ANNAQUISTA PYKOSZ, eleven, is an unschooler who lives on a homestead in central Vermont with her mother, father, and younger brother. Over the years her interests have included theater, horses, piano, cooking, and antiques. Presently, she enjoys attending flea markets, making discoveries on the computer, sewing, hiking, reading, traveling, gardening, and watching movies. Annaquista is editor of a newsletter for adolescent unschoolers. She plans to own her own business by the age of sixteen and is already saving for her first car.

JEAN REED was raised in Winnetka, Illinois. She studied music, dance, won trampoline medals, was a nationally certified ski instructor, loved to sail, play her guitar, and was pretty much of a goof-off until she met Donn in 1962. She is publisher of *The Home School Source Book.*

Brook Farm Books
PO Box 246
Bridgewater, ME 04735

Alternate address:
Glassville, New Brunswick E0J 1L0
Canada
Phone/Fax: (506) 375-4680

DONN REED worked as a carpenter, radio announcer, truck driver, dishwasher, librarian, teacher, foundry worker, peace marcher, psychiatric aide, tax assessor, sawmill edgerman, migrant field worker, reporter, columnist, newspaper editor, and publisher. He's been listed in *Who's Who in American Education.* He served three years in jail as a conscientious objector, where he received a Meritorious Service Award from the U.S. Bureau of Prisons for work with adult illiterates. Married thirty-two years, the Reeds homesteaded in Vermont and Canada, birthed four children at home, and spent twenty-four years homeschooling. Donn wrote and published *The First Home School Catalogue* in 1981, the very first of the homeschooling catalogs. He wrote *The Home School Source Book* in 1991 (second edition 1994). Since Donn's death in 1995, Jean has taken over as manager of Brook Farm Books, and is revising *The Home School Source Book* in preparation for its third edition.

BECKY AND RANDY RUPP, both cell biologists, have three sons—Josh, sixteen, Ethan, fifteen, and Caleb, thirteen. They live in very rural Vermont, where they garden, stargaze, skate, read, cross-country ski, juggle, and plow snow. Becky has written several books, including *Everything You Never Learned About Birds* (Storey Communications, 1995), *Good Stuff* (Holt Associates, 1997), *Committed to Memory: How We Remember and Why We Forget* (Crown, 1998), *The Dragon of Lonely Island* (Candlewick, 1998), *The Home Learning Source Book* (Crown, 1998), and *Getting Started in Homeschooling* (Crown, 1998). The boys, who have always been homeschooled, are all strong, good-looking, and above average.

WILL AND MARGARET SHAW have been home-schooling for thirteen years in rural Louisa County, Virginia. Their two younger children are still being homeschooled; the older two are in college. Will is employed as a physical plant superintendent at the University of Virginia in Charlottesville. Will and Margaret were both trained to teach in public schools, but they overcame this handicap to become successful homeschoolers. Will has been a lobbyist for homeschool interests and is president of Virginia Home Education Association.

> Virginia Home Education Association
> PO Box 5131
> Charlottesville, VA 22905
> Phone: (540) 832-3578
> E-mail: vhea@virginia.edu

SUSANNAH SHEFFER has edited *Growing Without Schooling* magazine for eleven years. She is editor of *A Life Worth Living: Selected Letters of John Holt,* and of Heinemann's *Innovators in Education* series, which brings radical education classics back into print. Her own books include *Writing Because We Love To: Homeschoolers at Work* and *A Sense of Self:*

Listening to Homeschooled Adolescent Girls. She is married to Aaron Falbel, who also writes about issues in education.

> Holt Associates/Growing Without
>   Schooling
> 2269 Massachusetts Avenue
> Cambridge, MA 02140
> Phone: (617) 864-3100
> Fax: (617) 864-9235
> E-mail: HoltGWS@aol.com or
> HoltGWS@erols.com
> Web site: www.HoltGWS.com

DEB SHELL has been unschooling for more than twenty years, since her oldest daughter was born. She is currently working as a clinical mental health counselor and home-study specialist. She has directed the Resource Center for Homeschooling since 1995. In her spare time, she is also a potter, enjoys quilting, writing, reading, and gardening. She lives with her husband, Fred, four daughters (Mae, Sara, Emily, and Eva), and their five noisy dogs in Georgia, Vermont.

> The Resource Center for
>   Homeschooling
> RR 2, Box 289-C
> St. Albans, VT 05478
> Phone/Fax: (802) 524-9645
> E-mail: shell@together.net

MAE SHELL has been an unschooler her whole life (twenty years). She works at a small public library, and is currently pursuing a career in graphic design. In her spare time, she enjoys reading, writing, watching classic films, and playing around on computers. She lives with her family in Georgia, Vermont.

(See Deb Shell for contact information).

SARA SHELL, eighteen, grew up in Vermont as a lifelong homeschooler. She started dancing at the age of eleven and hasn't stopped since, a love which brought her to Tisch School of the Arts at New York University where she is currently in her second year. She hopes to dance professionally when she graduates, and also enjoys writing, spending time with nature, and playing with her dogs.

(See Deb Shell for contact information.)

LUZ SHOSIE taught fifth grade in a public school for two years, and that's when she decided to homeschool. Now she grows food and flowers, studies and teaches t'ai chi, runs a support group, and publishes a newsletter for unschoolers. "I enjoy holding people's hands as they take the leap into self-directed learning."

Guilford University
22 Wild Rose Avenue
Guilford, CT 06437
Phone/Fax: (203) 458-7402
E-mail: guiluniv@javanet.com

NED VARE is sixty-three and has been homeschooling for eighteen years. He has enjoyed various occupations, usually with no connection to his "education." Ned adds, "I consider my schooling (private) and college (Ivy League) a waste of time—an expensive warehousing and even damaging experience because so much of it had to be unlearned, and also because it gave me an inappropriate or unrealistic world view. Like most people, almost all my valuable learning was done outside school and after my schooling ended."

(See Luz Shosie for contact information.)

CINDY WADE is an artist and homeschool advocate currently residing on a Vermont homestead with husband Todd and children Annaquista and Zebhdiyah. Cindy founded and directs Gnarly Birch Press, a mail-order company specializing in homeschool materials, and she publishes *Right at Home* newsletter. She is author of *The Vermont Homeschoolers' Directory*, among other publications, and speaks and presents workshops on homeschooling.

Gnarly Birch Press
RR 2, Box 145
E. Wallingford, VT 05742
Phone: (802) 259-3493
E-mail: cwade@vermontel.com

THE
Homeschooling
Book of Answers

CHAPTER ONE

Now That Homeschooling Is Legal and Safe . . .

O NCE UPON A time, the most frequently asked question about home-schooling was, "Is that *legal?*" I always thought it a strange one. If I say I'm taking responsibility for my own children's need for food, no one questions if that's legal. If I say I'm taking responsibility for my children's need to be healthy, again, no questions asked. In fact, I could be hauled off to jail if I *didn't* take care of those responsibilities.

Since taking responsibility for my children's need for education isn't very different than taking care of their need for food and health, I find this turn-around interesting. When it comes to "which books they read" instead of "which vegetables they eat for dinner," all of a sudden it's a legal issue. Please allow this book to help you ponder the significance of this.

That the question, "Is that legal?" is not today included in a book of the most important and most often asked questions about homeschooling says a lot about the growth and acceptance of this educational phenomena. Homeschooling's legality is today a given, in many respects a tribute to the countless families who fought to maintain—or reclaim—parental responsibility for children's education.

That something as personal as the art of education is tied to a series of legal hoops one must jump through in order to practice it is a fact worthy of deep—possibly life-altering—consideration, particularly to those who cherish the ideal of a free people living in a free country. That a question-and-answer book on homeschooling still needs a chapter on legal issues, and that those questions are important enough to be addressed in the first chapter of this book, says a lot about how much farther we have yet to go along the path toward *assuming,* instead of *allowing,* family responsibility for our own children.

I like to imagine a day when the art of education may be widely viewed as the private family affair it is, a day when those charged with the weighty task of educating future generations *en masse* let loose the reins they've held so tightly for the relatively brief, 150-year-long educational experiment known as public schooling.

> **W**hen it comes to "which books they read" instead of "which vegetables they eat for dinner," all of a sudden it's a legal issue. Please allow this book to help you ponder the significance of this.

Until that day, however, anyone contemplating homeschooling her own children; anyone who has a hand in running, regulating, or in any way supporting the business of schooling—indeed, anyone who would benefit from a microcosmic look at the effects of government influence in our personal lives—needs to know (1) what the hoops are and (2) the most effective way to jump through them. *You* are capable of grabbing those reins, allowing your children to move in a different direction more in keeping with your family's values, dreams, and hopes.

Why does a thirty-year veteran school teacher tell you you're lucky if you *don't* have teacher training before homeschooling your children? Would you like to know just what the legal requirements in your state are? And where to find the most accurate information about them? If you've always tiptoed gingerly about your school administrators, or have never had any dealings with them in the past, could you use a few tips on how to approach them? Can you stand to learn that they see your child much differently than you do? And that you can learn just as much if not more about your child's education than they in a very brief time?

Now that homeschooling is legal and safe, welcome to what you need to know about remaining legal issues to fully understand which legal hoops are still real, and which have fallen by the wayside. After addressing these necessary evils, we'll move on to the ideas directly relevant to truly educating children.

1

Can I teach my own children if I don't have any teacher training?

BILLY AND NANCY GREER Yes! In fact, teacher training can be a disadvantage in the home environment. Traditional teaching methods still tend to break up learning into several separate categories or subjects that are taught independently of each other. This may work well when groups of students are moved from class to class for each subject. In theory, this allows teachers to specialize in a particular subject so that the student gets a teacher with expertise in the subject. This is one of the key ideas in mass production—break a process into separate components and let a specialist handle each component.

In real life, there is no artificial segregation of subjects and there is often an amazing integration. Reading and writing are involved in every subject area; science involves history, foreign languages, math, art, and social studies. It is much more effective to integrate all of these items and treat them as part of a whole. In a home environment, it is easier to take this kind of approach. The payoff is that it is easier to relate what is learned to real life, and to make the material more interesting.

And guess what? Companies are finding that multidisciplinary team approaches work better than traditional mass production. When marketing, engineering, production, and finance work on a project simultaneously, the quantity and quality of work increase. The better and more innovative companies are already moving away from traditional mass-production models.

If you see that you have more freedom and flexibility to use techniques that would not be effective in a classroom setting, but are still worried about your own knowledge, just remember that your children are not limited to what you know. You do not teach your children; you help them learn. Coaches are not the best athletes. They help motivate, and provide resources and support.

NED VARE Teacher training—the kind of training given to public school teachers—is one of the main reasons for the failure of the schools in the first place. You are not expected to be a classroom teacher overseeing two dozen diverse strangers, anyway. Your job is to be a tutor, on a part-time basis only, for one or maybe a few of your own children—whom you know intimately. You are well qualified to do that; you've already been doing it for years. Children don't need schooling; they want to learn, and they know how to do it. If they have questions, answer them. If you can't answer them, find the answers together. The process is called life. It's not separate from education.

> **Children don't need schooling; they want to learn, and they know how to do it.**

JOHN TAYLOR GATTO Let me reverse that question. Can you teach your own children if you *do* have teacher training, did well in it, and believe its precepts of scientific pedagogy, its psychological principles of child development, its habits of time management, behavioral control, text selection, sequencing, assessment, and guidance? I don't think so.

Teacher training is not about assisting a mind and character to develop according to the principles of its own internal genius. It is not about education at all, but about successful *schooling,* which is a much different thing. Schooling is a comprehensive indoctrination process, designed—by Plato, Hobbes, Rousseau, and others—to isolate children from their natural sources of personal power, which accrue from family identity and experience, self-discovery, freedom to experiment in a safe and familiar setting, early guidance in metaphysical speculation and participation (what we call religion), access to highly personalized and particularized

text and experience matchings (what is called elsewhere in this guide "interest initiated" learning, knowledgeable mentors drawn from the ranks of the talented, not merely from the cohort of "certified" state agents), and much more.

Isolation, followed by controlled abstractions of reality and controlled "simulation" games, a controlled diet of materials, a highly tense setting (even in the very best of schools) in which authorities are essential for protection—all this is the stuff of schooling. And you know that in your bones because you have been schooled yourself. This is the reason the science of schooling is called "pedagogy" and teachers (sometimes with a secret, innocent pride) hear themselves referred to as "pedagogues."

The word has an ancient and very specific lineage. The *paidagogos* was a form of slave in ancient Greece who drilled children according to instructions issued by a master. He had no latitude, doing as he was told. What Comenius and Rousseau and Pestalozzi and Froebel—those wildly inappropriate saints of holistic/progressive schooling—all taught in the nineteenth century, which gave us mass forced schooling for the first time in human history, was how to do *pedagogy* efficiently. You study each child very closely, embed them in an unending context of undifferentiated "affection," stifle their intellect aborning by parceling out the stuff of experience (the only reliable foundation of character) relentlessly, all the while *wooing* the little charges from home, tradition, church, culture, and so on, bit by bit.

Once the child is fatally narcotized, and that job is largely done by third grade, the real schoolmasters—whoever they may be—have in theory an empty child to fill, a plastic substance to mold. Sounds creepy, right? Aren't you glad to have missed formal teacher training? The trouble is you didn't miss informal teacher training, or you wouldn't have asked this understandable but very dumb question!

Nature, God, common sense, history, or whatever other principle guides the best part of your intelligence should tell you that *you* are the only indispensable teacher your children need besides themselves. (Read Ben Franklin's autobiography for inspiration.) You may believe that you can *purchase* someone else's concern for your children through taxpayer-supported schooling or private-fee schooling, but then you may believe in the tooth fairy, too.

Don't.

2

I know that homeschooling is now legal in every state, but doesn't each state have its own requirements? Do some states allow more educational freedom than others?

DORIS HOHENSEE Homeschooling laws vary tremendously from state to state. There are three basic categories for homeschooling laws: private school laws, equivalency laws, and home education laws.

The best situation is when home schools are legally recognized to be private schools. Intrusive regulations cannot be imposed upon private schools. Private schools have fought long and hard to protect their curricula from state censorship and to protect their teachers from certification requirements. Numerous court opinions stand in defense of the right of private schools to be free from state regulation. Homeschoolers are fortunate, indeed, if they live in Alabama, Alaska, California, Iowa, Illinois, Kentucky, Michigan, Nebraska, Oklahoma, or Texas, all of which enjoy private school status.

Equivalency laws are those which exempt children from compulsory attendance laws if they are receiving "equivalent instruction" elsewhere. While these laws may vary somewhat from state to state, it's difficult to define "equivalent" and the burden of proof is on the state. For the most part, these states have little by way of regulation, as the vagueness in the law works in favor of parents. Homeschoolers in Connecticut, Delaware, Idaho, Indiana, Kansas, Massachusetts, New Jersey, and South Dakota have equivalency laws.

The most variable laws are the home education laws. Having been classified separately from the rest of the private school community, home education in many of these states is quite regulated. Though the requirements are enumerated, there is still considerable vagueness in these laws. However, many times the vagueness now works in favor of the state, not the parent. What's more, there is little restriction on the amount of regulation that is possible should the legislature decide that more regulation is necessary. Homeschoolers need to be constantly vigilant lest their rights erode still further in these states.

The following states have home education laws: Arizona, Arkansas, Colorado, Florida, Georgia, Hawaii, Louisiana, Maine, Maryland, Michigan (has both private school status *and* home education laws), Minnesota, Missouri, Mississippi, Montana, Nevada, New Hampshire, New Mexico, New York,

North Carolina, North Dakota, Ohio, Oregon, Pennsylvania, Rhode Island, South Carolina, Tennessee, Utah, Vermont, Virginia, Washington, West Virginia, Wisconsin, and Wyoming.

SUSAN AND LARRY KASEMAN Yes to both questions. Education, including homeschooling, is governed basically by state laws rather than federal laws. Requirements vary widely. Some states have no explicit requirements. Some require that parents notify public school officials that they will be homeschooling. In some states, parents must submit curriculum plans; in others, periodic reports. Some states require testing. Some states require several of these.

However, homeschooling laws are not as hard and fast as may first appear. As homeschoolers, we can influence the amount of educational freedom we have. We have the right and responsibility to read and interpret laws. We know more about homeschooling than most officials and have incentive to find reasonable interpretations that support children and families. Determined homeschoolers have increased our freedom by devising inventive ways to comply with laws. For example, homeschoolers are often required to have a curriculum. However, people, including professional educators, do not agree about what specific curriculum is best. In fact, conventional schools keep changing their curricula. As homeschoolers, we can give the widest interpretation possible within the law and choose or develop an approach to learning that meets our family's needs, whether this be a purchased curriculum, unit studies, or unschooling. (See Question 5.)

We can also refuse to comply with demands from officials that exceed their statutory authority, even though it is often tempting to just give officials what they request. For example, when we receive an official letter demanding more than the law requires, we may want to simply supply it and avoid any hassles. When school officials appear at our door, it may be tempting to give them as much material as we have in hopes that we will then be left alone. Or when filing required reports, it may seem like a good idea to include extra information to show school officials how well our children are doing or to educate them about homeschooling. However, in all these cases, doing more than the law requires sets precedents that may be difficult for us and other homeschoolers to follow in the future. It also increases the authority officials have over homeschoolers.

> **Standing firm in the face of excessive demands from officials requires a thorough knowledge of the law and constant vigilance.**

Standing firm in the face of excessive demands from officials requires a thorough knowledge of the law and constant vigilance. School officials often request more from homeschoolers than is required by law because they have inaccurate information about the law, or are convinced that homeschoolers need their expertise, or are trying to increase their power and authority. Fortunately, when homeschoolers challenge them with accurate information, officials generally back down.

Informing other homeschoolers about the law is also important. Inclusive state-wide grassroots homeschooling organizations encourage homeschoolers to work together to protect everyone's rights.

For more ideas about ways to increase and protect homeschooling freedoms, see Question 86.

For information on homeschooling requirements in a given state, contact homeschoolers who live there. (The National Homeschool Association, Holt Associates, and *Home Education Magazine* provide lists of contacts. See the resources in appendix A.) Contacting school officials is not a good idea; they often have misleading or inaccurate information. Similarly, contacting lawyers outside the state, including homeschooling lawyers, often results in misleading information.

PAT MONTGOMERY In states that have home education statutes, parents can read the statutes. Understanding and abiding by them is a fairly straightforward matter. Some, however, are marvelously vague. This allows for a wide diversity of home educating styles. It catches some parents off guard, however, if they feel the need to have every jot and tittle spelled out, but both camps are served. The implications here are that parents are expected to abide by what is written in the statute as it is generally applied throughout the state.

In states where home education is tucked into the private school category, parents must discover what legal power the state has to regulate private schools. In Illinois, for example, the state has no power over private schools at all. This is true in most states. In Michigan, on the other hand, the state does have some regulatory power over private schools.

Then, too, much of what is written in state law regarding private schools is not actually practiced. Heads of private schools can provide help explaining what is, in fact, expected of them. Librarians are almost universally helpful to parents researching this issue.

Looking at Michigan again, one part of the private school act refers to annual notification to local public school superintendents of the names and addresses of each private school student. This practice, however, is no longer expected of nor followed by private schools.

States that classify homes as private schools offer parents the same protection that private schools enjoy. Having no reference to "homeschool" in state regulations means that the term is not open to being defined by legislators or school officials who are unaware of the diversity of approaches to education. This is a desirable set of circumstances that bodes well for parents. Should any trouble arise, home educators find themselves with allies who are, for the most part, knowledgeable and fiercely loyal to their status as independent educators. Not bad company in the event of a skirmish!

CHRIS CARDIFF Generally speaking, statutory homeschool states (that is, states with laws specifically defining and regulating homeschools) are much more restrictive than states that consider homeschools as private schools. Failure to comply with the restrictive regulations within statutory homeschool states results in parents forced to place their children in government schools. These restrictions usually take the form of:

- mandatory curriculum approval by government officials (school district superintendent) or their designate.
- mandatory testing, where permission to homeschool is contingent on the child scoring above a certain percentage.
- education requirements for the parents (college degree or high school diploma, depending on the state) before the state allows them to homeschool their children.

In contrast to the direct regulation of homeschools, states that treat homeschools as private schools have fewer restrictions. In California, for example, private schools are subject to the same general curriculum guidelines and attendance laws as government schools. However, there is no government oversight of these general statutes and, more importantly, none of the harsher restrictions found in those states where homeschooling is regulated directly.

Because of this increased relative educational freedom, you will find homeschoolers in these states actively working to preserve their status quo as private schools. For example, the legislative policy of the California Homeschool Network explicitly states that "California Homeschool Network believes that current state law provides for the legal practice of homeschooling as private schools.

We stand opposed to any legislation which would: define 'homeschool,' 'home education,' or related terms; add to or change the definition of 'private school,' as it now exists in law."

While the private school option is much less intrusive than direct regulation, underlying both approaches is the assumption that government has the right to compel the education of children. True educational freedom will be achieved when this assumption has been successfully refuted by the repeal of compulsory attendance and mandatory curriculum laws.

3

How do I find out what is legally required of homeschoolers in my state?

MARY GRIFFITH You've got several options and it's always best to choose several of them. You can ask your local school district, county office of education, or state department of education. Depending on where you live, the odds of getting accurate information from any of these may be fairly low. You might get lucky and run into a school official who is knowledgeable and forthcoming about the homeschooling regulations; but some school officials often are not familiar with the laws regulating homeschooling (and some may tell you what they think the law ought to be instead of what it is). Some officials may have the additional problem of knowing that more homeschoolers in their jurisdiction may mean less average daily attendance (ADA) funding for their own programs.

You can go to the library and look up the applicable education statutes and administrative regulations for yourself. Sometimes you'll need to try a regional branch or a community college library. Be sure to check the updates in the pocket parts in the backs of the statute books to make sure you've got the very latest version of the laws. You might also want to check into any relevant case law that affects the ways those laws are actually enforced. You may find that some of the language is less than transparent, and you may have to do a bit of digging around to find out exactly how all the different rules interact to learn what exactly they mean for the everyday lives of homeschoolers.

Best of all, you can ask homeschooling organizations in your state. The best first choice would be a statewide homeschool association that maintains a legal and legislative watch and publishes a regular newsletter to keep its members informed. If the group seems to rely on other organizations to do this work for them, or provides only sketchy information about bills and hearings that concern them, watch out. You want a group that will help you help yourself, not one that takes over for you completely. If there are no statewide groups in your state, check with local or regional groups in the larger cities. At least one of them will probably be performing some of the same functions.

New homeschoolers are often leery of relying on information supplied by other homeschoolers as being somehow suspect or less reliable than information from other sources. But homeschoolers have a vested interest in getting the legal information right: If they are wrong, they are jeopardizing their children's education.

Get information from as many sources as you can. You may be confused by all the variations at first, but you'll sort it out eventually—and, by doing so, you'll know your rights and responsibilities thoroughly. The peace of mind you'll get that way is well worth the trouble.

PAT LINES Every state recognizes homeschooling as a legal way to meet state compulsory attendance requirements. Many state laws provide for options for qualifying your homeschooling program. All states require the family to file basic information with either the state or local education agency (SEA or LEA). Some states have additional requirements, such as the submission of a curricular plan, testing of students or, in a few cases, education or testing requirements for parents.

The basic rules are in the state's compulsory education law. It's a good idea to get a copy and keep it on hand in case there are questions about some particular of the law and your situation. In most states a few sections will specifically apply to homeschooling, but pay attention to other sections. If the age of compulsory education does not begin until eight, for example, you do not have to worry about compliance until your child reaches that age. In those states where there is no specific mention of homeschooling, a court, an attorney general, or the state board of education has ruled that private schools may meet in a home. In these states you must meet the rules for a private school to be "legal."

The law may also give the state board of education authority to make regulations regarding homeschooling. This authority is limited to filling in

> **E**very state recognizes homeschooling as a legal way to meet state compulsory attendance requirements.

Pat Lines

the details of the law, not to changing it. Most state education agencies have assigned an individual to serve as homeschooling liaison and to provide assistance on understanding the state law and regulations. As a practical matter, I would recommend first checking with your local or state homeschooling organization for tips and help on compliance. There may be some surprises in the way a state or local official reads the law. If there is a dispute over interpretation or a need for a new law, a homeschooling organization run by experienced homeschoolers is your best source for understanding the issues, and for advocating your best interests.

4

Since I don't have much experience dealing and communicating with school administrators, what's the best way to approach them about homeschooling?

PAT MONTGOMERY Do your homework:

1. Determine first of all whether your state regulations require any interaction between home educators and school officials. In most of the United

States, no contact is required, so parents need not approach the school administrators at all.

However, if your child has already been in attendance at a conventional school, it is merely an act of courtesy to inform the officials at the previous school. A brief note to the teacher or principal will do. It ought to state, very simply, that your child "is no longer enrolled in the school." A written note is preferable to a phone call for many reasons, the chief of which is that a note can be placed in the file folder.

The school officials then remove the student's cumulative file folder (school records) from the active files. If another school or program requests the records, the school personnel send the originals or copies of the originals to the next school. If no school requests them, the records are placed in the inactive files. This means they are, for all intents and purposes, "dead" files.

2. If you reside in a state where contact between home educating parents and school administrators is required by the regulations, ask other home-based educating parents how they dealt with the matter. Or you may choose to hand this task to someone else, like Clonlara School officials, who have a long and successful history with it.

Remember, you are engaged in a political activity: a parent, the primary teacher of her child, is approaching a school official who has, very likely, grown accustomed to believing that he or she bears that primary responsibility. Remember, too, that many school officials are sincere when they state they take their roles seriously.

Know for certain what the regulations require; use those as the yardstick. This coin has two sides: Parents are expected to obey the law; school officials must also obey the law. *Only* what is stated in the regulations need be provided; nothing more. Home education is enough of a job without restrictions and requests being hoisted by (perhaps) well-meaning officials.

Don't hesitate to point out to school administrators that both you, as parent, and they must obey what is written in the regulations. Don't hesitate to point out that when a school official asks for more than is required, this reveals underlying doubts and fears. Ask what prompts these fears. Most parents, after all, graduated from public schools. Is the official implying that the education given was riddled with error?

You are not approaching school officials with hat in hand asking for permission. You are in a position of power and status. You are notifying the officials, not begging or usurping or stealing what is theirs. Politeness, firmness, and humor are excellent tools to employ. Enter with a confident air. The lesson will not be lost on your ever-watching children.

MARY MCCARTHY When you make the decision to educate your children yourself at home, you also accept legal responsibility for your actions. The best way to approach local school administrators is with knowledge. Go to the library, look up your state's truancy and/or homeschooling law, and copy it. Talk with a local support group and buy its legal packet. Compare the two and analyze whether it all makes sense and is complete. When you are sure of the law, follow it. Some states require notification, others do not. If your state's laws do not require notification, do not notify. If they do require, follow the instructions you have assembled and comply. Give them only what they ask for and what you are legally required to provide.

Always send your correspondence registered with a "return receipt requested"; that way you establish that on a specific date you notified a specific individual. Always "get it in writing."

If someone from your district contacts you and requests information you did not provide, and which you do not think is legally required, write and ask for the specific law, statute, or regulation that impels you to provide this information. If it's by telephone, request the person write out the questions and send them to you. Always be polite but firm. Understand that the actions of your school district personnel may be nothing more than a test of your resolve to homeschool or a display of their ignorance of the law and your rights.

If you have complied with the law as written, and the school personnel continue to harass you, then you have to take the offensive. Always try to keep the ball in someone else's court. Sometimes a letter to the individual's employer, the board of education, will solve the problem.

You can hire your own attorney or wait until the school district begins legal action and then respond. The best attorney to speak with is a local one who may know the individuals involved as well as the local law, and be able to negotiate a settlement. Some attorneys now specialize in education law. But even if you cannot afford an attorney, you still have all your research and your written record that you are complying with your state's law. Don't be afraid if you are in compliance with your law.

Some homeschoolers choose not to comply with their law for one reason or another. That is your choice. And another question!

LILLIAN JONES A solid sense of self-confidence goes a long way in dealing with potential conflict—that and the effort to understand the point of view of the other side. Those of us who have been homeschooling for some time know that we are on the cutting edge of education and personal growth. The schools are also very serious about the mission they face. They feel that they hold the hope for the future and, whether we like it or not, they are raising more children than we homeschoolers are. The children they're raising are going to be right out there building tomorrow's world with our own. This is the overview I think is best to keep in mind when dealing with school authorities. Confidence with compassion.

Beyond a good knowledge of the laws, it helps to be comfortable with homeschooling itself. Prospective homeschoolers often ask where they can get "the books." It's a question that seems perfectly reasonable to someone who hasn't en-

tered the territory yet. We're all products of a long-standing system that seemed to materialize the books, the knowledge, the plan, the wisdom, the whole golden enchilada from some mysterious temple of higher education somewhere out there . . .

Those of us who once actually embarked on a journey to that holy temple, expecting to come away as "teachers," found that it was an illusion. There's no one out there in the school system handing out infallible wisdom about how to educate kids, but there are lots of administrative bureaucrats making their livings by pretending to be, or hoping to become, the ultimate authorities on that elusive body of knowledge.

In the homeschooling world, meanwhile, we have thousands of parents who are working full time on the commitment dearest to their hearts—providing their children with a good life and bright future. We network—we communicate in books, in newsletters, in magazines, on electronic bulletin boards, on the Internet, in national and state organizations, and in state and local support groups.

We don't have to settle for textbooks and policies

> **W**e're all products of a long-standing system that seemed to materialize the books, the knowledge, the plan, the wisdom, the whole golden enchilada from some mysterious temple of higher education somewhere out there . . .

that have filtered down from intellectual discussions in upper-echelon board rooms, to middle board rooms, and through local school boards. We investigate on our own and take in ideas we hear about from one another, ideas for encouraging our children to love life and learning.

Longtime homeschooling families offer many excellent catalog resources that make school texts and methods look pathetic in comparison. Some are specialized to various religious orientations, but many others are relevant for anyone. *The Drinking Gourd* carries child-friendly math and science materials, and all sorts of interesting materials aimed at self-directed learning. A company called Pennsylvania Homeschoolers sells, among other offerings, the deliciously well-written math books by Harold Jacobs. The Holt Bookstore catalog has long been a favorite source for an appetizing array of books and materials supporting the enjoyment of learning. Rebecca Rupp's *Good Stuff: Learning Tools for All Ages,* and Donn Reed's book, *The Home School Source Book,* describe hundreds of interesting resources for enjoyable learning, very few of which can be found inside a school.

Ironically, as rich as we are in resources, the longer people homeschool the less we tend to buy. We urge new homeschoolers not to make investments in the beginning because we find, to our surprise, that tremendous learning takes place with very little in the way of specialized resources.

The school systems, on the other hand, are not yet set up in a way to understand and explore the nature of education in the way we do. They face other challenges. Keeping all this in mind can help you avoid feeling intimidated and hold a feeling of compassion for what they're trying to do as you approach them about homeschooling. We can help in the long run. I hope we can eventually be mentors of a sort, people who have explored some very radical and successful ways of thinking that can help the school community become a better place for the kids who are there.

5

Am I required to teach the same curriculum as the local public school?

REBECCA KOCHENDERFER Although not required to, some of my homeschooling friends follow the public school curriculum when teaching their children. They like this method because they are comforted knowing that their children are learning the same things as their peers.

I don't use this method because I feel it doesn't take advantage of one of homeschooling's strengths—its flexibility. Whereas curricula are developed to fit the masses, homeschooling can be developed to fit the child. You can design your children's education to take advantage of their interests, their pace, and their learning style. For example, California's curriculum requires children to learn about missions in the fourth grade—whether or not they are interested in missions. With homeschooling, you can wait until your child *is* interested in missions, or perhaps even decide not to learn about missions at all.

Another reason our family has chosen not to use a curriculum is because we think it is too teacher-directed. We prefer learning activities that are more student-directed. For example, we have set up learning centers throughout our house. We have an art center, a science center, and a woodworking center. We set up these obvious learning areas because we want the children to initiate their own activities. We want that microscope out in the open where it can beckon to the kids to "come and explore."

The bottom line is: You are not *required* to teach the same curriculum as the local public school. Whether or not

you choose to use that curriculum is up to you.

DAVID AND MICKI COLFAX Yes and no. In some jurisdictions the education code requires that homeschoolers conform to a state-mandated curriculum, while in others there are few if any requirements. But even in states in which the code specifies what must be taught and when, homeschoolers have been quite successful in interpreting the law in the broadest possible of terms, with the result that parents have considerable latitude in what they teach and when. In states in which the work of homeschooled

David and Micki Colfax

children is closely monitored, most parents can creatively conform with the spirit of the law, if not its bureaucratic intent to exercise control. Who is to say that a brisk walk in the park does not qualify as physical education, or that an hour spent watching a television documentary on the Civil War cannot be construed as an American history lesson?

The task homeschoolers face under these conditions is to fit authentic educational experiences into conventionally defined categories in such a way that the authorities can accept them. It may take a bit of imagination and some creativity, but most homeschooling parents shouldn't have too much trouble completing the pedagogically meaningless forms that educrats and politicians, in their wisdom, have deemed such an important part of the educational process.

SUSAN AND LARRY KASEMAN No. One reason homeschooling works so well is that homeschoolers can choose curricula that meet their needs, sometimes using different approaches for different children and modifying their approach as their needs change. (Some states do require that homeschoolers submit their curriculum plans to officials.)

Some families follow curricula that are similar to those used in public schools, often purchasing them from a curriculum supplier and changing them to suit their own purposes. They spend as much or as little time as they need on specific topics, add subjects, change schedules, and take breaks from subjects that temporarily are not going well.

Other families develop their own curricula. Some use unit studies. (See Question 33.) Others base their curricula on the children's and parents' special interests and learn the basics while exploring their interests. Another approach is to do real-life projects and learn from building a garage or raising goats or gardening or cooking or whatever. (See Question 31.)

It makes sense for homeschools to use different curricula from public schools. Public school curricula were developed for a classroom, a very limited space where large numbers of children of the same age are all supposed to be learning the same thing at the same time under the guidance of one older person who does not know any of the children well. Curricula have been developed to make this unrealistic, contrived setting somewhat manageable and to reassure taxpayers that they are getting their money's worth from public schools. They were not developed primarily to meet children's needs. By contrast, homeschools have a few children of different ages; one or more adults who know them well, love them, and can give them lots of individual attention, the whole world to explore, and no taxpayers or administrators to keep happy.

Public officials sometimes try to make homeschoolers adopt curricula similar to public school curricula, either by requiring that homeschoolers submit curriculum plans to school officials or that homeschoolers take standardized tests which means homeschoolers have to adopt a curriculum similar to a conventional curriculum to prepare for the tests. Homeschoolers can use the points below to counter both these requirements. When we homeschoolers understand them, we understand more clearly why we can and should choose our own curricula. We are also better prepared to defend our rights and freedoms when we talk with school officials, legislators, friends and relatives, and members of the general public.

- Homeschools, in many instances, are private schools. Under both state law and historical tradition, private schools choose their curricula. For example, parochial schools can teach religious beliefs. Therefore, homeschoolers have the right to choose their curricula.
- Parents have the right to secure for their children an education consistent with their principles and beliefs. The state may not have a monopoly in education and may not demand a uniform education for all. This right is guaranteed by the First, Fourth, Fifth, Ninth, and Fourteenth Amendments to the U.S. Constitution. It has been upheld by U.S. Supreme Court cases such as *Pierce* v. *Society of Sisters* and *Farrington* v. *Tokushige*.
- Laws require compulsory school attendance but not compulsory education. Compulsory school attendance laws are enforceable; it is not difficult to check attendance for young people enrolled in public and private schools, including homeschools. However, laws that required compulsory educa-

tion would give the state control over education. The state would have to develop a clear set of definitions and criteria for what it means to be educated and a series of tests to determine whether people have acquired the knowledge, skills, and attitudes that the definitions require. This would cost us our freedom of education and learning and even our freedom of thought.

6

I've heard some families purchase legal insurance in case of future problems. How many families do this, and is this necessary?

SUSAN AND LARRY KASEMAN Legal insurance is not only unnecessary; it is unwise. Few families buy it, a reasonable estimate is less than 10 percent of homeschoolers.

Legal insurance is unnecessary because families are almost never taken to court just because they are homeschooling. (Court appearances by homeschoolers are almost always the result of a larger dispute, such as a custody battle.) Ironically, homeschooling insurance often excludes the people who are most likely to be involved in legal proceedings, such as families whose children were truant or in difficulty with a public school before they began homeschooling.

Purchasing legal insurance is also unwise.

- Purchasing legal insurance undermines the most valuable asset we have—our willingness and ability to take responsibility ourselves. Just as no one else cares as much about our children's educations as we do, no one else is as motivated to maintain our homeschooling rights and responsibilities as we are. Legal insurance makes us dependent on experts and less inclined to act on our own behalf.

- Homeschoolers working through state-wide inclusive grassroots organizations are more effective than legal insurance in preventing and solving problems faced by individuals and by the homeschooling community as a whole. For one thing, there is a fundamental conflict of interest between us homeschoolers and providers of insurance. We homeschoolers want and need as little government regulation as possible. In states like Illinois, this means living without a specific homeschooling law that says, "Homeschooling is legal as long as homeschoolers do such and such."

However, it is in the best interest of insurance providers to have laws that are clear cut (although these laws reduce homeschooling freedoms), so homeschoolers who comply with them are easy to defend in court. For example, insurance providers often favor testing requirements. It is easy to defend homeschoolers who have scored well on the tests.

But as homeschoolers, we ask, what about families who don't comply with the law? Those who don't want their children tested, either because they object to the content of the tests, or because they do not want the state to have that much control over their children's educations, or for other reasons? Or families whose children do not score well? Insurance providers can simply refuse to cover these families. This means that a substantial number of homeschoolers are stuck with a law with which they cannot or do not want to comply, and they are more likely to be taken to court than they would be with a less clear-cut, less lawyer-friendly law.

- National organizations that provide legal insurance pose a particular problem. Residents of a state understand the political climate, and have more at stake and stronger incentive than outside experts and will have to live with the resulting law or court decision.

- Legal insurance focuses on laws that sometimes undermine common sense.

For example, it is obvious that our homes remain homes and are not school buildings. We do not need laws that say that we do not have to comply with regulations intended for conventional school buildings. We do not need school bus turnarounds.

Reducing fundamental parents' rights to a set of legal rights would cost us a great deal. We have important rights and responsibilities because we are parents. These rights do not originate with the government, and we reduce them significantly if we ask the government to "protect" them through laws. Then the government is seen as the source of basic rights and responsibilities which it can change or reduce.

• Legal insurance is also unwise because people are willing to pay a fairly substantial sum for it. This gives an organization that provides insurance a large budget. Inevitably, such an organization will put a great deal of emphasis on the legal aspects of homeschooling. Also, if the organization has an agenda in addition to homeschooling, perhaps even more important to it than homeschooling, it may be willing to sacrifice our homeschooling freedoms for the benefit of its larger agenda.

Our greatest protection comes from working together through grassroots organizations and responsible individual actions rather than purchasing legal insurance.

WILL SHAW Many years ago, when the resurgence of home education was in its infancy, it was not unusual for a homeschool family to be harassed by public education authorities or others. Homeschooling was not clearly legal in all states, and the public education industry always wants to protect and strengthen its near-monopoly over the training of children. There really were people out to make life difficult for homeschoolers by using truancy and child neglect processes. Legal insurance for homeschoolers was desired by a minority of homeschoolers.

However, though there are still some nasty local officials, home education is legal everywhere in the United States, and any need for legal insurance is even further reduced. Most homeschoolers don't feel the need. The parents just examine and abide by their applicable laws, network with other homeschoolers and homeschool organizations, and keep abreast of events and practices.

Homeschool legal insurance is a big business, and scary stories increase demand. In my experience in recent years, the very few problems that homeschoolers have had with local authorities are usually due to genuine mistakes or bad judgment that is not motivated by ill will. You need to be familiar with the requirements for homeschooling in your state. You do not need to be an attorney to teach your own kids, and you are not likely to ever need any homeschool-related legal representation.

Realize, too, that the unelected leadership of an insurance provider has a political, social, religious, economic, and home education agenda that goes beyond providing legal insurance, whether or not you need such insurance.

> You do not need to be an attorney to teach your own kids, and you are not likely to ever need any homeschool-related legal representation.

7

Why should I homeschool my children when I'm paying taxes for the same public schools I attended?

JOHN TAYLOR GATTO First, they *aren't* the same public schools you attended, regardless of appearances. In every decade since the end of World War II, a complex, comprehensive social agenda has unfolded through the agency of public schooling. Each succeeding generation is much more "schooled" than its predecessor, making the movement of this agenda "progressive" through a process of simple addition. Each generation of parents knows less than the generation before it, and hence is less able to counteract the training of schools.

It's impossible to fully analyze this agenda and track it to its source in 500 words or even 5 million, but all of us can see the visible effects it produces in our children: short attention spans; a dramatic inability to spin out satisfactory lines of meaning in their own lives; a profound weakening of family bonds; an indifference to concepts of duty, loyalty, sustained commitment, principle; a substitution of law for morality; and a massive stupidity, even among the bright with specialized competencies, about the great historical, philosophical, religious, political, and narrative contexts that give the details of everyday life their place in a tapestry of meaning.

What does it *mean* (do you know?) that 100,000 retreating Iraqi soldiers were instantly incinerated by the explosion of simple gasoline over their heads, dropped by an air fleet with full intelligence in hand that the war was over? What is the theory of human life that allows such a thing? Unless you know how unique and almost un-precedented such an action was in the history of war-fare, you would be left with the notion such things hap-pened every day.

The agenda of public schooling has been, for the entire twentieth century, to remove the power of most people to think for them-selves. The methods by which this has been done were developed first in the north German states of Prussia, Saxony, and Hanover, the latter principality the source of the British kings our American revolution overthrew. A full analysis is impossible here; but you need to realize that because of the systematic, hierar-chical nature of schooling, your local teachers, principals, superintendents, and the like have almost no say in this—they are *pedagogues,* which means practi-cally that they administer routines made elsewhere far away. Whatever the facts of the case, the results are progressive, following closely a discipline created by the philosophical movement called Posi-tivism.

If you cannot find ways to counter-act what amounts to a mechanization of your children's minds and characters, and a low-grade mechanization at that, they will surely cease to be fully human.

> **The agenda of public schooling has been, for the entire twentieth century, to remove the power of most people to think for themselves.**

They might even be-come people who think it a day's work to burn 100,000 men to death. Break their marriage vows. Put you in an old age home.

Those are some rea-sons you should homeschool.

NED VARE Just because we pay for the public schools doesn't mean we have to consume their services. We pay for parks, roads, libraries, and many other things we never use. Taxes pay for the salaries of thousands of people whose services we don't use, from police and secretaries to architects and lawyers.

Children are homeschooled as an al-ternative to public and private schools because parents believe those schools will not provide what they want for their children. The problem of paying taxes to sup-port the government schools, whether we use them or approve of them, is a political problem and should

Ned Vare

not cloud the issue. Parents, being legally and morally responsible for the education of their children, have a de-cision to make: How can I provide my children the best education possible? That question does not go away when parents choose a school or homeschooling. It is a choice that can always change because of circumstances and/or events.

Government schools have now become so expensive for us all that they have reduced our ability to pay for alternative schooling—and that is part of their strategy of forcing everyone into their system.

Nevertheless, parents need to realize that no matter how much money we give the government, it will not produce the kind of schools we want. After we remove our children, we need to vote against tax increases whenever possible, and be outspoken about the failings and deceit and corruption that are part and parcel of the public school system. A specific step available is to join the Separation of School and State Alliance, an organization whose goal is to disconnect education from government. (See the resources in the appendix.) That will produce huge local tax cuts and leave parents the funds to choose the kind and amount of education they want for their own children.

DAVID AND MICKI COLFAX If you feel that the public schools can give you a good return on your coerced investment, then perhaps you shouldn't homeschool your children. But if you are suggesting that you should get at least *something* in return for your tax dollars—even if it is a bad education for your children—your interest in economic justice is probably misplaced. To send children to public school simply because you (like most of us) are compelled under penalty of law to support them is rather akin to taking public transportation to places you don't want or need to go simply because your tax dollars subsidize the transit system. Clearly, there are many things our tax dollars are spent on that don't benefit and sometimes even harm us. Too few of us realize that most public schools fall into the latter category.

CHAPTER TWO

Homeschool May Be Cheaper Than You Think

HAVE YOU EVER thought about how much money you wouldn't spend, and therefore wouldn't need, if you stayed home to educate and enjoy your children? Across the nation families are realizing the cost of a paycheck—in terms of taxes, time, and worth when compared to their children's futures—is too steep. It just might pay—literally—to take a close look at the answers to Questions 8 and 9. Your job could be more expensive than you ever realized.

Speaking of expensive, let's also consider the high cost of public education and the never-ending cries for more money to correct increasingly expensive mistakes. If you already know that the average per-pupil expenditure in American public schools is a whopping $6,993, you may at least want to keep closer tabs when your local school budget expands, especially after Cafi Cohen tells you about a family providing an excellent education at home for less than $25 per child per year.

Have you ever taken a hard look at how often the pendulum of educational fads swings back and forth, as failure in one direction sends your tax dollars flying in another direction, a direction just as likely to be abandoned as so many before it? Even when the fad is recognized as a failure, the nature of the beast necessitates that it continue for years because so much money was invested in it in the first place. You can't throw away millions of dollars worth of textbooks and teacher training and advertising after just two years! It takes time to scrape around for the replacement. It takes many committees to study the proposed replacements and offer counterproposals. Textbook publishers must be alerted to the replacement fad, find the writers, and get the new books to print. Taxpayers must be coerced into paying for it all.

With more than 46 million children in public schools, according to a National Center for Education Statistics estimate for 1997, imagine the dollars wasted with a system like this. Maybe it's time for more families to check out an alternative route. Stay home and use a textbook that your child picks out. Drop it if it doesn't work. Minimal financial damage, immediate correction. Better yet, read Mary Griffith's, Becky Rupp's, and Wendy Priesnitz's advice about how to keep the cost of homeschooling to a minimum; not one recommends purchasing textbooks—a staple of government schools' voracious dollar appetite—at all.

Hundreds of thousands of families have proven you can live on one income in a two-income society, with enough money left over to educate the children well with homeschooling. Still other families, with a reordering of priorities and deft scheduling, have found room for homeschooling *and* a job for both parents. A bonus, homeschooling lends itself to immediate correction should something be wrong. At educational bargain basement prices, and using the ideas you'll discover in this chapter, homeschooling could save your family a bundle. For just a little more fun, multiply that by 46 million children, and dream of the bundle it could save our nation.

8

How much does it cost each year to homeschool?

CINDY WADE Homeschooling need only be as expensive as you want it to be. We discovered that we didn't need all the trappings used in a public school classroom, like desks, chalkboard, art station, reading station. Instead, we stuff our house with lots and lots of good books.

We prefer the classics because they're proven literary works with good vocabulary and strong moral values. All these books are free at your local library or through the interlibrary loan system.

There's really no need to buy expensive curricula and textbooks. Many homeschoolers get by on $200 to $300 a year per child for instruc-

Cindy Wade

tion and activities. We've found success with simple department store workbooks, a library card, computer programs, and mentors.

Homeschooling can happen when both parents feel compelled to work outside the home. Many parents work split shifts to accomplish this, one parent working during the day and the other at night, sharing responsibilities.

Remember, older children are quite capable of handling many of the chores necessary for maintaining a peaceful and efficient household. Homeschooled children develop a much more positive attitude toward parents and responsibility. They learn cooperation is necessary for survival.

Even single parents find that with a little creativeness and ingenuity they, too, can homeschool. Single parents don't live in a vacuum. There are family members, neighbors, and friends willing to help with lessons, supervision, and resources. Much depends on how determined a parent is to take charge of her children's education and of her own life.

To fairly gauge the cost of homeschooling there are two more aspects, frequently ignored but vital to consider:

- Homeschooling saves you the expense of a school wardrobe, school lunches, transportation, extracurricular activities, field trips, and fund-raising activities.
- Factor in the cost of making money. What do you spend on wardrobe, gas, breakfast, lunch, car payments, insurance, gifts for office acquaintances, day care, increased income taxes, and any other rituals associated with going off to work each day?

> **W**ouldn't you rather live on less and spend more time fishing, swimming, talking, playing, laughing, and sharing with your child?

Wouldn't you rather live on less and spend more time fishing, swimming, talking, playing, laughing, and sharing with your child? You may discover, as we did, that homeschooling becomes a simpler, more enriching way of life rather than just an inexpensive educational alternative.

CAFI COHEN The first problem is defining cost. Do you count the computer your family would have anyway? Or the encyclopedia set? Or the trip to Washington, D.C., you would have made whether you were homeschooling or not? The following answer assumes that we do *not* count those things, even though they are educational and you can document them as "school." I will also not consider the second income one parent might give up. After that, "How much does it cost?" depends on how you homeschool.

I have known homeschoolers who spend less than $25 per child per year. These families use community resources. They frequent the library; attend school district book giveaways; accept other homeschoolers' discards; make their own math manipulatives; watch PBS and other instructional television programs; garner subject-matter expertise from neighbors, friends, and relatives; and buy occasional books and even science materials at garage sales.

Teenagers in these families often volunteer in educational settings like veterinary clinics and museums and community drama groups. These older children also trade babysitting or housework for piano or French lessons. Educational sweat equity!

A cost of $100 to $400 per child per year is probably a more common expenditure for materials, once you understand the homeschooling market and learn to shop carefully. The average text for one year of math or language arts costs between $20 and $40, and families may buy anywhere from one to six texts for each child each year. Those who rely less on textbooks, as well as those who

---

THE LITTLE THINGS

Delight in every day's little things. Cherish them. This is the stuff from which life—and therefore, learning—is fashioned. From the little things your children will shape their hopes, dreams, and eventual reality.

The little things remain when all too soon paths diverge, forming the threads that bind family together through space and time's inevitable tug.

And in the most quiet of moments, when those threads glisten brightly in love's pure light, it's the little things that move your heart to smile and stir your soul to sing. That's what it's all about, this homeschooling.

The little things.

do, spend money on computer programs, real books, field trips, paper and pencils, and materials for special projects (building model rockets, for example). Families who stay in this price range also often use the strategies listed in the previous paragraphs.

It is possible to spend $400 to $1,000 per year or more for each child if you enroll your child in an independent study program; and some of the online programs for grades six through twelve can cost $700 to $2,000 per year. A few programs are less expensive, but most fall into these price ranges. Private tutoring may also run up the tab. While most families successfully homeschool through high school with self-instructional materials and inexpensive community resources, families occasionally hire tutors for high school math or science or foreign language.

One category of increased expense surprised our family. When our children attended school, they had time for two or three extracurricular activities—maybe Scouts, piano lessons, and soccer. As homeschoolers, our children—with more time—could easily take part in five to ten activities each week. Of course, these additional activities generated additional expenses—for supplies, uniforms, dues, transportation, lessons, and so on.

9

If I homeschool, can I continue to work and earn the income we need? How can a homeschooling family survive on one income in a two-income society?

BILLY AND NANCY GREER First you have to define your "needs." The American way seems to promote living beyond one's means and turns "wants" into "needs." Look at the costs of work as well as the income, and you may discover that you do not really gain much by working. Day-care costs, clothes for work, transportation costs, and meals can quickly add up.

At one point Bill was working a sixty-hour-per-week job, Nancy was working a forty-hour-per-week job, and both spent Friday night through Sunday night at a residential home for handicapped kids (our children would go with us). Since then, we have both started to work from home and discovered that we can survive on less than half the income we had before.

REBECCA KOCHENDERFER I work fifteen to twenty hours a week *and* homeschool my children. Because my children are young (seven, four, and one), I have a babysitter come in to watch the kids while I work out of my home office. I have found several advantages to this arrangement.

Two of the biggest advantages are safety and flexibility. I know exactly what's going on with my kids at all times and I know how the babysitter is treating them. If the kids get hurt, or if something exciting happens, I am just a closed door

Rebecca Kochenderfer

away. It's also nice to be able to nurse the baby directly instead of pumping all the time.

Also, the kids are involved in my work. They help me test products and tell me what they like and don't like. As they grow older, I hope they will help me with my writing, editing, and bookkeeping. I think they learn a lot just by being around me while I'm working. And, when they're not helping me, I enjoy a break away from them and they enjoy a break away from me.

I'm lucky to have help with the kids. Our babysitter wants to be a teacher, so she loves doing science and art projects with them. She also helps with the

household duties, which allows me to spend more time on homeschooling projects.

It is also possible to work at home without hiring extra help. One homeschooling mom I know runs a successful catalog business. She has been quoted as saying, "My business has grown as my children have grown." She is able to spend more time on her business now since her children are older and able to homeschool themselves. Another friend of mine runs her husband's kung fu business while raising three young children. She takes her children with her to meetings, and they study or play quietly nearby.

You may not *have* to work. I quit my job in order to homeschool, and I was scared that we were going to starve. Everyone warned us that "it takes two incomes these days just to survive," but I have found that not to be the case.

When I quit work, our expenses dropped dramatically. I no longer had those sneaky work-related expenses like dry cleaning, lunches out, gas, day care, and higher taxes. By the time I subtracted the cost of working, I discovered

> **W**hen I quit work our expenses dropped dramatically. I no longer had those sneaky work-related expenses like dry cleaning, lunches out, gas, day care, and higher taxes. By the time I subtracted the cost of working, I discovered that my $25-an-hour job was really bringing home just $7 an hour.

that my $25-an-hour job was really bringing home just $7 an hour.

The book *Your Money or Your Life,* by Joe Dominguez and Vicki Robin, has really helped us get a grip on our finances by showing us how to spend money on the things that matter to us, and to stop spending money on things that don't matter to us. I know a number of homeschoolers who use the program in this book so that they can work less and spend more time with their kids.

Of course, even after reducing your expenses you may feel that you want or need to work. Talk to other homeschooling parents. I'll bet they will have some great ideas for you!

KATHARINE HOUK Some homeschooling families have found ways for both parents to bring in money, although most homeschooling families are two-parent families in which one parent stays at home and takes care of the children. After considering your own situation, you have to decide if it would be possible for your family to take the cut in income that would enable one parent to be primarily responsible for homeschooling. This belt-tightening would be temporary because children grow quickly, and within a few years they may be bringing in money themselves! Our son recently contributed financially to fix a leaky section of the roof on our house.

If it isn't possible for one parent to be at home full-time, it doesn't mean homeschooling is out of the question; it does mean it's more challenging. Some families have rearranged their work hours; some have willing neighbors, relatives, or other homeschooling families who help them out; others arrange to work at home. I know of some groups of homeschooling parents in urban areas who band together to help each other out so that families can still make enough money to get by.

If your children are old enough, responsible, and self-reliant, they could have times at home alone and find constructive activities to keep them busy. In some states it is possible to engage in part-time homeschooling, with children attending one or two classes at the public school. It comes down to looking realistically at your situation and ordering priorities.

If your child is just plain miserable in school, and you have a strong support network of friends or family willing to help you out, you could give homeschooling a try even though both parents need to work. Contact a local homeschooling support group and ask if any of its families have two working parents; talking to others who have found ways to do it may inspire you to try it yourself. If you decide it is simply impossible for your family to pursue home education at this time, you could instead strive to be as involved in your children's school education as you can. After all, it's your loving concern and involvement that make the difference.

SANDRA DODD If a family feels that they *cannot* live without two incomes, maybe they can't afford to homeschool. Some families split shifts, of necessity. Some single parents homeschool. When homeschooling is a priority, people manage to manage!

I've heard budgets described in terms of what it would have cost to have the children in private schools, to clothe them appropriately, and to pay athletic fees. Then there are the costs of having the job—dressing up, lunch out, and so on, for the mom. After all that is balanced, the loss of the second income doesn't seem so big after all.

Some families have decided that paying for a curriculum is a bad use of funds.

I was employed full time, pre-children. Luckily for us, my husband was just finishing the college degree he had procrastinated about when I first got pregnant. There were times in our financial history when it would have

been more difficult to live on one income. Even now, if we really cared about driving new cars and having expensive furniture, we'd be unhappy with our finances, but we settle for older cars, used books, used furniture, and happy kids. Certainly, my kids are satisfied with hand-me-down and thrift store clothes, and are not bound by the fashion dictates of the kids at school.

Our entertainment and education are one and the same budget item (ha, if we had a budget, I mean). We don't have to spend money to relax after a hard day of school, since we're unschoolers. Budgeting, cooking, investments, home businesses—these are worked into homeschooling by many families and made learning experiences in addition to moneymakers.

DONNA NICHOLS-WHITE Homeschooling is like starting a business: The more money you have in the beginning, the more you'll waste. It's been seven years since I made my initial homeschooling purchases and I'm still feeling aftershocks.

Take the time I spent $400 on a prepackaged first-grade curriculum for my five year old. We haven't made it past chapter three in any of the subjects. (As it turns out, we found we didn't need all those textbooks.)

When our first child was born, I didn't have a lucrative career. I was, of all things, a retired instructional aide for an intermediate school. Needless to say, we were already accustomed to living on one salary.

Over the years we have adjusted our lifestyles to our income. Instead of expensive clothing, your children can wear hand-me-downs. Many homeschoolers claim their favorite store is the local Goodwill. Being "in style" is not a typical need in children who do not attend school.

I have friends who participate in an organization called the "Gleaners." They pick foods in the fields after harvests to provide for their families and for charity. This practice was established during biblical times.

After harvesting, they freeze, can, and dry food for year-round consumption. During the winter months, an appointed manager receives overstocks and damaged goods from grocery stores. These items are picked up by the member families. One family of six spends only $200 per month on food. I find this amazing. Of course, they are mainly vegetarian and every meal is prepared from scratch.

Money for home maintenance can be saved by borrowing do-it-yourself books from the library. If you buy tools such as hammers, screwdrivers, and nails instead of junky toys, the children will become quite handy around the house.

Jobs like indoor and outdoor painting, floor polishing, and carpet cleaning cost quite a bit if you contract the jobs out. They can be done by family members at a fraction of the cost.

I'm acquainted with a family who charges all of their purchases (groceries, gas, stamps, and so on) on one credit card, which they pay off in full every month. They receive mileage credits for each purchase. Every two years or so, this family travels to a foreign country using the free tickets they've earned. On one vacation they camped through Europe!

Having a vehicle to get around in is a boon. One family who couldn't afford a car payment decided to work on a paper route. The mother and children delivered papers every morning. This supplied enough funds to finance a van.

Sometimes parents will find that their hobbies can pay off. Woodworking, pottery, and even freelance writing can increase a family's income.

Teenagers benefit immensely from home-based businesses. Babysitting, gardening, and window washing are some of the jobs that can provide the money needed for clothing and extracurricular activities.

Financial responsibility begins at home. Supporting a family with one income can be a very positive experience.

SHARI HENRY By and large, I think the whole notion of sacrificing things to stay home is a bit overplayed. We live in a culture where too many people think they're entitled to too much. I often think it must be insulting to the generations that came before us to listen to those of us raised in the 1960s to 1980s whine so much. It's never been easy for the vast majority of people to make ends meet keeping one parent home. Good heavens, think of the colonists, the pioneers, the Depression-era families! They made choices and did the best they could.

So, we made choices. We measured the benefits and consequences of keeping me home to "school" the kids and have never, not ever, regretted our choice. We've been through lean and fat years and, while the fat are certainly less stressful, we don't think our children's education has either suffered or benefited because of our particular financial status at any given moment. Classical music on NPR, great literature at public libraries,

and many art exhibits are free. Children raised helping their parents plant seeds in a garden then later chopping the harvested vegetables for dinner will have much richer memories than children coming home from school to an empty home and a microwavable snack.

Some families, by choosing to have mom home, make tremendous sacrifices. They live in a way that many people question, even judge. To all outside appearances, these families "need" a second income. The children roam and experiment and raise chicks and do a lot of other things lost on most twentieth-century American children. These families have changed their definitions of what is and isn't necessary. They learn to set their own standards and move forward with great conviction, even in the face of much criticism. They shop at garage sales and thrift stores and rummage sales, and barter and trade for a good amount of their goods and necessities. The tradeoff is that one parent is home, and the other parent is usually more available than those who work more mainstream, urban jobs.

I watch people run hither and yon with both

> **By and large, I think the whole notion of sacrificing things to stay home is a bit overplayed. We live in a culture where too many people think they're entitled to too much.**

parents working and children imprisoned in school all day. I think it's dreadful, really.

10

Even if we can manage to live on one income, how can I keep the cost of homeschooling to a minimum?

Becky Rupp Money.

Always a sensitive topic.

For the financially strapped, there are all kinds of possibilities for low-budget (even no-budget) homeschooling. Many educational resources are absolutely free. The public library, for example, is a great source—not only for books and periodicals, but for educational videos, audiocassettes, story hours, craft programs, discussion groups, and lectures. Many field trips, with their wealth of learning opportunities,

Becky Rupp

cost nothing: tours of local businesses, visits to craftspersons and other professionals, nature hikes, historical societies, museums. Flipping back through my homeschool journals, I find lists of freebie field trips. We visited a local orchard to watch the cider press in action, and in the process we learned how cider is made. A friend with a stable showed the boys how to take care of the horses, taught them how to ride horseback, and let them watch the farrier changing horseshoes. The local historical society (free) had a wonderful display of Native American artifacts, which sparked great interest in the history of arrowheads. A violinmaker in the next town let the boys visit his workshop and explained the process of putting together a violin.

Used-book stores are generally inexpensive sources for books, magazines, and maps—though browsers should be cautious of used science books, which can quickly become outdated. Some homeschool supply companies specialize in marketing used (and thus greatly marked-down) educational resources. One source is The Homeschool Exchange (see the resources in appendix A). An annual subscription to their newsletter costs $6.50 (six issues) and it can pay for itself fast.

If you own a computer, the Internet is a spectacular source for homeschool programs. Search and you'll find online books, poems, and stories, art galleries and museums, foreign-language dictionaries, tutorials in all possible subjects, biographies of famous people, history timelines, maps, quizzes, virtual field trips, science demonstrations, and much more. Once you've got the computer, this is all inexpensive; acquiring the computer, on the other hand, is a substantial investment, so perhaps this doesn't count as "keeping costs to a minimum."

Many homeschool resources can be made at home. Through our boys' elementary-level years, I wrote a lot of our materials, including science, history, and handwriting workbooks and beginning readers (precisely tailored to the interests of each child—how many first-grade science workbooks can you find that are all about submarines?); and we made a lot of our own games, equipment, and manipulatives. Making do can be an education in itself. Our boys probably learned more from making their own history board games (with cardboard, felt-tipped pens, and index cards) than from playing the commercial versions.

A local homeschool support group can be a wonderful resource for mutually beneficial tradeoffs of the "your skills for mine" variety. Ask and you'll find people willing, for example, to tutor your kids in French in exchange for carpentry lessons, or teach your kids quilting in exchange for creative writing classes.

One of our worst money drains in homeschooling—I continually kick myself for this—is what my husband calls "false starts," the purchase of stuff that simply didn't work for our kids. A good series of math books and manipulatives, for example, can be a terrific investment, lasting through many years and children—but if the kids don't like it, there it will sit, hated, on the bottom shelf of the bookcase, an educational and financial lost cause. A geography game, if the kids find it boring, is money down the tubes. I can't think of any single purchase that was financially devastating in and of itself ("Rats—the kids don't like the grand piano . . ."), but all the lesser goofs add up. Textbooks, for example, are pricey, and we've bought our share of blah ones.

There's no truly foolproof solution to this, kids being the unpredictable little intellects that they are, but wherever possible, it's a good idea to preview and pretest. Borrow the materials from someone who already uses them and see what the initial reaction is. Ask opinions and read reviews. But don't assume, just because a given program is popular ("Everybody uses it") that it's desirable for your family. I think of our experience with the (expensive) Saxon math texts, a series of much-praised math books available for all age levels, favored by many homeschool families. Our kids loathed them.

So what's the bottom line? It's certainly possible, with a little imagination, to homeschool very inexpensively, especially when your children are young.

Get the kids to share in designing the annual homeschool budget.

It's math enrichment and it doesn't cost a dime.

MARY GRIFFITH Homeschooling doesn't require much of anything you wouldn't already have around anyway. You don't need an expensive purchased curriculum (or even a cheap purchased curriculum!). You don't need special books or software or fancy manipulatives to "enrich your children's minds." In nearly ten years of homeschooling, the only thing I ever bought specifically because we were homeschooling was a teacher's planner book the very first year. I meant to use it to record, neatly organized by subject and date, what my children learned as they learned it. Within three days I realized I'd wasted my four dollars.

What you need to homeschool is the willingness to answer your kids' questions, to help them figure out what they want to know, and to help them find their answers. This could mean also buying books and equipment, but it doesn't have to. You can use the library, including interlibrary loan. You can haunt used bookstores, thrift shops, and yard sales. You can seek out people who know about whatever interests your children and get their advice. You can help your children figure out ways to make or grow or otherwise create what they need to learn.

After only a couple of years, you may find that you prefer the do-it-yourself route even if you don't need to watch your cash flow too carefully. There's much to be learned from searching out your own resources, figuring out how to make do with what you've already got to work with. (And keeping the everyday sorts of expenses to a minimum can allow you the occasional splurge on something you *really* want!)

WENDY PRIESNITZ Children do not require fancy curriculum packages in order to learn. They learn best by participating in the real world. After all, that's the way they learned how to walk and talk—two of the most difficult skills human beings ever learn. Mastery of these skills doesn't require textbooks, or even formal instruction for that matter. It requires a safe environment; somebody modeling the behavior; lots of opportunity for practice; plenty of encouragement; solace when something goes wrong; celebration when you're successful; and most of all, trust. Few parents ever doubt that their children will learn how to walk or talk. No formal instruction, no testing, no curriculum plans.

Think of learning as a drama that is unfolding with you and your children as active participants. Your role is to keep up with your child, ask questions at appropriate times, and help create bridges between new information and prior knowledge; it is not to contrive ways to teach skills or subject areas artificially. In this way, you'll do your children the honor of allowing them to be in charge of their own learning, with knowledge and skills developing in natural sequence through the exploration of an ever-expanding world. And you'll not have to spend money on curriculum materials!

Of course, books can be an excellent way to spark your child's interest in a subject, or provide more information about a topic he or she has discovered. Your public library can provide access to a whole world of historical fiction, newspaper articles, reference books, poetry and nonfiction, and is a valuable and well-used resource for most homeschooling families.

Some families feel more confident using a prepackaged curriculum pro-

> **Think of learning as a drama that is unfolding with you and your children as active participants.**

gram, at least when they begin their homeschooling adventure. But as children develop their skills as active learners, they inevitably demonstrate how much or how little instruction they require at any given time. It's up to us parents to listen.

11

With all the talk about the possibility of vouchers for education, can I wait and then use this money for homeschooling?

MARY GRIFFITH Don't hold your breath. Most of the voucher proposals I've seen specifically disallow homeschoolers receiving vouchers. And even if homeschoolers were eligible, they'd also be eligible for the accompanying regulation (and there is *always* regulation accompanying money). The price of vouchers for homeschooling is far more than I'm willing to pay.

MARY MCCARTHY Talk is cheap. You can no more spend a possible voucher than you can spend a possible lottery jackpot.

However, should vouchers ever become a reality, it seems reasonable that the taxpayers who are supplying the money—in the form of a voucher—would want you to account for how you spent their money. They might even want to exercise control over your curriculum choices, as demonstrated in the potential problem with using taxpayer dollars to purchase religious materials. As a taxpayer I would want to see proof that my money was being well spent and that your child was being educated. I can see where vouchers would lead to standards and mandatory testing in addition to paperwork and accountability procedures.

> I can see where vouchers would lead to standards and mandatory testing in addition to paperwork and accountability procedures.

DAVID AND MICKI COLFAX To do so would be a little like not buying a computer because you are waiting for them to come out with a faster model: You lose the use of what's available while you wait. And while you can be sure that a faster computer will be produced, there is next to no chance that we will ever see vouchers being used for homeschooling anytime in the near future. Indeed, there is some reason to fear that efforts to put a voucher system in place could threaten the interests of homeschoolers, even to the point of making homeschooling illegal in some cases. A recent California voucher ballot measure—which was rejected by the voters—contained provisions that would have required a redefinition of homeschooling by legislators heavily indebted to the public education lobby, a move all but certain to make homeschooling, in a voucher-providing state, far more difficult than it is currently.

In short, don't wait for something good to happen on the voucher front; governments that have been thus far so obviously reluctant to provide vouchers so parents can send their children to closely regulated schools are a very long way from providing them with money to spend on independent homeschooling programs.

NANCY PLENT Don't hold your breath waiting for vouchers to happen. Charter schools somehow got a foot in the door, but there's a fierce battle over their existence wherever they spring up. Charter schools and vouchers take money from the public schools, and the schools won't sit still for that.

If any voucher plans do make it, I don't think homeschoolers will automatically be included in them. We'll have to fight for that if we want it. And doesn't it seem likely that state money would come with some unacceptable strings attached? Would we have to test our kids, send in reports, or use certified teachers to get the voucher money, for example?

There's so many books out there on being a "tightwad" to stay afloat financially, so many ideas about making money from your home, that I think homeschoolers would be better off saying "No, thanks" to state handouts and cope with the expense in other ways.

READING TO HELP YOU SIMPLIFY

Many good books have been written on the subject of simplifying your life. Here are a few of my favorites.

Andrews, Cecile. *The Circle of Simplicity: Return to the Good Life.* Harper Collins, 1997.

Dacyczyn, Amy. *Tightward Gazette I, II, and III: Promoting Thrift as a Viable Alternative Lifestyle.* Villard Books, 1993, 1995, 1997.

Elgin, Duane. *Voluntary Simplicity: Toward a Way of Life That Is Outwardly Simple, Inwardly Rich.* Quill, 1993.

Halverson, Delia. *Living Simply.* Abingdon Press, 1996.

Luhrs, Janet. *The Simple Living Guide: A Sourcebook for Less Stressful, More Joyful Living.* Broadway Books, 1997.

McBride, Tracey. *Frugal Luxuries: Simple Pleasures to Enhance Your Life and Comfort Your Soul.* Bantam Books, 1997.

Mitchell, Jann. *Home Sweeter Home: Creating a Haven of Simplicity and Spirit.* Beyond Words Publishing Co., 1996.

St. James, Elaine. *Living the Simple Life: A Guide to Scaling Down and Enjoying More.* Hyperion, 1996.

———. *Simplify Your Life with Kids: 100 Ways to Make Family Life Easier and More Fun.* Andrews & McMeel, 1997.

Taylor, Robert, Susannah Seton, and David Greer. *Simple Pleasures: Soothing Suggestions and Small Comforts for Living Well Year Round.* Conari Press, 1997.

CHAPTER THREE

Can Homeschool Fit *Your* Life Situation?

B EWARE.

If you've ever said, "I'd like to homeschool but (fill in the blank)," the answers to the questions in this chapter just may blow your justification out of the proverbial excuse pile. If, as an educator, policy maker, or legislator, you've ever said, "Homeschooling may work for some but not for (fill in the blank)," you have found experienced voices to correct misunderstandings. If, as a reporter, journalist, or researcher, you've tried to pigeonhole the lifestyles of homeschool practitioners, get ready for a real eye-opener.

Chapters 1 and 2 illustrate how legally safe and affordable homeschooling is, and chapter 3 is a tribute to its astonishing flexibility. Homesechooling can be fashioned and shaped by its users into a viable educational approach suited to individual family needs and circumstances. The contributors to this book were asked if homeschooling could benefit children who are labeled gifted, have special needs, are diagnosed with Attention Deficit Disorder (ADD) or Attention Deficit Hyperactivity Disorder (ADHD), or have experienced discipline problems in school. They candidly reveal how homeschooling can fit the lifestyle of a single parent, a rural family, a child coming out of school after years of attendance, or a child who wants to homeschool

> **C**ombine the insights contained in this chapter with a good dose of creativity and a pinch of determination, and you just may find you can be as flexible as home-schooling itself.

part-time. Can homeschooling work if you're an ethnic or racial minority? If one child stays in school while another comes home? The answers are here.

As critics are all too happy to point out, not every family can homeschool. But it grows increasingly clear that many more of those who don't, can. Combine the insights contained in this chapter with a good dose of creativity and a pinch of determination, and you just may find you can be as flexible as homeschooling itself.

12

Is home a better place than school for my child, who has been labeled a "gifted child"?

NED VARE "Gifted" is a public relations term to make some parents believe the school recognizes talent in some children. It's self-esteem for parents; it does not benefit children. Gifted does not mean the same thing to a public school person as it does to a parent. To the public school, gifted means smart enough to be put into certain classes to be indoctrinated in ways different from the regular indoctrination. Do not make the mistake of believing that a gifted child is being given fast-track academic courses or advanced courses in those disciplines.

Yes. Home is a better place for almost any child to be educated—especially if the school considers the child gifted.

WILL SHAW Yes, and this was one reason we decided to try out homeschooling. After two years in public school, our oldest, Leah, then age seven, wasn't challenged or stimulated enough in her regular class. The so-called gifted program was, well, very inadequate. We feared her becoming a social outcast over time, so different was she from her classmates. She had already been "skipped" a grade, and we were stumped as to how to deal with the situation. As products of public schools and as former teachers, Margaret and I were burdened with conventional notions of what schools and education were supposed to resemble. But regular school was just not meeting our little girl's needs.

We heard about homeschooling and realized, "Hey, *this* is how we can make sure our child receives the variety and depth of instruction, knowledge, exposure, and room to maneuver that she needs and deserves." Homeschooling isn't as constrained by clocks and calendars or a one-size-fits-all curriculum.

You and your child can explore and pursue as deeply as you wish.

REBECCA RUPP "Gifted," surely, is one of the more conflict-laden words in the educational lexicon—what's gifted? We've all got gifted children, right?

Technically, giftedness is defined by standardized test scores: Children who score one or more grade levels above normal level are deemed academically talented or gifted. I don't know whether our children are "gifted" or not, since none has ever been tested. Josh, our oldest, is a talented and versatile writer (with a definite aversion to math); Ethan, the middle child, is intensely interested in and knowledgeable about the physical sciences (but can't spell); Caleb, our youngest, an extremely quick learner in general, is—according to his piano teacher—talented in music. Gifted? In the sense that some of their talents need more nurturing and support than my husband and I can give them, yes.

For children with unusual talents or highly directed interests, a homeschool environment is often ideal. It gives them the freedom to set their own agenda, concentrating on the development of their own special set of abilities, spending their time as they see fit. A notably talented or ambitious child, however, sometimes needs more input than is readily available at home. Caleb, for example, who taught himself to read music and play the piano, clearly needed a teacher to help him progress; Ethan, determined at the age of thirteen to learn college-level physics, had list after list of questions that demanded some high-powered physics expertise. We found Caleb a piano teacher and Ethan a kindly e-mail pen pal in the Cornell University physics department.

Josh, on the other hand, prefers to work on his own. We've tried a couple of creative writing and literature classes at different levels—most recently an online class through the local community college—but none has been too helpful. Fun, said Josh, but he thinks he learns more by himself. He writes daily and is working through a self-assigned reading list, including works by Kafka, Solzhenitsyn, Isaac Bashevis Singer, and Wallace Stevens.

> **For children with unusual talents or highly directed interests, a homeschool environment is often ideal.**

Gifted children—most children—are often skewed in their interests: obsessed with chemistry but indifferent to poetry; fascinated by art but unwilling to practice the clarinet; thrilled by astronomy but bored by Shakespeare. If anything creates tension in our homeschool program, it's this academic imbalance. Children given the freedom to pursue their own interests, do. The writers write; the scientists spend whole days in the basement where they've set up a chemistry lab. This means that not all academic subjects get equal enthusiasm, equal dedication, and equal time. My husband and I provide the fundamentals of a basic education, but the boys, inevitably, pick and choose. We lay it out; they take what they need. Each according to his own gifts.

13

Can my child, who's been diagnosed with ADHD, succeed at home?

Susan Evans Children who have been labeled ADHD, ADD, dyslexic, hyperactive, or any of those other labels may benefit most of all from homeschooling!

Conventional schools can be failure traps for children who are not by nature quiet, compliant, morning people who are able to concentrate for long periods of time on disconnected, unrelated tasks and who are able to screen out lots of distracting sounds and activities. That's not a description of very many children I know.

Some young people, especially boys, are active and curious, focusing on several activities simultaneously—building with Lego blocks, watching television, listening to a conversation on the phone, humming a song. These children need, thrive on, and deserve an environment where they can move freely, change activities as their minds shift gears, and be able to eat, sleep, dance, and use the bathroom as their bodies require.

Time and growing maturity allow children to develop healthy patterns of eating, sleeping, working, and playing in their own time—consistent with their own personalities and temperaments. Productive responses to frustration, anger, and enthusiasm develop over time in a supportive atmosphere. In such an environment, an impulsive, too active, easily distracted boy, for instance, can grow to become an empathic, energetic, multitalented delightful young man. And rather than being dependent on drugs or rigid routine to be likable, he grows with his independence and self-esteem intact.

Many overly active youngsters thrive on physical challenge: digging in gardens, building structures, moving furniture, and so on. Often they need to eat, rest, and use the bathroom on timetables different from quieter, less active children, and they can easily be overstimulated.

These children have an internal demand for activity and need for instant response to stimuli that seems overwhelming, and they can find spending large amounts of unsupervised time with groups of other children unsuccessful. But they are delightful and happy with people who are more mature and can accommodate their temporary social immaturity, while providing positive behavioral role models.

Homeschooling can do a superb job of giving young people this supportive environment while they are growing up and "mellowing out." After several years of quiet, appropriate support and productivity, these kids will move of their own accord into a group of peers (age, interest, or both) as pleasant, successful friends. In the meantime, they've learned more about the world in a useful context than they would have as singled-out, different children in a class, who absorb the lesson that they're not quite acceptable as they are, and often can't

> Conventional schools can be failure traps for children who are not by nature quiet, compliant, morning people who are able to concentrate for long periods of time on disconnected, unrelated tasks and who are able to screen out lots of distracting sounds and activities.

figure out what they're doing wrong or what's expected of them.

As homeschoolers, they are useful, valued members of their families and their communities. They're the ones folks turn to when something needs to be fixed, hard work needs to be done, or a puzzle (physical or social) needs to be solved.

LUZ SHOSIE ADHD, in most cases, is a teaching disability. It means that your child learns in ways other than the way school chooses to teach. It is likely to disappear once your child is allowed to choose what, when, where, and with whom she wants to learn. Read Thomas Armstrong, Susannah Scheffer, John Holt, Daniel Greenberg. Remember that children want to learn and they know how.

Luz Shosie

CINDY WADE Many families new to homeschooling tell me they see the greatest change for the better in their children in the first two weeks after they begin to homeschool. They say their children seem more relaxed, more secure, and more loving. Many tell me their child's ADD or ADHD symptoms all but disappear.

I'm convinced that ADD and ADHD are conditions created by the schools to shirk accountability. Pick up any book on ADD or ADHD and just look at the "symptoms": fidgeting, stares out the window, won't wait for a turn, speaks out of turn, talks loudly, unable to learn to read, accident prone, given to tantrums, noisy, mischievous, dawdles, loses things, daydreams, impulsive, needs constant stimulation, gets angry and frustrated, restless, low self-esteem, can't concentrate, and awkwardness at sports. That describes just about everyone on this planet! These are things that all children (and many adults) do innocently and naturally.

Nature provided children with short attention spans for a reason. It's part of their survival instincts. A child will, however, spend hours doing one thing providing that one thing holds his interest. My six year old can spend an entire day playing in his sandbox, if I let him, taking short breaks only for food and potty-runs. Try getting him to sit still at a desk for an hour or so. It's just not possible. But then sitting at a desk for four to six hours a day isn't natural, either.

I'm also convinced that children under the age of ten shouldn't be forced to attend any kind of institutionalized training such as preschool or public school. These children should be out catching frogs, building forts, raising chickens, going on hikes, playing in sandboxes, baking cookies, riding bikes, and playing make-believe. A child's play is his work. While he plays, he learns. Children this young are not psychologically, biologically, emotionally, or physiologically ready for structured learning. This is the reason so many of the male youth in this country spend much of their frustrated childhoods labeled as ADD or ADHD and are legally drugged into submission and dependency.

I once got into a heated discussion with a mother of a teenage boy diagnosed as ADD. By her description this boy was a real terror; but after listening to her lengthy diatribe about her son's upbringing, I came to the conclusion that the boy's major problem was a combination of his public schooling experience and her parenting. She'd hauled that boy from psychologist to psychologist, yanked him in and out of any number of programs, homeschooled him, then put him back into school because it was too much trouble for her and she couldn't "handle" him. He was put on drugs only to be taken off and put back on again. The boy's life seemed like one endless experiment and psychotherapy session. All of this was done with the countless advice from the countless "experts" in the school system and psychiatry industry.

Early on in my discussion with this woman, I told her I didn't believe ADD or ADHD even existed. She argued it had to exist because "just look at all the books written about it." I took the liberty of reminding her that just because something is discussed and written about extensively doesn't mean it really exists. Take the Loch Ness Monster, for example. She eventually ended our conversation by walking away from me.

Children, especially boys, shouldn't be required to attend formal instruction until they are at least ten years old. They should be allowed the freedom of learning by doing. Let them build forts, climb trees, have lengthy conversations with their parents, raise animals, go fishing, and play while they are young, unlabeled, and drug-free.

But, you ask, what would society do with all these little boys running around loose? Maybe society would tolerate them better. Maybe society would love them more. Maybe the tolerance and love would be returned to us when these

same boys reach adulthood and they do not abuse drugs or other people.

14

I'd like to homeschool my child, who has special needs. Is this possible?

MICHELLE BARONE Yes, the benefits of homeschooling for all children extend to those with special needs, including serious or multiple disabilities. I truly believe these children do extremely well being nurtured at home. I was a special education teacher in a very small, self-contained, special education classroom for five years. This classroom had no more than eight students and one full-time aide. Additional staff was available when I needed it. I cared deeply for these children and gave them my best, but I knew I could never spend enough time with each one individually, as they deserved. The need for classroom management increased as my students "learned" a variety of disruptive behaviors from each other. This cut down on the time I had to cover the material assigned by the powers that be.

In my heart I knew what I was teaching them could easily have been taught at home. Most of my students would have been much happier there, with their families, going on errands, participating in programs that truly fit their needs. Instead, so much time was spent on the bus to and from school, waiting for everyone to be ready, interruptions for snack, lunch, or outside time. I often wondered why they had to be in this classroom learning about cooking and self-care when they could learn the same things at home. This was all before I had children or had even heard of homeschooling.

When parents decide to homeschool their exceptional child, it takes great courage and love. But it is being done successfully. Here are a few suggestions: Get support from friends, homeschoolers with special-needs children, family members. Find professionals who support your decision to keep your child home. Pick their brains for ideas and good resources, and use whatever services your community offers. Always remember, you have the final decision on what is best for your child and your family.

Because you know your child better than anyone, you are in the best position to assess his or her educational needs. Consultation with experts, like speech or physical therapists, can be very help-

> **In my heart I knew what I was teaching them could easily have been taught at home. Most of my students would have been much happier there, with their families, going on errands, participating in programs that truly fit their needs.**

ful. With love and patience, you can learn to work with your child in these areas. You don't have to give your child over to others, but you can use others as resources so you can care for your child at home. A family I know with an autistic child hires a teacher to come in their home three times a week. This gives the mom a needed break and brings another caring adult into this child's life.

Working one-on-one gives you the opportunity to help your special needs child with daily living skills based on her individual needs. Your child will get much more attention in these areas with you than at a school.

Homeschooling a special needs child is a difficult task—you need to make sure your needs are also met. Time for yourself and a good support group are essential. Caring friends and relatives can also be of tremendous help with your child's care.

WENDY PRIESNITZ Many families find that their special needs children blossom in the homeschool environment. For many children, the typical classroom style of teaching is not the most suitable learning method. Their cognitive or motor skills may be developing slower or faster than their age peers. They may learn better by listening than by reading or writing. Or they may simply not be interested in the subject matter being discussed and tune out. When these children have difficulty with their school work, the blame is often laid at their feet and they are said to be "learning disabled." This label adds to their already high level of frustration and low self-esteem, contributing to a downward spiral of poor school performance and antisocial behavior.

Many parents have told me that, to their astonishment, these so-called learning disabilities often turn out to have been more like teaching disabilities. In many cases they disappear once the parents are able to cater to their children's unique style of learning. Away from the pressure of a competitive classroom in which they couldn't keep up, and finally able to make academic progress at their own pace, their self-esteem returns and their behavior improves.

Children with real disabilities also tend to do well in the home-based learning environment. As a parent, you are able to provide just the right amount of individualized attention in a caring, supportive environment, which is often just not possible in a school setting.

15
Should I do anything special for a child who is coming out of public school after years of attendance?

CHRIS CARDIFF The key to a successful homeschooling transition starts with the parent, not the child. The best thing you can do is *relax.*

This is an extremely difficult assignment for most parents. After seeing their children struggle inside the traditional institutional school, they are frantic to "do something" to correct the situation. Recognize that "doing nothing" may be the best "something" you can do for them at first.

Allow your children the freedom to explore areas that interest them without placing them on any artificial schedules. They need time and space to decompress from the public school experience. The methodology of public schools (and many private schools) discourages their inborn curiosity and desire to learn. It may take some months away from that environment before a child's natural curiosity reawakens. Look for ways to encourage the reawakening rather than stifling it.

The most common mistake new homeschooling parents make is attempting to recreate the public school environment at home (aka the "school-at-home" syndrome). While "school-at-home" is a natural mistake (for many of us, it's the only model we're familiar with), it's an unfortunate one because it puts unnecessary pressure on both parent and child. For the parent/teacher, there is the frantic scramble to duplicate the schedules and curriculum of an institutional-based style of teaching. For the child/student, it's a return to an environment and style of learning that probably was the source of problems before—except now there's no way to escape it by going home.

One of the strengths of homeschooling is the freedom and flexibility it provides in contrast to the rigid structure required for mass schooling. It takes time for both parent and child to adjust to homeschooling's freedom and flexibility and decide how they want to take advantage of it. Neither of you should make any hasty decisions or rush to spend money on some fancy (and expensive) prepackaged curriculum.

To help you explore and understand your homeschooling options, get involved with a local homeschooling support group. Support groups are available in most areas. If you can't find a group

> **A**llow your children the freedom to explore areas that interest them without placing them on any artificial schedules. They need time and space to decompress from the public school experience.

(or the existing group doesn't suit you), you can always start your own or get involved with one of the online groups. These groups can be a major source of group activities for your children as well as an important source of information for you as a homeschooling parent.

Every family develops its own philosophy and style of homeschooling. Spending time evaluating and discovering your child's learning style and matching it with an appropriate homeschooling philosophy is time well spent. Be patient with yourself and your child as you explore the world of homeschooling together. Give yourselves time to relax and enjoy learning again.

JOHN TAYLOR GATTO Only you know the answer to this question. Government schooling is set up structurally to produce incomplete people. How and why that happened is far too complex and bewildering to tackle here, but suffice it to say the folks who did this were *sincere* ideologues who believed what the students

John Taylor Gatto

were about to be in the best interests of the human race. They still do. This "true belief" is what makes them so dangerous. It fuels their cause—sometimes referred to mystically at the turn of the twentieth century as "The Work"—much more effectively than greed or self-interest or class hatred (and all the motives attributed by the best school critics to school policy-makers to explain the otherwise inexplicable nature of public school).

So your child will have been made incomplete by his or her experience. How radically incomplete and in what areas your own close attention and analysis will have to determine, although in a great many cases *your child will know what is missing,* what needs priority attention, and will tell you or try to tell you. So listen. Fortunately, the human spirit is very resilient; all the theories of child psychology, including the best ones, are based on partial truth dimly seen. Read hundreds of biographies to see just how resilient Washington, Franklin, Farragut, and Edison really were. Read the brilliant modern masterpiece *Angela's Ashes,* by Frank McCourt, to realize how a child who is regularly beaten, starved, humiliated, embedded in continuous poverty of a type that makes Harlem seem like Utopia, reared without safety of any sort, becomes in adulthood a fine man and useful citizen because his ignorant mother (Angela) had courage, and his drunken father told him hero tales and gave him imagination, resourcefulness, and pride.

LILLIAN JONES The wonderful new lifestyle you're entering is almost like a different dimension from the one that seemed normal up until now, so it might take some time to get oriented. You'll want to be especially sensitive to your child during the transition. Take care to support his unique style of being and learning, and try to avoid thinking in terms of a thing called homeschooling.

Children just coming out of school will often go through a withdrawal or decompression period, and will almost certainly balk at any attempt to reproduce elements of school. The intensity is in direct proportion to how long they went to school, and to how difficult the experience was for them. You might think the summer break would have taken care of that, but it just doesn't seem to work that way.

> **The wonderful new lifestyle you're entering is almost like a different dimension from the one that seemed normal up until now, so it might take some time to get oriented.**

It might be a bit unnerving for you at times, but your child really does have an internal wisdom about his needs. Remember that he's been in an unnatural situation for a long time, one in which he wasn't always trusted or respected as an intelligent, self-directed person. Time taken for the internal process of refinding himself and his equilibrium is every bit as legitimate as any academic study might be.

Try not to take it too seriously if you have some nervous moments—times when you worry that you might be doing the wrong thing, that your child is not a good candidate for homeschooling, or that you aren't cut out for this. It passes. As you gradually let go of the school model of being and learning, a new and richer way of life will emerge.

This is a special and sometimes delicate time for your family, a time for getting to know and trust in one another all over again. Relax and enjoy, read wonderful things to him, and let your child know that he's wonderful and loved just as he is. Listen to him, and respect his way of being. Provide things that interest him, science experiments, time outside in nature together, field trips, play time with old and new friends, and lots of time to vegetate in whatever way he's drawn to. It's easier if you don't watch for the kettle to boil: Occupy yourself

with something else, and it will be easier to let him be. He's doing what he needs to do, and it's a healthy process. Moreover, your child very much wants and needs for you to remain available as his parent. It can unnecessarily stress your precious relationship if you turn into a teacher.

You, too, will need time to adjust. You'll need to reexamine lots of expectations. If you trust your child, give him space, and promote mutual respect, you will become a trusted facilitator. You will begin to witness the magic of homeschooling. It won't look anything like what you expected—and it will amaze and delight you!

16

My child has had discipline problems at school. Can homeschooling help?

PAT MONTGOMERY Problems are symptoms. They indicate that something needs to be fixed. Determine the reasons for your child's discipline problems. If they can be traced to the way he relates to the teacher and/or classmates, or to time scheduling and the other aspects of the school environment, home-based education may be the way to go. It may be necessary for you to observe your child in the school environment and make a judgment on whether or not he would benefit from being in your one-on-one setting (home).

It is not an uncommon situation. Parents and students alike have reported  a great release of pressure because of the move from institutional schools to home. Problems often disappear. Critics claim this is

Pat Montgomery

catering to a child's whims, as in the oft-repeated myth, "A child has to learn how to tough it out in this world."

Consider how a gardener tends new shoots in the nursery. Never would she take them from the heat and light of a deliberately planned nurturing environment before they have the strength and stamina to withstand the elements. Parents almost take this approach for granted when it comes to babies and toddlers. Yet children of any age have growth needs that must be met humanely if they are to develop into healthy human beings.

DR. RAYMOND MOORE AND DOROTHY MOORE
Yes, usually, depending on the problem and how mature they are. If under eight or nine, be wary about their readiness for school, especially boys—who are as bright as girls, but are a year less mature. Children who aren't ready physically, mentally, or emotionally, or who have recently witnessed death or family separation, should rarely be placed in special education or anywhere their self-worth or ability is in question. (See Question 37 for more on this topic.)

The highest concept of discipline is "the fine art of discipleship." Children who spend most of their time with exemplary parents instead of peers learn to reason like them and avoid peer dependence. Such children normally achieve adult-level reasonability or cognition between the ages of eight and twelve instead of the typical fifteen to twenty.

Our suggestions for good discipline are first preventive. Good habits of eating and sleeping with a reasonably regular, consistent mealtime and bedtime from birth will help avoid problems later. As toddlers, not yet able to reason, children should be taught to obey, using gentle encouragement, persistence, and diversion. When they begin to reason, help them understand reasons for rules. As reasonability grows, give them more choices and authority, helping them make many of their own decisions until they are self-disciplined, your ultimate goal.

A balance of authority and responsibility with practical work experience is the soundest route for well-behaved children. They can and should work as soon as they walk, picking up their toys before they have other privileges. Teach them gradually from the list printed by the Ozark Folk Center Old-Time Print Shop many years ago: "If you open it, close it; if you turn it on, turn it off; if you unlock it, lock it; if you break it, fix it; if you can't fix it, report it; if you borrow it, return it; if you make a mess, clean it up; if you move it, put it back; if it doesn't concern you, don't mess with it; if you don't know, ask."

Remedial methods should start with checking diet; our *Home Made Health* will help you here. Allergies and food sensitivities account for many behavior and learning problems. The sweetest and best solution is work, combined with service. Aside from chores, it may earn money and teach practical math, management, writing, and personal relations. It builds skills to earn a living instead of developing couch potatoes and TV/sports fanatics. Our work-service books, *Minding Your Own Business* and *Home Built Discipline,* offer peace and save a lot of pain.

WILL SHAW Many are the children who don't fit in the "box" of the conventional school classroom. School can be an oppressive, intimidating, boring, confining, unimaginative, failure-reinforcing, spirit-crushing place. Behaviors may be taught, learned, or tolerated in school that are unacceptable or even destructive. School is a social pressure-cooker, and the other children can be brutal. A teacher can be plain lousy. These and other aspects of conventional schooling can contribute to major behavioral problems.

Homeschooling may bring relief, break the cycle, allow kids to grow and even flourish academically, socially, spiritually, and emotionally.

We are delighted when people say, "My, aren't those homeschooled children in the Whosit family so well-behaved and bright, blah, blah, so we should consider homeschooling, too." I heard this once from a couple who didn't recognize that their own children were obnoxious little snots because they, the parents, were inconsistent regarding their children's behavior and discipline and not supportive of each other.

So good parenting is still good parenting. But clearly, homeschooling can often help behavior problems, restore self-confidence, jump-start or launch a kid's academic progress, and bring parent and child closer.

DAVID AND MICKI COLFAX
The only possible answer to this kind of question—and we have been asked it many times at home-schooling conferences—is . . . *probably.*

Some so-called "discipline problems" are so trivial or school-specific that getting the child out of school will obviously help. Less obvious are instances in which the discipline problems are more serious or less directly related to school functions. Discipline problems relating to drugs or alcohol abuse, for example, need to be taken seriously, and rehabilitation may require more than simply removing the child from the school setting. And serious discipline problems that cannot be attributed to the school setting itself may be manifestations of more general problems, such as psychological or physical disorders and family dysfunction, and are unlikely to be helped by homeschooling programs that do not directly address these possibilities.

In general, we recommend that parents of any child who is not enjoying or doing well in school should at least consider removing him or her from that

While homeschooling cannot *guarantee* success—particularly where the damage inflicted, from whatever source, is substantial—patient and understanding parents who are prepared to take very seriously the at-home reeducation of their "discipline problem" child will substantially increase the odds that homeschooling will indeed help.

setting. But every case is different; and while homeschooling cannot *guarantee* success—particularly where the damage inflicted, from whatever source, is substantial—patient and understanding parents who are prepared to take very seriously the at-home reeducation of their "discipline problem" child will substantially increase the odds that homeschooling will indeed help.

SHARI HENRY This was not our situation, but I'd like to answer it based on the situations I've seen. A friend pulled her son (he was nine at the time, third grade) out of school halfway through last year. He had been loaded up on Ritalin and was known far and wide as one of the most difficult children at school. This particular school is widely thought of as the best public school in the area, and is located in a wealthy district full of successful, well-educated parents. I listened to various conversations about this boy over lunch at the swimming pool. If it weren't so sad, it would have been laughable to hear these people's reasons for why this child should have been made to tough it out in school. The fact is, many of these parents liked having children lower in the pecking order than their kids. It's all a big race to them—who wanted to be moved down the ladder simply by having a couple on the bottom rung pulled out?

I got tired of listening to their elitism disguised as concern. I asked why anyone would care if this kid was gone. He was nothing but trouble to the teachers; the other children didn't like him; and by removing him from school, his parents were saving the school district thousands of dollars.

The mother has since dropped the dosage of Ritalin incredibly and the child's behavior has improved dramatically. Sometimes this child comes over to play. Once, his mother forgot to send along his Ritalin and phoned, nearly panicked, to ask if he was okay. I asked him. He said he was fine and he stayed to play with my son another five hours. No problem. The most recent time they played, my son, TJ, and this friend walked through the woods to the school's playground. The boy showed TJ where he usually sat during recess. "Over there, in that corner by the fence." TJ said, "You mean you didn't swing and slide or play with the other kids?" "No, they were always mean to me. I just sat over there and played with the rocks."

The imagined scene grieved my son. It infuriated me. Did those teachers try hard enough to integrate this child into the lives of the others, or were they too exasperated by his difficult behavior? Did the other parents encourage their children to respond more kindly, or did they only use this child as an example of how not to behave? Was the boy ever, ever held up as an example and acknowledged for what he did well (he is headed toward national rankings in swimming), or was the school environment so determined to set him straight and the other children so trained to keep others in their place to maintain what is theirs that no one dared say a thing?

Words can not express how privileged I feel to watch this young man emerge from his prison-like cocoon, his wings glistening with possibilities.

17

I'm a single parent. Isn't it hard for single parents to homeschool?

MICHELLE BARONE I have been homeschooling as a single parent now for three-and-a-half years. Single parenting certainly has its challenges, but the rewards are many. Homeschooling as a single parent is not much different than for couples. I have the same concerns, questions, frustrations, and joys as most families because only one parent is usually with the children all day long. The real difference—the big difference—is in not having the support of another parent, and money.

For this reason, gathering a strong support system around us is vital to my family, and is probably the most important step in being successful. I have friends who take my children when I have to work nights, a brother who puts up my bookshelves and fixes the light switch, a mother who buys my children their nice Christmas presents when I cannot, and a support network of other homeschooling friends who keep me connected and sane.

Find a rhythm that works for your family. As a single parent, you may be working either outside the home or in a home business, or maybe even both. This means your family may not operate on the standard nine-to-five schedule. This requires creativity and flexibility from everyone in the family. This struggle to support your family can be the most difficult task as a single parent. If you are responsible for earning an income, how do you do that if your children are not being taken care of all day in school? There are lots of different ways to tackle this problem. Some find a home business works well. For some, a job with flexible hours can work well. I know of single

moms who have done manicuring, sewing, bookkeeping, direct sales, house cleaning, baby-sitting, typing, writing, crafts, tutoring, teaching, anything they could so they would be home with their children most of the time. This dedication and commitment are a tribute to the unshakable belief that our children deserve to learn at home with us.

Homeschooling provides you with the time and opportunity to be with your children in a loving and healing way. If you are single as a result of a loss from divorce or death, then both you and your children need time together to heal. Time and closeness can provide you with the strength to mourn the loss of dreams, and courage to make new ones. The first few years of homeschooling on our own were hard, both financially and emotionally. I tried to keep my focus on the long run, knowing my children would not be children for long and we could do without a bigger house, better toys, or new clothes, but we could not do without each other.

18

What is the homeschooling situation among ethnic and racial minority populations?

DONNA NICHOLS-WHITE When I began homeschooling, I entered the world as a triple minority. I was African American, an at-home mother, and I homeschooled my children. Living in Washington was an additional problem; this state's population was, at the time, only 2.6 percent black.

I felt as if I was the only black woman who homeschooled. Whenever we attended a homeschooling function, our family stood out from the rest of the crowd.

Over the years I discovered my original premises were incorrect. Homeschooling is as diverse as the rest of American society. It's just finding the folks that is hard. Many parents shy away from going public with their lifestyle. The harsh reactions of some communities to home education can often hinder a family's desire to be noticed. Let's not forget that many advocates of schooling think families such as mine should think like them.

When I was a child, black people were fighting to get into supposedly better schools and therefore have access to equal opportunity. It's pretty painful to leave an institution that has always been credited for being the road to upward mobility and have enough trust to go it alone. It is also a relief when we discover how wonderful the homeschooling experience is.

Many ethnic and racial groups are noted for having a firm belief in education. The more degrees a person has, the more prestige offered. Homeschooling in many communities is not considered the road to a higher education. I remember a browbeating I received at a child development convention. I was accused of cheating my children out of a decent education and also harming others by supporting family education. Whenever I pointed out the plight of black children in schools (which was the reason this particular organization was formed), and noted how homeschooled children fared better, he berated me more. I thought it strange that a male of my race would defend the schools so adamantly while accusing me of harming my children. (I knew, from experience, that I couldn't help but offer an education that far exceeded that offered through institutionalized education.) John Holt once noted that the least served communities were the strongest advocates of institutionalized education.

> When I was a child, black people were fighting to get into supposedly better schools and therefore have access to equal opportunity. It's pretty painful to leave an institution that has always been credited for being the road to upward mobility and have enough trust to go it alone. It is also a relief when we discover how wonderful the homeschooling experience is.

I've been honored by having had the opportunity to meet, and be in contact with, a very diverse group of home-schoolers. We are here but we just aren't yelling about it.

19

My family has chosen to live a natural lifestyle. Are there enough educational opportunities available to homeschool in a rural area?

WENDY PRIESNITZ There are educational opportunities everywhere. Life itself is an educational opportunity, and children learn by being part of it. While rural children don't have easy access to muse-ums, art galleries, and libraries, like their urban counterparts, they can learn by wading in streams, growing their own gardens, and interacting with nature.

For many rural families, the Internet opens up a vast array of information rivaling that found in the best libraries and science museums. In addition to Web sites that inform and entertain, Internet access provides people of all ages with opportunities to correspond and communicate with both age peers and communities of interest from around the world.

HELEN AND MARK HEGENER There are more than enough resources in the smallest community, even on a remote

---

LOTS OF WAYS TO UNCOVER RURAL RESOURCES

- The Internet
- Educational television, videos, books on tape
- Interlibrary loan programs through your local library
- Homeschooling magazine subscriptions
- Oodles of catalogs
- Join or start a local support group
- Utilize online support groups
- Enjoy and learn from your natural surroundings

homestead, to enrich the life of a child beyond measure. Just as it is in the city, homeschooling in a rural environment is mostly a matter of finding and supporting your child's interests. Computers, the Internet, educational television, videos, books on tape, and other resources bring a world of learning to everyone's door. Even the smallest community libraries are often connected to a never-ending network of other libraries, and interlibrary loan programs can provide almost any book in print.

Subscribe to a homeschooling magazine, and send for educational resource catalogs. Many large school supply catalogs are free, and offer every learning resource imaginable. Sometimes the smaller, less polished catalogs will have just what your child is interested in, and often for much less money.

If you or your children need socialization with other homeschoolers, join or start a local homeschool support group. Or join an online support group via the Internet or a service provider—if you haven't been online yet, the resources and support available there will astound you! The *Home Education Magazine* Forum on America Online

> **I**f you live in a rural area, count yourself and your children lucky. Fresh air, green grass, animal friends, and all the rest are usually well worth the loss of a few museums and well-stocked bookstores.

includes a very active message folder specifically for rural homeschoolers, who discuss everything from cabbages to goats to strange weather patterns! If you don't have a computer, check your local public library. They often have computers available for accessing the Internet at little or no cost.

But even without any of these resources, homeschooling rurally can be a rich and rewarding experience. What does any child really need besides love and encouragement and someone to share discoveries with?

For many years children raised on farms and ranches and coastal islands have learned by doing—raising animals, growing gardens, doing chores, tending crops, overseeing herds and flocks. A lot of what most children learn sitting in school seats is learned by these children first-hand: reading, writing, and math as they read instructions, keep records, compute feedings, adjust recipes, and so forth. In the same way, homeschooled children can find endless ways of learning and applying what they've learned.

Most of all, if you live in a rural area, count yourself and your children lucky. Fresh air, green grass, animal friends, and all the rest are usually well worth the loss of a few museums and well-stocked bookstores.

20

Is homeschooling an all-or-nothing situation, or can I homeschool one child while the other is enrolled in school?

Luz Shosie Self-directed learning takes place wherever the learner chooses. If one child in the family wants to experience learning inside a school building, it should not interfere with the learning of other members of the family. If it does interfere, then compromises may have to be made—but that's learning too, isn't it?

Sandra Dodd *Sandra's answer originally appeared in the August/September 1996 edition of* Network News, *now called* California Homeschool News, *published by the California Homeschool Network, PO Box 44, Vineburg, CA 95487.*

Some people are solidly homeschoolers and happy to be so. Others are wholly involved in and supportive of the public schools their sons and daughters attend. Then there are those with a foot in each world.

Using my sister as a test case, I made a radical recommendation that she chose

to implement, and it turned out well. Since then, I've given this advice several times and haven't been sued (yet). Nobody's even asked for a refund!

Here is the way my sister overcame her school codependency: She divorced herself emotionally and politically from the public school. I have one sister, three years younger than I am. I was a star pupil, junior honor society member, extracurricular queen, member of the band, all-state chorus. Younger sisters in the readership are already sympathizing with my B-student sister. She went out with the younger brothers of my boyfriends a couple of times. She couldn't get out of my shadow. She dropped out of high school not long before I became a teacher. I was invested in the system. She had rejected it.

Years passed, and we each had three children. While I opted not to send mine to school at all, my sister was a "room mother" and gifted-program advisory board member, and she chaperoned field trips. Her older boy wrote at the age of five. Mine didn't *read* until he was eight. The evidence that she was right and I was wrong was increasing, which must have been a great feeling for her. (It happens more and more as the years go by, and I don't mind it at all.)

Another thing was increasing, though. From once a month, to once a week, to every other day, my sister called and complained about something at school, and I would play devil's advocate, or give her considerations the teacher had that my sister might not have known. At first I was sympathetic. Then I was apathetic. After a while I got irritated, and one day I cut her off in advance of the tale of woe, saying, "You already know what I'm going to say. You don't *have* to send them to school."

It was springtime. She decided to spend the summer preparing them for the idea of staying home if they wanted to, but meanwhile she needed a way for their being in school not to ruin *her* life. I recommended that she just detach. She was not to enable the teachers to torment her children. She quit forcing them to do homework. She quit even considering punishing them for bad grades or rewarding them for good grades. Their grades were theirs, and not a reflection on the family, and not an indicator of learning. They were just grades, a contest, a competition like who sold the most candy bars, only my sister quit buying the candy bars, as it were. She quit helping with the homework.

> Some people are solidly homeschoolers and happy to be so. Others are wholly involved in and supportive of the public schools their sons and daughters attend. Then there are those with a foot in each world.

The year after that her daughter, the oldest, stayed home instead of going to fourth grade. The boys went to school. When they felt ill they were allowed to stay home without having to have a fever or puke to earn the privilege. They became more honest. Sometimes they just said, "I don't want to go to school today." She would say, "You don't have to then. I wish you just would never go again." So their first reward was renewed and increased honesty. (When I called my sister to read this to her for verification, she asked me to add that if she had it to do over, she wouldn't be so honest as to announce to the principal, "School is optional at our house." She advises you to make assorted excuses, like the other parents do.)

The next year the daughter went back because she had missed her friends. The dynamics of that school year, though, were phenomenal. Neither my sister nor I had foreseen the extent to which this detachment would free the entire family, and hadn't considered the effect on the relationship between the children and their teachers. No longer were these children in school against their will, their parents having submitted them to a lock-up situation. On one hand, they had teachers who wanted them to stay in school. On the other hand, they had parents who wanted them to say home. How much more "wanted" could they feel? Each moment they were in school they were aware, and the teacher was aware, that they were there because they, the children, *wanted* to be there! These factors changed the way the kids responded to assignments, to interpersonal problems, and to threats from the teacher (which have little power without the backing of the parents).

In late winter, the daughter contracted a staph pneumonia and was in a hospital ninety miles from home for a couple of weeks. After that she didn't want to return to school (and her recovery was better served by staying home, too). One of her brothers left school at that time as well, and next year all three plan to stay home. When school starts and they don't go, how different it will be for them than it is in those families in which the children pine for school but their parents forbid them to go.

There are different reasons for homeschooling. School might not be an option at all in a family in which religious or social considerations take precedence. In families in which stu-

dent-directed learning is the primary focus, children taking control of their own learning by deciding whether to pursue it at home or at school can be liberating for all involved, and educational in the extreme for their teachers.

Although the ideal might be children who have never gone to school a day in their lives, reality isn't always ideal. If your children press you to let them go to school, this detachment option might be a way for you to have your cake and eat it, too. The philosophies of choice, freedom, child-led learning, "bliss-led learning," and personal responsibility can be honored and spread to new audiences by parents treating children as humans with rights and responsibilities whether they are sixteen, twelve, or eight years old.

21

Can my child go to school for some classes and homeschool for the rest?

DORIS HOHENSEE When my children were young, I never considered using the elementary school for classes while homeschooling. I was concerned that teachers might not understand our open approach to learning. What if a teacher found it necessary to criticize my child if he failed to meet some arbitrary expectation? As I saw it, the benefits of school never outweighed the potential for damage.

However, when my children turned fourteen years old, I encouraged each of them to attend high school to discover for themselves what sort of learning activities actually take place in school. At that age I felt my children were capable of giving an accurate accounting of what transpired in the classroom. Regardless of what happened, we could work it through together.

For my oldest son, the well-equipped science labs were extremely appealing. After being given the grand tour, he could barely wait to set up a course schedule so he could start. Two days later, however, he wanted to quit. The teachers, students, and course material failed to meet his expectations. The most startling thing about school, from his perspective, was the manner in which teachers treated the students. The atmosphere was hostile. Students were considered irresponsible and little individual attention was given.

It was extremely difficult to adjust to this environment because my son was always expected to be responsible. He quickly decided he could learn more and be a lot happier back at home.

PAT LINES The most interesting new development in homeschooling is the emergence of public school–home school partnerships. Alaska pioneered such arrangements, assigning teachers in Juneau to work with students located all over the state, staying in touch by mail, telephone, and occasional visits in person. Although designed for students in remote areas, Alaska made this service available to all, and today a majority of its students live in the Anchorage area. North Dakota has had a distance learning program for older students for many years, and is now extending it to younger ages.

Elsewhere, these kinds of partnerships have emerged at the district level. In California, for example, a child can enroll in a public school in an independent study program, and base his or her studies in the home. In Washington and Iowa, state law requires public schools to enroll children part time if they apply. (The district can claim a portion of the basic per-pupil assistance for the enrollment.) In these states interested districts have organized education centers where families may obtain resources, find instructional support, and/or sign up for scheduled classes. Some other states or districts also allow part-time enrollment, "shared schooling," "dual enrollment," or similar part-time school attendance. Often, children may enroll in programs anywhere in the state.

These fledgling programs often rely heavily on electronic learning and communications programs. They offer a preview of education in the twenty-first century, where the electronic workplace and the electronic school bring back neighborly communities.

HELEN AND MARK HEGENER The answer to this question depends on your state's homeschooling laws or regulations, local public school district policy, and the "climate" for homeschooling in your area. Within any given school district, one school's superintendent might welcome the opportunity to work with homeschooling families while another superintendent might prefer not to have anything to do with them. Your local homeschool support group will generally be the best source of information about what's possible and what's recommended.

There are many schools of thought on the subject of "blending" schooling and homeschooling, some favorable, most not so favorable. On the one hand, it seems like the best of both worlds for the student. But there are many legitimate concerns about the precedents that are set when homeschooled students become involved with the schools. Familiarize yourself with the pros and cons, and then do what's best for your family and for other homeschooling families.

SUSAN AND LARRY KASEMAN Yes, many states provide free public education for everyone of school age. The term "shared services" is used when private school students, including homeschoolers, take courses in public schools.

However, before participating in shared services, many families ask:

- Are there better ways to learn, perhaps an informal tutorial, an apprenticeship, or volunteer work?
- Will the benefits justify both the disruption to our family life and the time, energy, and expense involved?

Susan and Larry Kaseman

- Will our children benefit from school social life? How will they be influenced by "the culture of school"?
- Will attending school really meet our children's needs? Are there better ways of accomplishing whatever goals led us to consider shared services in the first place?

Attending a conventional school is not necessary or even an advantage. Many homeschoolers learn math, science, foreign languages; make friends; and play sports on community teams without attending school. One homeschooling mother observed: "There is nothing public schools offer that I can't find, and probably in a better way, in the community."

Increasing numbers of grown-up homeschoolers are showing that experience in conventional schools is not necessary to get a job, do volunteer service, travel abroad, or go to college. In fact, many of these young people are doing so well because they chose home-schooling over conventional schooling.

Participating in shared services can undermine homeschooling freedoms. It puts homeschoolers under the jurisdiction of public schools, promotes the idea that conventional schools are a necessary part of learning, blurs the distinction between public schools and homeschools, and sets precedents of government control over homeschoolers that may then be applied to homeschoolers who do not even want shared services. For example, public schools may require that home-schoolers pass tests to show that they are qualified to enroll in certain classes. Critics of homeschooling will then find it easier to argue that all homeschoolers should be tested.

In short, homeschoolers who are considering shared services should ask themselves whether the benefits

> **In short, homeschoolers who are considering shared services should ask themselves whether the benefits they hope to gain are worth the costs involved.**

they hope to gain are worth the costs involved.

If homeschoolers want shared services despite the downsides, it is better to make arrangements with local schools than to seek a law requiring school districts to provide shared services to homeschoolers. The following suggestions may help.

- If officials claim that they are not required to provide shared services to homeschoolers, remind them that the statutes require that free public education be provided to everyone of school age.
- If school officials claim there is no precedent or policy for shared services, explain that virtually every public school in the nation regularly enrolls private school students in special education classes on a part-time basis.
- If school officials claim that the district cannot afford to provide shared services to homeschoolers because the state does not reimburse them for the costs, remind them that in most states property taxes cover a substantial part of the school budgets.

• If school officials fear that home-schoolers' participation in shared services will disrupt their planning, explain to them that homeschoolers are a very small minority (less than 2 percent) of the school-age population. Of these, only a few home-schoolers will be interested in shared services.

22

If our circumstances change, by choice or otherwise, are there any problems when a homeschooled child returns to school?

HELEN AND MARK HEGENER The problems children face by returning to public school are the same ones they would face if they had never been homeschooled, because the problems of schooling are inherent to the system, the bureaucracy. Some children can work with them, can learn to fit into the schedules, the expectations, the unfairnesses, but other children never will, especially if they've been unschooled for any length of time.

If your child needs or wants to re-turn to school, the best source of infor-mation will probably be your local homeschooling support group. They should be able to tell you if problems have been experienced with certain dis-tricts or individuals, what the school

personnel will be looking for, how best to make the transition.

In the January/February 1998 issue of *Home Education Magazine,* in an arti-cle titled "My Daughter has Special Powers," Martine Palmer writes:

> I don't care too much for schools. I went to one. It wasn't that awful, but still it stifled my life. I learned some good things, but looking back, I see now how much I missed. And now, I've seen that schools have become even more stifling. Even more rigid. Skewed reward systems, commercial-ism, more emphasis on behavior manage-ment than on asking questions and being curious. Books and subjects so watered down and "politically correct." Not much juicy learning. Overcrowded classes with disruptive students.

Still, Martine's daughter wanted to attend school, and Martine agreed to let her go. She continues:

> I sent my daughter fully expecting her to see the light and quit. Well . . . she loves school, and her teacher and her classmates. She gets up early, gets dressed, eats, eager to get on the bus. She comes home happy and exhilarated. What's not to like? I even like her teacher. She supports many of my homeschool philosophies. No homework because kids should play after school, no grades, lots of moving around in class, lots of singing and dancing, and much emphasis on children being read to by their parents "in their laps." Lots of manipulatives.

Heavy emphasis on home life. I feel so lucky that Olivia is in good hands.

On the other side, I miss my family being together. I want to read to her some more. Take her to parks and to dance class. Want to see her running free in the grass and laughing. I want her to quit.

Nancy Plent I had homeschool friends who divorced, and the mother had no choice but to return her children to school so she could work. One son adjusted pretty well. She left the other one crying at the school door every morning while she hurried off to her job, also crying. The oldest son's teacher blasted at my friend during their entire first parent-teacher meeting for "ruining him." By the middle of the school year, that same boy was above grade level. Today both children, now grown, have positive memories of their homeschooling. Yes, there were painful problems, but the same grit that made this mom try homeschooling helped her get through the rough places.

Most of the parents who change their minds and return children to school still have good things to say about the experience. Often they used

> **M**ost of the parents who change their minds and return children to school still have good things to say about the experience. Often they used the time to reconnect with their children, or enjoy a peaceful hiatus in lives that had been too hectic.

the time to reconnect with their children, or enjoy a peaceful hiatus in lives that had been too hectic. Many have told me that, even if they couldn't see themselves continuing, it had given them and their children a fresh start with a positive attitude.

In either case, I think children are different persons for the experience and will cope. You will have taught them that school isn't the sacred necessity we all grew up thinking it is, and that they are really the ones in charge of their learning and their lives.

School officials generally don't offer much resistance to returning students, except in high school. High schools are often reluctant to admit a student at the level his mom-teacher places him unless he brings some kind of certificates or testing results.

23

Is there an ideal situation for homeschooling?

Deb Shell I'm sure the most important factors regarding a positive homeschool experience relate more to family beliefs about how children learn, interpersonal respect, effective communication, and unconditional love than they do to location or money. We could have done what we did anywhere—in a tent or in a high-rise. This isn't to deny that some situations are naturally more conducive to homeschooling and lend support to parents who may be feeling a bit outside the norm of popular culture.

For us, homeschooling evolved out of our attachment-parenting lifestyle as set forth by Jean Liedloff in *The Continuum Concept: In Search of Happiness Lost*—from the start I trusted our children to develop according to their own needs. So right away I found myself seeking out like-minded parents who also supported these values. Meeting people with similar sensibilities has always been a priority, since friendships made life so much more fun. This was how we built community wherever we lived. Once, before the listings were available from *Growing Without Schooling,* I put an ad in the local paper to find other homeschoolers hidden in the mountains of rural northeastern Washington state. It worked. So, for the most part, actively seeking kindred spirits has paid off a thousandfold.

We worked hard toward creating the extended family supports that weren't available readymade for us. We identified what would make us happier and really went after creating as best we could, a situation that supported our needs. For me, it was especially important to be around other women; and for our children, it was important to have easy access to other unschooled kids. Another issue in our ideal setup was privacy—not only did our kids like to roam about during "school" hours, but we too, being self-employed, tended to work nontraditional hours.

We did carefully consider where we wanted to raise our kids, and the criteria fit our particular needs. Every family is unique in this respect—you need to consider how you function not only in the present, but how you want to function in a few years. I'm glad we chose to live within commute distance to a small city because this helped our teens find diverse cultural opportunities such as training programs, mentors, and classes when they began to crave community interaction. I'm also glad we live in the country and have been peacefully left alone to homeschool in the manner which we see fit. The natural world has always been important to us; and so having opportunities to raise vegetables, flowers, animals, to be near the water, and to observe the seasons has satisfied our particular needs as well.

I don't think everyone could agree about where the right place to homeschool might be; only knowing what you'd like to have around you will tell you what's right for your family. I believe that people are more important than material things and so relationships, and opportunities to nurture them, have taken precedent over other things in terms of choosing how or where to live. Although we sacrificed material goods and financial security to raise our children this way, we invested wisely. After all, they are truly our family jewels.

JEAN REED Are you living your idea of an ideal life in the ideal place? If not, are you making the best of your particular circumstances? Everyone has a mental image of an ideal place to live and raise a family. We would have our ideal house, in an ideal place, and enough income to do just what we want. A nice dream, and there's nothing wrong with it, except that life isn't like that for most of us. Most of us don't have everything we want. In reality,we have to make the most of what we have. Homeschooling is a way of life and, as with the rest of our lives, we have to make the most of whatever we have.

History proves that neither location nor financial status place limitations on great thinkers or the ability to learn. Some great men and women have come from impoverished homes, and some of the sons and daughters of the very wealthy have been idiots. Learning can take place anywhere, anytime. Money can buy resources, but it can't insure learning any more than it can buy happiness.

We ship homeschooling materials all over the globe. No matter where you live you can learn. Where you live is, or should be, an irrelevant detail in respect to learning. It's taking advantage of wherever you live that is important. There are advantages and disadvantages to all places. If you lived someplace else you would learn something different. If you live in the city you will learn some things you wouldn't learn on the farm and vice versa.

Jean Reed

We couldn't live in the city, which doesn't mean that our children went without some of the advantages of city living. Although there is nothing like being at a live concert or visiting a good museum, we found reasonable substitutes through books, magazines, on radio, CD, videotape, and television. The television, for all the junk shown, can be a very useful tool. Sometimes you see more than you would if you were there in person.

You can't have an extensive garden, orchard, or raise a lot of animals in the city, but you can grow many plants, even small trees, in pots or in a small yard. You can raise a number of small pets even in an apartment.

I think it's up to us as parents to help our children be aware of the great variety of human experience, cultures, beliefs, and places to live in this world. Books, magazines, field trips, radio, television, videos, computers, and libraries can make the world accessible to us all. These are tools we can use wherever we live.

Most of all, I think homeschooling parents want their children to be happy as children; to grow up to be strong, happy, productive adults. All we can do is provide them with love and encourage them to make the best of their own lives. This is a matter of philosophy, not location. This can be achieved wherever and however you live.

> All we can do is provide them with love and encourage them to make the best of their own lives. This is a matter of philosophy, not location. This can be achieved wherever and however you live.

LILLIAN JONES Every homeschooling scenario offers unique advantages and disadvantages, although people often think someone else has the ideal setting.

Hard Times in Paradise, by David and Micki Colfax, is an inspiring and thought-provoking book—the fascinating account of the personal hardships and challenges the whole family had faced and mastered while struggling to build a homestead, eventually creating a successful goat farm. That ongoing project, along with the family's social/political activism, was the kids' education! Academic preparation, which started in early adolescence, was basically just a means to an end, a way to get into and through college, and on to the real and important things they would later want to do with their lives. Their pragmatic education in learning how to learn got the kids scholarships to Harvard, not anything they learned in a book.

I fretted a bit, when I finished that book, to think of how underprivileged my own son was. Poor kid—born into a relatively affluent family, raised in a snug house, no particularly important work to do, destined to miss the opportunity to struggle and to have to figure out the mechanics of survival. So sheltered. Soft. What would become of him? I chuckled later, as I recognized my own exaggerated perception of the grass on the other side of the fence. I'm sure the Colfaxes might have had a moment or two during their adventures when they would have traded with us in a flash, too.

There is no ideal situation for home-schooling, any more than there is an ideal situation for living in general. Once you let go of the notion that there is an almost tangible plan or pattern called "homeschooling," it's a lot easier to appreciate the opportunities life has to offer in any number of settings and lifestyles.

Those who don't fit into the prevailing lifestyle, religion, or racial group of their region might have a tougher time because of isolation. On the other hand, there are a growing variety of home-schoolers in most places. If you look hard enough, and with an open mind, you can usually find like-minded souls. It might take some creativity to find your niche.

One of the marvelous things about homeschooling is the way it forces us to let go of old familiar notions of how things should be. The whole family benefits deeply from an ongoing process of growing into new ways of thinking. Parents who have had basic educational needs handled by schools for many years often unconsciously expect homeschooling to be much the same way. They want a format. They want to know how it's all supposed to be. The good and the bad news about homeschooling, they discover, is that it's all up to them. That may feel scary at first, but it's inevitably the thing we value most.

Now that you've read Lillian's account of the Colfaxes' homeschooling situation, here are the Colfaxes' thoughts on the same question.

DAVID AND MICKI COLFAX The ideal setting for homeschooling? On a remote moutaintop in northern California—with plenty of electricity and water, great soil, and a pile of money! But as our book, *Hard Times in Paradise,* shows in sometimes too painful detail, one can do a fair-to-middling job of home-schooling without *all* of those things. "Ah, but your situation was ideal for homeschooling," is a line we've heard many times from homeschoolers and non-homeschoolers alike. All that space, few distractions, the opportunity to learn new things, do real work, no television—

Unlike realtors, however, home-schoolers have little reason to concern themselves about "location, location, location." By now we have plenty of evidence that homeschooling both flourished and floundered in urban and rural areas, in all parts of the country, and in homes rich, poor, and somewhere in between. Indeed, every homeschooling family, to a greater or lesser degree, constructs its own image of what constitutes a "good" or "ideal" homeschooling situation, the elements of which often vary radically from family to family. Elsewhere, we have compiled a list of some of the characteristics of what we regard as successful homeschooling efforts—parental commitment to keeping the love of learning alive, a skepticism of educational fads, intellectual openness and flexibility—which, without exception, are *attitudinal* rather than *spatial* or *circumstantial.*

Unfortunately, too many parents who hear about homeschooling are made to feel that it is something they cannot do because their home or economic circumstances are so different from what they perceive to be the "ideal." Those of us who are homeschoolers perhaps need to consider the extent to which we have promulgated—however unintentionally—the idea that homeschooling is a Dick and Jane, June Cleaver sort of activity, best conducted in a middle-class, two-parent family living in a nice house with a big yard in a nice neighborhood, a family in which the children are bright and well-behaved, mom stays home, dad has a good job (or they all work together in a family business), surrounded by supportive relatives and friends who are themselves homeschoolers. The realities of homeschooling are infinitely more diverse, and we do a disservice to the movement when we fail to remember that homeschooling does, indeed, take place everywhere, and under all kinds of conditions.

CHAPTER FOUR

Rest in Peace, Fears About Socialization

N O OTHER ASPECT of homeschooling has garnered more attention, commentary, and criticism over the years than the socialization of its children. I can't believe anyone really thinks we make the decision to homeschool so we can lock our children in closets, chain them to the kitchen table, or otherwise see to it that they don't interact or communicate with other human beings. Think about it for a minute: Wouldn't that make it that much more difficult to educate them? Wouldn't that make it that much more difficult to be around them for large portions of each day? Wouldn't that be downright counterproductive to a parent's natural inclination to raise well-rounded children into adulthood?

So why the big fuss over socialization? Rather than being related to any real problem homeschooled children have meeting and mingling with fellow humans, it seems to be a problem with the thinking of some adults. These folks think it's "weird" that families would have the audacity to decide for themselves with whom, where, when, and how much or how little "socialization" occurs. The converse of this, of course, is that someone outside the family decides these things for our children. Thus, in recent history, it has been decided that children's socialization occurs in the institution of school, away from the rest of the world, much as the prison institution keeps inmates away from the rest of the world. And the constancy and intensity with which this

> **L**isten to the voices of experience, those who dared to by-pass control and decided to define, value, and actually practice "socialization" on their own terms.

decision is defended, mostly by those with a vested interest (read paycheck!) in making sure the institution stays full, is cause for pause. This focus on school as a children's socialization device is an even more recent invention than public school itself.

What can we learn from this? That (a) the educational decision makers believe the public school system's job extends beyond teaching academics; (b) these same decision makers need a strong criticism of a growing educational alternative that by-passes their control; or (c) both of the above.

The proliferation of topics addressed in schools, from drugs to sex to health to peer counseling to values training, coupled with the giant "strings attached to federal aid" programs such as Goals 2000 and School-to-Work, shows that choice "a" above is definitely true. And it is all accomplished under the seemingly benign term of socialization.

Research and personal evidence show that homeschooled children get along with others as well as, and in some cases better than, their publicly schooled counterparts. If what the educational decision makers mean by socialization is the ability to get along with others, familiarity with even a small amount of research would reveal the criticism as absurd.

But if their definition of socialization reaches beyond the ability to get along with others, and encompasses a standardized list of behaviors, attitudes, values, and thinking they wish to implant in all children, then, indeed, homeschooling has by-passed their control and choice "b" is also correct, making "c" the right answer.

If you didn't choose answer "c," don't worry. I'm a home educator; I'm not in the habit of grading people like slabs of beef. It just means it's most important for you to read this chapter carefully. Get the other side of the story from those who don't hire public relations firms to put their own spin on this issue. Listen to the voices of experience, those who dared to by-pass control and decided to define, value, and actually practice "socialization" on their own terms.

From this vantage point, it's easier to put the modern definition of school socialization into perspective. From this vantage point, you and your family can see how homeschooling offers you *real* choice now that the importance of parental choice in education grows increasingly important to our children.

24

How can my children meet other children and find friends if they don't go to school?

DONNA NICHOLS-WHITE I do not believe my children need to be surrounded by hordes of peers. A few close friends contribute more toward character development than, say, forty or more acquaintances. Consequently, I do not go out of my way to replace school by recruiting friends. Instead, I choose to follow Khahil's, Latif's, and Rukiya's hobbies and interests.

I wasn't always like this. When I decided to homeschool, I put my oldest children on soccer and baseball teams, in swimming classes, in extracurricular lessons, and eventually in dancing school. For four long years, I trudged from practices to games to classes, to lessons and back. It seemed as if I ran a private school on wheels.

Upon noticing my husband was always out of town during soccer or baseball season, and admitting I really didn't like the competitive nature of organized children's sports (I especially wasn't interested in fraternizing with their teammates' parents), I decided not to sign up for the next year's sports season. Instead, I let my children take more dance classes.

This has worked for us. My daughter studies ballet and tap and my sons take ballet, tap, and jazz. Initially, my sons were the only boys in the dance classes; but as more people saw them perform, the male population increased. For the past two years, Khahil and Latif have participated in a performance troupe. They dance year-round at shows, recitals, and festivals.

One day my eldest asked if he could begin to act, model, and perform in commercials. Reluctantly, I took both boys to an agency that a friend recommended and lo and behold, my sons are now professional models and actors.

Since my daughter is seven, and I've already homeschooled two children before her, I have realized that learning to live with oneself is very important. Peer dependency develops between the ages of one through eight. Having plenty of at-home family time is essential during these formative years.

Our family, first and foremost, is our peer group. Forming an attachment with an adult is of premier importance in the healthy development of a young child. These are the years when I can prepare a safe and loving environment for my daughter while we get to know each other.

I noticed that when the neighborhood children began preschool, they changed for the worse. Aggressive kids became bullies and many nice or shy ones became fearful. Since Rukiya was naturally "feisty," I knew she needed the calm environment of our home.

Having all three children in one venue, dance, is great. It's an indoor sport that requires a lot of self-discipline and associates them with others of like interests. Through dance my children have traveled, performed, and matured while developing close, noncompetitive, and wonderful friendships. I know I'm fortunate that things turned out this way.

BILLY AND NANCY GREER This is part of the big "socialization" question that always seems to come up when discussing homeschooling. First of all, we think it is important to point out that socializing and socialization are two different things. Socializing is basically talking and playing with other kids; socialization involves learning the proper rules of behavior for a culture.

Neither of these tend to take place in a school environment (at least, not in a beneficial way). Socializing is typically punished in school. Kids are not supposed to talk and play in the classroom. During the day they have little opportunity to socialize, except perhaps briefly at lunch or recess.

The socialization they get is very artificial because the environment is very artificial. They are grouped with kids their own age. The rules for behavior in their culture say that older kids don't play with younger kids. If you like computers you're a geek, if you like sports you're a jock, if you're small you're a target for bullies.

Our five-year-old daughter and a nine-year-old homeschooled girl are best friends. This probably couldn't happen if they were in school. It's common at homeschool activities to see children of all ages working and playing together.

There are lots of activities available for homeschoolers now. Field trips, clubs, activities, and sports are readily available. In fact, you have to be careful not to overcommit yourself. There are probably more homeschoolers who are doing too many activities and meeting too many people than there are those who are isolated. Our opinion is that it is better to have a few deeper friendships than to have a lot of acquaintances you don't really know very well.

JANIE LEVINE HELLYER Because school is where most children spend the bulk of their waking hours, it's naturally the place that comes to mind when considering the opportunities children have for meeting others and developing relationships. The traditional classroom, however, can be compared to the workplace in that children do not choose those they are grouped with. While a "working relationship" may develop, there is little time to actually get to know others and nurture true relationships. No matter where a child is educated, true relationships seem to be formed outside of the classroom.

Let's first consider the young child. Is there a need for young children to be surrounded with agemates all day? No. Before young children can interact with a social group in a positive way, they must first have established their own identity and feel secure. Too often, young children are placed in social situations before this develops, and so are not sure that it's "okay" to be themselves. This is the first step to lifelong peer pressure and control.

The home, family, and neighborhood are natural places for children to begin to explore relationships at their own pace and as they are ready.

The home is the first social unit. Young children at home learn to recognize the structure of the family, and acquire important values and skills that will assist them as they move out into the world. As children grow strong and secure in the concept of self, it is natural that they will begin exploring the world

When strong relationships are developed with various age groups, peer pressure is less of a factor, leading many to view the social opportunities of homeschoolers as superior to those of schooled children.

outside the walls of their home.

Most youngsters grow up in neighborhoods, play with neighbor children, and get to know them well. An important aspect of this stage of social development is that children playing in their own neighborhood are free to leave a group or activity when they are tired, uncomfortable, or when they choose not to participate for some reason. Real friends are those we choose to spend time with, not people we are forced to be around, and the experiences youngsters have in their neighborhoods allow them to freely choose the time, place, and individuals with whom they wish to spend time and develop lasting relationships.

As children grow older, no matter where they are educated, there are many positive social activities to choose from outside of the classroom. Homeschooled youngsters participate in the same positive activities as their schooled peers. These include things like Scouts, 4-H, YMCA, sports activities, church groups, and community-based youth groups. Most communities also have special activities and organizations for homeschoolers. As our children grow into young adults, most homeschoolers are out in the community pursuing their interests. This provides opportunities to meet others who have the same interests.

Homeschoolers are not confined to friendships with those exactly the same age as they are, and so tend to be comfortable with a wide variety of ages. When strong relationships are developed with various age groups, peer pressure is less of a factor, leading many to view the social opportunities of homeschoolers as superior to those of schooled children.

25
But what about the prom?

NANCY PLENT Strange thought, isn't it, that no childhood is complete without a formal dance at the end of it, wearing expensive, uncomfortable clothes! We've certainly bought into the school lifestyle when we ask this question. Families who have a lingering regret about their children missing the prom (a highly overrated affair to many, by the way) may have a lingering doubt about whether they're doing the right thing by homeschooling. You can't blame them; rituals are comforting and important, a way to mark certain passages in life. If we give up traditions, something feels a little incomplete.

I think it may be important for homeschooling families to develop meaningful rituals of their own. I know one mom whose traditional graduation gift to each of her children was a short European trip. It probably meant at least as much to them as a ceremony. As support groups grow, many will probably duplicate school functions like the prom. In a way that's too bad, to copy what we've left behind; with a little more time, maybe we can come up with something better.

SHARI HENRY After chaperoning a youth group trek to the local roller rink, then subjecting myself to watching children aged nine to fourteen "slow dance" at set aside times, then watching boys skate while girls lined up alongside the rink with their hands held out and the boys passing by to "smack" the hands of the "cute" girls and then vice versa, I became even less concerned about the prom than ever. Certainly, nine to fourteen year olds could much better spend their time preoccupying themselves with a host of other activities than pre-mating games. So, about that prom, it would be my desire that my kids have plenty of friends of the opposite sex by the time they're prom age, and perhaps (but perhaps not) they would be asked to attend a dance as such. But I'm glad they won't be in school where the event takes on undue importance. It's just not, nor should it be, that big a deal.

SUSANNAH SHEFFER The simple answer is that homeschoolers can usually find a way to go to a school prom if that's what they want to do, or to create a parallel opportunity by organizing a homeschoolers' dance (or a community dance for both homeschoolers and schooled teenagers). Long before they reach prom age, homeschoolers have had many ways to meet and interact with school students, and one easy way to go to a prom is to be invited by someone who attends that school.

Susannah Sheffer

But not all homeschoolers (or, for that matter, all school students) actually want to go to the prom. When *Growing Without Schooling* magazine asked one homeschooled teenager about missing the prom, she replied, "I didn't go to the prom because I would have had to go with someone who went to the high school, and my boyfriend goes to college. I probably could have gone if I really wanted to, but it wasn't

that important, and all my friends ended up having a horrible time. It wasn't something that I felt I missed out on."

I love this comment because of the reality check it provides for adults who may romanticize the trapping of conventional teenage social life more than the teenagers themselves do. And even if the prom was truly the highlight of one's teen years, who's to say that experience is intrinsically more fun than a weekend-long gathering organized by homeschooling teenagers, for example?

The question, "But what about the prom?" may seem to be a simple question about access, but I think on a deeper level it's about parents' fears and hopes for their children. What will it be like if my children's experiences are different from mine? parents wonder. Homeschooling may attract parents precisely because it offers something different from schooling, but "different" is also scary. After all, what usually happens to children in school who are "different"?

A school student who doesn't want or can't gain entrance to the popular crowd, the conventional social arena, may have little choice but to be an outcast. Homeschoolers, however, can redefine the

> **The question, "But what about the prom?" may seem to be a simple question about access, but I think on a deeper level it's about parents' fears and hopes for their children.**

terms and can think about what kind of social life they truly want rather than only what the movies, or even their own parents, tell them they should want. It's reassuring to hear about homeschoolers who go to dances and football games and parties, who date and have groups of friends. I know plenty of homeschoolers who do all these things. But I find it equally reassuring to know homeschoolers who don't date and don't have to defend that choice, or who prefer a few close friends to a large group, or prefer adult friends to peers, or like to spend a lot of time alone, or whatever other variation suits them. I like seeing that, in the social as in the academic arena, homeschooling means that young people can find—and create—the kind of set-up that best works for them.

26

I've always considered public schools the place where children learn how to get along with each other. How do you compensate for this at home?

DEB SHELL Most people believe schools are teaching young people how to get along with each other. Unfortunately, this is probably true. Sassiness, disrespect for the personal property of others, fighting, and cheating, as well as

succumbing to peer pressure at younger and younger ages (resulting in early sexual experiences, body mutilation, and drug and alcohol abuse), are behaviors now considered by many educators, social workers, and mental health professionals to be the normal developmental stuff we should expect our kids to exhibit as they mature.

I've had a very different experience raising four children at home. Just from living in our family, and as members of our community, my children learned how to get along from birth on. Their models for appropriate social behavior were other adults who valued individual differences and demonstrated effective interpersonal communication skills. Our children learned fairness by being treated fairly, respect by being respected. They learned to trust themselves because we gave them real opportunities to explore self-responsibility. They held others in high regard because we held them in high regard. Their self-confidence increased as their real skills improved—as measured against their own development, not some arbitrarily standardized concept of achievement.

The value of not using grade levels or grades enables children to feel right about themselves, no matter where their stage of development happens to be. The effects of manipulation and coercion into activities that hold no appeal or meaning may produce behavior that, when taken out of context from its cause, may result in the child being pathologically labeled (for example, ADD, ADHD, oppositional disorder). Very often, children who are labeled in school have their symptoms disappear once they are removed from the social system that supports such coping behaviors.

My favorite book about the socialization of children, *The Continuum Concept*, by Jean Liedloff, is a tribute to what many homeschoolers know to be true: Children learn how to get along while naturally living as integral members of their family and community. Like all children, ours also wanted to participate, to be included, to be contributors. A loving family is the natural place from which to learn how to get along. Schoolchildren have to learn how to get along as members of an organization that sets up within-the-ranks competition, supports the use of rewards and punishments as motivational tools, and sets up unnatural consequences for disobeying rules that may benefit the school bureaucracy rather than the educational needs of its students.

Now that my children are teenagers and beyond, I am frequently met with amazement from parents and educators of schooled peers. My children get along

with each other and with their parents, as they do with all ages and races of people. Who wouldn't be proud to say their children are compassionate, considerate, responsible human beings?

SANDRA DODD At school, children learn to get along in a pack environment. They create their own little culture among others their own age, and their mediations and solutions are often discovered and resolved without adult advice or modeling. In other words, the tricks they learn are sometimes good to use in committee meetings or gangs later on, but not in "real life," by which I mean everyday situations involving groups of people of varying ages doing real-world things.

At home, children can be talked through difficult situations, and can be given a range of options by the parent. Teachers don't have time to hear the details of why Johnny's feelings are hurt, but moms do. Unless a family moves around a lot, the children learn to get along with their neighbors, relatives, and friends on a long-term basis. At school, children come and go. A carefully maintained friendship can be broken up abruptly by a school district's remapping, or by class assignments that split up the children so they can't even have lunch together. Even school children who *do* manage to build and maintain friendships can't necessarily keep them.

My own children have never been to school and I'm glad they have friends of varying ages. Nobody ever told them fifth graders aren't supposed to play with third graders, and they're rarely sure what grade they would be in if they were in school, anyway. Their relationships are built on mutual interests, proximity, and shared humor and experiences, not on having been thrust together arbitrarily.

Homeschooled children are usually spared the situation where they are set up as a separate species from adults, with adults as the "other" or the enemy. In school, certainly, the teachers and the students are more different than officers and enlisted. More like royalty and peasants. This doesn't happen with homeschooling.

When people ask, "What about socialization?" they're usually thinking of socializing with same-age peers. I've never seen homeschoolers with a problem in that area, but I have seen *many* school attendees who have problems with older children, younger children, parents, teachers, kids their age who dress differently, kids their age who talk differently, kids their age from a different school, and more. I think schools produce some profound socialization problems. Children are thrust into a sit-

uation that is unnatural and in which they are powerless. That's no place to learn socialization.

When *teachers* ask, "What about socialization?" I quote back to them what I've heard dozens of teachers say to children in school: "You're not here to socialize."

CAFI COHEN First, examine your assumption that public schools are "the place where children learn how to get along with each other." Visit your local school for one entire day and simply sit and watch. Watch how the children treat each other, in and out of class. Watch how teachers treat the children and vice versa. Total the amount of one-on-one adult attention for each child.

I have done this in schools in three different states and always found three things. First, there is not much time for meaningful interaction, certainly no time for in-depth relationships. Second, the atmosphere is—more often than not—petty and mean-spirited. And last, the social pecking order leaves many kids more isolated than they could possibly be in any home-based program.

If I were to design an environment to enhance my children's ability to function socially, I would never propose anything resembling school. I would never design a place where my children principally see those born in a one- to two-year period who also happen to live in our zip code, a place where they have little adult contact.

Instead, to enhance our children's abilities to get along with others, we focused on our community. Our children satisfied their needs for age-peer socialization through groups like 4-H and Civil Air Patrol and church choirs and softball teams. In addition, they had friends of all ages through various community activities—classes, drama groups, political campaigns, hobbyist organizations, various volunteer jobs. Our teenage homeschoolers befriended people of all ages from a much larger socioeconomic spectrum than is present in most schools.

Our children meet and make friends much as you and I do—through their interests and through current friends, neighbors, and relatives. We always knew when school dismissed because the phone started ringing. Finding social opportunities was not a problem. Our real problem was keeping a lid on it: "No, you cannot go out again tonight; you have been out every evening this week, and I need the car."

I never worried about compensating for school "social" experiences. We did

If I were to design an environment to enhance my children's ability to function socially, I would never propose anything resembling school.

not want what schools provided. Our family and the larger community presented more opportunities to meet a greater range of people. And homeschooling provided something attendance at most schools precludes—*time* to develop and maintain friendships with people of all ages.

CHRIS CARDIFF Actually, if you think about it, exactly the opposite is true. Many of the pathologies of youth are associated with public schools—peer pressure, age segregation, cliques, isolation, and persecution of nonconformists. Logically, how could it be otherwise? Yes, children *are* learning social behavior from other children. However, what

Chris Cardiff

most parents want is for children to learn social behavior from adults. The home is the natural environment for this training.

Homeschooling does *not* mean that children interact only with their parents and siblings. This popular homeschooling myth (also known as "The Isolation Myth") suggests that homeschoolers have no academic or social interactions outside the family. Reality is far different, as homeschoolers work, play, and learn within the community in ways that resemble "real life" much more than the artificial environment of the institutional school.

Homeschooled children participate in their full share of traditional extracurricular activities: 4-H Club, Little League, Cub Scouts, Brownies, dance, karate, gymnastics, music, and more. All of these activities provide boundless opportunities to interact with other children, both homeschooled and public schooled.

Moreover, as the popularity of homeschooling soars, any activities normally found in institutional schools are being duplicated by entrepreneurial members of the homeschooling community. Spelling bees, choir, band, sports leagues, science fairs, foreign exchange students—homeschooling specific versions of these are all available somewhere, providing more opportunities for children to work, play, and learn together.

A primary source of additional academic and social opportunities for homeschooling families is local homeschooling support groups. Weekly park days provide opportunities for social interaction (for kids *and* parents!). Field trips and group learning opportunities are also typical activities sponsored by individuals within the group. Children

are usually not age-segregated (although age guidelines are provided for some activities) and parental involvement is high, ensuring more positive interactions. With their flexible schedules, homeschooled children have much more opportunity to interact with a wider variety of people than children confined to institutional schools. The results of these interactions are children who capably communicate and interact with people of all ages.

27

Without siblings in the house, how does my only child learn social skills as we homeschool?

Mary McCarthy Oh, my dear Linda, are you implying his parents don't have any social skills?

Luz Shosie We learn social skills by interacting with people. We included Cassidy in our interactions as much as we could when he was a baby and as much as he wanted as he grew older. He learned to interact with all kinds of people of all different ages.

We get together with homeschoolers, neighbors, friends and relations, and coworkers, not to learn social skills, but to live a full life.

My favorite answer to the socialization question comes from Mary Beth Nelsen, the president of the Connecticut Home Educator's Association: "We did tend to over-socialize when we first started homeschooling, but I think we have it under control now."

WENDY PRIESNITZ When we think about socialization, we need to consider quality as well as quantity. How much social interaction do children actually require? What is the quality of the socialization at school compared to what is available outside of school? Do speaking and other social skills get as much attention as listening skills?

Life for children in school is public. They have virtually no time or space to which adults can be denied access. Children who find psychological privacy by daydreaming are labeled as inattentive or disinterested. On the other hand, life for unschooled children— even ones without siblings—is a mixture of personal and shared time, which allows them to get to know themselves, at the same time as they learn to value—

yet be discriminating about—the time spent with others.

My observation of thousands of home-educated children over the past twenty years suggests that another factor outweighs any kind of peer or sibling interaction in its influence on social development. Feelings of security and self-confidence are created in children who have the freedom to venture into sophisticated social situations at their own speed. This positive self-concept is nurtured by warm, loving interaction with parents who respect their children. As some of the main ingredients in a child's proper social development, these even outweigh the contribution of continued social contact in creating a child who functions well in society.

These observations are reinforced by developmental and social psychologist Dr. Urie Bronfenbrenner of Cornell University, who has spent many years studying children in various societies. He has noted that overexposure to a peer group during a child's early years can be damaging and has found that until the fifth- or sixth-grade level, children who

> **My observation of thousands of home-educated children over the past twenty years suggests that another factor outweighs any kind of peer or sibling interaction in its influence on social development. Feelings of security and self-confidence are created in children who have the freedom to venture into sophisticated social situations at their own speed.**

spend more time with their peers than with their parents or older family members become peer dependent. This, he claims, leads to a loss of self-worth, optimism, respect for their parents, and trust in their peers.

At any rate, even homeschooled children with no siblings often have much more contact with a wider variety of people than they would if they were in school. They interact on a personal basis with people in the community from all walks of life, with the result that they learn about the adult world without losing any sense of the child world. Because they're not segregated in a school building all day, their lives can be full and integrated into all aspects of community life.

28

Have there been any studies about how homeschooling affects a child's ability to get along with others and make the transition into the adult world?

PAT LINES First a word about studies: There is no conclusive research suggesting that time with same-aged peers is preferable to time with individuals of varying ages. Limited testing of a self-selected group of homeschooled children suggests above average social and

psychological development. At the very least, anyone who has observed homeschoolers will notice a high level of sharing, networking, collaboration, and cooperative learning.

People disagree on whether homeschooling helps or hinders a child's social development. Children engaged in homeschooling spend less time with same-aged children and more time with people of different ages. Most spend time with other children through support and networking groups, scouting, churches, and other associations. Many spend time with adults other than their parents, through community volunteer work, running home-based businesses, tutoring or mentoring arrangements, and in other ways.

The stereotype of the isolated family does not fit any homeschooling family that I have met to date. To the contrary, homeschooling families seem highly connected to other families and other institutions. I would suggest that you make an effort to meet experienced homeschooling families and talk to their older children. If you enjoy meeting them, and they can discuss a variety of topics knowledgeably, then that may be the best test.

KATHARINE HOUK There have been research studies done in which homeschooling children score high in self-concept, leadership skills, and community involvement—all reflectors of positive socialization. These findings are borne out by my experience with my own children and hundreds of other families. "Getting along with others" means being able to move beyond oneself to consider the position and point of view of another. It is the realization of and ability to live with the fact that something other than oneself is real. Another word for this process is "love." What better place to foster these realizations and skills than in the family? Such family learning stands children in good stead when they come in contact with those with different opinions. A strong sense of self is what enables people of any age to move beyond themselves for mutual solutions when dealing with one another.

When my own children found themselves in disagreement with each other to the point of tantrums, each learned that in order to retain a playmate, he or she would have to work things through. The family can be a safe place for this to happen, and it behooves us as parents to learn and pass on conflict-resolution skills. Because children

> There have been research studies done in which homeschooling children score high in self-concept, leadership skills, and community involvement—all reflectors of positive socialization.

are involved in their communities, they also learn social skills from friendships with people of all ages, church, classes, volunteering, and jobs—in other words, in the "real world." People homeschooling today are at an advantage because of their flexible schedules and the large number of opportunities available to them through homeschooling groups, learning centers, travel networks, and other places where people meet and share their knowledge and ways of life. The ability to get along well with others is valuable to homeschooled teens as they begin working or applying for college; and by the time they have reached sixteen or seventeen, most homeschoolers have a strong sense of their aptitudes and their direction in life and are not afraid to pursue their dreams.

A friend of our family once told me that what impressed her most about our children was that they could, with ease and confidence, carry on a conversation with adults. I've noticed that they also take pleasure in carrying on conversations with babies and toddlers. They've never learned that younger people and adults are stupid or somehow inferior because of age differences. This stands in sharp contrast to what I learned in school, where upper-class students always looked down upon younger ones and peers "ruled." Psychologists and counselors are dismayed that so many teens today behave as though they hate their parents.

When we began officially homeschooling many years ago, the superintendent of schools told us that our choice would ruin our daughter's life. I suppose there may be families who isolate their children and stunt their growth; but if these families exist (I don't know any personally, though every once in a while one reads a horror story in the papers), they must be a tiny minority. My husband and I have seen many young people, including our own, become independent, self-supporting, involved members of their communities. Homeschooling can facilitate getting along with others and moving into the wider world.

29

How can I be sure my child is growing socially without trained school personnel assessing this growth?

CINDY WADE As a homeschooler, you spend most of your waking hours with your children. No one knows your children better than you. You know their likes and dislikes. You know their favorite foods and the ones they detest. You know how well they're developing social skills or where they need improvement.

School personnel tend to assess a child's growth by rather bizarre standards. Is it really that important little John-John learn to stand in line, raise his hand for conversational purposes, or base his self-worth on team training?

As a homeschooler, you can focus your energy and resources on basic skills like reading, writing, and arithmetic, and on the social skills your children need. Throw in business, law, world history, the U.S. Constitution, and language for good measure. Time is on your side. Time to relax into well-rounded academic and social lives.

When little John-John learns to read at the age of seven or eight by using phonics in a one-to-one learning setting, his self-esteem will remain intact, giving him a boost when it comes to developing better social and academic skills.

JOHN TAYLOR GATTO How can you be sure you got a good haircut? How can you be sure that wearing a bikini to your sister's church wedding is the wrong thing to do? How can you be sure whether the soup you just ate was tasty? A huge part of professional assessment is fraud.

I don't mean to be flippant, but forced schooling can only ensure its own sovereignty by making its clientele mistrust their own judgment. And the more you do mistrust your own judgment, the worse your judgment will indeed become. Formal assessment is institutional school's mechanism to mediate this fatal process.

Think of it this way: Abundant models of success (as you personally define success) are available everywhere in profusion. Look at them for your indices. There are no templates of "social growth" a trained schoolperson is charged with conveying except these:

- Stay in the "class" to which you have been assigned.
- Respond to the bell and other reflexive commands.
- Do what you are told.
- Confine yourself to your specified place in a world of children.

> Forced schooling can only ensure its own sovereignty by making its clientele mistrust their own judgment. And the more you do mistrust your own judgment, the worse your judgment will indeed become. Formal assessment is institutional school's mechanism to mediate this fatal process.

Does that sound like a formula calculated to produce what any sane person would call "social growth," or is it a formula for making a hierarchical, intensely corporatized, fundamentally totalitarian future work by providing a trained proletariat for it? A hive world.

You can be sure your child is "growing socially" if he or she is curious about all kinds of people, the details of their lives, their motives; you can be sure your child is okay if he can find pleasure, satisfaction, profit in talking to all different ages, responding appropriately to the challenges and opportunities presented by those older and those younger than himself. You can be proud of your child's social growth if he relishes responsibility and looks on work as a lovely thing instead of a mere duty; if he can be alone with himself for long periods without boredom; if he confronts his own cowardice with people unlike himself and is learning to swim easily, like some noble fish in all human environments.

But most of all, you can be "sure" by learning to trust yourself. Study those people you admire yourself with great and continuous intensity, analyze precisely what it is that makes them socially valuable people, show your child by your own example, your conversation, and your choices that you yourself are growing socially (for surely none of us is ever fully done with this challenge).

And for pity's sake, encourage your children to develop at least one social talent: play the piano, sing, fill a room with humor, listen creatively, be graceful, whatever. Look at the people you *like* to be around and you'll see that every one of them has some attribute which makes her socially valuable. Many such attributes are natural and only need a little encouragement in youth to blossom on their own; some are more sophisticated and require disciplined effort to acquire. It can't hurt to make your child self-aware—which is not the same thing at all as being self-conscious.

But throw away your fears about what school calls "socialization." You'd have to be nuts not to see the dehumanization/depersonalization intended by that deadly umbrella word.

MICHELLE BARONE The first issue we must make clear is this: Just what *is* socialization? I define a socialized child as one who easily and cooperatively fits in with other humans, someone who has the skills to live in society. The next question then must be, Do children learn to be social beings in a confined, same-age group of other children? Studies have shown that children learn to socialize in a positive

Michelle Barone

way by spending time with people who love them and have a compelling interest in helping them learn to be a part of society. They learn this skill by being with people of all ages and by following the models of the adults around them in a healthy way. They learn by being with friends and siblings, shopkeepers, and neighbors, learning what works and what doesn't. You will know your child is growing socially by simply observing, seeing her mature before your eyes. One month she will have such difficulty sharing her toys, and the next month she is loaning her things to everyone. My experience has shown that children who have been with their families as their primary teachers are truly socialized. They are a part of the world, learning what is most important to them, to their families, their community.

We have been led to believe children learn to socialize by being only with

---

A PRESCRIPTION FOR FAMILY EMPOWERMENT

Take the experts with a grain of salt. Then do what you know is right in the morning.

At their best, the "experts" spread advice based on families and children they know. At their worst, many do and say whatever will bring in the most money. Child care and public education are quite susceptible to "fads" that are based on the expert-of-the-moment's ideas, fads that come and go with the wind.

But each and every child is unique, just like every family—and its circumstances. Whether you need to address silly everyday problems or major crises, *you*, the parent, are the expert on your child. *You* are the best informed about your child at any given time in any given circumstance.

Give over your time to discovering within yourself the means to raising your children. Both you and your children will be better people when you do.

---

children of their own ages in a very structured setting, with punishment and shame as the motivating force for behavior. The truth is, children want desperately to belong to the world of adults, to become competent, contributing members of society. This can only happen when a child is allowed to be a part of the world, not apart from it.

A child's temperament also influences his social growth. It is important to honor your child's pace and temperament. If your child is slow to warm up to a new setting, give her the time to adjust. If you have a very social child, find enjoyable activities and people for him. Socialization is always the big question with new homeschooling families. In reality, it is usually not a problem to find friends and activities. If you live in an isolated area it may take some effort; but again, children truly learn to be happy, well-adjusted social beings by spending time with their families, with other adults, and the world at large.

PAT MONTGOMERY Since when are school personnel trained to assess social growth? This reminds me of a story the Swiss scientist, Jean Piaget, told. He wanted to study children of various ages, so he went to schools. In a short time he gave up this quest because, he explained, schools are not natural habitats. If one wants to study rats and truly get a well-rounded picture of ratdom, one must go to sewers and dumps and nests—to nature—where rats are free to be rats. If one goes to laboratories where rats run in artificial mazes, one will learn only the habits of imprisoned rats. Schools are artificial places; children are not free to be themselves there.

Look at the social opportunities permitted in the schools. In my forty-four years of teaching, I have seldom been to institutional schools that allow for socializing, that is, interacting at work or at play with other people of different ages and backgrounds and interests.

To start with, children are segregated into age levels at school. Nowhere else in our society is this done. Not in hospitals or grocery stores or churches. The reasons for this have nothing whatsoever to do with a child's social needs. They have only to do with control.

When children are free to socialize with old and young—in home-education support groups, in boys' and girls' clubs and the like—they have older people than themselves to look up to and admire and younger people to assist and to learn from as well. Children learn by imitating. Being with children who are of identical age for the better part of a day can hardly be classified as a maximal social growth opportunity.

Home-educating parents and students are free to choose to read to elderly in nursing homes or convalescent centers, to bag foodstuffs at the food co-op, to plan and execute stage productions in the town drama group . . . the possibilities are too numerous to cite. This is socializing in the real world, not in the artificial confines of institutional school.

What is even worse, today's schools have inherited the problems of society at large—drugs and violence. They are scarcely models of healthy socialization opportunities.

CHAPTER FIVE

"Educationese" You Can Understand

T HE TOOL MOST frequently used to make parents think long and hard about removing their children from public schools is criticism of home-schoolers' socialization. The secret language of education runs a close second.

Fearing they won't be able to toss out the right jargon to explain their concerns, many parents don't question teachers and administrators. Those parents who do dare to speak up are often barraged by unfamiliar terms, and quickly fall prey to the "professionals'" implications that *they* know a lot more—and better—than an untrained parent.

If you are trying to stay involved with the education of a child in public school, you might want, for example, to bone up on the differences between types of assessment: authentic, alternative, group, valid, peer, portfolio, or self. Which does your child's school use?

You could study the implications of outcome-based education (OBE), and whether your child's school is in the stage of traditional OBE, transitional OBE, or transformational OBE.

Heard talk about CIMs and CAMs? Do you know what they are? Where they came from? Whether your child's school plans to drop traditional diplomas when adopting them?

Did you wonder what was wrong with "old" math when you studied "new" math in school? Do you know how "new new" math differs from both? (I'm not making this up, folks!) And, by the way, how do your child's metacognitive skills measure up?

Truth is, each of the "educationese" terms can be explained in a few, plain English sentences. Within fifteen minutes you'd have a handle on it all and be capable of discussing it with anyone. (And I strongly recommend doing so!) As easy as the jargon is to translate, though, it's totally unnecessary to the practice of home education. Educationese is the language of an institution concerned with management, efficiency, teachers' unions, and funding. This language needn't be applied to a home where the only concerns are the needs of one or a few children surrounded by supportive family.

> **Educationese is the language of an institution concerned with management, efficiency, teachers' unions, and funding.**

Ironically, many of the current educational reforms are attempting to take what works in a home setting and institutionalize it, mostly with disastrous results. It stands to reason that if you take what works in an institutional setting and put it in the home, the results will be equally calamitous. Indeed, personal reading and anecdotal evidence suggest that it's those homeschoolers who create "school at home" who suffer the highest incidence of stress and burnout and send their children back to school in frustration.

There are many ways to go about homeschooling without resorting to school at home, and an explanation of just a few of these approaches are all the "educationese" you'll need to better understand homeschooling. Unschooling, interest-initiated learning, and unit studies will help you see how many different ways there are to go about helping your child receive an education, and probably get you thinking of a dozen more ways.

For a special treat, read the fascinating essays about some of homeschooling's earliest advocates. First, Susannah Sheffer, author and editor of the popular *Growing Without Schooling* magazine, and Nancy Plent, who founded the Unschooling Network twenty years ago, share their memories of John Holt and his work. Then Dr. Raymond Moore and Dorothy Moore describe their world-famous Moore Formula, a customized low-cost, low-stress, readiness-oriented plan for achievement, behavior, and sociability through a study-work-service balance.

It's "educationese" you can understand—and enjoy.

30

The name John Holt comes up frequently in articles about homeschooling. What was his thinking about education when he began to encourage homeschooling?

Susannah Sheffer Holt had been a schoolteacher for several years when his book *How Children Fail,* published in 1964, brought him to public attention. It was an account of life in a fifth-grade classroom, and it looked closely at why the students—supposedly bright, privileged, successful—weren't learning what Holt was trying to teach. He was surprised and puzzled to find that most of the children in his classroom were bored and frightened, intent primarily on figuring out what the teacher wanted. The classroom was not the place of active learning and exploration that Holt had imagined it would be.

While teaching in school, Holt was also spending time with the young children of relatives and friends. He saw in these young children the energy, enthusiasm, and skill at learning that were almost wholly absent in fifth-grade students. What was it, he wondered,

> **The whole idea of compulsory learning and of a society that judges people on the basis of their schooling seemed wrong to John Holt.**

that turned such active and curious human beings into the timid and evasive strategists he met at school?

He began to suspect that the fault lay in the way children were treated in school and in the entire assumption that learning was something separate from life that children had to be made to do or shown how to do. Children are good at learning, Holt eventually asserted, and that phrase is a good short summary of his beliefs. (In his second book, *How Children Learn,* he wrote, "Everything I am saying in this book can be summed up in two words: trust children," so there's an even briefer summary.)

Holt spent many years at the forefront of the school reform movement, talking, writing, and working for more freedom, choice, and innovation in education. For a while he felt hopeful; it seemed as if many people were interested in the ideas he and others were putting forth, and change seemed forthcoming. But, by the mid-1970s, many "free schools" closed; innovative teachers were fired; audiences seemed less receptive. Holt later wrote that he came, slowly and reluctantly, to see that "very few people, inside the schools or out, were willing to support or even tolerate giving more freedom, choice, and self-direction to children."

At the same time, Holt's own thinking was being challenged and expanded by his contact with Ivan Illich, author of *Deschooling Society*. Holt began to consider that school might not be "a good idea gone wrong," but rather "a bad idea from the word go." The whole idea of compulsory learning and of a society that judges people on the basis of their schooling seemed wrong to him. Holt began to imagine what growing up without schooling would be like; at the same time, he began meeting parents who had actually taken the step of allowing their children to learn outside of school entirely. To support such families, to provide a forum in which they could communicate with one another, and to explore and develop his own ideas, Holt founded *Growing Without Schooling* magazine in 1977.

NANCY PLENT John was one of those rare people who adjusted his vision when new information came his way. His thinking about education was in Stage III when I met him. First he had tried teaching in public school and began to talk and write about how they should change.

Then he encouraged families who couldn't wait for change (which might take years, the way bureaucracies move) to get together and form their own schools (Stage II). It turned out that these schools rarely lasted very long, and he saw that.

So to parents who were discouraged with the membership wars that went on in co-op schools, John suggested the most direct route to get what they wanted was to take on the job themselves.

I often wonder what insights we may be missing because he's not around today to point out what Stage IV should be.

31

What does "unschooling" mean, and how is it different from homeschooling?

NANCY PLENT I was stunned when my first homeschooling friend showed me her basement schoolroom. She started lessons from her teacher's desk every day right after breakfast. Her kids had desks lined up in front of her, just like in public school. I couldn't understand it. Wasn't that what we were all trying to escape? She was what I would call a "home schooler"—somebody who duplicates school at home to a high degree. I've since realized that my reaction was because *I* was trying to escape everything that looked like school, but that by itself didn't make me an "unschooler."

Each person's definition of *unschooling* is a little different, and that's appropriate. Unschooling is about helping your child learn by doing the things that excite him, that fit his inner drives, rather than trying to motivate him to work at a generic "Goals 2000" curriculum.

Biographies of famous people are packed with examples of how well child-centered education works. Read about Thomas Edison, Noel Coward, Andrew Carnegie, Woodrow Wilson . . . and hundreds of others, all lucky enough to have parents who helped them travel their own unique unschooling road.

MARY GRIFFITH Having written a book on unschooling, I've acquired quite a collection of definitions for it. My favorite is one from my friend Carol Edson: "Unschooling means learning what one wants, when one wants, in the way one wants, for one's own reasons."

Unschooling is the way we all learn most of what we know and do. It's learning by reading, by creating, by trial and error, by figuring out what we're doing as we do it. Unschooling is learning as a process, not as a sequence of products.

Sometimes unschooling doesn't look much different from other forms of homeschooling, but the difference is that choice and control reside with the learner. With unschooling, learning is not something imposed from outside, not something *done to* the learner. It's something the learner does *for herself.* She may find outside help in the form of parents, mentors, books, or formal lessons, but *she* is the one making the decisions about how best to proceed.

Unschooling is trusting that your children are at least as clever and capable as you are yourself.

KATHARINE HOUK Most people understand homeschooling to mean learning outside of the institution called school, yet some families refer to what they do as unschooling. The term unschooling has been used in a couple of different ways.

Katharine Houk

Unschooling sometimes refers to homeschooling without a set curriculum, wherein what happens each day is based on the interests and curiosities of the people involved. Sometimes this process is called natural learning, the discovery method, or experience-based learning. Many families, including my own, have enjoyed this family- and community-centered way of living and learning for many years. To some this may not look like "education" at all because it so closely resembles daily life.

And daily life it is—with a focus for both adults and children on exploration, problem-solving, discovering where to look for answers to the hundreds of questions that naturally arise, all intertwined with the tasks involved in keeping a household running smoothly.

Becoming unschoolers was an evolutionary process for our family. At first I was worried about "covering" the same topics that children in school were learning. I borrowed books from my local district but found that my children's daily explorations at home and in the community went far beyond what they would have learned from those books. Using our home and public libraries, going fun places and meeting interesting people, taking care of home, pets, and the garden, and attending homeschooling gatherings filled our days with discovery. My task as an unschooling parent has been to create a rich learning environment (which has included everything from dance classes to textbooks to travel), provide guidance and direction when appropriate, and nurture interests. This is not to say that a family homeschooling with a set cur-

> **The term *unschooling* is also used by homeschoolers to describe the process of shedding notions that institutional education has bestowed on us, both parents and children. These notions may include the idea that learning is a chore and must be coerced with rewards and punishments, or that teaching is necessary for learning to take place, or that there is a uniform timetable for learning certain things such as reading.**

riculum cannot also do these things, time and energy permitting.

The term *unschooling* is also used by homeschoolers to describe the process of shedding notions that institutional education has bestowed on us, both parents and children. These notions may include the idea that learning is a chore and must be coerced with rewards and punishments, or that teaching is necessary for learning to take place, or that there is a uniform timetable for learning certain things such as reading.

Letting go of these ingrained ideas is a recovery process, best helped by developing trust in our children and ourselves, which can be nurtured by learning from experienced unschoolers whether in support groups, online, or by reading articles in publications. My children have been my best teachers in my efforts to unlearn what my schooling has taught me and it's an ongoing task. It's been my love for them that has opened my eyes to what they really need, to what captures their minds and hearts, to what has helped them grow up to be healthy, knowledgeable adults.

One scary aspect of unschooling, if you live in a state that requires reports, is translating this kind of learning into a form that school officials can understand; therefore my husband and I have put in valuable time explaining to education officials what we are doing and how it is working. Translating our children's natural learning into "educationese" can be tedious, but doing so has enabled us to keep on with what has been working best for our family. Some unschooling families enroll with a support group such as Clonlara, which acts as a buffer/translator between them and school officials.

The flexibility of unschooling has allowed our children to develop in directions that might not have opened to them had we stuck to the school's (or some other) curriculum. They've become self-directed learners. Unschooling has worked well for our family and for many others, but there is no right way when it comes to homeschooling. You and your children are the experts on what is best for your family.

Donn Reed (edited by Jean Reed) There are as many ways to homeschool as there are people and families. Unschooling is one way of homeschooling, just as dif-

ferent religions are different ways of celebrating life and worshiping God.

Differentiating between unschooling and homeschooling requires a definition of homeschooling. I believe homeschooling occurs when parents take personal responsibility for a child's development and education outside of the traditional public school environment. That's a simplistic definition. Homeschooling is actually much more. It's a lifestyle involving and bonding the whole family. For us it means recognizing that learning takes place at any time or place; that life itself is an ongoing education not confined to a particular time, place, or age.

Homeschooling allows us to give our children more than test-taking and money-earning skills. Our global society is changing. We feel it our responsibility to give our children more than just academic skills to meet these challenges. Our children need the ability to evaluate, make responsible judgments, and resolve conflicts peacefully with open minds and creativity. We also want our children to be happy now. We feel that childhood is important in itself; it shouldn't be spent only in preparation for adulthood.

Unschooling advocate John Holt said, "Children do not need to be made to learn, told what to learn, or shown how. Given access to enough of the world, including our own lives and work in that world, they will see clearly what things are truly important to us and to others and they will make for themselves a better world than we could make for them." Some parents feel allowing children freedom to learn "by doing" without interference constitutes unschooling; that parents shouldn't offer advice or "teach" unless asked or "invited" to share their knowledge as opposed to teaching how to do it: a statement of faith in children's innate curiosity and abilities.

We found that leaving our kids alone, letting them study when and what they wanted, worked at some times, but not always. It worked for Mowgli and Tarzan; other times we've wondered why so few of the great educators have children of their own. If I interrupt my son's woodworking to show him a way to start the saw-cut without nicking a finger, am I interfering with his ability to learn by himself? If I withhold the same information from an adult, and he becomes aware of it, he may very well resent me. Letting a child struggle with a task without offering advice that would make it easier is not showing respect; and, once he realizes you could have

helped but chose not to, probably will not increase his respect for you. Perhaps it is the manner used to convey the information.

Our experiment with different learning styles continued throughout twenty-four years of homeschooling. Our conclusion: Any philosophy, carried to its "logical," consistent extreme, can become ridiculous and indefensible. We all learn in different ways at different times. Homeschooling should allow each child to learn in the manner that is best for them at that particular time. We've always liked Emerson's comment, "Consistency is the hobgoblin of little minds."

> **H**omeschooling is . . . a lifestyle involving and bonding the whole family. For us it means recognizing that learning takes place at any time or place; that life itself is an ongoing education not confined to a particular time, place, or age.

32

What is "interest-initiated" learning, and how do I learn how to do this?

LUZ SHOSIE Have you ever watched a baby learning to pull herself up to reach a toy, or a seven year old figuring how many weeks' allowance it takes to buy that new game, or a sixteen year old planning college-entry strategies? That's interest-initiated learning. Humans, and all other living beings, come into the world with the ability and the need to learn and grow into adults. They know how to do it.

Many of us who spent a lot of time in school were taught that we must be forced to learn, that learning is difficult, and that only experts know how to do it. For us, some unlearning is required. I recommend reading John Holt, carefully observing young children, and joining (or starting) an unschoolers' support group.

Our son, Cassidy, and I have made several cross-country trips and stayed with homeschooling families. Usually one of the first topics of discussion when we meet a new family is how do we do it? I would always say that we don't do lessons, that we answer questions or give help when asked. They would say, "That's the way we do it, too, but we thought we were the only ones because our support group always talks about how to teach math or how to choose a curriculum."

So I decided to start a group for those of us who are struggling to overcome our years of schooling and trust ourselves and our children to be learning all the time. We meet at each other's homes on Saturday afternoons so the

> **I**t's Schoolaholics Anonymous—when you think you can't make it through another minute without *teaching those kids a lesson,* **get out your phone list and call an unschooler. We all have those days. It will pass.**

children can play and the parents can reassure each other and exchange ideas. We publish a mailing list so people can get in touch. It's Schoolaholics Anonymous—when you think you can't make it through another minute without *teaching those kids a lesson,* get out your phone list and call an unschooler. We all have those days. It will pass.

SANDRA DODD You're asking how to learn something? You're asking someone you think would know? *That's it! You've got it!*

You could have taken a course in interest-initiated learning, maybe, and bought a $60 book and read the chapters in the order the teacher listed, at the speed the syllabus recommends, taken two tests and a final, written two papers . . . that is *not* interest-initiated learning. That's submitting yourself to scheduled torture. That's lying down and letting someone else tell you to learn more slowly, learn more quickly, don't ask *that* question, it won't be on the test, anyway.

Sandra Dodd

THE DEFINITION OF "TO EDUCATE"

Educate: from Latin: *ex* (out) + *ducere* (lead). You have to look long and hard to uncover this original definition in your dictionary, but you will search forever to find evidence of it in the way we typically approach our children's learning lives.

To lead out—what does this definition tell us? It tells us that perhaps we are experiencing so many problems teaching our children because we are going about it backwards. We consider education as putting information into our children when true education is the act of "leading out" that which already exists inside.

This simple definition can transform your family's perspective on learning. Through it we recognize learning's natural connection to life. The artificial experience of reading and memorizing (pouring in) pales in comparison to real life learning through which your child learns by discovery (leading out). Only you as parent can allow your child the opportunity to touch true education.

Memorize this definition. Let it lead your entire family to the joy of learning.

If I need to be at a meeting in a neighboring town at a certain time I would plan time to get there, no side trips, no stopping, no changing my mind. If I'm going to drive for four hours without a destination, turning where fancy leads, staying as long or as short a time as seems good to the children, we will do and see things we could never have chosen in advance. A flexible willingness to experience what comes will open up the world.

If, after a lifetime of schedules, deadlines, and year-ends, you want to experiment with interest-initiated learning, I think the best way is to play. Play board games, word games, work jigsaw puzzles side by side with your children (even if they are seventeen years old). I predict two things will happen: You'll be surprised at the connections to history, geography, math, language, culture, science, and so forth that will unfold from your game *if* you can consider it an opportunity instead of "just" a game. You will have an opportunity to talk with your child on a calm and personable level. The game or puzzle creates a space in which you are facing the same direction, and you have a need and excuse to sit still, without jumping up out of anxiety or discomfort. It creates a calm area and a shared space.

Another shared learning experience can be reading aloud. With younger children, this is obvious. With middlin' children, you can read books that would be too hard for them to read on their own, a chapter or two at a stretch, or read them to sleep. They'll gain vocabulary and a feel for written English beyond what they can get visually. With older children who are proficient readers, you could take turns reading, maybe in the car, or they could read to you while you sew or do dishes. You could read to them while they work on a model or draw or work puzzles or sand furniture. Reading in the car or listening to books on tape can be a great way to share literature, and car trips are good opportunities for long discussions.

Once you've seen half a dozen instances of getting to a subject area you hadn't expected to reach, or of the children asking questions you would never have thought to set up or to coax from them, you'll gain confidence. I can't tell

you what your children will ask or learn because that would be a curriculum, a set of facts or activities you all could pass or fail. I'm talking about cross-country thinking. Get off the paved road and explore.

What if you don't "do history in order"? Probably you'll learn a lot more history! Just get out there and play around with words, ideas, concepts, and connections.

Another approach is to think of the things you have learned outside of school, and how you learned them. What hobbies or authors or subjects or crafts have you learned just because you developed a curiosity and burning interest? What collections do you have, what skills or special knowledge do you have that you've developed gradually or quickly without paying a teacher, without being tested or certified?

DONNA NICHOLS-WHITE Watch your children while they play. I know this sounds weird, but I believe learning begins in this way. Observe while they build, create, and resolve conflicts. Notice what interests them.

Ever notice a little one become fascinated with machines like bulldozers? Some will sit quietly for hours observing construction workers. One of my sons would kneel beside a stream while waiting for a bug or lizard to show up. Activities such as these are rarely considered academic, or worthy of note.

Discover your child's hobby. My daughter loves music and dance. I take her to performances, the theater, and concerts. I buy books about dancing. Of course she attends classes and spends hours observing others who perform at more difficult levels.

Through dance, if I desired, I could cover math, science, language arts, foreign languages, and a host of other subjects. One hobby or interest can open up a myriad of subjects for a child. I shy away from making a lesson out of every experience, for I believe that children should be independent learners. They don't need me as a crutch.

This means that I lead them to the answers for their questions instead of just handing them over, I offer plenty of free time for them to think and create, I limit television, and I have a home that's filled with self-teaching tools like books, building toys, and art supplies.

I have found resources that not only reflect my children's interests, but mine. Usually, when they want to know something, they can research it at home using our library or the Internet.

Letting go of the antiquated idea that I have to pour knowledge into my children comes pretty easily for me. For one thing, I'd be exhausted in no time at all if I did their thinking for them. I easily become annoyed with the robotic tendencies of schooled children. Their spouting out the correct answers, their asking permission to perform life's natural functions like eating and sleeping, and their absolute obedience to learning what and when others tell them to learn. The thirst for knowledge is very important. I've met too many academically burned out children for my tastes.

I have chosen my battles. Supporting their interests is a lot less hassle than pushing what is supposedly necessary.

33

A friend told me she finds out what her children are interested in learning about, then turns that into a unit study. Is this an effective way for children to learn?

PAT LINES I'm not experienced in child-directed learning over time, and I know of no studies on this topic, so I must give a very general answer. I don't know how you can "teach" a child who is not interested in the subject. On the other hand, I don't know how a child can become interested in a topic unless there is some initial exposure. In a rich environment, where there is much natural exposure to many topics, I would expect this approach to work. Most children have a natural curiosity about a wide range of things, even those that are more focused on a single topic. We do expect children to learn a range of skills and subject matter, but I don't think the order in which they learn it will be that important ten years from now.

SHARI HENRY I imagine it is an effective way for many children to learn. We don't work that way in our house, at least not formally. My children do take off on learning tangents, but I've never felt the desire to turn it into a formal unit study. My middle child, at age seven, became fascinated with Greek mythology thanks to a fantastic Renaissance art exhibit in town. A painting of Europa and Jupiter spurred months and months of reading myths, creating books of her favorite gods and goddesses, making paper dolls with changeable goddess clothing, playing make-believe myths with friends (where they would each transform into a famous mythological character and role play for hours), and decorating her bunk beds with leaves and grape clusters to make it look like a "Greek island." There, she'd escape for hours at end. This all led into a study of the planets and filtered into other areas of study as well. She now knows more about mythology than most college graduates, helps bail her father out of tough spots in crossword puzzles, and is on her way to what I consider a high school level study of space and the planets. I didn't do anything but help her browse shelves at the local bookstores, place a few catalog orders, and look up some pronunciations.

> **My middle child, at age seven, became fascinated with Greek mythology thanks to a fantastic Renaissance art exhibit in town.**

While I know unit studies work well for some families, they feel a bit contrived to us. And, to be honest, I'm not looking for more work!

34

What is the Moore Formula approach to home education?

DR. RAYMOND MOORE AND DOROTHY MOORE In contrast with conventional homeschools, the Moore Formula provides a great deal of freedom within guidelines that target (1) readiness for formal learning, (2) the student's interests, and

(3) a balance of study, work, and community service. This offers a certain security that most curricula don't provide, with little or no burnout. It also contrasts with packaged curricula that fit nicely into conventionally minded families but sharply restrict creativity and lead to burnout.

Freedom embraces the *readiness* principle for all tasks. Whatever children need or want to do—physically, mentally, or spiritually—if they are mature enough, they learn faster, with less stress. Although they are ready for simple physical jobs as soon as they can walk, such as putting away toys, they are usually not ready for formal study until at least age eight to ten or twelve. Until then, there should be much informal learning, including useful work, learning games (phonics, math, and so on), life experiences (bakery, market, fire station, post office), and true stories read to them on many subjects (language arts), including religion (history), nature (science), biographies (history), and travelogues (geography). The longer such learning continues, at least until age ten, the better the foundation for their superstructure of formal learning. Meanwhile,

> **O**nce you have their interests, motivation seems automatic, instead of being dilemma to both teachers and students as in conventional programs.

some skills naturally develop, although never through parental pressure. If you live in a state requiring school at age six or seven, label your informal learning with typical subject names as above in parentheses.

The Formula's love for freedom isn't slap-dash. It fosters sound educational tools—reading, writing, phonics, grammar, spelling, and math. Our materials emphasize student interests and therefore motivation. So there are more lively but thorough games, biographies, and practical materials than workbooks and traditional textbooks. We insure that students are ready or mature enough for formal studies. They reach higher-than-normal achievement levels.

Freedom here is a principle that measures to responsibility. Kids thrive on freedom that rhymes with authority. Yet integrity and common sense say authority must be limited to ability to accept responsibility. So states require maturity and responsibility levels before it awards driver's licenses. When youngsters see this clearly and sense the meaning of authority, motivation reigns. The Formula doesn't function exactly the same in every family or with every student. There is a built-in flexibility that's limited by student mastery of learning tools. Given that prospect, we customize to the interests, aptitudes, attitudes, and abilities of each student. The big thing we have going for us here is targeting student interests instead of giving each grade the same stack of books, which tells them we think they are all alike. Once you have their interests, motivation seems automatic, instead of being dilemma to both teachers and students as in conventional programs.

So we follow the three guidelines above, which aren't optional. For example, *study* with balanced *work* and *service* usually means as much or more work and service as study. Work usually relates to earning money, and service here is volunteering without pay. Together they shatter selfishness.

CHAPTER SIX

Okay, the Kids Are Home— *Now* What?

F OR SOME FOLKS, the *decision* to homeschool is a piece of cake compared to actually facing the first day of complete responsibility for their children's education. I know; I've been there. There can never be a definitive "how to" book for this occasion, no matter how loudly a title may shout it. Why? Because that momentous "first day"—and, for that matter, all subsequent days—are unique to each family. Let's meet just a few of the broad "groups" of new homeschoolers to help you understand how the experience that all call by the same name—homeschooling— starts from many different places.

Let's begin with the I-Always-Knew-I-Would family. They've known since their first child was born—and maybe even before—this was the only way to fly. For them, the first day of homeschooling is not the first day of school during the year their child turns five or six years old. Rather, their child simply turns five or six during the learning rhythm of day-to-day life, and they're well aware from the get-go that each day provides opportunity and experience galore for learning. There is no easily recognizable first day of homeschooling for this family.

The Oh-No-He's-Almost-School-Aged family makes the decision to homeschool when the day to sign up for kindergarten looms ever closer. Likely, friends and acquaintances with children the same age busily go about the rituals associated with starting school: taking their children to "readiness tests"; buying new clothes; checking bus schedules; making sure all vaccinations are up to date. The Oh-No-He's-Almost-School-Aged family is less likely to recognize the learning rhythm of all the days that have passed before and enter into what may be termed "substitute" rituals: a quest to find the magical list that outlines what all the other kindergartners will be learning that year (aka curriculum); a frantic materials- and book-buying spree; a series of late-night "Are we doing the right thing?" conversations; a tenth phone call making sure they've got the right day and time for the next homeschool support group meeting. For the Oh-No-He's-Almost-School-Aged family, there will be a first day of homeschooling, and it will be a "happening."

> **For some folks, the** *decision* **to homeschool is a piece of cake compared to actually facing the first day of complete responsibility for their children's education. I know; I've been there.**

The first day of homeschooling is different still for the I-Don't-Want-Him-in-School-Anymore family. Each of this group's families has their own reason for this, be it religious, philosophical, academic, social, growing fear for their child's safety, or an intricate combination of some or all of the above. One or several of their children have gone to school for a year, maybe a few years. Their children are still quite young, but even in this relatively short time period, the family has grown assimilated to the school routine. The I-Don't-Want-Him-in-School-Anymore family will not only have a first day of homeschool "happening," this family is likely to make sure it starts on time and occurs in specific subject areas at specific times of the day, to boot—just like school!

And last, meet the My-(Pre)Teen-Is-Coming-Out-of-School family. They have spent a *long* time in the school routine, and their child may be bored or overwhelmed academically, ditto for socially, acting out, caving in to peer pressure, or sensing that school isn't all there is. The idea to homeschool may have been Mom's or Dad's, or it may just as easily have been suggested to them by their child.

This child may have many strong ideas about where he wants to go with homeschooling and jump right in with little or no help or guidance from parents. Another teen, used to having others set the learning schedule and agenda, could easily require—or even demand—strong guidance from a parent. In either case, the first day of homeschooling is different here than it is in the I-Don't-Want-Him-in-School-Anymore family's house, as an increasingly independent teen approaches *everything* differently than an elementary school-aged child does.

We could go on, but from even these few examples you can begin to see how many varied places there are from which a family begins to homeschool. Homeschooling is neither easier nor harder for any one of these broad groups of new homeschoolers; it's simply different. And with so many different starting points, you can begin to see how each family will soon be traveling its own homeschooling path in its own way.

This chapter addresses the practical aspect of homeschooling, and the included questions and answers were chosen to be useful no matter where you're starting from. Here you'll find out what experienced homeschoolers do all day. Equally important to notice is what they *don't* do all day! You'll find out how they feel about the use of textbooks, curriculum, and computers. They share ideas on finding the best resources, keeping records, and meeting the needs of several children of different ages at the same time. From sports activities to motivation to learn, this chapter is guaranteed to help you get off to a great start, no matter where your starting place is!

35

What do you *do* all day?

CINDY WADE My favorite response to this question is: "Whatever we want!"

Much depends on the weather, the time of year, finances, level of energy, or whim. We laugh, we talk, we cry, we share, we write, we read, we travel, we stay home for days on end, we work, we play, we touch, we shop, we sleep late, we learn our constitutional rights. We do what comes naturally.

Winter is a great time to hunker down with lots of new books obtained at summer tag sales, a few new educational CDs for the computer, a ready supply of sleds, skis, and new long-johns, and a cupboard full of Ovaltine.

Summer naturally lends itself to bike riding, hiking, flea markets, outdoor auctions, horseback riding, the sandbox, swimming, gardening, day trips, and lounging. Books get tossed aside for beach pails and barbecues.

So when do you "school," you ask? We don't! We actually make a concerted effort *not* to "school." A trip to the grocery store, approached with the right attitude, provides education in home economics, physics, math, health, and nutrition. We ask questions but we don't try to turn everything into a "lesson."

We threw out the desks, bulletin boards, textbooks, and chemistry set a long time ago. We kept the reference books, art supplies, Legos, and cookie cutters for a more natural learning environment. We've discovered the computer makes a good tutor.

We read lots of books about homeschooling and how others are doing it. We meet with other homeschoolers to play, chat, and bounce ideas and thoughts off each other. We attend programs, performances, weddings, funerals, graduations, and meetings.

What do we do all day? We live life!

CAFI COHEN Our teenage homeschoolers do what needs to be done. That includes shoveling snow, planning and cooking dinner, practicing piano, bathing the dog, volunteering at the hospital, working math problems, attending diving practice, memorizing a speech for 4-H, and teaching a rocketry class at a Civil Air Patrol meeting.

We also do whatever strikes our fancy. On this list are biking, drawing, playing games, seeing old movies, reading for hours on end, entering writing contests, and getting together with friends of all ages.

We have no typical days, no set schedule. Our activities vary tremendously, in accordance with the children's changing interests. One day my son might spend five hours with a new computerized flight simulator and the remainder of the day mowing the lawn, helping his dad with car maintenance, and reading—all of which we count as "school." The next day might include science homework (from his community college class), piano practice, math problems, weight training, and a 4-H meeting.

Sometimes the children are very productive. On other days it looks like they do very little—maybe just some household chores, visiting friends, and curling up with a favorite book for the fifth time. And we drop everything for family crises, unexpected travel opportunities, and great weather (best time to hike and ski!).

I do not worry about these apparent down times. Every day need not be the educational equivalent of the Fourth of July. Often enough (two to five days each week) the children are busy with activities that many professional educators would not only approve of, but envy.

It looks messy, but it works.

LUZ SHOSIE We create for ourselves a life worth living and work worth doing and try not to do what doesn't fit into that framework. We invite our son to participate in our activities as much as he wants and is able. Sometimes we insist that he join in the work of keeping a house and family operating. Sometimes he invites us to participate in his activities or asks us to help in his work.

We try to remember that we are all learning all the time, that life is not divided into math, social studies, science. Whatever we choose to do or pay attention to will teach us and lead us to the next learning experience. We do not choose or create activities for the sake of learning; we learn by doing what interests us and what needs to be done.

SUSAN EVANS The activities in our home change week to week and season by season. There are times when big projects overtake all of our lives for a period of time: an upcoming conference, finishing requirements for a Boy Scout Eagle badge, painting the house during the last week of nice weather in the fall. Mostly, though, life is pretty low key, variable, and focused on what any, few, or all of us are interested in at the time.

For many years our family life looked much like "advanced preschool at home," even when one of my "preschoolers" topped six feet tall! Our days were built around daily chores, errands around town, cultural enrichment (trips to the library, museums, zoos, plays,

> **After almost twenty years, I've come to see the truth in the statement that one can get straight A's in classes and yet flunk real life.**

concerts, movies), field trips (farms, small businesses, factories, restaurants), time to think, time to read and dream, attention to personal interests (collections, crafts, research), time for hugs, laughter and tears, long-term focused obsessions (Lego bricks, drawing, poetry, gardening).

For a while I described our approach to living and learning as being like the "gifted and talented" curriculum (while successfully skipping much of the "grade appropriate" curricula): hands-on exploration of interests; lots of messy projects; quiet, deep, long-winded conversations; scientific, spiritual, and philosophic wonderings, with no pressure for a final, definitive answer.

The main focus of our "homeschooling" time has been real life, taking care of important matters like homemaking, housekeeping, family rituals. Our most important work has been loving and supporting one another by taking the time and energy to deal with personal crises (large and small) in a direct, open, and honest manner. We've tried to attend to the real issues in life rather than artificial ones. So challenges like growing up to be ourselves, becoming responsible for ourselves and our actions, finding our true work in our lives, and creating the kind of lives that nurture our souls and challenge our spirits are in the fore.

What we've put aside are the issues and pressures that seem manufactured and rather pointless in comparison: "Are you ready for the science quiz?" "Did you write the 500-word paper that will count for half of your final grade?" "Are you wearing colors that start with the letter P today?"

After almost twenty years, I've come to see the truth in the statement that one can get straight A's in classes and yet flunk real life. What we do is real life: making a home, being actively involved in our geographical and cultural community, seeking and doing worthwhile work, seeking ways to support ourselves financially, spiritually, and emotionally.

36

How do I develop a curriculum or plan of study?

PAT MONTGOMERY The question is not "How?" but "Why?" I taught in public schools and parochial schools for fourteen years prior to starting Clonlara School in 1967. For fourteen years I never used that word, nor did my associates, teachers, or administrators. Textbook companies studied whichever curriculum a school district adopted.

The textbooks were what teachers used in classrooms. Sometimes these were the only teaching devices employed.

Curricula are designed by committees of teachers and administrators or by university college professors. These compilers of curricula usually observe and test children on each grade level to find out what the average child is interested in and can learn relatively easily.

It was only when home-based education became known to school officials sometime in the early 1980s that the word "curriculum" took on significance in relation to home educators. It was as though school officials, initially threatened, strained to find something that would discourage parents from opting out of schools. How could mere parents have access to the inner workings of schools—to curriculum? It became a buzz word.

Many home-educating parents bite the bait. They accept the myth that educating is about curriculum, textbooks, tests, and lesson plans, the trappings of institutional schools. I submit that the design of a child's education ought to be about the child. What are his interests? Her needs? His capabilities? Parents are not bound by the constricts of schools, which deal with such large numbers of students that they find it easiest to teach to the average students.

Parents are in the enviable position of being able to observe their own children and to develop a curriculum based upon their real interests and abilities and needs. This has been the practice at Clonlara for its entire thirty-plus-year existence. We have no other curriculum than the individual child herself.

Everyday life in the home can be the basis around which a plan is built. The ordinary has a magical aura for very young children. Building on a sense of wonder, following trails from how a key works to where the squirrel ran off is curriculum aplenty. As children grow, the home and the wealth of activities and wonder within it open out to the neighborhood, the community, even the world. Listening to a child's questions, finding answers together, and creating more questions is living curriculum. Those things that in schools are broken down into twenty- or fifty-minute segments can be studied for as long as an interest remains.

Curriculum and a plan of study are not mystical things. They were designed to let the student know facts about the

> **It was only when home-based education became known to school officials sometime in the early 1980s that the word "curriculum" took on significance in relation to home educators. It was as though school officials, initially threatened, strained to find something that would discourage parents from opting out of schools.**

world around him. We would never dream of establishing a curriculum for a baby or toddler, yet we know that a child learns more in the first three years of life than in all the rest of it put together. Why destroy this method of education in favor of an institutional school approach designed to pour facts into a child's mind? Your child has been making connections and using her mind actively since birth. She learns in ways peculiar to her own style. Study *that*. Then design a plan to nurture and support *that*. Education ought to be the parent's goal, not schooling. Education and schooling are not synonymous terms.

JOHN TAYLOR GATTO I'm glad you asked this. Nobody can develop a curriculum for you that isn't, at the very best, *second* best and, at the very worst, a rather diabolical exercise in mind control—even if its intentions are honorable.

Consider that the term "curriculum" comes to us from the classical period of ancient Rome and refers to a race course upon which animals, chariots, and drivers are "run." You don't have to be a rocket scientist to see similarities

---

**JOHN TAYLOR GATTO'S RECOMMENDED READING LIST
FOR CREATING A CURRICULUM**

1. *Autobiography of Benjamin Franklin:* Franklin provides an account of his middle years, prior to his role in the early U.S. government. He started without wealth or position, but achieved greatness as a well-rounded citizen—from scientist to entrepreneur, from public servant to national leader—all the while adhering to the guidance of industry and thrift.

2. *Autobiography of John Stuart Mill:* John Stuart Mill was the subject of a massive experiment by his own father to test how much a mind could be force-fed in childhood. You can derive two genuine values from Mill's later musings about his own experience. First, how criminal an abuse it is to trivialize a young mind with thin, insubstantial garbage; but second, how it is possible (though not likely) to err on the other side of exploitation of intellect at the cost of the affections. You will learn in detail the actual curriculum used and Mill's mature thinking about what he missed, and the effect it had on his character.

3. *The Autobiography of Norbert Weiner:* Weiner, a legendary teacher at MIT, is often called the "father" of cybernetics, the creation of artificial intelligence. Mill's curriculum was adapted by Weiner's father to deliber-

---

between race courses and mazes through which rats are run for the amusement and satisfaction of academic masters. Curricula, by their very nature, assume the surrender of volition—free will—for some presumably valuable goal that will be achieved in some presumably worthwhile future.

These are pretty big assumptions (and there are more assumptions inher-ent in the idea, had we the time to think about them) considering that the most efficient schoolmen and curriculum de-signers of history were the north Ger-man states of Prussia, Saxony, and Hanover, where every moment of the day fell under orders and directives of one kind or another—including the di-rective that women must report the onset of menses each month to the local ately create a scientific genius. Again, the precise curriculum is reflected on in detail, with its glories and inherent contradictions.

4. "The Lost Tools of Learning," a 1947 essay by Dorothy Sayers (not difficult to find): The famous detective story writer and social thinker (she created Lord Peter Whimsy) generally analyzes how people, of the upper classes mostly, were taught to think for themselves for hundreds of years through the classical tradition preserved in every one of America's elite private boarding schools. Whether this is your cup of tea or not (and I confess it is mine) if you think about what you are hearing from Sayers you will have no difficulty realizing that an aristocratic education—unlike the education of a technician—costs absolutely nothing to deliver and is accessible to all. Read this short piece at least six times on different days.

5. *Angela's Ashes*, by Frank McCourt: Pick up this book that's been atop the bestseller list for a year. You will learn how a boy with weak eyes can be beaten, starved, humiliated, and hounded every single day of his young life, in the worst curriculum the twentieth century has to offer, and still—because his mother and drunken father provided him a curriculum of tough love—could grow up to be an honorable and successful teacher in America's most prestigious high school, an entertainer in his spare time, and a multimillionaire from writing about it.

---

police. These social planners caused the three biggest wars in modern history so far, although everyone agreed the "education" was superb.

The problem with buying someone else's *comprehensive* curriculum for personal development (limited curricula—like those for mastering a musical instrument, are not part of my warning) is that it will be certain not to fit you. I say certain because the assumption that there are only a few types of humanity, and that all are sufficiently plastic or empty to take on whatever shape is imposed upon them, is an insane utopian idea contradicted by common experience. It *is* possible to shoehorn people into a few kinds of *classes* or types and spend oceans of energy and money convincing those so confined such a course conforms with human nature. Schools do it every day. But the mutilations necessary to achieve the appearance of regular human ordering cause a lot of problems in an open society. Run to the library and read H. G. Wells's *The Island of Dr. Moreau,* which dealt prophetically with this very social initiative one hundred years ago.

To develop a curriculum of your own, you must be determined to know yourself and what you expect of yourself. This is a wholly different thing than studying and guessing what others expect of you. As you begin to know yourself (and the roads to self-knowledge are multiple but always begin with silences, solitudes, intense reflections, and self-study done obsessively until the programmed layers begin to flake away), you will begin to see what racecourse you *want* to build for your family to run on, and begin to fashion it by arranging experiences and planning time dispositions which lead in that direction.

Think of it this way: If the goal of your race is to have your child go to Harvard, work his way up an international corporation's ladder, and get rich, you will move the foundations of his day in such a fashion that attitudes, habits, and interests suitable for such a competition are pre-

pared. I hope that isn't your goal, but what the hey, I'm not you.

On the other hand, if a strong, independent person filled with courage, resourcefulness, curiosity, humor, and in possession of a livelihood not dependent on fitting into a collective is your hope, then a *much* different course has to be run. (For this latter I again recommend the eminently readable *Autobiography of Benjamin Franklin.*)

Some important part of the curriculum of growing up will have to be supplied by the young person, even in babyhood. I think it's a bad idea to be doctrinaire about this—how much exactly is something you have to play by ear—but the guardians have to be enthusiastic about it as well as the guarded or else it will degenerate into a bad thing for everyone. In the words of the immortal Chris Mercogliano at the Albany Free School, you have to make it up as you go along in this regard.

Reading and studying other people's curricula, as long as they are explicit about selection of items, methods, justifications, outcomes, and assessments over time of the life results, can be extremely useful in showing you different ways such thinking can proceed. I don't mean you copy necessarily what others do; but by observing how and what they think you can sharpen your own mind.

But remember, it's not a contest. There are many, many ways to grow up right, and many "good" lives that can be enjoyed. Too many for any person to have them all.

SUSAN EVANS Fortunately, every homeschooling family comes equipped with curriculum experts: curious children.

What are your children's interests?

What sorts of places do they like to visit: airports, parks, libraries, museums, malls, the backyard, rock shops, zoos, factories . . . ?

What sorts of questions do they ask or wonder about?

What do you and your children enjoy doing together: talking, eating, dancing, playing sports, reading, singing, swimming, arguing, shopping . . . ?

The world and everything in it are connected. You can start your exploration anywhere and keep traveling intellectually. Interests lead one to another, and you're sure to run out of time before you run out of new adventures.

If you live in a state with reporting regulations, it's not difficult to translate what you love to do into educationese.

If you live in a state with required testing, you might want to add political activism to your curriculum (it won't hurt the rest of us, either). From what I've seen, most children who are following their hearts and their passionate interests do well enough on the tests so that they needn't sacrifice real learning in order to meet arbitrary state requirements.

In every state with excessive regulations, though, there are parents who have figured out how to put their family's education ahead of bureaucratic paperwork. It's worth the time to seek out these parents in your state and learn from their experiences.

Back to curricular considerations: A good rule of thumb from the time your children are small is to think of purchasing tools rather than toys for holiday and gift giving. Beyond the obvious books and art supplies, think of other useful materials and resources: fabric, pins, hammers, nails, a sheet of plywood (what would *you* make out of your own sheet of plywood?), rope, duct tape, Lego bricks, embroidery thread in a rainbow of colors (good for jewelry, hanging pictures, twisting into dog leashes, weaving), shovels and rakes and a corner of the yard.

What are your children longing to "mess with"? Can you think of creative ways to oblige them?

Do what's fun, what's intriguing, what keeps you up at night wondering about. Don't worry about grade level or the paperwork, if you absolutely must make your life conform to a state's idea of a curriculum, you can always write it up later, in the afterglow of newfound wisdom and knowledge.

37

Can I find a ready-made curriculum to get started in homeschooling?

DR. RAYMOND MOORE AND DOROTHY MOORE
Yes, although twenty-five years ago they were scarce. Many Christian publishers resented homeschools and would not sell to them. Today, mass-produced textbooks, workbooks, and videos make big money for these publishers, and perform a service for conventional schools. As a university teacher-education dean and curriculum specialist, I authored and coauthored many such books. Parents often choose them because that's the way they were taught. Many often are uneasy with programs that encourage freedom for imagination, and sometimes they are right; it can be overdone. Yet those who use mass education for homeschools are the most frequent burnouts.

If you want creativity and exciting quality with the best chance at major scholarships, customize to your children's abilities, aptitudes, and interests. Ready-made curricula seldom produce creative children, balanced in head, heart, hand, and health.

> **T**hose who use mass education for homeschools are the most frequent burnouts.

Dr. Ed Dickerson, who supervises Iowa homeschools, wrote about curricula for our *Moore Report International*. He says when upset parent-burnouts misunderstand and misuse curricula, he tells them a story about an imaginary shopping trip for a boy, age nine. They tell a clerk, "We'd like some nine-year-old boy shoes." He brings a shoebox clearly labeled "nine-year-old boy shoes." But the shoe doesn't fit! So the clerk concludes, "His foot must be deformed!"

Children's minds are even more individual than their feet. A nine year old in a ready-made curriculum at home or school will seldom fit right. So we have many "special education" misfits, especially boys, whose maturity is often misdiagnosed.

If you want to know how to teach with freedom, recheck our answer to Question 34, read our Moore Formula books, *The Successful Homeschool Family Handbook* and *Minding Your Own Business*, and send for a free basic information packet (BIP) from Box 1, Camas, WA 98607. These books are based on our research, which is the main reason that Moore Academy students are known for their creativity and many major scholarships.

Whatever your curriculum route, for your own well-being and for your children's sake, be sure that it is consistent with the research on readiness. It is a form of child abuse to force children to enroll for studies for which they are not equipped by age, maturity, ability, and aptitudes, especially for boys.

Some ask about correspondence schools. If they provide personal tutorial help, they are especially useful for college-age students or for odd courses for high school diploma needs. Be sure they provide the freedom and creativity of a sound work-study-service curriculum customized to students' interests, abilities, and aptitudes, and also embrace readiness. The president of a highly rated correspondence school recently visited us, saying he'd like to follow our plan. Given these conditions, he will come closer to producing vibrant, creative children at low parental stress levels than with average packaged curricula.

NED VARE Yes, but don't ever take them seriously.

38
At what age do I have to start formal lessons with my children?

JANIE LEVINE HELLYER Before children reach what our society has come to call "school age," they acquire an amazing amount of skills and knowledge without benefit of formal lessons. These things are learned in a very natural way, and most parents know that when children are ready, they will learn. Consider how our children acquire language skills and learn to talk.

From the time of birth, we talk to our children, sing to them, and some of us have been known to make funny sounds and faces in an effort to communicate with them. No one expects an infant to be born talking. Most of us realize that there is a lot of learning that takes place before a child speaks his first word, and that our healthy children will talk when they are ready. Do we expect our children to speak their first word on a strict schedule, at a certain month? Of course not! Everyone who has been around infants realizes that our babies are on their own learning schedule, and the exact age that a little one speaks his first word is something that cannot be planned. If we were to formalize a learning plan to teach our children to talk, it might go something like this:

"Good morning, Susan. Today we are going to have the first lesson in how to talk. I want you to be still and quiet and listen very carefully as I introduce the first sound of language to you. The first sound we will learn is, 'Ahhhhh.' Can you say 'Ahhhhh?' Ahhhhh." After a time, the baby cries, and the teacher/mother says, "Very good, Susan! That's the sound! Now I want you to practice that sound until you have it down and remember it. Once you have learned it perfectly, we will add a new sound!"

Of course none of us teach our children language skills in this way. We do not break down "learning to talk" into neat and tidy lessons, nor do we expect the sounds our children learn to be acquired in any particular sequence or any particular time. Most mothers know exactly what to do. We talk to our babies, sing to them, and expose them to the language that we use in our daily lives. We realize that in their own time, they will talk.

Acquiring language skills is very complex, yet we understand that babies learn to talk naturally in a nurturing environment. Why is it, then, that when children turn five or six years of age, we think that how they learn changes and everything requires formal lessons and teaching? They don't. Most of the things taught in school during the early years can be easily learned in a more natural way at home. Children naturally want to learn to do the things they see their parents and other people doing. They want to explore the world around them. Young children ask questions and are excited about learning new things. This is because the learning that is taking place is that which is of interest to the child at that moment, not some pre-

planned information that someone has determined that children of a certain age should know.

The answer to the question of when formal lessons should be started is very individual. Your child will let you know when it's time for this to happen. In the meantime, enjoy the company of your child as you introduce her to the world around you.

LILLIAN JONES Life offers so many things that are fun to learn, interesting to learn, good to learn, or necessary to learn, but formal lessons are not generally helpful for the learning process—there's something clumsily unnatural about them.

A young child wants to learn about the world, about people, animals, places, the seasons, weather, the night sky, the sun and moon, natural processes like plant's growth—all things that come about naturally in the course of living, questioning, and observing. If you pay sensitive attention, it will be obvious when your child is ready to learn something.

Young children mostly need relaxed time to play and to imagine. They thrive on having wonderful books read to them from an early age. There's no hurry for independent reading—lots of time spent snuggling together while being read to will bring a deep love of reading, learning, and imagining. The places you can go together, the characters you can get to know, and the experiences you can share through reading aloud are indescribably wonderful. I've always felt sorry for families who missed out on this because of feeling their kids need to be reading on their own at young ages.

You'll eventually want to have some specialized books for a few subjects like math or science, but any learning can be approached in just the same way as helping a child to get a kite off the ground; you can be a partner in learning rather than a teacher. Children will also learn an amazing amount on their own, and you'll recognize this more and more throughout your homeschooling years. If you provide trips into the wider world, a good play environment, good conversation, construction toys, books, tools, craft supplies, dolls, and models, their growth and learning will flourish.

Parents' worries behind the issue of "lessons" are usually around the question of discipline, or whatever might need to be mastered for college entrance exams,

> Children will also learn an amazing amount on their own, and you'll recognize this more and more throughout your home-schooling years. If you provide trips into the wider world, a good play environment, good conversation, construction toys, books, tools, craft supplies, dolls, and models, their growth and learning will flourish.

and academic success toward a career. This is where you might want to seriously reexamine the nature of learning. A child can labor for years over those things from an early age, or he can wait until much later, and get through them pretty quickly. If he's had a healthy childhood, with plenty of time for growth and exploration, his enthusiasm and imagination will be ready for meeting the challenge of more formal study in later years—if he decides to choose that path.

Wonderful materials are available for facilitating self-directed learning, but you'll be surprised with the great amount of tangential learning kids' special interests will stimulate. Any number of little boys I know of, for instance, have been motivated to teach themselves to read by deciphering their video game strategy guides! Parents often worry about how they can teach something they don't know about or don't remember; but parents tend to underestimate the ability of kids to learn on their own, or better yet, alongside their parents.

When should you begin formal lessons? Ideally, you never will. You'll be too busy growing, learning, and enjoying life together.

PAT MONTGOMERY The human brain grows and develops in spurts. It lays out networks of axons and dendrites over which a network can be etched. For maximal growth, the child is compelled by her brain to do certain tasks over and over until the network can operate with no (or minimal) conscious thought. Grasping a rattle, pulling open a drawer, tossing a ball, assembling a balsam model, and so on, are all dictates of the brain in its quest for maturity.

Play and motion are the natural brain-developing activities of the young child. They ought not to be interrupted by lessons that an adult thinks might be more appropriate. (It helps to bear in mind that no adult had a hand in designing this magnificent creation, the human brain. Any one of us, however, can interfere with its growth and development if we are careless or ignorant.)

The child who has opportunities to explore in a safe environment (home) is learning all the time. By the time a child is twelve years old, she is ready for more formalized learning. By this time that child has a brain that has, in fact, grown to the point where all of the necessary networks are in full working order and are ready for outside direction and guidance. It is as though, having been free to explore—to play—the child possesses within herself a view of the world that makes sense to her.

At Clonlara, teachers and parents and students expect more of a formalized approach to learning. My own eldest child attended Clonlara School until she was twelve years old. In those days (mid-1970s) we did not serve high school-aged students. She played with dolls and in the sandbox and with checkers and chess and board games and letter puzzles and number games . . . you name it.

She entered public school for the first time in sixth grade. On the second day of school, she came home with her assigned textbooks, an impressively heavy assortment of them. "Look, Mom," she glowed, "they gave me all of these, and if I complete them they'll give me more."

Her teachers expressed delight and surprise at how eager she was to work and how interested she was in what was presented

> It helps to bear in mind that no adult had a hand in designing this magnificent creation, the human brain. Any one of us, however, can interfere with its growth and development if we are careless or ignorant.

in the classes. They often wished that the other students were as involved in learning as she. I submit that she would have been as burned out and turned off as the other students had her play been continually interrupted during those developing years. Maria Montessori called play "the work of a child." I am always grateful there is a place like Clonlara where children are free to play and develop their minds and souls without coercion and interference from well-intentioned adults.

39
How do I schedule and organize our days?

JANIE LEVINE HELLYER Homeschool families can organize their days any way that meets the needs of their family. It's important to keep in mind that we are families, not institutions, and free to create what works best for the individuals in our home. We can start out with an idea of what it takes to keep our home running smoothly. Things like shopping, cooking, laundry, and housework must be done. Each of these activities are opportunities for working and learning together.

Homeschool families tend to be busy and active people. Something that is often overlooked is the need of the parent at home and her (or his!) needs and interests. While it is true that our children are only young once, and that as they grow and become independent there will be more time for us to pursue our own interests, it is also very important for parents to be active in things they enjoy. As we go about pursing an interest, finding answers to problems, information and resources, our children are watching and learning how to do these things themselves. For this reason, it's important for us to make time for the interests of parents, too.

As for a "learning schedule," you know your children best. Some children get up in the morning and want to dive right into their projects immediately, while others do better later on in the day. Don't attempt to duplicate what goes on in traditional classrooms, for this defeats the real advantages of homeschooling! If your child is busy working on a science project, there is just no need (and no sense) in interrupting her at 2 P.M. so she can work on English literature. Over time, your youngster will learn everything she needs to, and will most likely learn it "better" than had she been taught in a more traditional way.

Possibly the greatest advantage of homeschooling is that our families can find a balance in life. Members of the family can pursue their interests and learn in their own way, come to know what it takes to run a home and family, what work is, and become active participants in our communities. That balance of learning, real work, and community creates an environment in which young people thrive and grow into caring and concerned adults, capable of meeting each new challenge as it comes along in life. Finding that balance is different for every family, so take the time to create what will work best for yours.

40

Do I need to use textbooks?

JOHN TAYLOR GATTO You need to use *texts*, and the best ones available, because they are the cheapest, most reliable way your children can come to grips with the whole range of human intellect, and how different minds see the world, develop their arguments, and reach their conclusions. Notice I've said nothing about the content, the "facts," these classic texts will contain. With that you are welcome to make any use that suits you for it is much less important.

Textbooks, on the other hand, have been for at least a half-century, and probably longer, creations

> Textbooks . . . have been for at least a half-century and probably longer, creations of publishers or ambitious academics written not for children, but to please textbook adoption committees.

of publishers or ambitious academics written not for children, but to please textbook adoption committees. The standard followed is almost always what the states of California and/or Texas will tolerate because those jurisdictions bulk-buy for the entire state centrally; hence adoption by either of these assures the financial success of the book. In order to be acceptable, numerous concessions to the preferences of politically powerful groups of many persuasions must be made; hence not only is the information suspect (a Scott-Foresman "history" book in 1991 announced that the atomic bomb had been dropped on Korea), but it has *always* been politically doctored to reflect prejudices thought/known to exist in the textbook adoption committees. Hence you may read an expensive textbook allegedly written by a Pulitzer Prize–winning historian upside down and inside out, and in the section on Western contact with Japan in the 1850s, you will be unable to detect the interesting fact that Tokyo harbor was forced open by American gunboats. Similarly, in the references to Tibet, there will predictably be no hint that a "punitive expedition" under British General

Younghusband forced open the sacred city of Lhasa, which had declined to accept intercourse with the West. Or that the international drug trade was created and militantly policed by the British government for at least a century and a quarter—and it fought two wars to protect its monopoly.

It is not only history that is inevitably politicized in textbooks, but math, science (especially science), literature—you name it. I said "inevitably" because I mean just that. Far too much is at stake in arranging the strength and contents of young minds to allow that to occur uncontrolled.

The answer is easy and inexpensive. The core of your text material should be primary materials, not secondary ones, and especially not books written by committees for committees. The only utility in reading those, not an insignificant one by any means, is to illustrate their deficiencies. By turning first to the index rather than the table of contents, then doing a graph by number of text lines devoted to each major and minor topic occupying more than a brief space in the textbook, you will—and your children will—be able to penetrate the code sufficiently to recognize what the book is actually selling. If rockets and space travel, for instance, occupy 180 column inches in a history of modern

times, and the economic engine of capitalism only six, even a thirteen-year-old will have no difficulty understanding how his mind is being regarded once the discrepancy is pointed out to him.

CINDY WADE My answer is an unequivocal *no*. I have always found textbooks dry and void of any real learning value. Textbooks tend to make a subject choppy and uninteresting. My children find them dull and cumbersome. They prefer workbooks for the simple reason they can write in them without recopying the information or questions.

Additionally, modern textbooks have become so politically correct and void of any values we find them offensive. Use your money instead for CDs for the computer or buy a good set of encyclopedias.

Although I consider workbooks to be more valuable than textbooks these, too, are subject to misuse. The younger the child, the less inclined they are to need or want workbooks. Before a child can read well enough to understand the directions, he's better off with quality educational manipulatives (a fancy word for toys). Workbooks imposed too early will only frustrate your child.

If you know your child is capable of doing workbooks but balks at the idea of sitting down with mom or dad to work on them, you can try what I did. When my daughter was six or seven years old, she was a very good reader. I knew she was capable of reading the instructions and completing the written work in these workbooks. When we tried to sit her down and "instruct" her, though, we would all be in tears before the session was over.

I learned to purchase several workbooks and leave them scattered about the house in conspicuous places. After a week or so, the workbooks didn't seem to budge; but when I picked them up and looked inside, they were completed with little or no mistakes! Without the need to "perform" or "be schooled," the pressure was off.

Today, my daughter is eleven. We still purchase workbooks but she helps select them, and they disappear into her room where she does them at her leisure still. And there are still few, if any, mistakes.

Our six-year-old son, on the other hand, doesn't yet read but loves to sit down with workbooks. He likes the interaction with the person reading the instructions more than he enjoys the actual work. In the meantime he fills his hours with manipulatives, such as Legos (with gears—he can make cars with front and back wheel suspensions), calculators, computers, and lots of picture books and children's magazines. He may never use a textbook until he takes a college course someday.

41

Where do I begin to find the resources and materials I need?

JEAN REED You're going to look at the world with new eyes, starting with yourself. You know much more than you think you do. You've learned where to find information if you don't know about something. That's one of the most important gifts you can give your child. You've been teaching or showing your children by example how you live and learn in this world since they were born. You started the minute you first smiled and talked to your baby. Family unity and good values aren't taught so much as shown by example. Some things you can't buy.

Very young children use their immediate surroundings to explore and learn. You can start the same way. Your own house is full of resources! Your best tool is yourself: your love, playfulness, laughter, and encouragement.

Older children will need books and materials that are harder to find. Successful homeschooling isn't so much a matter of how much you spend, as how creatively you use what you have. According to several surveys, the average spent per homeschooled child is $500. I'm sure we never spent that much. Mary Potter Kenyon's *Home Schooling from Scratch* has lots of good ideas. Use your library card (don't forget to check for library discards), yard sales, cheap workbooks, and occasionally good reading books at Wal-Mart.

It's amazing how much paper you'll use. Check your local newspaper office and print shop for rolls of newsprint and odds and ends left over from printing jobs. If you're part of a support group, make a list of books you'd like to borrow or lend, organize a book sale, or create a group resource library.

Look for homeschooling magazines and books that review other books and products, preferably by an author you know and trust. Donn did the very first of the homeschool catalogs years ago because we learned by trial and some expensive errors that all that is hyped as educational ain't necessarily so. As a reviewer and supplier for homeschoolers, I'm getting mounting pressure from big businesses and publishers to recommend their products. They know there are over a million homeschoolers. They want your money. They'll try to sell anything they can with big, glossy, impressive looking ads. Some homeschool publications will take any ad because advertis-

ing pays the bills. Don't discount all paid ads. Some of the books and products are excellent. Use your discretion. You'll make some mistakes; who doesn't?

Resources: Ask homeschoolers who share your learning philosophy what they like. I recommend (and admit prejudice) *The Home School Source Book*, because it covers learning resources from pregnancy through to adulthood, and liberal arts subject matter, including other homeschooling resources: everything is reviewed, satisfaction guaranteed. Second is *Home Education Magazine* because you'll find resources and how-to articles from many different points of view. *Growing Without Schooling* magazine is extremely valuable. Even if you are not an unschooler, you will find valuable ideas. Becky Rupp's *Good Stuff* is also excellent. For Christian-based resources, I like Ted Wade's *Home School Manual*.

REBECCA KOCHENDERFER It used to be difficult to find quality educational materials that were designed for home use. Everything was designed to be used in a classroom setting. These days, however, there is an abundance of materials available.

One of the easiest ways to find supplies is through the Internet. You simply type the word "homeschooling" into your Web browser and hundreds of homeschooling sites are listed. There are Internet sites for Christian, Catholic, and Jewish homeschoolers; for those following a school-at-home approach and those leaning towards un-schooling. And these sites usually have a resource page that lists resources and materials that fit that style. If you don't have Internet access at home, you can use the computer at the library and print out any information you find.

Homeschooling magazines are also helpful. I read my magazines with a pen in my hand so that I can circle those product reviews that sound interesting. *Home Education Magazine* is one of my favorites because their articles reflect a variety of homeschooling styles. *Growing Without Schooling* is a great magazine for unschoolers, and *Practical Homeschooling* is very popular with Christian homeschoolers.

If you're worried that homeschooling may be too expensive for you, I'd like to put your fears to rest. Although there are lots of educational materials now available, I think you will find that you need less than you originally thought you would. Mary Kenyon's

> **W**henever my children are "hot" on a particular topic we run to the library and come home with books on kitchen science, dinosaurs, sharks, and art.

book, *Home Schooling from Scratch*, has lots of great ideas to help keep costs down.

We also get a lot of our supplies from the library. Whenever my children are "hot" on a particular topic, we run to the library and come home with books on kitchen science, dinosaurs, sharks, and art. Plus, I read lots of historical and biographical chapter books to the kids and that has helped them learn about Native Americans, American history, mythology, and famous inventors.

I don't think you'll have any difficulty finding good resource materials. Homeschooling has helped me broaden my horizons, and I find myself becoming more and more creative at helping my children learn.

BECKY RUPP Educational resources are a challenge these days simply because there are so many of them—and so many different opinions about their relative appeal, usefulness, and worth. Choosing resources for a homeschool program is always tricky. No matter how well you know your children, occasionally you make a choice that leaves them cold. A project, program, or book series that fascinated one child (a success, you've decided triumphantly) will bore another to tears. Homeschooling, in our hands, has always been a process of trial and error. The errors, for me, have always been a bit of a mental struggle—that math text cost $40, I mutter to myself, watching the youngsters squirm miserably at the very sight of it. But sometimes a flop is a flop, and the only solution is to drop the thing and try something else. If the children aren't interested, they're not going to learn—or at least they're not going to learn very much or very well.

For resource-hunting parents, there are a wealth of educational supply companies and catalogs: most are reviewed in Rebecca Rupp's *Home Learning Source Book*.

Our prime information resources—for tackling such questions as "Where's Timbuktu?" "Who was Grandma Moses?" and "What do penguins eat?" —are our personal library, an ever-mushrooming collection (our kids have learned to build bookcases), the public library, and the Internet. The Internet, with its phenomenal store of information, conversation, and educational activities, is an invaluable resource for homeschool programs. One child or an-

other around here is always logged on, searching for Civil War timelines, physics tutorials, software reviews, virtual museum tours, or foreign-language dictionaries. A good starting point, incidentally, for young Internet browsers, is the American Library Association web site (http://www.ala.org), which includes a list of over 700 excellent sites for children, categorized by academic subject.

Our children's education over the past years has involved a lot of varied resources: games, science kits, building sets, carpentry tools, popular books, textbooks, reference works, art and music supplies. We've invested in a microscope and three violins, a lot of laboratory glassware, assorted math textbooks and an excellent American history series, several educational video series, computer software, cross-country skis, and hockey skates.

Many of our most successful educational resources, however, have been simple and homemade. The boys' favorite math game for years was a family-designed buying-and-selling game which consisted of a pack of index cards, each with a picture of some desirable object—a robot, a pony, a rocket ship, the state of Colorado, the Great Pyramid of Giza, the Hope Diamond—and a (wholly imaginary) price. The kids started the game with a standard amount of money, and—in turn—bought, sold, traded, and made change, attempting to acquire their favorites.

You could get the Hope Diamond, as I recall, for a cool $1.75.

Their favorite geography game consisted of a National Geographic world map tacked to a bedroom wall, with accompanying pack of index cards, each with a geography question or challenge: "Find the country that Paddington Bear came from." "Where would you find kangaroos?" "Where did Charles Lindbergh land after his famous solo flight across the Atlantic Ocean?"

I suppose, looking back, if I had to name one resource that I found absolutely essential to our homeschool program, it would have to be index cards.

Or maybe not.

Some of our best learning experiences—the ones I truly cherish—used nothing at all. These were the times when we sat on the rug in front of the woodstove or sprawled on the back porch and simply talked—conversations that ranged from astronomy to Chinese philosophy to current events to cows, that covered books we'd read and places we'd like to visit, ideas and inventions, and just plain curiosity: "What's the

difference between a hurricane and a tornado?" "Which do you like better, Beethoven or Bach?" "Do you think President Truman was right to drop the atom bomb?" "How do you engineer a gene?"

Our single most important resource is the one I never seem to have enough of.

Time.

42

Do I need to keep records? If so, how?

DEB SHELL Even though I didn't do it initially for the sake of complying with school or state requirements, keeping records of my daughters' work (the tangible stuff anyway), has served a good purpose. When they were young, I always treasured their little scribbles and hieroglyphic writing as well as early drawings, just as I had treasured  their first spoken words and sentences. These were the tangible evidences of their current thinking; these attempts at communication and individual expression represented a process of learning about the world and themselves

Deb Shell

in it. So I've always saved stuff—at the beginning of each calendar year I would make a new folder with each girl's name on it. Whatever they produced (after it came off the designated "artist's" wall or the refrigerator) eventually went into their folder. This turned out to be a great record of each child's progress. What I am compelled to remind people, especially those who want a tangible record representing every designated area of study, is that just one drawing, or poem, or design, represents a holistic understanding and becomes a point of reference from which to appreciate future development.

When end-of-the-year assessments approached, I chose the certified teacher option (we live in Vermont, where there are several measurement options available to homeschoolers). The folder of collected works provided evidence of development. Proof of progress is the purpose of any assessment method used.

Personally, the benefit of saving stuff or keeping records of their work included helping me to appreciate how our children progressed. As drawings be-

> **H**elping my daughters to examine the learning components entailed in a seemingly general activity not only helped them to develop transcripts that related specifically to things they really knew about, but also helped them to see how our unstructured homeschooling really did fulfill state high school requirements.

came more detailed and representative, so letters became articulated; developing handwriting reflected individual styles, as did designs, stories, and poems. Themes became evident as areas of interest appeared. When she was five, our eldest daughter began taking photographs of projects she and her sisters created, which I see in retrospect as another way of recording the less sustaining yet equally important developmental events that occurred so frequently in our house full of active children.

When my daughters became teenagers, I created divided folders headed with departmental categories that roughly followed the expected areas of study represented on a high school transcript. For example, the learning components of an experiential activity such as raising a purebred Shih Tzu puppy to adulthood, selecting a sire, breeding, preparing for whelping, and caring for the litter, may be broken down into several areas of study: science (developmental canine physiology); math (accounting); geography (breed discovery, ancient Tibet and Chinese Empire);

literature (James Herriot's *All Creatures Great and Small* series). Helping my daughters to examine the learning components entailed in a seemingly general activity not only helped them to develop transcripts that related specifically to things they really knew about, but also helped them to see how our unstructured homeschooling really did fulfill state high school requirements.

Rather than viewing record keeping as a negative requirement, we used it to our advantage. The difference is that our record keeping simply chronicled progress; it was never intended to influence the course of study or exploration by looking for deficits. We assumed that by the time our children were about graduation age, they would have covered the areas of study that adults consider important for adequate functioning. The big secret is that when left to follow their interests, children really do a fantastic job of this.

43

Do I need to buy a computer? More important, do *I* need to know how to use the computer?

DORIS HOHENSEE Computers are certainly very powerful, time-saving tools. Net communication has revolutionized the rate at which information can be exchanged. People no longer need to schedule meetings, or even consider the geographic distance between participants in the discussion. The possibilities are only limited by one's imagination.

This may not be important for younger children; but for teenagers, not having a computer is a serious disadvantage. Where else can they find people to ask questions on almost every topic available with such relative ease?

Maintaining a computer can seem overwhelming. Yet, with some assistance, teenagers are often more than willing to help out. My son installed our operating system using installation manuals, getting the occasional pointer from his father in the evening. With a Net connection, he found an Internet relay chat group where he could discuss his computer problems. There he found solutions to several of his networking problems so that he was able to successfully link our machines together.

In return for the favor of allowing my son all these wonderful learning opportunities, I'm given an account and some computer time. I do have to be patient when a system upgrade temporarily—or perhaps even permanently—misplaces a few of my favorite files. These occasional mishaps are a small price to pay for such learning experiences and they do happen less frequently over time.

I believe job specialization is here to stay. I manage to find the time to maintain the household, while my son happily maintains our computer system.

> **W**ith a Net connection [my son] found an Internet relay chat group where he could discuss his computer problems. There he found solutions to several of his networking problems so that he was able to successfully link our machines together.

REBECCA KOCHENDERFER When television first came into use, it was hailed as a great educational tool. Now the computer (and especially the Internet) is considered to be an educational must. Although I use the computer for my work and am very comfortable using the Internet, I have concerns that computers, like television, may not be all that great for my young children.

Before you buy a computer, you may want to consider the following:

• What will your child *not* be doing when he's using the computer? Will he sit in front of the computer instead of riding his bike? Will he draw pictures on a computer screen instead of using chalk outside in the fresh air? Will your children really be learning from their computer, or will it just be-

come another electronic babysitter?

• Jane Healy (author of *Endangered Minds*), Thomas Armstrong (author of *Awakening Your Child's Natural Genius*), and Joseph Chilton Pearce (author of *Magical Child* and *Evolution's End*) all warn that computers are not good for young children. These authors believe that young children should learn about their world through their physical senses and that they should be interacting with people, not machines.

• Most child-development researchers believe that children are not developmentally ready for computers until they are about fifteen years old. After that age, these same people believe the computer to be a great asset to a child's education.

• The Internet can be a great tool, but it also has certain safety considerations. When your child watches television, it's easy for you to see and hear what's going on. Computers, because they are one-on-one, are much harder to monitor and you will have an easier time keeping your child safe if you know how to use the Internet, too.

So, do you *need* to buy a computer? If your children are young, you may be better off without one. But then you'd miss out on this great tool for yourself. I must admit that I have not come up with a great computer plan for our family. Television was easy. We simply moved it to the garage, where it's available if we *really* want to watch something. I can't keep the computer out of sight, however, because I use it every day for my work. And since my children see me using the computer so often they naturally want to use it, too. Until I come up with a better plan, I'm just going to keep reminding myself that the computer is a tool and should be used not so much for entertainment, but to achieve a purpose.

DONNA NICHOLS-WHITE The way I figure it, a person will need programming skills in order to make a piece of toast within the next ten years. We've owned two VCRs and I still haven't figured out how to use them. (It's a good thing I don't like to watch television.)

I need a computer in order to run my company, and I need my children in order

Donna Nichols-White

to teach me how to use that confounded piece of machinery.

Programming skills will be essential in the future. Computers today are like books were when the Gutenburg press was invented. (I know it's hard to think of mere books as being technological advancements.)

And then there is the Internet. A child introduced me to that, thank goodness. I couldn't tell a search engine from an e-mail address.

A basic knowledge of how to utilize a computer is important. It's just one more way to obtain information, but owning a computer isn't essential. Like any other item in your home, you purchase it based on the needs and desires of your family. A child can have access to computers outside of the home. Our libraries provide free Internet access. Baby-sitting, in exchange for the use of a friend's computer, can also offer opportunities for learning.

A parent doesn't have to know anything about computers. My children have even showed me where the on and off button was (after they explained what it was for). I cannot help but stress that if you own a computer, and are over the age of thirty, being humble is a good asset. There's nothing like having a six year old guide you through the Internet or show you how to change the fonts in a word processing program.

Children are born programmers, as far as I'm concerned. Whenever we acquire an appliance or machine that requires this skill, I forego reading the instruction booklet and just let them figure out how to use it. I've met children who have efficiently taught themselves how to program in Logo, C, and Visual Basic languages. Some have parents who wouldn't be caught dead using a computer.

Some parents are very uncomfortable with modern technology. They feel that computers are invasive. This should be respected. They can offer their children programming skills by playing binary games like Othello, Dr. Nim, and Oh Wah Ree. They don't even have to know what these games offer.

Computer technology has proven that a child's knowledge isn't limited to that of the parent; if it were, we wouldn't have companies like Microsoft and Apple around. It's also proven that we parents can learn a lot by just watching our kids, working with them, and asking questions. Skip the manuals, it works for me.

I rely heavily on my computer and on the help and assistance that the young people in my house have to offer. So the next time you need to make a piece of toast or program your VCR, feel free to call on the computer experts in your home.

CHRIS CARDIFF Families were homeschooling long before today's personal computer revolution arrived. You and your family can homeschool perfectly well without one. From the 3 R's to history, science, and shop, there is no subject that requires a computer (with the possible exception of computer science). There are no educational materials available on computers that aren't also available through other media.

Having said that, I believe a computer can be a fabulous addition to your family's educational resources. Just as businesses large and small invest gazillions of dollars in computers every year because computers make jobs easier and faster to do, the same can be true in homeschooling—a computer can enhance a learning experience, make learning easier and faster with new tools, and allow access to enormous informational resources not easily available by other means.

Guiding your child through this informational maze is easier if you understand it yourself. However, one of the more joyful aspects of homeschooling is learning together with your children. And remember, this is how most families have done it. We are the generation that lived through the personal computer revolution and had to homeschool ourselves in their use because they didn't have computers back when we went to school.

Learning about computers, the different software programs, the online universe—all of this is an amazing learning opportunity for you to share with your child. Here are just a few samples of what you may encounter:

- Reading: "Living Books" not only tell a story but also allow a child to interact with elements of the story on the screen. Many programs teach reading through a phonetic approach. The Internet's Online Books project contains the complete texts of hundreds of classic books whose copyright has expired—Twain, Shakespeare, Kipling are all online for reading, searching, printing.

- 'Riting: Once you've used word processing software, it's unlikely you'll ever return to a typewriter or handwriting. Basic word processing today allows onscreen editing, spell checking, grammar checking, and control of what your text looks like. More advanced software created the phenomenon of desktop publishing.

- 'Rithmetic: "Edutainment" programs drill kids in basic math operations through games where success is based on correctly answering math questions. More sophisticated programs focus on real problem-solving skills. These programs seek to engage the children without boring them and provide analysis of their progress to the parent.

- Research: An entire shelf of encyclopedias is now contained on a CD-ROM disk that includes words, pictures, sound, and video. An Internet search can turn up a multitude of Web sites with information and references on a particular subject. Thousands of subject-specific Internet newsgroups provide discussion forums for people around the world.

- Geography/History: More fertile fields for edutainment software. You can travel the Oregon Trail yourself with one program, or chase an international thief all over the world with another.

44
Do I have to stay at home all day with my children?

JANIE LEVINE HELLYER When some people think about homeschooling, they have a notion of mother and children sitting around the kitchen table from 9 A.M. to 3 P.M. The fact is, most of us are out in our communities doing real things, meeting real people, learning through exploring the world together. Homeschooling does not necessarily mean doing what schools do or keeping their schedule. Our learning is home-based, but this doesn't mean that we are locked in the house all day.

Most of us have homes to run and families to care for. We do the same things that parents with children in school do. We shop, run errands, visit friends, we do work in our communities. Homeschooling parents are among the most active people I know. Many families integrate their community activities into their learning plan, introducing their children to the real work that adults do. Some of the best volunteers at our food co-op are home-schoolers! As homeschooling has grown in popularity, our community has become a diverse cross section of the general population. Homeschooling families are not necessarily two-income families with one parent at home full time.

> The truth is that many homeschooling families find it necessary to limit the available activities in which they participate because there is just so much available. With all the opportunities available today, most of us find that having a quiet day at home with our children is an enjoyable experience.

Every year, we see more working and single parents successfully homeschooling their children. These tend to be creative people who, when confronted with a challenging situation, go out and find the resources they need to accomplish their goals. I can think of no better role models for our children than parents who are actively creating the lives and lifestyles they want for their own family. We are seeing more cooperatives, networking among parents, and more resources available in our communities.

Our communities also offer a variety of experiences and resources for homeschooled youth. Homeschool support networks offer things like informal play days, group learning experiences, and interesting field trips from which families can choose. There are also interesting places in every community to explore, such as museums, businesses, and special events. All of these things can become learning experiences for our families.

The world around us becomes our classroom, and few of us are home with our children all the time. Our options are limited only by our imaginations.

The truth is that many homeschooling families find it necessary to limit the available activities in which they participate because there is just so much available. With all the opportunities available today, most of us find that having a quiet day at home with our children is an enjoyable experience.

SANDRA DODD At home? Why? There are stores, museums, libraries, theaters, parks, rivers, mountains, beaches, friends' houses, historical sites, factories, construction sites, churches, caves, animal shelters, art galleries, fish hatcheries, foundries, and blacksmiths and . . .

What was the question?

KATHARINE HOUK Very few homeschooling parents, in my experience, stay at home all day every day with their children. In any town there are opportunities for children to do things on their own—story hour at the library, music and dance classes, Scouts and 4-H, field trips with other homeschoolers—and you have a life of your own, as well! In my own case, the children went with me to work at the food co-op, to lay out and print newsletters in a friend's office, to spend the day in their dad's office, to meetings in the Capitol to lobby for improved home education regulations, to visit friends . . . the list goes on and on.

To find out what's happening locally, check the bulletin boards at your public library, community center, or church, and read your local paper. Homeschooling support groups can provide a place for social contact outside the home by organizing a wide range of activities for both parents and children. One group in western New York sponsors an annual family camping trip—in winter. They have lively and chilling stories to tell upon their return!

An important gathering place in my small town has been the learning center I founded with friends six years ago. It grew out of the needs of families in our local support group, and it provides a place for classes, workshops, and activities two days a week for homeschooled children. The parents themselves and people from the community and surrounding area offer their skills, and classes have included astronomy, singing groups, art and craft projects, American Sign Language, French, math, first-aid, history, drama, career exploration, auto maintenance, and more.

The center also organizes field trips, group excursions to plays and museums, and trips to interesting businesses and workplaces. As a parent cooperative, it provides a place for parents as well as children to socialize and learn. The number of families involved has ranged over the years from four or five to about thirty, which is pretty impressive, considering that only 3,000 people live in the town itself. Twice a year, in December and May, children bring their projects, sing their songs, and perform their plays for Display Day. The bonds formed by all involved with this community space are marvelous to behold, and have grown and deepened over the years.

It may take some extra effort on your part to find the community resources available to your family, or to determine whether you have the time and energy to invest in a support group or learning center, but the possibilities are there. Home education need not be an isolating experience. I do wish to add, however, that being at home isn't such a terrible thing, and that engaging in too many outside activities can become burdensome and stressful. Sometimes slowing down and spending some time at home with our families feels just right and is the best thing to do.

LILLIAN JONES The homeschoolers I know relish those days when they can stay home together. There are always so many other things calling—classes, support group events, shopping, errands, and the lure of interesting field trips.

We also love to be out in the world, and homeschooling allows us more free-dom to do that. We jokingly refer to some of our travels by name: American History 101, for instance, was a trip to historical sites along the East Coast. Our school friends think we're being outrageously irreverent, but I think we're actually learning more from these trips than we could from books. Notice I said "we." We learn together.

We were at the Museum of Natural History in town yesterday, gawking and talking as we went—learning and enjoying ourselves enormously. We were surrounded by school kids with worksheets they were dutifully filling in. They weren't enjoying the displays so much as going through prescribed motions and bouncing off of one another. I asked my son if he ever missed that aspect of school, the crowds of kids working together on projects and all. He looked at me quizzically, and then exploded into laughter at the idea.

Early in the game I learned not to make field trips into "lessons." Years ago, when visiting a museum, I kept calling my son's attention to this display or that, reading him the display cards, and generally making a pest of myself to nudge him to "learn" something. After all, that was what we were supposed to be doing, wasn't it? Homeschooling? Suddenly, a guide with a stern, booming voice said, "Hey, *you!* You look bored! Come with me!" We followed him upstairs. There he dressed my son in an old soldier's uniform and took him behind a roped-off area, where he got to try out the soldiers' beds and poke around in their old tools, ammunition, and personal belongings. My husband and I got the guide to share fascinating historical stories we would never have heard otherwise. Our son got to follow his own imagination, and we all enjoyed a veritable feast of food for thought by following ours at the same time.

We often stop crowds in museums or historical sites by talking to guides about their area of expertise—their passion. These people are treasures of knowledge. One of our favorite finds was on the sidewalk in town near home. We saw a man coming up out of a manhole. A manhole! What an opportunity! We asked him what was down there, and he was delighted. He had marvelous things to tell us, *and* he let my son climb down to look around. Learning is everywhere, and the world quite literally is our classroom.

We do need ways of getting off to exercise or do things alone once in a while. That gets to be easier with time, but you really need to get creative about meeting your own needs, whatever they are. No situation is perfect, but home-

schooling is by far the most natural and easy way for a family to live.

45

I hated (fill in a subject) in school. How can I possibly teach this subject to my child?

WILL SHAW I hated math. My worst subject. I routinely fell behind and received poor grades. I now know that, with math, before you move to chapter 4, you'd better have a good handle on chapter 3.

Regarding math or any subject, homeschooling can allow your child to learn more thoroughly and to move ahead with more security. In school the class would move on when I wasn't ready, when I didn't get it yet. I'd be lost in no time, and I never recovered. But in home education, you can spend as much time as needed to master the subject. You move ahead or stay put. Make sure your child doesn't experience what you did.

You can actually learn some things, and you can teach what you do know, and you can help your child to learn even when you don't fully understand it yourself. I'm not saying it's a breeze, but it's not at all impossible. The math texts, workbooks, videos, and other materials available to homeschoolers are fantastic, so much better than what I ever had in school.

There are sometimes other home-school parents with whom to share teaching cooperatively, each handling his or her favorites. If you want, you could look for a correspondence school that will take your math questions. Since you're not cooped up in school all day, the opportunities to apply math are greater and learning is reinforced. We called a publisher when we thought there was a mistake in a textbook. (There was.) One of my children once called a local college to see if the professor would explain something. (He did.)

You don't have to be a professional, and you don't have to personally know and personally teach every aspect of every subject. If that were true, then only the teacher-trained chemist could teach chemistry, only the teacher-trained historian teach history. The public education industry would have us believe this is what happens but it's simply not true.

We've found that once our children have a firm foundation, they can go ahead on their own. You can help them learn to self-teach. Our two oldest, now in college, went way beyond their parents in math, way beyond what we ever knew or could (or can) do in what

seems such a daunting subject. Our third child is doing it now, and our last one will, too.

Our oldest will graduate from Virginia Tech next semester with a BS in math. Go figure.

DORIS HOHENSEE My major concern was not to destroy my children's interest in learning. Any subject can be ruined if it's forced on a child before he's ready or interested.

When I attended school, I developed many strong dislikes for certain subjects. Later, I discovered that each of these subjects was truly fascinating when approached in a different manner.

The subjects weren't the problem. Coercion was. It can kill curiosity dead in its tracks. I had to find a reason to want to learn these subjects before any genuine learning could take place. But this is hardly a recent discovery.

"Bodily exercise, when compulsory, does no harm to the body; but knowledge which is acquired under compulsion obtains no hold on the mind." Plato, circa 400 B.C.

MARY MCCARTHY By not teaching. You can talk, and preach, and scream, and beg, and plead until you are blue in the face; but if you don't let your child discover her own ways and interests, she is not going to learn.

Homeschooling isn't about teaching—it's about learning. Instill in your child the love of *learning* and you won't have to worry about the teaching. Spending three hours doing a single page of division problems does not teach math—it teaches "I hate math."

Remember?

JEAN REED Homeschooling is a fantastic challenge! If you didn't want a challenge, I don't think you would be homeschooling or considering it. It is also one of the most fantastic opportunities. The obvious answer to this question is to learn the subject along with your child or find someone willing to teach it for you.

I can't think of one valid reason why we should know all about everything we would like our kids to learn before starting to homeschool. Some things we can learn about before beginning to actually do it. Some things are learned best by doing. Some things require a combination of approaches. I believe homeschooling needs the combination of both approaches.

Only very young children believe their parents know everything. Kids ask the craziest questions; and by the time they are five or six, they certainly know

we don't know everything and they love us and have learned from us anyway.

Except for the time I attended public school, I've never felt that admitting ignorance about something was shameful or wrong. One of the most important things we wanted our kids to learn was that the only really stupid thing you can do is to not ask a question when you don't understand something. In homeschooling, admitting we don't know something puts us on equal footing with our kids and they love it.

Whenever you search for tools or materials so you can learn something together with your children, you double your rewards. By saying, "Let's find out" you'll have the fun of doing something important together and you'll have learned something new.

I hated school. Period. I was a terrible student. The idea of teaching our kids scared me just about witless. I never wanted my kids to go through the humiliation and fear I experienced. At the other end of the spectrum, Donn did well in school. He found it an all right experience, but felt it could have been much better. From opposite ends of the spectrum, we had a common goal. We wanted something better for our children. In the first month that Donn and I were together, we met a family using the Calvert School correspondence program. Whenever we went to visit, the kids met us at the door bubbling over with excitement, immediately wanting to show us what they were learning and doing. Their excitement was tangible. It was our first glimpse of something that would shape our future.

Hundreds of parents have written and told us that they've felt this was a glorious second chance to go back and learn so many things they had missed in school. You may be challenged if you were a poor student in some subjects and you take your whiz-kid teenager out of school, but there are a lot of great books to help you. If the material your child needs to learn is important, then you'll find the resources you need. You may just get educated in the process!

> **H**undreds of parents have written and told us that they've felt this was a glorious second chance to go back and learn so many things they had missed in school.

46

Can others help me educate my child?

DONN AND JEAN REED Give me one good reason why we should restrict our kids to just one teacher. Would you limit yourself? Maybe for a year; maybe for very specialized study, but not for an extended period of time, especially if you are studying many subjects.

If you're thinking about finding others to help your child learn, you'll be amazed at the number of people with something to share. One of the really great things about having your kids learn with other people is that you'll be surprised by the contributions others will make that go beyond what you expected.

We always wanted our kids to learn more than just facts. We wanted them to find their own persona, what values were important for living in peace with themselves and others; to aim high; to reach for their dreams. Learning facts and figures is important, but doesn't necessarily make for happier people or better living. You and your spouse will impart through words and example what you believe. It's not likely that your kids will grow up to be imitations of you. Working and learning with others will give them the opportunity to view other lifestyles, values, skills, and points of view that will become grist for their minds.

We all need friends. Working and playing with others is the way we all live. There are lots of ways you can involve others with your kids. You may choose to find someone to tutor in a subject you feel you can't teach adequately or find someone who shares your child's interests to act as a friend or mentor.

Children enjoy being with other children. Take advantage of your support group. You can take turns teaching different subjects or go on field trips together. Reading and discussing a variety of books is a great way to share thoughts, explore new ideas, and learn from others. If you don't have a support group, start one, or just take field trips and do things with other families even if their kids are in school. If you live in an isolated area, you will have to work harder to find others to work with your children; but determination can accomplish a great deal.

You can help older children find a part-time job. Getting paid in cash is nice, but working in exchange for learning a skill can work just as well and lead eventually to a paycheck. One of our daughters volunteered in the local library a couple days a week, then was offered a full-time summer position. Her experience led to an excellent job when she left home. Explore hundreds of possibilities through some of the Peterson Guides (*Learning Adventures, Internships, Summer Jobs for Students, Summer Opportunities for Kids and Teenagers,* and more).

Life is an ongoing learning process not limited to age or place. Our world is full of people who know so much that we don't know! If we keep our minds open we can learn something different from each person we meet. Our children can do the same, especially if we don't narrow the definition of learning to just the standard school subjects.

Susannah Sheffer Of course. They do already, whether you're conscious of it or not. Living not just in a nuclear family but in the broader community, children surely learn from watching or helping or simply being around other people. But homeschoolers do reach out to teachers and mentors in more purposeful ways, too, forming connections that may be informal or highly organized, occasional or quite regular.

Sixteen-year-old Eva, for example, sought out a math mentor by putting up signs at a local university asking for a graduate student who could help her see math in a new light. Twelve-year-old Christian's chance to volunteer at a biologist's lab grew out of his involvement in another activity: He and his mother went to local Audubon Society meetings and happened to meet the biologist there. And Mika's mother gave art lessons to a neighbor's children in exchange for the neighbor's helping Mika with algebra. This worked so well that Mika herself offered violin lessons to another family's son in exchange for

Spanish conversation practice with the boy's mother.

Mentoring and support from adults outside the family can come through the mail, too. For several years I've served as a writing mentor to homeschoolers (roughly aged ten to eighteen, though some have been younger); they send me their work and ask for critical comments. I've formed close and rewarding connections with kids all around the country.

So, seeking out mentors, being open to opportunities, and thinking creatively about what you can offer or where you can find help—these are the kinds of things homeschoolers get good at. But I'm not that resourceful, you say? It gets easier with practice, and there are so many great examples by now that no one has to start from scratch. The main thing to realize is that parents don't need to be a homeschooler's only source of information or help. To be sure, homeschooling does quite frequently strengthen family bonds, but parents don't need to know all the answers or even be interested in everything in order to help a child learn. Parent and child don't even have to work well together in all respects. Fourteen-year-old Amanda, for example, found

> **S**ixteen-year-old Eva sought out a math mentor by putting up signs at a local university asking for a graduate student who could help her see math in a new light.

that she and her mother had trouble working together on math: "On some days Mom and I would work really well together, but on other days we would both accidentally irritate each other, and when you're crabby and tired it's much harder to understand a math concept." They found a family friend who was happy to help Amanda with math and, as Amanda said, her mom "was really nice about understanding that and not getting offended."

The world is full of interesting people who have a lot to offer. Access to a wide range of helpful adults gives homeschoolers the opportunity to learn whatever specific skills they desire *and* to have a team of caring adults in their lives.

47

I know homeschoolers who only "work" in the morning. How can the homeschooled children possibly learn as much as the children who go to school all day?

BILLY AND NANCY GREER Most homeschoolers will tell you that their kids can accomplish more in a few hours at home than in a full day of school. What really surprised us, however, is that the board of education in most states will tell you the same thing. At one of our local support group meetings, Bill was talking to a woman who was considering homeschooling. Her son had been ill the previous year and spent most of the last semester at home. The school board assigned a pupil services worker to continue his school work at home. The school board said that six hours of this instruction at home was equivalent to full time school attendance! (It was provided in three hour sessions two days a week.)

Bill was surprised and decided to ask members of an e-mail list about requirements in their states. The typical requirement was six to ten hours a week of in-home instruction.

Now please note that Bill was only surprised that most states would *admit* that a couple of hours a day of home instruction was equivalent to a full day in school. If you think about a typical school day, you can see how much time is wasted. There is attendance to take, time spent changing classes, time wasted in classroom management—and there is little individual attention. It's similar to going to the doctor's office. You may be there for hours even though the doctor only spends ten minutes with you!

> **M**ost homeschoolers will tell you that their kids can accomplish more in a few hours at home than in a full day of school. What really surprised us, however, is that the board of education in most states will tell you the same thing.

Time is wasted in more subtle ways, too. Have you ever noticed children when they are engrossed in something new? They may spend hours on one activity before they are ready to move on to something else. A good teacher may get a classroom of kids excited about a topic, but just as they are getting warmed up—rrring! The forty-five minutes are up and it's time to change classes. Some kids may need more time to get a concept; or if they get excited about something, they may want to spend more time quickly moving ahead to other concepts. On the other hand, a child may get a concept in the first five minutes of class and the rest of the time she is bored to tears. An artificially predetermined time schedule disrupts a child's normal learning patterns.

SHARI HENRY We tackle our schoolish sort of work in the mornings. It's quite possible to pack twelve or thirteen years of traditional schooling into about five or six at home by waiting for readiness and desire. Most children will buck a lot of sit-down work at eight, but seem to want it at twelve or thirteen. They know what they want to accomplish and are ready to do whatever it takes.

Otherwise, as far as school days go, there are no interruptions by difficult students, no passing out papers, no hanging up coats, waiting in lines, taking breaks for recess, or wasting time with frivolous studies. Realizing how relatively simple being well educated is, and how relatively little time it takes, shines a light on just what a waste of children's lives conventional schools are.

> Realizing how relatively simple being well educated is, and how relatively little time it takes, shines a light on just what a waste of children's lives conventional schools are.

JANIE LEVINE HELLYER In a study done in Washington state, standardized tests were used to compare the academic outcomes of homeschoolers. The study concluded that the number of hours per week in formal learning has no apparent relationship to academic outcomes. (Jon Wartes, "The Relationship of Selected Variables to Academic Achievement Among Washington's Homeschoolers," 1988). The same was found for the level of school-like structure.

In traditional classrooms, there is a great deal of time spent "getting ready" to learn. When there are twenty or more children, organizing efforts are tremendous. Considering this and the fact that there will always be some children intent on disrupting the classroom, and you can see that the full school day is not devoted to learning.

Another important aspect to consider here is that while a child at home may be doing "school work" for only an hour or two, learning continues to take place in less traditional forms throughout the day. From "art" to "zoology," children at home doing real things are learning. Not only is learning taking place, but children see the relationship between subjects and skills and real life. Everyday activities provide opportunities for learning and practicing skills, making repetitious exercises unnecessary.

A good example of this type of informal learning is meal planning and grocery shopping, something all of us do without thinking in terms of education. Meals are planned according to nutrition, thrift, and the tastes of the family. Nutrition, budgeting, and research take place every time we plan a shopping trip. Other opportunities include writing lists and comparative shopping.

Many of us have no formal school schedule at all, yet our children learn, grow, and thrive. In my own home, it is the individual learner who chooses the time, place, and subject he will pursue. He is also free to spend as much or as little time as he wants or believes he needs. My job as parent becomes helping the young person learn to find resources and materials, and to find a balance in his life. Two things grow from this type of learning environment. First, the young person is not dependent on having someone stand over him and tell him what to do, when to do it, or how it should be done. Instead, he becomes self-motivated and an independent learner. Second, learning is internalized as a positive thing, interesting, and enjoyable, so the young person is likely to become a lifelong learner.

Education is how we prepare our children to function in the adult world. Homeschooled children have the advantage of observing adults in their everyday lives as they go about their work, and also working with their parents. Pursuing their own interests in meaningful ways nurtures a love of learning. What we do at home and in our communities is often more experiential, and doesn't look much like what takes place in traditional classrooms, so is often overlooked when considering the number of hours homeschooled children learn.

SUSANNAH SHEFFER Ask a child in school how much of the six-hour day that particular child spends in active learning, exploration, or engagement. How much time is spent getting one's own questions answered or experiencing the "click" of a fuzzy concept suddenly becoming clear? If we're honest with ourselves, we don't even have to ask a child because our own memories remind us that much of the school day is spent waiting—waiting in line, waiting for the assignment to be handed out, waiting for the teacher to come help you, waiting your turn with a piece of equipment. Children in school spend more time than we'd care to admit staring out the window, either because they're not following the lesson and feel lost and confused and frightened of being called on, or because they already know what's being taught but aren't allowed to move ahead or do something else. Studies of how much time schoolchildren actually spend "on task" show that only a small portion of the school day is really spent in direct instruction. And even when a teacher is offering direct instruction, there are all sorts of reasons that it might not be reaching a particular child at a particular moment.

One indication that schools themselves recognize how little of the school day is spent "on task" is that when a school student is absent for an extended period—home with a broken leg or an illness, for example—and the school sends home a tutor to help the child keep up with the class, the tutor comes anywhere from two to seven hours a week, and that's considered enough. (See John Holt's book *Teach Your Own* for confirmation of these figures.)

Because homeschooling is so different from schooling—it's individualized and flexible in schedule, pacing, and approach—comparing how much time homeschoolers spend "doing schoolwork" with how many hours a day school students are in attendance is really comparing apples and oranges. If you hear that homeschooling families only "work" in the mornings, what you may be hearing is that the mornings are when they sit down for formal lessons, or for quiet activities like reading and writing, or simply for focused time with their parents. But this tells us nothing about what they may be doing with their afternoons and evenings: going on field trips, getting together with other homeschooling families for a vast range of academic and social activities, volunteering at an adult workplace, having a great discussion at the dinner table or at bedtime, spending time on any one of a million independent projects. Even if it doesn't look exactly like school, you can bet that a lot of learning is going on.

48

Can my child participate in sports programs if we homeschool?

Rebecca Kochenderfer Yes and no. Twenty-four states allow homeschoolers to participate in interscholastic sports.

Interscholastic sports are those programs in which one school competes against another school. Those states that welcome homeschoolers include: Alaska, Arizona, California, Colorado, Florida, Georgia, Idaho, Illinois, Iowa, Louisiana, Maine, Massachusetts, Michigan, Minnesota, New Hampshire, North Dakota, Ohio, Oregon, Rhode Island, Utah, Vermont, Washington state, Wyoming, and Pennsylvania. (A Pennsylvania homeschooler, Jason Taylor, played football, received a full athletic scholarship to college, and was eventually drafted by the Miami Dolphins.) Vermont allows homeschoolers to participate in individual sports, like golf and tennis, but not in team sports. In those states that allow participation, the schools have found that very few homeschoolers actually do choose to participate. Oregon has the most participants, but that still only represents 200 homeschoolers.

If your state does not allow "homeschoolers" to participate in its interscholastic program, your children may still be able to join a school team if they register with the school as independent study students.

Of course, there are other ways to participate in sports. Community athletic programs are easy to find, but generally end at the age of fourteen. One national organization, the Amateur Athletic Union, provides sporting activities

---

THE FOLLOWING IS A LIST OF STATES, COMPILED BY JOAN HARRISS, THAT ALLOW HOMESCHOOLERS TO PARTICIPATE IN INTERSCHOLASTIC SPORTS:

Alaska	Iowa	Ohio
Arizona	Louisiana	Oregon
California	Maine	Pennsylvania
Colorado	Massachusetts	Rhode Island
Florida	Michigan	Utah
Georgia	Minnesota	Vermont*
Idaho	New Hampshire	Washington
Illinois	North Dakota	Wyoming

Vermont allows participation in individual sports, but not team sports

---

for all ages. Quoting from the January/February 1997 issue of *Growing Without Schooling*: "Homeschoolers who want to play team sports but, for whatever reason, can't do so with local school teams can instead play through a national organization called the Amateur Athletic Union." Here is a quote from their brochure, which is available by calling 1(800) AAU-4USA:

Founded in 1888, the Amateur Athletic Union (AAU) is the largest not-for-profit, volunteer, multi-sport organization in the United States dedicated solely to the promotion and development of amateur sports and physical fitness programs. The AAU is the only sports organization in the country which provides a multi-sport program for all age groups. The AAU has focused itself on providing developmental and participatory programs to all Americans beginning at the grassroots level.

You may also be able to find sports programs at local athletic clubs. For example, an athletic club in Brentwood, Tennessee, has a recreation and athletic program specifically for homeschooling families. Home schoolers throughout the Nashville area use the club's facilities for swimming, tennis, dance, and endless other recreational activities.

If you would like more information on homeschoolers and sports you may wish to e-mail Joan Harriss (JHarr77840@aol.com). Joan has conducted research on homeschoolers and interscholastic sports and is the contact person for the New York State Task Force for the Participation of Homeschoolers in Interscholastic Sports. I am indebted to Joan for her help in answering this question.

HELEN AND MARK HEGENER

There are many options for sports programs for homeschooled children, but there are also many potential problems when they want to take advantage of public school facilities.

In the July/August 1997 issue of *Home Education Magazine,* Peggy Daly-Masternak addressed the question of school sports programs: "A handful of other homeschoolers, both here in Ohio and across the country, are pursuing their local school districts, departments of education, and legislatures, forcing statutes for the right not only to play sports, but for 'core' classes, extracurricular activities, even scholarships and diplomas. And sometimes, the results are much more than homeschoolers may have bargained for."

Peggy outlines how well-meaning proponents in several states are introducing bills that could lead to increased governmental regulation. She cautions, "Many of us are aware of the initiatives that are coming down the road to 'improve' education in our state, as well as the current requirements placed on enrolled students, both publicly and privately schooled. Proficiency tests are a big deal already in Ohio and School-To-Work is gaining momentum daily."

> **S**ometimes a vision is all that's needed. A vision, and a few kids who want to play ball.

Peggy suggests finding alternative routes, such as community sports teams or organizations such as the Amateur Athletic Union, whose stated purpose is "Sports for All, Forever." Many homeschooling support groups organize formal and informal sports teams, ski trips, gaming tournaments, and more. Often all that's needed is someone interested enough to organize an event, and kids interested in playing the sport.

In the July/August 1989 issue of *Home Education Magazine,* Earl Gary Stevens described his group's Homeschool Family Baseball: "This is fun baseball. This is fooling around, three-mistakes-per-minute baseball. Catch the ball, miss the ball, nobody cares. There are no sign-up sheets, no try-outs. Come when you can, leave when you must. There are no practices, no extremely important games, no obligation to be on time."

Several years later, Earl describes how their game was started: "At the beginning I was feeling my way along and having to make many decisions. One parent thought the game should be more challenging for bigger kids. Another parent wanted it to be less challenging for little kids. Another felt it was too disorganized, while still another believed that any adult direction at all was too coercive. I listened to everybody and kept to my vision."

Sometimes a vision is all that's needed. A vision, and a few kids who want to play ball.

49

How do I meet the educational needs of several children of different ages at the same time?

CHRIS CARDIFF Have you ever tried juggling? It's a lot like that sometimes—

keeping several balls in the air while you handle one specific ball.

This juggling act is more challenging when younger children are involved who don't yet have the patience to wait their turn. It is much easier with older children who have developed into self-directed, independent learners. In this respect, this is a problem that will take care of itself over time.

I don't have an easy answer to the juggling question, only some suggestions that work sometimes in our family (three girls, ages twelve, nine, and three). There are times when all three of them want help simultaneously on different projects. When the kids outnumber the parents, someone must wait for attention.

First, consider taking advantage of the fact that your children are at different ages. Where it's appropriate, older children can teach the younger ones, a technique popularized by Joseph Lancaster in the early 1900s. This method leverages your time and benefits the older child as well as the younger. Explaining and communicating a subject requires a different way of thinking about it and results in a deepening of their own understanding.

> **W**here it's appropriate, older children can teach the younger ones, a technique popularized by Joseph Lancaster in the early 1900s. This method leverages your time and benefits the older child as well as the younger.

Second, some subjects or projects lend themselves to appreciation or participation at different levels, making it easy to include children of different ages and understanding. We have a Geography/Culture club in our local homeschooling support group that includes kids age five to fourteen. Each month we study a different country. Older children may give in-depth reports on a famous person, historical event, or cultural difference, while younger children make drawings of the flag or a famous building. Everyone, including the adults, participates at a level they enjoy—and everyone enjoys the ethnic food served at the end!

Finally, let's return to juggling. Successful juggling involves patterns, rhythm, and timing. You develop a pattern and rhythm for catching and throwing the balls so that you always know where they are and what's coming next. This translates into scheduling and time management for homeschooling—planning. Each child needs individualized attention at some point, and sometimes the best way to accomplish this is to structure your time to make sure it happens.

As you work on your own juggling act, remember that each family has its own rhythms and patterns. And, just to keep it challenging, those rhythms and patterns change over time. But with a little experimentation, you will find what works for your family.

DEB SHELL I never bought the idea that meeting the educational needs of my children meant teaching them what I (or someone else) thought they should be learning. Although I felt personally responsible for meeting the educational needs of my variously aged children, I assumed my children would inquire about and explore their interests as their needs arose, and that my role was to provide opportunities for discovery. The fact that we had four children spaced about two-and-a-half years apart never conflicted with our ability to meet their specific needs. Just as one child might have been learning to crawl backward down the stairs, another might have been learning how to unbutton and button her overall straps. My job was to foresee potential accidents and otherwise to stay out of their way while they were busy mastering new skills. Later on, while one might have been learning the written language of fractions or long division, another was hard at work putting together her first poetry book; my role was to guide according to the questions asked and follow the pace presented to me.

While my husband and I worked hard at facilitating opportunities for each of our children to develop their particular interests, neither of us felt compelled to specifically teach anything other than what we were asked. Our girls, like most children I know, did a very good job of asking.

So I relieved myself of the responsibility that compels most teachers; I didn't have to find the "right" curriculum, the "best" learning aids, nor did I have to be vigilant about discovering each child's so-called deficits or specific moments of readiness. When my children were ready to learn to read, they asked appropriate questions. We answered them. As adults, it's clear that the responsibility to learn rests within each of us. I don't believe children learn any differently or from any other sense of motivation. Observing young children learning reveals the pure motivational drive that compels all education. We really do self-educate, even when we ask others to teach us.

So for me, the key to educating several children was listening to each child's requests for knowledge and providing opportunities for them to learn what they desired. We rarely had conflicts about me spending more time with one than another. Time spent with one in-

evitably spilled over to whoever else was also interested. Interests were contagious, too. For example, when one child read about children living in Japan and designed paper dolls fashioned in Japanese dress, she also invited her sisters to play "Japan" with her. Thus she taught them about what she'd found out. Reading books aloud also crossed many ages—the younger ones may not have gotten the same thing out of the story as the older ones, but they got something because they stayed and listened. When read again a few years later, new insights were brought to light. Because I didn't have preset goals in mind, each child was free to explore at her own discretion and sense of appropriate need. This really eliminated any responsibility on my part in terms of having to guess what each child supposedly needed. I was able to spend time with each child when she requested it, without excluding anyone else from the experience. Much like a one-room schoolhouse, a large family can reinforce each member's personal responsibility for guiding her own learning. Knowledge also moves up and down—what a younger child may become interested in and learn about may not have occurred to an older child. Respecting each person's individual sensibilities helps foster alliances between children, which thereby increases opportunities for learning and makes being part of a large family truly beneficial.

> **"They don't need us anymore," I say ruefully to my husband. "That's the point," my husband says.**

BECKY RUPP We have three sons, all of whom have always been homeschooled. Though we've had our share of problems, the joint homeschooling of children of different ages has not been one of them. For most projects—say, a study of the Civil War, an investigation of astronomy, or a pottery-making activity—the boys all learned together, each participating to the best of his abilities. They didn't necessarily do exactly the same things—the older children, for example, might read books about American Indian pottery and try making coiled pots, while the youngest made mudpies—but all shared the experience. In many cases, joint learning had an added plus: the boys helped and learned from each other. ("Look, Caleb, you roll the clay out like this and make a little snake . . .")

For basic subjects, like reading and arithmetic, the boys used different materials and got individual attention. Ethan, our middle son, who had a rocky time learning to read, had a special phonics program all his own; each boy progressed at different rates in math; and each preferred different kinds of math books and workbooks. Which means that our boys, through their elementary-level years, got a mix of (mostly) joint and (some) private homeschooling. It seemed to work fine.

Juggling the demands of children at different skill and age levels wasn't difficult; juggling the demands of children with wildly different interests was trickier. ("Let's do physics experiments this morning!" "No, ancient history!") Sometimes there simply weren't enough hours in the day to discuss English literature with Josh, work on chemistry problems and experiments with Ethan, ferry Caleb to his piano lesson, read Josh's latest creative writing project, help Ethan set up the telescope, and write an interactive workbook for Caleb ("I want one of my own") all about ancient Greece. Then, as the boys grew older still, demands on our time lessened as they became increasingly independent learners. "They don't need us anymore," I say ruefully to my husband, watching Josh buried in *The Black Arrow,* Ethan absorbed in building a robotic arm, and Caleb, on the computer, lost in the geographic adventures of Carmen Sandiego.

"That's the point," my husband says.

50

How do I ensure my children are motivated to learn at home?

SANDRA DODD It's pretty hard to ensure anything, but motivated to learn? People are born with the desire to learn. If your kids have never been to school, you won't have many problems (unless you try to play school, in which case you can create the same problems school creates). If your children *have* been to school, and there have learned what they should avoid (math, writing, and so on), now you have a job to do. You need to help make those things interesting, relevant, fun, tricky, amusing. One way to do that is to find them where you didn't think they were. Find writing at the movies. Find math at the swimming pool. Mix life up. Scramble ideas. Sprinkle your days with granulated information. Whatever you do, don't "do school" just like you think school is doing it. After all, if that works, why would you keep your children home?

> **M**ix life up. Scramble ideas. Sprinkle your days with granulated information. Whatever you do, don't "do school" just like you think school is doing it. After all, if that works, why would you keep your children home?

School teaches that there is a minimal set of information that will guarantee a child success. That is simply untrue and unfair. There is no end to information, and rather than try to guarantee your child enough of the right information, you will do better to present him with the freedom and means to find it joyously and to want more.

We've found the best way to make information interesting is to show an interest ourselves. If I were to say, "Oh, I hate Egypt, but *you* go read that book about Egypt, and you make a model of a mummy, and just keep me out of it," what I'd really be saying is, "Egypt is stupid. You have to do something because you are a kid. Learning about Egypt is a kid-thing and when you're grown you can forget the whole thing." Interest and enthusiasm are infectious. Cynicism and derision are harmful. A positive attitude and a sharing of interest are motivational.

When we first bought pattern blocks, my husband and I played with them ourselves and wouldn't let the kids mess up our patterns. We talked about the degrees of the angles and the kids overheard it, but we weren't talking to them. They were saying, "Let me try!" and we'd give them just a small portion of the blocks. They were dying to get the whole set, and we told them they would be next. Ever since that first night, they see those blocks as something so fascinating that adults love them, and very often I still put them out when adults will be over and we play with them on the table while we're talking.

SUSAN AND LARRY KASEMAN Homeschooling parents find that their children are usually motivated simply because they are curious and eager to learn. Many families use the following suggestions to help motivate their children or to deal with times when parents wish children were more motivated.

• Arrange your house so children have easy access to interesting stuff: intriguing books (often from the library), catalogs, magazines, and other printed materials; supplies for writing and arts and crafts, including different kinds of paper, pens, markers, paint, and general office supplies; math and science equipment such as a blocks, calculators, cash registers, scales, thermometers, collections of specimens (rocks, feathers, pressed flowers), anatomical models, charts or models of the solar system, and perhaps a microscope or telescope; social studies materials such as maps and time lines on the walls, map puzzles, a globe; a chance to explore natural settings as simple as a backyard or nearby park; perhaps a computer; and any other materials that particularly interest them.

• Don't worry about what's missing. Choose materials based on your family's needs, interests, and budget. Your attitude is more important than what's available. Relax! Select things that children can use on their own. Store things so they are easy to find and get out. Help children learn to restore order when they are finished. Let go of other people's ideas about how houses are supposed to look and arrange your house to suit you. Add an art table and a cupboard with supplies to the dining room. Put up maps and posters. Provide space where projects in process can be for several days or weeks, if necessary. Then let the environment do the teaching. Resist the temptation to follow your children around trying to get them to learn.

• Include children's interests as much as possible. If you are using a purchased curriculum, look for supplementary materials about birds or baseball or whatever fascinates your children. If you are developing your own curriculum, start with their interests whenever you can.

- Let children make choices when feasible. With a purchased curriculum, consider letting them decide whether to do reading or math first. Let them skip a subject and spend extra time on another. Families developing their own curricula may focus on one or two subjects and then move on rather than trying to cover each subject every day. Don't over-schedule children's time with either academics or fun activities. Children learn a lot from time they can manage themselves.

- Encourage children to learn at their own pace. Something a child is not ready to understand now will be much easier in a month or a year or two. As homeschoolers, we can use our time flexibly. Our children's self-esteem and love of learning are much more important than whether they learn to add fractions today or even this year.

- Learn to recognize all that children learn outside formal schoolwork. Often children who seem unmotivated are actually highly motivated to learn things not usually considered school subjects. One of our most important jobs as homeschooling parents is to recognize the importance of such learning and if necessary, describe it in conventional school terms for spouses, friends, relatives, school officials, and others. For ex-ample, playing store, building with Legos, and keeping track of sports statistics are all math.

- Expect and accept down time when children don't seem to be doing much at all. Maybe they are processing major concepts they have just mastered or preparing for their next step forward, large or small. We all need time to relax and just be.

- Children who are beginning homeschooling after attending a conventional school, especially if they had negative experiences, benefit enormously from time, perhaps a month or more, to do constructive things they choose without worrying about academics: play games, go for long walks, learn to cook, read things that interest them. Some families find their children learn so much this way that they do not need to do formal academics.

- Many families find it helps to limit or eliminate television; to eat nutritious foods with a minimum of sugar; to plan quiet times at home when children can do what they want to do; in short, to simply relax and enjoy life and each other.

Wendy Priesnitz Children learn as surely as they grow. Watch a toddler, motivated by her boundless curiosity to explore her surroundings, and you'll understand that children are hungry to learn. It's only when their urgent questions have been brushed aside too many times, when their innate learning agenda has been sacrificed to the more aggressive plans of a well-intentioned adult, that they become passive learners who have to be artificially motivated to internalize facts.

It may be difficult to envision young children getting enthusiastic about arithmetic or history, because we have few role models to demonstrate this internal motivation. So, with their permission, I like to use my unschooled daughters, who are now twenty-four and twenty-five years of age, as an example.

Heidi and Melanie learned math, language arts, history, geography, and science because it was part of their everyday lives. Having never been told to sit and listen to an adult teacher, they just naturally explored their world. They constantly looked for meanings and for patterns in what they were experiencing; sometimes they asked questions, sometimes they introduced discussions about what they were learning, sometimes their father and I did. They learned by living, in other words.

Our family ran a home-based magazine and book publishing business. So when Heidi was eight years old, she started to publish a newsletter for other home-based learners. This was a real business, with real, paying customers. The experience involved bookkeeping, writing, editing, graphic design. Interaction with her subscribers led to explorations into geography, history, and foreign languages. She ran this business until she decided to enter our local public high school five years later. The knowledge and skills she'd picked up along the way were far beyond what her peers who'd been to school had managed to retain—and she'd never had a formal lesson in her life, never been tested, and never read a textbook.

CHAPTER SEVEN

It's Effective! Assessing Your Child's Growth

MANY PARENTS BEGIN the homeschool journey full of doubt in their ability to assess their children's educational development (there are "experts" who do this, mind you!). They find it reassuring to believe that there is some sort of "yardstick" to measure progress. Yet with only four questions, this chapter on assessment is the shortest of the book. Why is what seems to be a very important aspect of school given such short shrift?

Because it's not really necessary. Experience has shown homeschooling parents that a school's need to constantly test children is a direct result of the way it goes about teaching children, not a necessary component of the learning experience itself. When you gather a large number of children together, and present to all the same information in the same way, a test to see how much was absorbed by each is the only measure available.

But if you change the way you go about teaching children—and, better still, if you proceed from the idea that the child is learning as opposed to being taught—a different, improved option of assessment automatically becomes available. This may come as a shock, but all the necessary indicators of progress come naturally—from the children themselves. Combine this with a parent who spends a lot of time with the children, understands the way they learn best, knows their strengths and weaknesses as well as she knows her own, and is attentive enough to the children to remain aware of the indicators they share, then the tests we associate with the measure of academic progress become unnecessary, time-consuming burdens.

Let's look at unnecessary measures from another angle. Many regulations exist to constantly test products from a factory. Let's use a grape jelly factory, for instance.

Experience has shown homeschooling parents that a school's need to constantly test children is a direct result of the way it goes about teaching children, not a necessary component of the learning experience itself.

Lots of hands touch various aspects of the product as it passes through the assembly line, and not one of the people working for a paycheck is responsible for a jar from start to finish. Due to the methods of production, these tests are necessary to ensure the desired final product, time after time after time after time.

Now, one day Grandma decides to make some grape jelly in her kitchen. Grandma is not mass-producing; hers are the only hands touching the product (she knows she should wash them first!), and she alone handles the process from start to finish. Grandma's not making jelly for a paycheck. She's making it because she knows her grandchildren enjoy it. Grandma can be trusted to make sure the final product comes out right: She has an inherent, loving interest in making sure the jelly doesn't make her grandchildren sick when they eat it! Wouldn't it be a waste of time and money—not to mention downright silly—to expect Grandma to use the same regulations and tests as the factory does?

This is why homeschoolers fight so hard against regulations that would require the implementation of testing where it doesn't exist, or any increased testing where it is already required. These tests serve no purpose and hold no value to the homeschooling way of life and learning. They're just as silly for homeschooled children as factory tests are for Grandma's jelly.

So we've addressed assessment, but in a very small space, for several reasons. New homeschoolers tend to want some means of measuring success; the few methods included will serve you well. Those who want to increase test requirements for homeschoolers need to understand there are other, family-centered methods to ensure our children are learning; the methods outlined will help you realize any other way is simply a waste of taxpayers' hard-earned money.

Most important, we've used a very small space because no more is required. After all, we all know there's no jelly on earth that tastes as good as Grandma's.

51
Do I have to give my child tests?

REBECCA KOCHENDERFER Some states require yearly, standardized testing, others do not. Some charter school programs require testing and others do not. Your local homeschooling group can tell you about your state's regulations.

In California, we are not required to test our children, although the local homeschooling charter schools strongly encourage it. As a former special education teacher, I must say that I am rather negative toward it.

First of all, I don't believe that tests can accurately measure a person's intelligence or abilities. Since I doubt their accuracy, I naturally doubt their worth. Second, for a child to do well on standardized tests, you generally have to teach to the test; and I really don't want my children to learn something just because it might appear on some test.

Finally, I'm trying to raise my children with the belief that they are the most important judges of their work. If I were to ask them to take an academic achievement test, I would be giving them the impression that somebody else's opinion of how they are doing is more important than their own opinion.

But these are just my own beliefs. Lots of homeschooling parents appreci-ate these tests. They like to know how their children are doing compared to their peers and they like to see growth from year to year. Once again, the beauty of homeschooling is that you can choose for yourself what you think is best for your child.

SUSAN EVANS What we're really asking is, "How do I know if my children are learning?"

There are many stereotypes about learning—testing, resistance, and the need to provide external motivation—that feed into worries and misgivings in this area.

But look at children who've not yet attended school. One and two year olds who endlessly ask, "Whazzat?" are building their vocabulary skills. Three year olds who talk through all of their waking (and some of their sleeping)

Susan Evans (with daughter)

hours are editing and revising their oral narratives. Five year olds join Socrates and Plato in trying to figure out the order of things and forces in the universe: "But how can Santa deliver *all* those presents in one night? And what about houses that don't have chimneys?"

So it is with eight year olds writing to pen pals: "How do you spell 'Connecticut?'" "What does 'G' look like in cursive?" And with ten year olds reading *The Hobbit:* "What are runes? Are they still around? Can you drive me to the library *now* to get a rune book?"

When we pay close attention to the paths of our children's interests, I think we'll very often discover that their understanding and insights about particular pieces of knowledge are much deeper and wider ranging than what any tests could capture.

Over time, it's become apparent to me that, for a self-directed learner, tests not only waste time and break the flow of inquiry, they miss the whole point of seeking out and internalizing information and knowledge.

Looking back over my schooling and the patterns of testing I experienced, it was as though we had a chunk of information given to us on Mondays through Thursdays in class. On Fridays we were tested to see if we got the point. Then we were finished and started anew the next Monday. (Studies show that we forgot huge portions of the information as soon as we finished taking the test— *even if* we got a good grade on the test!)

When I look at my children's understanding of the world, and when I tackle

> **O**ver time, it's become apparent to me that, for a self-directed learner, tests not only waste time and break the flow of inquiry, they miss the whole point of seeking out and internalizing information and knowledge.

new ideas and experiences myself, I see a very different process: New information is considered from several perspectives, filed away in relationship to existing understandings, and is brought out periodically and reconsidered. Learning about Leonardo da Vinci, for example, can be an inquiry into early theories of flight, or intense studying of the art of drawing, or an ethical debate in the use of cadavers. It would be silly—and useless—to say one knows all there is to know about the man upon completion of a 500-word essay on the meaning of the Mona Lisa's smile, or a matching section on titles of his paintings. A month-long inquiry may only be laying the groundwork for larger consideration of some bit of information about the Renaissance five years or fifty years down the road. Again, any test would be useless, misleading, and a waste of time.

So when do we worry and when do we not when it comes to getting past the insulting stereotype of children resisting learning?

I always figure that if the television is off most of the time (or out of the house completely); if the children are engrossed in projects of their own choosing several times a day, or across several days; and if my calling for help with chores elicits a response of "Just a minute, I'm at a good part!" or "I need to finish this before the glue dries!" or "Fine, I'll never figure this out anyway!" then their minds are perking along, they're figuring out lots of new things, and if I listen carefully, maybe they'll let me in on the secret of how airplanes fly, how to write beautiful poetry, or cut perfect mats for framing, or to design and make lovely glass beads. I just hope they don't try to test me before I'm ready.

52

How do homeschooled children compare academically with traditionally schooled children?

PAT LINES People disagree on whether homeschooling can help a child academically. There is no research involving controls that indicates whether the same children could do better or worse in homeschooling, or in a public or private classroom. A multitude of data does exist, and analyses of test scores are available, based on data from states that require testing or from homeschooling associations. Both sources may provide information on a select group, as not all families cooperate with state testing requirements and private efforts rely on

volunteers. Keeping these caveats in mind, virtually all the available data show that the tested homeschooling children are above average. The pattern for children for whom data are available resembles those of children in private schools.

SUSANNAH SHEFFER I could answer this question by telling you how well homeschoolers generally score on standardized tests and about the research studies that compare homeschoolers' test scores with scores of other students. But I don't think these facts get at what's most interesting or most important about homeschoolers or their academic experience. What distinguishes homeschoolers, in my mind, is not just their often impressive skill and accomplishment, but their attitude toward their work, their reasons for doing what they do.

A homeschooler who's now a junior at an Ivy League university told about working on a paper for class. He turned in the paper on time, but afterward he went to the professor and said that he was still interested in the subject and would like to keep working on the paper. I don't know what grade he received, but let's suppose for a minute that it was an A, and let's suppose (because it's quite likely) that another student in the class also got an A but wrote the paper simply to fulfill an assignment, not as something that he'd willingly continue on his own time without a further grade forthcoming. By conventional measures, these two students seem the same, but to my mind, the difference between them is significant.

But there's a question that is even more relevant than how homeschoolers compare to schooled students. How is a child who was once in school now faring as a homeschooler? In other words, how does she compare to her former self? I always think of the fifteen year old who told me, just after she had become a homeschooler, that she didn't like to learn through reading. She'd always felt bad about her reading, was embarrassed to be one of the class' slowest readers, and seldom read unless she had to. After she had been out of school for a few months, she mentioned to me that she'd spent the day in the library and that she was reading *Anna Karenina*. "Wait a minute!" I exclaimed. "How did this happen?"

Things had changed; her view of herself and her capabilities had changed. Later, writing about this process, she said, "I guess because I was just doing it for me and no one else was making it

> **H**omeschooling, for me, is less about making sure that the children do as well as their schooled peers (or become superior to them) than it is about making it possible for each homeschooler to flourish.

horrible for me, I began to get interested in the books themselves, in the stories, instead of thinking so much about myself and how I was doing."

Again, this strikes me as a difference that makes a difference. It tells us so much about people's capacity for change and about how varying the circumstances and assumptions can allow for new possibilities. Homeschooling, for me, is less about making sure that the children do as well as their schooled peers (or become superior to them) than it is about making it possible for each homeschooler to flourish.

53

How can I do my *own* assessment of my child's academic standing in relation to her peers?

Mary McCarthy Why would you want to? What difference does it make if the kid next door built a full-scale working replica of the space shuttle in the backyard using just the recyclables? Your child is an individual. Celebrate the individual. *No* one is good at everything, *no* one is going to be perfect in every subject, so why would you want to compare your child to someone else's? Diversity is the blessing of humanity; individually, we lack certain skills, but put together we make a whole. If your child is learning—and enjoying it—that's success.

SUSAN AND LARRY KASEMAN Your interest in your child's academic standing is understandable. Fortunately, we homeschoolers have many opportunities to observe our children's development. We watch them exploring the world and, when necessary, translate what they do into conventional academic language. (Sorting rocks is science. Building with blocks is geometry and spatial relations. Recognizing one's name is reading.) We can see the processes our children go through and support their early efforts just as we recognized and responded to their first words. We gradually come to understand that learning about baseball or horses develops basic academic skills.

When we get concerned about academics (yes, even confident, experienced homeschoolers sometimes worry):

- We can talk with other homeschoolers, especially those with older children. They'll know what we mean when we say, "Did you wonder if your children would ever learn to multiply?"
- We can review what our children have already learned. What can they do

today that they couldn't do a few months ago? Write a note? Discuss current political issues?
- We can look at the big picture. As homeschoolers, we know our children better than we would if they were attending a conventional school. We see their increasing understanding of the world; their growing ability to interact with others; their increasing self-reliance as they learn to ride a bike, drive a car, travel abroad; and their increasing maturity as they take responsibility for increasingly complex projects.
- We can realize that to become mature, responsible adults, children don't need to follow the path prescribed by conventional schools. Children learn best by following their own timetable, at different rates in different subjects. As homeschoolers, we have the flexibility to encourage this. Many grownup homeschoolers who are doing well didn't learn to read until they were eight, ten, or older. Many who write well and are comfortable with math would earlier have been considered "below grade level." Had they been pressured to learn these things earlier, they might have concluded that they could not learn them.

A great gift we can give our children is the ability and courage to be true to themselves, to set their own standards, to identify problems and not be overwhelmed by them, to consider a wide range of alternative responses and then act. This will serve them well whether the problem is a car that won't start, a health crisis, or simply the causes of the Civil War.

- Perhaps the best preparation is the ability to learn new things. (Consider people now using computers who did not study them in school.) We can ask: Do our children recognize when they don't know something? Are they confident enough to admit that they don't know it? Do our children know how to find information they need using resources such as their common sense, the library, the Internet, and assistance from other people?

Finally, it's great that you want to avoid standardized tests. They interfere with learning and are inaccurate, unfair, and biased against minorities, women, and anyone who does not have the same experiences and values as the developer of the test. Taking a test often undermines self-esteem. Test scores show only how well a given person performed on a given test on a given day, not how much one knows. But test results tend to be self-fulfilling prophecies. Why would we want to put our children through diffi-cult experiences that produce unreliable results that may be harmful to them?

JOHN TAYLOR GATTO You must understand the poisonous assumption buried in the simple words "standing" and "relation to her peers" before you can trust yourself to do the best by your offspring. Woodrow Wilson didn't learn to read until he was eleven—in what hell would he have ended up if his standing in relation to his peers had mattered much? I understand the footrace/contest aspect of growing up in a competitive society is important to most of you, and I won't try to deter your concerns—because experience has taught me that's a waste of energy, and probably arrogant, too. But I can say that after thirty years of classroom teaching, I'm utterly convinced that every single stage theory of child development is dangerously flawed; "dangerous" because all of them suggest overtly or covertly that unless the abstract sequence is followed, great harm will result.

But that is nonsense. Profitable nonsense, I'll grant; without it, we couldn't have a big chunk of the psychological industry, many academic departments and specialties, consulting contracts and experts. I know all this, but there you are. Every child I ever had much success with seemed to have his or her own internal sequencing logic. These logics have some flexibility to them but not an infinite amount. It's when these personal logics of mental growth are profoundly violated by shoehorning them into someone's theory of what should be happening at every stage of a child's life that real damage is certain to happen—*even* if the child complies!

All this is not to say that intellectual growth doesn't benefit from outside attention and guidance. It does. But you need to set aside the fears that if your child can't, say, program computers by third grade, that she will be hopelessly "behind" by sixth.

But I can say that after thirty years of classroom teaching, I'm utterly convinced that every single stage theory of child development is dangerously flawed; "dangerous" because all of them suggest overtly or covertly that unless the abstract sequence is followed great harm will result.

54
How can I tell if my children are learning what's important?

NED VARE Decide for yourself what's important for them to know. Be specific. Not geography, but where is New York? Not math, but how much money do I need to buy a baseball?

Second, decide whether it's really important for them to know it *now*. Have a good reason.

SANDRA DODD How can you tell if children at school are learning what's important? How can a teacher at school tell if children are learning what's important?

First of all, what's important? Assuming that's a simple question for you to answer, maybe the next question is, How do you know your children are learning that, the important thing? You can tell because their behavior will change, their questions will change, their actions will change. They will display the knowledge in everyday ways. If it's math, they will be able to calculate, measure, estimate, whatever. If it's reading, they'll be able to read. If it's writing, using maps, understanding mechanics . . . they will use what they've learned.

What if you think everything is important? Everything is connected, and learning is important. Consider the idea that it's not important where people start, and that people never quit learning until they finally do quit, after which *lots* of things are no longer quite as important. If a child is learning, and active, and inquisitive, and if the parents are open, and helpful, and encouraging, they are learning important things.

WENDY PRIESNITZ "What's important" is a highly subjective phrase! It depends on one's world view, definition of education, ambitions (or lack of) for a child's career, and much more.

Your family should decide on a set of learning objectives for your children,

Wendy Priesnitz

aside from any legal requirements of the jurisdiction in which you live. If you want your children to learn exactly what their schooled peers are learning, you can obtain an outline of the curriculum that's followed in your local school.

My own personal goal for my children's education was for them to retain their curiosity and love of learning, and to develop their research, learning, and communication skills. The skills and facts they picked up along the way were largely a function of their own interests, rounded out here and there with what my husband and I perceived to be missing pieces of their own personal knowledge puzzle. But the actual body of knowledge is ever growing and changing (for instance, Saturn has more rings now than it did when I went to elementary school!) at an increasingly enhanced pace. So I felt they'd be better served by developing a questioning nature and sound literacy skills than memorizing the dates of the battles of the World Wars!

No matter what you feel your children should be learning, don't worry about being able to tell if that learning is occurring. Because you're intimately involved with each youngster on a day-to-day basis, you'll be in the happy position of observing each burst of growth and sharing each new insight.

You might get concerned from time to time that your child's development seems to have stalled. At those times, it's important to remember that learning does not proceed in an orderly fashion. It's a chaotic, fits and starts, trial-and-error sort of experience. Brains need time to process new knowledge. Your learner will move from frenetic bursts of activity through slower periods of seeming hibernation, only to surprise you one day with a pronouncement that makes you marvel at what was going on in her brain while you thought she was vegging out!

Some homeschooling families test their children on a regular basis—and some laws require that home-educated children be tested regularly. But a good number of families object to testing as a way of measuring learning.

One of the main objections to testing is that it tries to judge the growth of knowledge by measuring the performance on one test at one moment in time, rather than as a process of growth that occurs over a period of time. It's a quick and easy measuring stick that is a poor substitute for the observation which you have the opportunity to undertake.

Test scores may be unreliable for a variety of reasons. To be at all useful, a test must reflect learning; standardized tests and those administered to home-educated children by school boards cannot, by definition, be directly relevant to the individual's learning process.

An alternative used by many families as a way of assessing their children's learning growth and needs is the portfolio. A language arts portfolio, for instance, could include compositions, reports, letters, stories, favorite poems, taped recordings of oral reports or readings, book reviews, lists of favorite books, photographs of plays being presented to family members, and even artwork. The format can be whatever is suitable for the material being collected ... from a file folder for language arts to a large cardboard box for science projects.

HELEN AND MARK HEGENER Before you try to determine whether or not your children are learning "what's important," take a moment to reflect on your own life and what has proven to be important for you to know as you live from day to day. How much of what you were taught in school has been helpful to you, and how much of what's truly helpful was learned beyond the classroom?

Some of the most important lessons you can teach your children won't be found in any textbook or curriculum. Things like love, responsibility, caring, compassion, respect, sincerity. These lessons will last them a lifetime, when all the math, science, and history are long forgotten.

But math, science, and history are important in their own right, so how can we tell if they're being learned? In the same way we can tell if our children are learning to be kind and thoughtful: by observing them, interacting with them, asking questions and discussing the answers with them. In short, by involving ourselves in their lives.

When we truly live with our children, as only homeschooling allows, we see them grow in many ways. Not just physically, or emotionally, but we also see them growing in learning and knowledge. We're aware of their interests, their hobbies, and their plans to a greater degree than parents whose children spend their days in classrooms and their free time with school activities or peer groups. If we see a child struggling to understand a computer program, we can search for something a little easier to help him over the hurdle; he can return to the more difficult program when he's gained skill and confidence. Bingo! We've got a reading on his math (or science or spelling) skills. If our child asks questions about the Civil War, we can help him find books at the library, and notice which titles, in which skill levels, he chooses. It's a sure sign of his reading/comprehension level. We see evidence of reading skills while driving, when a child sounds out road signs; at the grocery store, as he reads labels; playing games, as he calls out board instructions; watching movies, as he keeps up with the subtitles or credits.

Schoolish subjects are all around us: math in a million places, science everywhere we look, history found around

When we truly live with our children, as only homeschooling allows, we see them grow in many ways. Not just physically, or emotionally, but we also see them growing in learning and knowledge.

each corner, literary skills a part of daily life. There's no reason to chop them into curricular blocks— that's just a convenience to teachers and bureaucrats who need to keep paperwork filled out so the dollars keep flowing. We need only pay attention to know what our children are learning, and what they may need help with.

So how do we know "what's important" to know? It's important that a child knows learning is a key which unlocks wonderful opportunities in life. It's important that they know that key will always be available to them. Instill a love for learning, and let your child determine what's important for him or her to know.

CHAPTER EIGHT

You Mean I Don't Need to Know Algebra?! The Teen Years

Q UICK—DO YOU remember irrational numbers? How to factor a trinomial? Did you use the quadratic formula today?

When my oldest child was ready for algebra, he wanted my help. The terms above rang a bell but, unfortunately, it was a very distant bell. Like many other parents, it had been two decades since I'd tackled the math puzzles known as algebra, and there'd been no reason to visit them again since leaving high school. But something was different this time—my son and I had the answer book!

It's amazing what having the answers can do for your self-confidence. You don't do the problem once only to be told you did it wrong. You go back to the drawing board. You know you can figure this out and transfer what you learn to other problems. Your child gets an idea at the same time as you do and you compare notes. You play with the problem. Did I say play? You bet I did.

Armed with the answers, a "one day at a time" approach, and the notion that one could actually have fun viewing algebra as number puzzles—strolling quickly through sections we understood and slowing to a crawl when we felt we needed a little more practice—my son and I made it to the end of the algebra book.

I often wonder how many parents who are seriously considering homeschooling stop dead in their tracks when, in their mental imaginings, they reach the years they remember as high school and consider the subject matter beyond their scope. As Cafi Cohen and Luz Shosie explain in this chapter, homeschooling a teen is different, but far from impossible. Sandra Dodd, Donna Nichols-White, and Rebecca Rupp help you see how your teens can learn the "tough" subjects even if you don't understand them.

> **L**ike many other parents, it had been two decades since I'd tackled the math puzzles known as algebra, and there'd been no reason to visit them again since leaving high school.

And our homeschoolers answer still more questions about teens who learn at home and in the community. You may be worrying about diplomas, college, scholarships, and jobs. Or you may like to know how so many homeschooled teens find apprenticeships as they enjoy freedom from school schedules. The Hegeners, the Kasemans, and Susan Evans will give you and your children plenty of ideas and starting points.

I got to "play" with algebra one more time with my daughter. But just as I was looking forward to a third and last time, my youngest declared he was quite capable of doing it himself, thank you very much. You mean I don't need to know algebra? I *love* homeschooling in the teen years!

55

Is homeschooling a teenager different than homeschooling an elementary school–aged child?

CAFI COHEN Teenage homeschooling presented a new set of challenges. Our children wanted to try all sorts of things with which we were only vaguely familiar. Our son wanted a private pilot's license. Our daughter needed outlets for all kinds of creative endeavors: writing, speaking, performing, drawing, even cooking. In addition, both kids decided to tackle subjects in which we lacked expertise, most notably foreign language.

As parents of homeschooled teenagers, we began to worry about college admissions tests like the SAT and ACT. Our kids were also eager to begin researching colleges. One had a clear-cut goal, and our questions centered around the best way to help him attain it. The other could not begin to decide on a goal; and, of course, we worried about that.

In short, the kids seemed to need more expertise than we could personally provide. And we, their parents, worried more about the future than when they were younger. Were we doing The Right Thing?

Fortunately, as we discovered, teenagers can do more for themselves than younger children. Contrary to what many educationists would have you believe, teenagers *can* learn trigonometry and biology by themselves for the SAT. They *can* read college catalogs on their own. They *can* teach themselves computer skills with little outside help. They can even find resources on their own—like community drama groups and free flying lessons. When challenges arose, more and more often as the kids got older they would find a solution before we even realized there was a problem. Sometimes we brainstormed together to generate solutions.

What was the biggest difference we noticed in homeschooling our teenagers? Our role evolved from networker to facilitator. Our earlier research and our talking to experienced home educators had served two purposes: (1) We found resources, and (2) we provided a networking role model. Eventually, our kids adopted our techniques and became good networkers themselves. As they assumed more responsibility for their education, we, their parents, found we had an altered job description. We had moved from planning, motivating, and teaching to discussing, providing wheels, and writing occasional checks.

Luz Shosie Our philosophy and style of learning are not different—we have always let Cassidy know that he is in charge of his own learning and we are in charge of ours. Our job has been to keep him safe and help him gain access to whatever he needs or wants to learn about. We did not ever tell him he should learn to do math, learn to read, or say please and thank you. This was not easy for a couple of former schoolteachers, let me tell you!

What is delightfully different now is seeing the proof that children can be trusted to learn and grow. The first few years of homeschooling, we pretty much had to take it on faith that what John Holt, Daniel Greenberg, and others said was true—children are born learning and they want to grow up to be responsible, effective adults. Now Cassidy is eighteen and knows enough reading, writing, and arithmetic to hold two jobs and get high scores on GED and SAT tests. And he's

> **W**hat is delightfully different now is seeing the proof that children can be trusted to learn and grow.

one of the most polite people of any age I know.

56

How will my child learn the "tough" subjects, like algebra and chemistry, if I don't understand them?

SANDRA DODD You don't need to be your children's only teacher. Maybe learning alongside your children would be best for both of you, if you want to go that route. You can help them learn by learning *with* them. If you find yourself being surpassed, rejoice! Your child can teach you, or can go on to learn without you. There are other people in the world to help, and there are books, computer games and courses, flash cards at university bookstores, courses at local colleges or trade schools, correspondence courses and videos.

If a parent expects to be everything to a child, it limits the child's world. If I teach my children everything I know about history, they won't know as much as if I get out of the way and let them have all the books, people, photos, museums, maps, and sites in the whole wide world. I prefer to expose the children to as much as possible and let them make connections between things (with my help sometimes, but never at my insistence).

When a child has an actual need or desire to learn something, he or she can learn it. And it won't take an hour a day for nine months, either.

DONNA NICHOLS-WHITE It is an erroneous belief that in order to homeschool, a parent has to have an intense knowledge of every subject offered in the schools. When in school children are told what to think, when to think it, what to learn, and how to learn. Everything is supposedly accomplished on a rigid schedule.

Teachers are considered the experts in these fields and are hired to pour this knowledge into willing and ready children. (That Goals 2000 readiness for schools bit is preposterous.) And don't forget the importance of textbooks, drills, and exams.

Fortunately, our job is parenting, not teaching. Instead of schooling our children, we can have them actively participate in real-life experiences like grocery shopping, house cleaning, cooking, read-aloud sessions, theater, and more. We can model diplomacy and kindness. We can demonstrate self-teaching whenever we tackle a new subject of interest. This will assist our children far more than any amount of prescribed curriculum will.

Homeschooling is a process, not a school curriculum. Our children experience the real world and not the fake world of schooling. We have the unique opportunity to allow our children to learn how to learn. Since we aren't hindered by curriculum guidelines and timed schedules, we don't need to impose a rigid lock-step methodology on them. Instead, they can learn on a need-to-know basis, which is a reflection of how we, as adults, realistically learn.

One example is basic math. I've met hundreds of children whose primary school years were filled with activities like building, shopping, going to the post office, and counting the money they made while doing real work instead of sitting down daily working in basic math textbooks. By the age of twelve, these children could perform the required mathematical functions on paper easily and accurately. When they needed, or desired, to learn algebra, they had the tools to teach themselves the subjects.

My children have acquired a knowledge of many subjects of which I haven't got a clue. They aren't limited to my knowledge base or that of an imposed school curriculum (thank goodness for this). I've also met children who "filled in their gaps" of knowledge by attending adult education or college classes. Whatever they didn't learn at home, they quickly figured out while attending adult-level courses.

You can easily bypass the elementary, junior high, and high school–level textbooks if you go to a university bookstore and look for their self-teaching manuals, which are situated right beside the school-type books. These were designed to help adults survive and understand classroom-oriented materials. Usually, these books offer far more realistic explanations than school texts.

Homeschooling parents are so diverse that children are bound to come in contact with the practitioners of various arts and disciplines. Many are more than willing to apprentice interested children in their field of expertise. This is great because instead of schoolteachers, a child gets to learn alongside mathematicians, computer programmers, artists, writers, or a host of other practitioners in fields of interest to all.

REBECCA RUPP Everybody, sooner or later, hits a tough subject or two. Randy, my husband, and I, are both scientists, and we took algebra and chemistry in stride. Our sticking points in the course of our children's education were music, Latin, and Japanese. We coped by finding music teachers, a friendly language tutor, and a set of self-explanatory programmed texts.

In my experience, however, the "tough" subjects don't necessarily arrive in tidy blocks (LATIN) with tidy solutions (TUTOR), but surface every ten minutes throughout every homeschooling day. No matter how knowledgeable and well-educated parents are, children—with their absolutely endless curiosity—are impossible to keep up with. "How does a television work?" "What's inside a battery?" "I just read a book that says cows have four stomachs. Why? Do they all work the same? Are they all the same size?"

"I don't know," you say, dropping your dish towel, hoe, or fountain pen. "Let's go look it up."

In that sense, the tough subjects have always been my favorites. It's that experience of looking it up—of mutual discovery, of learning together—that makes homeschooling so special. A good education, to my mind, is not simply information acquisition; it's an active process of exploration, of learning how to learn.

When it comes to learning, kids are astonishingly well equipped to teach themselves. Looking back over our homeschooling years, I realize how much our children know that neither of us ever taught them: computer skills, philosophy, classical music, origami, and rocketry—to say nothing of the afore-

> **The tough subjects have always been my favorites. It's that experience of looking it up—of mutual discovery, of learning together—that makes homeschooling so special.**

mentioned Latin and Japanese. All our children have immense subsets of knowledge that we, their parents, don't share; and in many cases their "tough subjects" haven't been the same as ours.

That, in fact, may be the answer to the whole thorny question.

Kids don't know there are any tough subjects.

Don't tell them.

57
Will my child get a high school diploma?

LUZ SHOSIE If he or she feels the need to have it, yes. There are many ways to go about it. One way you may not have thought about is to hire a calligrapher to make one (or learn calligraphy and make it yourself).

CAFI COHEN There are several ways that your child can get a high school diploma.

• Grant your own! Easiest, cheapest option here. The family, acting as a small private school, grants a diploma. Just check with your local print shop or stationary store and ask for a blank diploma form. Several large mail-order homeschooling catalogs also stock. Alternatively, you can design and print one on your computer. Fill out the form when your child has satisfied your requirements for high school graduation, sign it as the principal, date it. Voila! Your child has a diploma.

Will this work? Is this official? Interestingly, "official" has no official meaning—other than the school is saying, "We issued this document." You, as a small private school, can do the same thing. Put a seal on it and call it official if you want. It will work. Whenever your child is asked if he has a high school diploma, he should check the "yes" box.

Cafi Cohen

- Hundreds of local umbrella schools (private schools that help homeschoolers homeschool) and dozens of national independent study institutions (for example, Clonlara, American School) award high school diplomas to homeschoolers. Some of these programs are accredited, some not. What that means is that some have sought and received the approval of an accrediting agency like the North Central Association of Schools and Colleges. When shop-

ping for an independent study school, do not be overly concerned about accreditation. After all, most colleges—being much more interested in transcripts and portfolios and test scores—do not require diplomas or transcripts from accredited institutions. Look first for a program that fits your child and your family.

- In a few states, your child can earn a state-approved high school diploma by satisfying certain requirements (for example, Pennsylvania) or by completing a public school independent study program (for example, California). This is still not an option in most places. Contact your statewide homeschooling organizations for more information.

- Finally, in all states, homeschoolers may take a GED, Tests for General Educational Development, or a state-approved equivalent (California High School Proficiency Examination in California, for example). Age eligibility for the test and passing scores are established by individual states. Passing the test is equivalent to a high school diploma. The GED is considered substandard by some, most notably the military, which restricts the number of GED holders they will enlist. Nevertheless, many homeschooled students have successfully used the GED for college admissions; and, despite the restrictions, some homeschooled teenagers have enlisted in the military with a GED. Your local libraries and community colleges should be able to direct you to a source for GED testing.

DEB SHELL When we began homeschooling in Washington state, and a few years later in Vermont, we declared ourselves a private school. The private school laws at that time were inclusive of families who unschooled, and that's the niche we found ourselves most able to relate to. Even when the Vermont law changed in 1987 and unschooling families such as ourselves were excluded, we identified ourselves as a private school: The Four Seasons Center for Natural Learning. So regardless of whether we complied or not with external regulations, we maintained our homeschool name and sense of identity throughout the years. As our children grew, they inquired about the legalities of homeschooling and our place in it. What about being able to "graduate" and get a job or go to college? We explored these questions and what evolved was the development of an unschooler's high school plan of study.

This can be a very confusing concept since, as I said earlier, we didn't use a curriculum. We approached this issue of a high school diploma as follows: First we found out what general requirements were expected of public high school graduates. Then we began to break-down areas of study into learning components (see Question 42 on record keeping). I had already done this in a college class titled "The Assessment of Prior Learning," intended to help degree-seeking adults attain college credit for life experience. This made a lot of sense to me, especially since the concept supported this unschooler's approach to learning; I could get college credit for having learned experientially, over the course of my adult life, things that could also have been learned through structured college classroom experience. Incidentally, I was granted enough life-experience credit to shave off an entire year of college study, which enabled me to quickly earn my BA and go on to graduate school.

> **A**s our children grew, they inquired about the legalities of homeschooling and our place in it. What about being able to "graduate" and get a job or go to college? We explored these questions and what evolved was the development of an unschooler's high school plan of study.

So, if this worked for adults, it surely would work for homeschoolers. After a lot of inquiry and study about how to interpret time spent on an area of study, including writing, projects or "labs," and reading, in terms of what would actually constitute a course, we felt confident designing courses around areas of interest that included work already done. What we did was translate experiential learning into titled coursework and attached credits to them. We used resource material from Clonlara, the homeschooling catalogs (especially Genius Tribe, *Growing Without Schooling,* and *Home Education Magazine*), Judy Gelner's book, *College Admissions: A Guide for Homeschoolers,* and my college course guides. In 1995, I began working for Burlington College, where I developed a resource center for homeschoolers, my main job being consultant to high school–aged homeschoolers who wanted help writing their transcripts. I began investigating college entry requirements and was able to tailor an unschooler's transcript to fit college requirements. This process could also reveal deficits or voids that, if desired, could then be remedied by studying what was necessary to comply. At that point, the motivation to study is high and the work is typically accomplished in short order through home study,

community college classes, or private tutor.

From the point of view that a high school diploma constitutes a minimum course of study equivalent to a certain number of credits, we granted our daughters diplomas issued from their own homeschool: The Four Seasons Center for Natural Learning. So far this has happened between the ages of fifteen and seventeen. They also had a very detailed transcript, which they could use to get into college, for jobs, or anything else anyone finds useful about a high school diploma. This type of homemade homeschool diploma has been acceptable to many colleges, including the Boston Conservatory, Hampshire College, New York University, University of Massachusetts, Amherst, and Johnson State College.

Since colleges are becoming more interested in having homeschoolers apply (they make such motivated students of impeccable character!), a general overview of high school–age work may be all that's necessary, along with any other specific requirements such as the SAT or GED. Letters of reference flesh out specified areas of interest, as do in-person interviews and essays. For those who desire a diploma and transcript from an outside source and have the resources to do so, Clonlara or Oak Meadow may be excellent alternatives.

58

Will my child ever be able to get into college if we homeschool, or receive financial aid or scholarships for college?

SUSANNAH SHEFFER A homeschooler who is now at Williams College told *Growing Without Schooling* magazine, "None of the colleges that I was interested in had any difficulty with my homeschooling background and none required me to have a high school diploma or take the GED." Homeschoolers have been admitted to Ivy League schools, small liberal arts colleges, state universities, conservatories, and community colleges, and are engaged in all sorts of work, so homeschooling is clearly not a liability. Stanford University, for example, has this to say in the letter it routinely sends to homeschooled applicants who inquire: "[Homeschooled] students are no longer unusual for us, and several are usually admitted and enroll at Stanford each year . . . We are scrupulously fair in evaluating these applicants, and they are not at any disadvantage in the admissions process."

Colleges are primarily interested in what students have been doing and learning during their high school years, and homeschoolers convey this through transcripts they create or through a portfolio of work. Another option is to enroll with a homeschool program that provides a diploma after students have completed high school credits. The main thing to remember is that many colleges are more interested in seeing the best evidence you can provide of your readiness to do college work than they are in having that evidence fit a particular format. Homeschoolers generally try to convey two things in their applications: (1) Although we've done things in a nontraditional way, this student is indeed prepared for an intense and fairly traditional academic experience; and (2) Because we've done things differently, this student stands out in some particular ways and has had a chance to develop in some particular ways. Homeschoolers also fulfill the other parts of the admissions process—writing essays, describing their activities and achievements, getting recommendations

> **As the homeschooling population grows older, we're able to see increasing evidence not only that these students can get *into* college, but that they can have an unusual and refreshing take on the experience once they're there.**

(which they typically get from adult mentors or employers), and taking the SAT or ACT if the college requires it. Colleges have so far been impressed with the self-motivation homeschoolers demonstrate and the interesting activities that lead to scholarship opportunities, as was the case with a student whose many volunteer and service activities throughout her homeschooling years led to her receiving the Community Service Achievement Award, a scholarship that her college gives to a few incoming students each year.

As the homeschooling population grows older, we're able to see increasing evidence not only that these students can get *into* college, but that they can have an unusual and refreshing take on the experience once they're there. One lifelong homeschooler, for example, said she was the only one of her friends who chose the courses she wanted to take, as opposed to writing down what her advisor told her to take. Interesting self-motivated students aren't just good admissions candidates; they're also valuable members of a college community.

WILL SHAW Ours have. Home education was no handicap whatsoever as our two oldest kids applied for admission to college and for financial aid.

Most college admissions applications ask the same basic questions, and some are kind of funny, such as class ranking. Unless you are enrolled in a correspondence school that keeps records and prepares transcripts for you, you'll have to make your own transcript, a fun project.

It helps to keep basic records so you can remember just when it was that you did that special one-semester course in whatever. As they hold weight for all college applicants, your homeschooled child will need to take the same admissions tests ("college boards") as other children (PSATs, SATs, and so on). You don't have to be a student in a conventional school to take these, and there are ready sources for them.

Many community colleges don't require college boards, or they administer their own tests to applicants.

Admission to college can seem fairly competitive, especially if you are intent on going to a particular college or if your child is not exactly an Albert Einstein. But I don't know of any public or private college or university that refuses admission to homeschoolers. Still, there may exist some prejudice here and there. As a representative of homeschool interests, a couple of years ago I participated in a panel discussion at a convention of college admissions officers. The subject was what to do about homeschoolers.

WEB SITES TO HELP IN PREPARATION FOR COLLEGE

The following sites were selected and reviewed by the staff of Excite for the Personal Technology section of the Sunday *Seattle Times*, February 1, 1998:

Financial Aid Information—http://www.finaid.org

Sallie Mae: Helping Make Education Possible—http://www.salliemae. com/home/index_e.html

KapLoan: Student Loan Information Program—http://www.kaploan.com

Texas Guaranteed Student Loan Corporation—http://www.tgslc.org

College Edge—http://www.CollegeEdge.com

Scholarship Search—http://www.collegeboard.org/fundfinder/ bin/fundfind01.pl

Kaplan's Amazing College Simulator—http://www.kaplan.com/precoll/ simcoll

Your Best College Buys Now—http://www.pathfinder.com/money/ colleges98

GoCollege—http://www.gocollege.com

College Board Online—http://www.collegeboard.org

Mapping Your Future—http://www.mapping-your-future.org

WebWare for the SAT Skill Lessons—http://www.testprep.com/ satmenu.html

Main Quad—http://www.mainquad.com

One admissions officer from a stuck-up university sniffed, "They always put down that they're top in their high school graduating class." Well, the application forms ask for it, so we honestly answer!

You're on at least a level playing field regarding SAT scores and the like. And your child should have advantages on some of the other qualifications that colleges like to see, such as participation in extracurricular activities and community services. Home education offers so much greater schedule flexibility and opportunities for these. So unless you have been an especially unimaginative and unambitious homeschool parent, your child should have a fine application for admission.

Paying for college is a concern for all parents, not just homeschoolers. Home-schoolers have access to financial aid, as others do. Most financial aid is need-based, with minimal connection to academic record. Of course, once your child is in college, he could be disqualified from more aid if he does poorly in his studies. There are many kinds of scholarships, loans, and grants, and the college admissions offices appear to assist their applicants equally and well. Home-schoolers can and do compete for those various merit-based and need-based moneys. There are books full of scholarship opportunities. At the time of college application, and even well before then, homeschoolers can fairly compete for financial aid.

59

What happens when my child graduates, doesn't have a diploma, and wants to get a job?

CINDY WADE I feel very strongly that diplomas are overrated. I have a bachelor's degree and don't have a job. I worked in professional theater, where performers with their master's degrees worked for $50 a week plus room and were thankful for the job. There is a world of difference between having an income and having a job.

Having a "job" conjures up all kinds of images for me, including sweat factories, assembly lines, and flipping burgers. To me, having an income means freedom, independence, choices, and self-employment. It's what so many adults long for. The number of home offices and home-based businesses is growing each year at a tremendous rate. Computers, fax machines, modems, and overnight mail service have allowed many working parents to stay in the comfort of their homes and still earn a living. The side benefit to this arrangement is the added time they can spend with their children and spouses.

Our goal for our children is to raise healthy, happy, self-sufficient, intelligent individuals. The only requirement we expect from them is that they own and operate their own businesses by the time they are sixteen years old. Our eleven-year-old daughter is already saving for her first car, which will assist with her business. Other than that we don't concern ourselves with acquiring certificates, diplomas, or degrees. If our children decide for themselves later on they want to pursue a degree, then we'll assist them with that pursuit. Until then, we'll continue to prepare them for one of the greatest and most demanding jobs they'll ever have—parenthood.

KATHARINE HOUK In working with many homeschooling families, I've found that their teens are almost never asked to produce a high school diploma in order to get a job. In the event an application asks, "Do you have a high school diploma?" a young person could honestly answer that yes, she or he has successfully completed high school–level work. Some families have a name for their home-schooling endeavor (Smith Family Academy or Pine Ridge Homeschool), and in some states it may be legal for the parent "principal" to award a diploma. Homeschoolers also have the option of registering with independent study programs that do give diplomas upon graduation, such as Clonlara in Michigan or Cambridge Academy in Florida.

A third diploma option is the GED. Our daughter took the GED test to obtain her general equivalency diploma when a college became stubborn about awarding her credit for courses she had taken (most colleges are not this fussy about diplomas). The test was not difficult, and there are published guides to help people prepare for it. In some states a child must be a certain age before being allowed to take the GED, but it may be possible to obtain an age waiver. Still the chances are, contrary to popular belief, your child won't need to produce a high school diploma.

In reality, most homeschoolers have held down part-time jobs—paid and/or volunteer—all through their high school years, which are a contribution to the community and enhance their learning. Such endeavors are valuable not only in developing work experience, commitment to the community, and skills in getting along with others; they also look great on job applications, and the relationships developed with employers and supervisors often provide marvelous references and good leads to other jobs. A young person's intelligence and skills, willingness and ability to learn, strong work ethic, and respectful attitude toward others are the things that are valued more than a diploma by prospective employers.

JEAN REED A diploma from a high school or college is just a piece of paper. Colleges and employers all know that having that "paper" doesn't necessarily mean the owner knows anything. That's why we keep reading about how the educational system is failing. More than ever before, it's how skilled you are and how you present yourself that counts.

All four of our children are grown and have been independent for a number of years. I've asked them all if they ever had trouble getting into college or getting a job because they were homeschooled. I got back a unanimous "no." Three out of four of them have attended college for a while. They had no admissions problems. One did have to take admissions testing, but scored well enough so they didn't ask any questions about Brook Farm School. She now teaches software design at one of Boston's top colleges.

When filling out job applications that asked specifically where they went to high school, they wrote in the name of our school. No one has ever questioned this enough to contact us. During interviews, the children have found their homeschooling advantageous. Not that many people entering the job market are homeschooled, and there is a lot of curiosity. Cathy says it's an advantage because you definitely stand out from the crowd. She says sometimes the interview has turned out to be more about homeschooling than her skills and she has had to work to keep the interviewer on track.

Why shouldn't your child have a diploma when he graduates from your school? You've done all the work of being a "school," educating your child. Why not make your own diploma? We did. You can buy them from most office supply stores. Can't find one? I can make one for you.

We created our own graduation ceremony, used the community hall, and invited neighbors and friends. We had music, speeches from our other children, a baccalaureate address by the minister, and Donn created a class history, class prophecy, and yearbook. Cathy wrote and read her Last Will and Testament. We presented awards to our other children and gave the graduate a diploma. The local newspaper came and took pictures and wrote a very nice article.

I've watched our children move around the country and work at different jobs. None of them has had a problem because she or he lacked a public school diploma. Sometimes they didn't get the job they wanted because there were others more qualified. Sometimes they wanted the job so badly, and had so much confidence in themselves, that they bluffed their way into the job and just learned what was needed before anyone found out. Homeschooling has been to their advantage in many ways.

> **W**hen filling out job applications that asked specifically where they went to high school, they wrote in the name of our school. No one has ever questioned this enough to contact us.

They have a great deal of confidence in themselves. When they have wanted to change the direction of their lives they know where to look for new information and learn what they need to know; sometimes by returning to formal education and sometimes learning on their own.

Diplomas are pretty pieces of paper, and occasionally useful. P. J. O'Rourke says, "Politicians are interested in people. Not that this is always a virtue. Fleas are interested in dogs."

60

Should my child go to community college while still high school aged?

CAFI COHEN One of our homeschoolers took community college classes, the other did not. Certainly, for either child, I had no worries about the material being too challenging. When our oldest requested enrollment in the classes, he was first asked to take math and language arts placement tests. At the math testing, the proctor told the thirty-plus people taking the test that they could opt for either a general math (arithmetic) or basic algebra test. When he asked how many people wanted the basic algebra test, my son was the only one to raise his hand.

After our son had taken a couple of community college courses, we estimated that the level of challenge, at least for the introductory classes, was roughly the same as that at the local high school. When you look at it this way, it almost seems silly not to accumulate some college credit when the kids are teenagers. Indeed, it would have been fairly easy to earn an associate's degree by age seventeen by taking two or three classes year-round beginning at age fourteen or fifteen.

Certainly, there are benefits to taking even a few courses. Your teenager can study subjects like foreign language and laboratory science that might be too difficult to tackle independently. He will accumulate college credit in a relatively inexpensive way, even if you have to pay for it (in some cases, you will not have to pay for it as you will be able to take advantage of agreements that the colleges have with local high schools).

The eventual transcript that the college generates will serve as independent, outside verification that your homeschooler can handle formal academics at the college level. Our son's admission to the Air Force Academy and other selective schools, plus full-ride scholarship offers, probably would not have happened without this demonstrated ability to handle college-level work—especially since he did not have sky-high SAT scores. This is not to imply that you need junior college classes to qualify for admission to good colleges, only that taking such courses may be a relatively painless way to convince an uncertain admissions officer at a selective school that your child deserves a second look.

On the other hand, if your teenager displays no interest in taking classes, or if he or she has no reason to pursue formal academics, I cannot see any benefit to taking college courses as a teenager. I have known many homeschoolers—working at everything from cartooning to emergency medicine to writing—who were better off spending their time on those activities. These teens had excellent community support and mentors for these activities; college courses would have slowed them down.

Another caution: Not everything your homeschooler takes at a given community college will be accepted for credit at a four-year college or university. If this concerns you, do check on transferability with the four-year colleges where your son or daughter will be applying.

DEB SHELL Our teens have found the local com-munity college to be an excellent resource. Since our family approached homeschool from the unschooling perspective, when the girls became focused on areas of study that suggested outside-the-home learning, our community college became an option from which they could pick and choose specific classes.

These classes may not have been the entire way (or necessarily the best way) that an area of inquiry was explored—but oftentimes community college classes served either as a jumping-off point for more serious study, or, simply as a way of getting a taste of something that intrigued them. While they were satisfying the need to further explore interests, they were also doing double duty by earning high school transcript credit (in terms of Carnegie Units, that is, the number of credits used to calculate high school graduation requirements, one semester of community college work is equal to an entire year of high school) as well as college credit, which we've found to be fully transferable to the four-year colleges our girls applied to. Also a bonus to our family, Vermont financial aid will pay for graduated student's classes.

> **W**hen the girls became focused on areas of study that suggested outside-the-home learning, our community college became an option from which they could pick and choose specific classes.

Most of the time people we mention this to assume community college is also good preparation for "real" college. While our experience with community college classes has been positive, with such qualities as excellent teacher-student ratios, well-prepared syllabi, interesting formats, and up-to-date resources being the norm, these classes also rival the quality offered in many large four-year schools, where tenured staff and overcrowding may bring quality down.

To date, our eldest daughter has taken four community college classes and discovered that they were also good preparation for *not* going to college! She discovered that limitations placed on her by the very nature of structured classroom study were not helpful or appropriate to her way of learning about something. She earned high grades, so having been unschooled wasn't a factor in terms of her having to learn how to study or whatever else the fear is regarding people who haven't been coerced into following a curriculum. She could and did easily apply herself to accomplish this—the real issue remained: For her, was this the best way to explore an area of interest and to develop skills? Instead of spending a great deal of time and money just going the college route, community college offered her a chance to realize why college wasn't the way she wanted to further her education.

61

How can my child find an apprenticeship opportunity?

HELEN AND MARK HEGENER Finding opportunities beyond the home starts in the home. If your child is interested in an apprenticeship or mentorship, first determine whether or not you have friends or acquaintances who work in the child's field of interest. If so, ask these friends or acquaintances about possible situations where your child would have an opportunity to learn more. If you cannot find someone already involved with the area of interest, try asking around. Chances are someone you know will know someone who's involved with the subject. Personal recommendations are often the quickest way to locate potential apprenticeship or mentor situations, and often the easiest for a child to follow up on. In most cases, finding help is a simple matter of locating an adult who can relate to the child's interest in or love for the subject. Recalling their own early experiences, they can be the best source of advice on how to proceed.

Volunteering can be an excellent way to learn more about an area of interest, and to meet new friends who can advise a child on becoming more involved. Many volunteer positions have led to further training and even to careers in the chosen field. Sometimes public libraries will keep lists of volunteer positions available in a community. Or, again, just ask around. There are also many books on volunteer opportunities; check your local library or bookstore.

Mentor and apprenticeship situations were commonplace before schooling became the accepted standard, but in these times it might be a foreign idea to the person your child will be talking with. When approaching a potential apprenticeship or mentor situation, it could be helpful for the child to bring along a portfolio of work he's done that relates to the field, whether it's informal essays on the topic, photographs he's taken, or perhaps a model he's constructed. A listing of books read, related computer programs used, Web sites he's familiar with, and so forth will show a grounding in the subject and a knowledge that could make all the difference to a prospective contact. If the child has experience in the field of interest already, try to obtain personal reference letters from people he's worked with.

> Mentor and apprenticeship situations were commonplace before schooling became the accepted standard, but in these times it might be a foreign idea to the person your child will be talking with.

If your child is interested in travel, there are many options—from short trips to visit friends and relatives to extended voyages of exploration in far-off lands. As we write this, our seventeen year-old daughter Jody is traveling alone in Washington state. She flew from Anchorage, Alaska, to Seattle, then took a multistage trip of several hundred miles, all arranged on her own. She wanted to visit friends and go snowboarding in Canada with them, so she worked out the details to make it happen and we trusted her ability to plan well and to be prepared for unexpected turns. Know your child's abilities and limitations, and be willing to help when needed and to stay out of the way when that's what's needed.

If you're not comfortable letting your youngster travel alone, and are not able to travel with him, perhaps a friend or relative will be taking a trip and would welcome the company. Check out student travel programs. They usually welcome homeschoolers, and some are planned specifically for homeschooled children.

The Kasemans felt much more comfortable giving their answer directly to teens and those searching for apprenticeships rather than to the parents.

SUSAN AND LARRY KASEMAN One way to begin is by thinking about your interests and what you like to do. A book like Richard Nelson Bolles's *What Color Is Your Parachute?* may help you identify areas you might want to explore.

You may decide you're interested in a formal, recognized apprenticeship run through the state department of labor or its equivalent in an area like plumbing. You can request information and apply, explaining how your homeschooling experiences qualify you for the apprenticeship. Or you may be interested in an informal apprenticeship in an area where apprenticeships are less common, rare, or even unheard of. In that case the following suggestions may help.

Think about what you are willing to do in exchange for the learning experience. Are you willing to wash test tubes in order to see what goes on in a working science lab? Build sets and manage props to get firsthand theater experience? Do data entry and other general office work to see how a legislator's office functions? Potential providers of apprenticeships are more likely to be receptive if you begin by explaining how they would benefit from having you as an apprentice.

Explore resources and opportunities available in your local community. Talk with people you know about their work, what they know about the community, and whether they know anyone who works in the areas you're interested in. Run an ad in your local paper, asking for help or volunteering your services. Don't hesitate to ask anyone who is doing something you would like to participate in. Many people who have not thought about working with an apprentice become interested in the possibility when someone proposes the idea.

To find an apprenticeship outside your local community, a book like *Internships*, published each year by Peterson's Guides, may be helpful. This book lists thousands of apprenticeships and internships available throughout the country. The book may give the impression that it is primarily for people who have completed at least two years of college, but homeschoolers who have not attended college have used it successfully. Some homeschoolers have found that it worked well to do an internship or apprenticeship that was readily available even though it was not in their area of primary interest, either so they could spend time in a different part of the country or could gain experience in a different area of work.

A contract that you write and both parties sign helps assure that both of you agree about ideas and expectations for the apprenticeship. It also helps ensure that you will not be stuck only doing routine work that no one else wants to do. When you have completed the apprenticeship, ask the person with whom you have been working for a written letter of recommendation, addressed "To Whom It May Concern," that you can include in your credentials and use when you are applying for future apprenticeships or employment.

SUSAN EVANS An apprenticeship is an age-old process to help children have the opportunity to learn the skills they will need as adults to make tangible contributions to their communities. It is an efficient, practical way to develop the means to feed, clothe, and house themselves and their families.

Families who have spent the younger childhood years with hands-on, learner-led education find that older children and teens move rather undramatically into situations we've labeled "apprenticeships." That is, they spend concentrated amounts of time with one or several adults learning about a specific body of knowledge.

For instance, a young person who loves animals and has spent several years caring for pets and making posters for 4-H fairs (or simply for hanging on a wall at home) would quite logically volunteer to help out at a vet's office or the local Humane Society. Within a short time, this capable teen would probably be invited to assist during simple (or not-so-simple) surgeries or be left in charge of the care and feeding of the animals over a holiday weekend.

I know one young man who took stained glass and lapidary (forming and polishing rocks and stones) classes as a lark. When his manual dexterity and visual skill at assessing workmanship was noticed by some senior members of the lapidary club, he was invited to work one-on-one with a skilled faceter and gold caster. He worked on new techniques and entered some local competitions, winning several blue ribbons. When his enthusiasm waned, he went on to some other interests. But he maintained several close friendships, valuable life lessons, and some exceptional skills, which will be available to him in the future if he decides to get involved in lapidary work again.

Several companies in our local geographical area offer more formal apprenticeship programs in pipe fitting, tool and die making, and other skilled trades. Most of these programs coordinate efforts with local community colleges to also confer associate's degrees upon successful completion of the training. All this while making a decent wage during forty-hour work weeks.

What interests does your child have which are shared by other people in your family or local community? Are there clubs or businesses in your surrounding area where your child could visit (alone or with you) to learn more about the skills or processes which intrigue him or her?

A field trip can provide an opportunity to ask lots of questions before approaching a possible mentor. Doing a short research project can be a perfect excuse to shadow someone for an afternoon, a month, or a year.

Apprenticeships can be formal arrangements, tied in with college credit programs, or they can be casual, informal relationships that a young person wanders into and out of as his passions lead him on the way to productive adulthood.

Like so many aspects of homeschooling, the spark of interest, the process of finding out about the world, is much more important than a finished product, a certificate, or becoming a master craftsman. In many cases, the human bonds may be many times more valuable than the original sought after skills or knowledge.

CHAPTER NINE

Kids Say the Darnedest Things— About Homeschooling

WHEN YOU HEAR GOOD things about homeschooling, it's always from the parents, complained a letter written to Dear Abby late in 1997. I have to agree with the letter writer, but I wonder if she ever thought about why this is so.

While a few homeschooling parents were themselves homeschooled (contributor Helen Hegener among them), most of us attended public school, and many spent time teaching in them. This makes it quite easy to see the difference between the two approaches to education. Mostly, our best clues come from our children. There's that gleam in their eyes as they realize they have painlessly learned how to read. There are those questions that know no end and grow ever more challenging. There's that way they jump out of bed in the morning knowing exactly what they want to do, and set about doing it, free from worry about tests, the school bus bully, or being bored. As parents, we know they are approaching learning from a different place than we did, a place we can only wish we had had the chance to experience.

Seeing the difference, it's easy to get excited about what we do. We'd like other parents to know they have an option—a true choice—and that homeschooling isn't as difficult as they probably think it is. We live with proof positive of a very basic difference between the two approaches every day, and it's wonderful to share it.

On the other hand, many of our children are not making educational comparisons. Their gleaming eyes, never-ending questions, and morning enthusiasm are, in their experience, as much an expected part of the day as the sunrise. *Homeschooling is the way they live.* They're no more compelled to shout about homeschooling than they are about eating breakfast in the morning.

Many of our children are not making educational comparisons. Their gleaming eyes, never-ending questions, and morning enthusiasm are, in their experience, as much an expected part of the day as the sunrise. *Homeschooling is the way they live.*

That is, unless asked. In response to her reader's comment, Dear Abby put out a call for homeschooled children to share their own feelings about homeschooling, and they did so with articulate letters that spoke about homeschooling in very general terms. So I wondered. If they were asked, would homeschooled children answer far more specific questions for *The Homeschooling Book of Answers*?

The answer was a resounding *yes!* and their contributions are a valuable addition to this book. We are fortunate enough to glimpse homeschooling "from the other side of the fence." As the soon-to-be writers volunteered, I found out a little about their background—age, number of years homeschooling, interests and hobbies, current activities—so that answers would reflect each unique experience. As their answers came in, I was struck by several elements:

- No one asked for a "different" question.
- The essays required very little or, in most cases, no editing.
- The writing is straightforward, open, and powerfully honest.
- Most thanked me for the opportunity to share their thoughts and feelings.

Our glimpse comes from a wide age range, from the eight- and eleven-year-old Dodd brothers to preteens TJ Jones and Annaquista Pykosz; from young teens Theresa Hyland and Adam Dobson to mid-teens Megan Kaseman and Lindsey Johnson; from "finished-with-high-school" teens Michael Hohensee, Sara Shell, and Adam Grimm to Mae Shell, the "old lady" of the group in her early twenties. Don't miss their biographies; they're very interesting people.

I'm happy Dear Abby printed a few of the letters she received. But I'm happier still that our writers will take us beyond the cursory treatment of homeschooling so often found in the short, generic mass-media portrayals, and share more meaningful thoughts on what they're discovering through homeschooling as the way they live.

62

On a day when you are doing things you like to do, what is it that you're doing and why do you like it?

KIRBY DODD I like going to my friends' houses because they're fun to play with. *[Mom's note: we know several homeschooling families, and visits don't have to wait for weekends or vacations.]*

Board games and Nintendo are fun, because it's fun thinking fast.

Kirby and Marty Dodd

I like watching videos, and movies at theaters. I like the entertainment and the stories. I enjoy voices, accents, special effects, costumes, music, and things like that in the movies.

MARTY DODD I like to play with Legos. "Why?" Now that's a harder question. Because it's fun. No, no, no. Not because it's fun. Because I like to. No, because I have them.

I build with Legos. And if I don't like the thing I built, I put it back to how it used to be. While I'm playing with Legos I make the Lego men talk. I make the guys pick up the things and go. I make them pick up the

pieces and put them into place. I like Aquazones.

I also like to play with Darda cars. I play with them because you can build any track you want.

I like to listen to tapes of Weird Al while I build things.

63

Who are the most important people in your life? Why? What do you consider the most important things you do? Why?

ANNAQUISTA PYKOSZ The most important people in my life are my mother, father, and my younger brother. Also, my great-grandmother, whom I call "Babcia" (that's grandmother in Polish). I think my mother and father are the most important people because they are the people who brought me into this world. Zeb, my brother, is important just because he is my little brother and I love him. Babcia is important to me in a way that is hard to describe. Babcia is just very special to me. When I go to visit her she makes me feel welcome and important.

I think spending time with my family is one of the most important things I do. I also think that helping my mom at the flea

> **I** enjoy voices, accents, special effects, costumes, music, and things like that in the movies.

markets we go to is important because I enjoy that kind of work. Reading and using the computer are important parts of my life also. Reading and using the computer are very enjoyable and relaxing for me.

Spending time with my family is very important. You can never spend too much time with your family because you never know how long you'll have them. So always spend plenty of time with your family.

> I think spending time with my family is one of the most important things I do.

64

What are some of the favorite books you've read over the years, and why are they your favorites?

TJ JONES Some of my most favorite books were written by Roald Dahl. I especially liked *The BFG, James and the Giant Peach,* and *Danny the Champion of the World.* Roald Dahl is a great storyteller. You can't really predict where he is going to go with a story. His books are completely unique.

As I've gotten older, I've enjoyed biographies and historical novels. I especially enjoy Landmark books. They have books such as *America's First World War, Remember the Alamo,* and *The Winter at Valley Forge.* I liked how the books told

about the actual events while also weaving interesting stories about people throughout the pages. For instance, in *America's First World War,* the author told about how if you were in school at the time of the war, you'd have had to knit socks for soldiers.

Other historical books I've really enjoyed are The Childhood of Famous Americans series. For one thing, they're very easy and fun to read. They go into the child's life and tell what it was like to live back in the days the particular individual lived. My favorite ones so far were Daniel Boone and Davy Crockett. When I read those books, I liked to imagine myself in the story. I keep begging my mom for a shotgun based on the fact that boys like Davy Crockett and Daniel Boone got their first guns at my age. So far no luck, though!

Two books that my Dad and I both have liked around my age are *Johnny Tremain* by Esther Forbes (an all-time classic) and *The American Boys Handy Book.* My grandfather gave a copy of the *Handy Book* to my father on March 13, 1968. My dad signed it over to me on November 19, 1995. I've spent hours reading through it. It has great ideas and instructions for easy-to-make items, equipment, and generally interesting things. For example, I've made slingshots, blowguns, bird buoys, and traps. It also tells how to make camping equipment and other things for outdoor life, survival, and fun.

> **My grandfather gave a copy of the** *Handy Book* **to my father on March 13, 1968. My dad signed it over to me on November 19, 1995. I've spent hours reading through it.**

doesn't have an official "start" or "end" date. You can keep going no matter when it is. You have plenty of "free time," which you can use to expand your interests. And you can interact with people of a much wider age range than you can at school.

65

You've been homeschooling for three years after attending a parochial school. What are the major differences in these two learning experiences? Could you share a couple of your favorite activities since you started homeschooling?

THERESA HYLAND After homeschooling for three years, it's easy to see the differences between the two learning experiences.

"Classes" are much smaller when you homeschool and you can learn at your own pace. If you want (or need) to spend more time on certain subjects, you can. There's no time limit. Taking field trips, visiting museums, and talking to experts are ways to learn more, and you can do these things more often in homeschooling than in parochial school. Additionally, learning

Theresa Hyland

Parochial schooling restricts the amount of time you spend on a subject. The classes are much larger. You don't take as many field trips. You also don't get to socialize as much.

Two of my favorite activities since I started homeschooling are the field trips and meeting other homeschoolers. Two of my favorite field trips were to the 1812 Homestead and Gettysburg. At the 1812 Homestead I saw what a typical day in 1812 might have been like. At Gettysburg I saw the hallowed ground of the battlefields, which gives you a good idea of what those soldiers went through at the turning point of the Civil War.

Homeschooling gave me the opportunity to meet people from different countries. In one case they even spoke a foreign language. I might not have had that chance in parochial school. I was excited to meet homeschoolers from Japan. They brought some traditional

Japanese toys with them so we got to see how Japanese children play. The visit also spurred a wish to learn Japanese and origami, the traditional art of paper folding.

I have enjoyed my homeschooling experience thoroughly, and I will continue to homeschool for as long as I can.

I was excited to meet homeschoolers from Japan. They brought some traditional Japanese toys with them so we got to see how Japanese children play. The visit also spurred a wish to learn Japanese and origami, the traditional art of paper folding.

66

What do you see different about your life compared to the lives of friends who attend school that can be directly attributed to the homeschooling lifestyle?

ADAM DOBSON First and foremost, all the free time is an excellent advantage. Getting done hours before those who go to school gives me an opportunity to spend time doing things that really interest me. For instance, I've had a lot more time to practice my electric bass, practice basketball, surf the Net, and so on. I've had a lot of time to learn about computers, then teach it to my parents!

I also use some of my time in an apprenticeship at a local rock and gem shop. The owners, Kean and Kasey Riley, have taught me a lot, not only about rocks and minerals but about how a business works.

Some of the greatest minds of all time were homeschooled. Thomas Edison, Ben Franklin, Pearl S. Buck, C. S. Lewis, Charles Dickens, John Quincy Adams, William Henry Harrison, Abe Lincoln, James Madison, Franklin Delano Roosevelt, George Washington, and Woodrow Wilson were all homeschooled, just to name a few!

I also use some of my time in an apprenticeship at a local rock and gem shop. The owners, Kean and Kasey Riley, have taught me a lot, not only about rocks

Adam Dobson

and minerals but about how a business works. (The Twin Crystal Rock Shop on Broadway in Saranac Lake, New York—now that's advertising!) Both of my older siblings' former apprenticeships have led to jobs for them.

Also it's been great to choose my own curriculum. I can take a more advanced math course instead of wasting time learning things I already know. I'm not the greatest with history, so we might spend a little more time reading, watching videos, and talking about it.

There is definitely a big advantage in homeschooling.

67

Could you share with us the evolution of your work in Shakespearean theater?

MEGAN KASEMAN When I was seven, I saw "The Winter's Tale." That evening changed my life.

The play was performed by the Young Shakespeare Players (YSP), actors ages seven to eighteen who perform full-length Shakespeare plays. During the play, I became convinced I wanted to share the magic and perform myself. The next summer I badgered my parents to get information about YSP, and I joined.

Since the directors, Richard and Anne DiPrima, don't believe in auditions or presuming to decide who will make a "good" actor, everyone is welcomed heartily. I remember with enormous fondness the experienced actors who encouraged me in my first play. They are a

> **W**hen I was seven, I saw "The Winter's Tale." That evening changed my life.

big part of why I stuck with it; they helped me know I could do it. Now I love supporting younger actors. It is a perfect cycle with special relationships on all sides and an example of the benefits of mixed age groups.

Megan Kaseman

During nine summers with YSP, I've learned that what seems impossible (such as young people performing full-length Shakespeare plays after only seven weeks of rehearsal) is actually possible to do very well if there are people who love and believe in what they're doing and work hard at it.

From the beginning, Richard and Anne and the experienced actors shared their deep love of Shakespeare's language, making it totally unintimidating and allowing me to see for myself that it is fun and beautiful and, once you realize you can understand it, very, very cool. For example, Romeo responds to a joke from Mercutio by saying: "O single-soled jest, solely singular for the singleness."

At first this sounds like a meaningless tongue twister. That's understandable; we don't speak Elizabethan English; we need a little explanation.

"O single-soled jest" refers to the fact that a shoe with a single sole (instead of a stronger double sole) is weak, just as Mercutio's joke is weak. "Solely" means only, "singular" noticeable, and "single-ness" silliness or stupidity. So we have: A joke as weak as a poorly made shoe, only noticeable because it is so stupid. Pretty cool!

Most Shakespeare is easier to understand. (If you convince yourself you can't understand Shakespeare, it's a lot harder. But if you say, "Shakespeare was a person, too; what he wrote made sense to him. I can make it make sense to me," it will be easier.) In "The Winter's Tale" Leontes greets his guests: "Welcome hither / As is the spring to the earth." The meaning is clear: You are as welcome here as spring is after winter. Living in Wisconsin, I appreciate how welcome spring is.

A suggestion for parents who want to find activities kids will love: Share things you love with your kids, but don't pressure them to do things. They'll know if something's important for them. When that happens, listen to them. One interest branches into many.

Kids: Trust your instincts. If something sounds interesting, *do* it. Try different things. You never know when an evening will change your life.

68

You're just finishing a third semester at Tisch School of the Arts at New York University. How are you feeling about the future? What are your immediate plans? What are your hopes for your next ten years?

SARA SHELL I am a dance major, which means this semester I took ballet and modern dance, improvisation, acting, dance history, and music history. I handed in my term papers for the latter two courses last week, and this week I will take my exams. It is with mixed emotions that I complete my

Sara Shell

final assignments, because this may be my last semester at Tisch. I have learned a lot here and made some wonderful friends, but there are things I want to study which I am unable to here, namely environmental science, and for that reason I have applied as a transfer student to Smith College. If I am accepted, I will probably go there. It is very difficult to be in this limbo of uncertainty, having to say good-bye to my friends and teachers without knowing if I will see them again in January, but I find my comfort in the knowledge that whether I stay here or transfer, I will learn valuable things and have great experiences.

When I graduate, whether it is from NYU or Smith, I want to live in New York and try to dance professionally. If I am not successful here, I will try other cities, possibly in Europe. I also hope to have children eventually, and when the time comes for that I want to move to the country. Someday I want to get my master's degree in environmental science or ecology and have a second career in that field. All of these goals are important to me, but I don't expect them to happen exactly as I plan them. I know that people change—two years ago I never would have thought I'd leave a great dance school for a school with a less professional level of dancing and more academics. At that time, dancing was so strongly the center of my life that nothing else could come close to comparing.

One thing which I have always planned on having is a family. I wanted this even before I started dancing, and when I did, I knew that a dancer's career is short, leaving plenty of time later for children.

Her immediate plans: I took three courses at my local community college when I was fifteen. I was interested in expanding my educational process by learning in a group setting, and taking a U.S. history course with my older sister, Mae, seemed a good way to go about this. I also had a second agenda I was less eager to admit, which was that I wanted to prove to myself and the world that I measured up and was capable of college-level work. I learned a lot of history in that course, as well as how to write a formal essay and take an exam. The next semester I took psychology and environmental science, and had equally rewarding experiences. Most of the other students were at least ten years my senior, and I found their opinions fascinating and their company enjoyable.

My community college experience was really invaluable when it came to applying to four-year colleges. I am sure that having a few grades (grading was never a part of my homeschooling) and letters of recommendation from teachers were important factors in my acceptances from New York University, Hampshire College, and University of Massachusetts

> College is very different from homeschooling, and community college is a great way to ease the transition. For these reasons I recommend it most highly to any homeschooler planning to attend college full-time.

Amherst. Once at college, it was a help to know what to expect and what was expected from me in college-level work. The classroom skills that were easy to learn when I was taking one or two courses and living at home would have been much more difficult when I was not only taking a full course-load, but getting adjusted to a whole new life in an unfamiliar environment. College is very different from homeschooling, and community college is a great way to ease the transition. For these reasons I recommend it most highly to any homeschooler planning to attend college full-time.

Beyond all the practical concerns, however, I think community college is wonderful purely for its own sake. I learned a huge amount and treasure my memories of it. Speaking from my second year at NYU, considered a very good school, I know that the quality of teaching at the community college is high, in my experience achieving standards many NYU professors I know have difficulty reaching. Perhaps even more significant is the quality of students. The people in my community college courses were mostly thirty-plus, and had kids and jobs and mortgages. They were coming back to school to improve themselves and their positions in life, bringing determination, enthusiasm, and a richness of opinion that only life experience can give. They were out to get the most from each course, and because I shared that goal, I discovered I had more in common with them than I do with the NYU students who share my age and more privileged background but skim through their courses without interest or dedication.

Her hopes for the future: The woman I consider my mentor is Jae Diego, my modern dance teacher from the ages of thirteen to sixteen, and my friend. I met her at the age of twelve when my ballet class learned a piece of her choreography. I loved the dance and was eager to have the opportunity to take her class the next year. What she had to teach me was a dance technique that excited my body and mind even more than my beloved ballet, and her class quickly became the highlight of my week. I also found in Jae someone I greatly admired—she was the best dancer I had ever seen, as well as funny and smart and liked by everyone. A compliment from her meant more than five from another teacher. The next year I took her class three times a week and relished every second of it. We also found an arrangement that gave me a wonderful chance to get to know her better, as well as save my parents time. She would drive me to her house after class, where my dad would meet us to take me home, saving him half an hour of driving.

At that time, I saw Jae as perfect, and I wanted to be just like her, a goal that led to unhealthy consequences. The summer before I turned fifteen I came to realize that Jae wasn't perfect, and that I could learn just as much from her with this understanding, but follow my own path and not hurt myself by making her mistakes. At that point in my life I was making a lot of discoveries about who I was and wanted to be, and also making big choices about my future as a dancer. Jae was there every step of the way, sometimes to give advice, but more often to help me discuss and understand myself and my choices so I could come to my own decisions. I decided to audition for dance programs at colleges, and the support and knowledge she gave me were a tremendous help.

I was accepted at Hampshire College and University of Massachusetts, neither my first choice. At the same time Jae and her husband decided to move to Portland. I didn't like the idea of spending another year at home without a modern dance teacher, but after attending a summer orientation at UMass, I realized it was my best option. I stayed home, taking the classes that were available and applying to colleges again. I talked to Jae on the phone periodically, and although I missed her classes it was still a help. I was accepted at the Boston Conservatory and New York University, both top dance schools.

I still call Jae, especially when I need advice. She has been a big help to me, and I know she's always there. I didn't decide she should be my mentor—it just happened as an extension of the student-teacher relationship, and has been an important and valuable connection in my life.

69

Now that you're settled in at Rensselaer Polytechnic Institute, what are your thoughts on homeschooling as an educational choice?

ADAM GRIMM Homeschoolers make up a colorful and diverse nationwide community. They have chosen homeschooling for almost as many reasons as there are homeschoolers, from those who want to include religious instruction not available in local schools to those whose children's educational needs just

Adam Grimm

are not met in the school system for whatever reason.

Homeschooling allows parents to collaborate with their children, if they wish, on learning. They can decide together what learning pace is appropriate without having to worry about forty other students. This is equally helpful for slow learners and those who are quick to grasp concepts. Self-paced learning is one of the things that homeschooling advocates love to point out as something the schools are ever attempting to move towards while homeschoolers have been doing it for years.

Homeschooling is another case of getting out what you put in. Parents who are able and willing to put in the necessary time and energy will be able to find the resources needed by their children. Those who are not may not find the homeschooling experience as advantageous.

So homeschooling is viable, but is it beneficial? Does homeschooling produce well-educated and well-adjusted citizens? This is a heated debate that has been going on for quite some time between homeschooling proponents and those who advocate for public school.

Those who argue against homeschooling say that children not educated in group environments do not get enough experience at dealing with large

> **O**ne of the reasons that the reasonable education debate has persisted for as long as it has is that many homeschoolers have ideas about what is meant by "well educated" that are different from the schools.

groups of people. They also say that a parent who doesn't have a teaching degree could never educate a child as well as a trained professional.

Homeschooling advocates say that these are mostly red herrings. Most homeschooled students spend a large amount of time out in public and with groups of friends. They play sports, belong to clubs, participate in scouting, and do many of the same things as, and sometimes with, their traditionally schooled peers. Socialization, then, is not an issue. Besides, as one well-adjusted former homeschooled student said, "How does learning all the four-letter words help me learn to work in large groups?"

The education issue has been largely shown as a red herring also. By one standard, in fact, homeschoolers seem better educated than their public school counterparts. On standardized tests normed to the public schools, a majority of homeschoolers generally score in the top thirty percentile points. By other standards, too, homeschoolers seem to be well educated. Many colleges are actively recruiting homeschoolers because, among other reasons, they tend to be more self-motivated and have an easier time adjusting to the looser college environment.

One of the reasons that the reasonable education debate has persisted for as long as it has is that many homeschoolers have ideas about what is meant by "well educated" that are different from the schools. In general, the public schools use easily quantifiable standards for education. Test scores are popular. Being able to achieve a certain score at a certain age says whether or not a child is well educated. Many homeschool parents, however, use different standards to judge their children. They prefer to measure their children's total education. For many children it is more natural to read at eight instead of six. By school standards a child like that would not be considered sufficiently educated. However that same child might, at six, know more about American history than most high schoolers and be learning multiplication. Most people would consider that child pretty well educated even though s/he doesn't know how to read.

This is not to say that all homeschoolers are well adjusted geniuses, although some are. There are cases where parents shelter their children to an unhealthy extreme or fail to provide the necessary resources for their children's education. These cases, though, are the exception not the rule. Much the same thing sometimes happens in schools, too, with large class sizes and underfunded budgets taking a toll on school activities.

So homeschooling can be a good thing. It may not be the right thing for everybody but then neither is public school. Whatever the educational philosophy there is one important goal: Make sure the education of the child comes first. Everything else should be secondary to that.

70

Looking back, what do you think are the most important things you've learned growing up with homeschooling?

MAE SHELL This is a difficult question to answer, in part because I have learned so many things growing up with homeschooling, and also because the most valuable things I have learned are so broad it feels almost impossible to put them into words. So, here goes.

Mae Shell

The first thing that comes to mind is the importance of my family life. And I mean this in every sense you can imagine, not simply loving but being friends with my family, enjoying their company, supporting them and knowing they support me no matter what happens. I feel very lucky to have wonderful parents who love me unconditionally, who support and respect my lifestyle choices. More than being "just parents," they are my friends, mentors, teachers, and counselors. I also cherish the friendship of my three younger sisters, and older half-brother and sister. As other friendships come and go (something that is inevitable in life), I know that I will always have these rich, wonderful relationships with my siblings.

Because my three younger sisters and I were homeschooled, we spent a lot more time together than we would have if we had attended public school, and by doing so were able to form true friendships with each other. Looking back on my childhood and adolescence, and remembering all the special times I have spent with my family, I realize that it is impossible to really describe what "family life" is. For me, being part of a family was, and continues to be, much more than just living together in the same house; there are fights, apologies, differ-

> I feel that I have a sensible belief in my abilities, in my strengths and talents. This faith was instilled in me by my parents, who always believed in me even when I didn't believe in myself.

ences of opinion, quiet times spent watching a movie or playing a board game, animated discussions in the car and at the dinner table, listening to one another read out loud . . . I value being a part of this intricate living quilt above everything else.

The second thing that comes to mind is the ability to believe in myself. Some would call this "good self-esteem," but to me it is so much more than that. It means having enough faith in one's instincts to choose seldom traveled paths because they "feel right"; to make objective, yet exciting choices, based on past successes; to honestly critique one's own work; to know that one is right even when everyone else disagrees; to know one's own limits yet create masterpieces within those boundaries. I feel that I have a sensible belief in my abilities, in my strengths and talents. This faith was instilled in me by my parents, who always believed in me even when I didn't believe in myself; who never criticized the bad but praised the good; who have always, and continue to, let me know they will always be there for me, no matter how far away from the nest I fly.

71

What would you suggest to a teen new to homeschooling about how to make the best of educational freedom?

LINDSEY JOHNSON Make the best . . . well, the best is different for different people, so it's not easy to tell how one should make the best of her educational freedom. It depends on her own goals and ambitions and dreams. It depends on the person. The whole point of having autodidactic freedom is to be able to direct her own path, to drum out her own direction. I shall try, though, to give some suggestions for un-

Lindsey Johnson

learning what school has taught, and for freeing oneself from the oppressive ideas of this institution most are so often dependent on.

I have never been to school. I have arrived at these conclusions by talking to friends who go or have gone to school, by reading many books on the subject, and by being in school-like situations such as driver's education that showed me what school is like. It showed me that school is not a place I'd enjoy, nor is it, in my opinion, a very good place. While there was only one "subject," it showed me that, if I went to school, I wouldn't be able to spend my life doing what is probably the best part of life—living it.

Knowing what I know now, I wouldn't dare give up my educational freedom to an institution. First, I would suggest to another teen to take a break from anything academic so as to unlearn what school has taught about learning. In school, the idea is presented that learning is a chore and a race to the finish. It is not. It is a wonderful aspect of life and a great journey. In school, she has also been told to learn what everyone else is learning. What is learned should be the choice of the learner. She should try to allow herself to be inquisitive about anything that betides her curiosity and wonder. I think that all too often people are dependent on others to decide what should be learned instead of finding out what the individual heart desires to learn. That is something we must unlearn . . . something school has instilled in us from the time it was created. She should dismiss the idea that she cannot direct her own education . . . when this is done, it will be found that she is the only one who can direct her education authentically and rightly.

She should unlearn the notion that learning must happen at specific times; it should instead be realized that learning is as breathing: It happens all the time.

She needs to stop thinking in terms of "subjects" and realize that everything is dovetailed together. Everything is connected into a unified whole. She should try and rediscover this interconnected unity that she was previously turned away from. She has been taught, while being given irrelative information, that knowledge is very limited because schools separate it into "subjects" with a precise line. This is not true; everything is connected.

She should try to allow herself to question everything. In school, she is taught to focus on the answers instead of the questions, but answers are dead ends. Once one has the answer, that's it, there's nothing left to say. She should allow herself to ask questions—as immense as the Milky Way.

Most of all, don't be afraid to be real. If real means studying only cars or stars, whatever real means, be real. Be yourself. Know yourself. Find the good in yourself . . . because only when you find the good in yourself can you truly find the good in the world.

> **M**ost of all, don't be afraid to be real. If real means studying only cars or stars, whatever real means, be real. Be yourself. Know yourself.

MICHAEL HOHENSEE The best thing a teenager can do with his new-found freedom is to do whatever it is that he thinks is best. The point of being free to choose how and what you are going to learn is to set and achieve goals that are worthwhile to you. *You* have to discover what you think is worth doing. All anyone else can tell you is what *they* think you ought to do.

But don't worry, you don't have to decide what you want to do for the rest of your life just yet. All you need to do is find a subject that you think is interesting. If you're like me, you like science, engineering, and computers, but can't decide which of these fields you like best. Just find a general area of study which you'd like to pursue. Do you like literature? History? Mathematics? Bird breeding?

Once you've found an area you'd like to focus upon, you need to determine the best way to pursue it. Are you going to raise birds? You might want to find some professional bird breeders to "apprentice" yourself to, to gain experience raising birds. When I set out to breed our cockatiels, the local bird aviary was only too happy to help me choose equipment and give me tips about the care and feeding of baby birds. You'd be surprised at how much you can learn by simply doing.

If you want to go into a professional field, you'll probably need to go to college. Not only do colleges provide diplomas with which to impress prospective employers, but (if you select your college wisely) they also provide you with access to people who are interested in the same subjects as you are. A further advantage of setting your sights on college is that it helps keep your options open. You can always change your mind and set a new goal.

Since most colleges require some evidence of preparation before they will accept you, you'll have to either remain in high school, take a battery of tests, and/or take some college courses to demonstrate mastery of high school material. I recommend the latter, for I found the local high schools to be a waste of time—too much regimentation and lack of interest in learning. They were more like factories than places of learning. You are much more likely to find teachers interested in *teaching* students in college than you are in high school. Generally speaking, one semester of college is equivalent to one year of high school.

> **T**he point of being free to choose how and what you are going to learn is to set and achieve goals that are worthwhile to you.

Not only is the quality of education greatly improved at college, but sampling different colleges allows you to determine what kind of college you really want to attend. I've gone to schools of different sizes and have found that I prefer smaller schools to larger ones. If you happen to live nearby the college of your choice, you may be able to attend classes and get to know the faculty. This not only may increase your chances of getting accepted, but also helps you learn whether the school is right for you. In any case, college courses look better than high school courses on your college application.

Above all else, remember that you, and only you, can decide how you're going to learn something. This has always been the case, even when you had no choice about where you were going to study. Only you can decide whether or not to learn anything. Others can only give you advice and opportunities to learn. It is, and always has been, however, your responsibility alone. Keep in mind that you not only have the freedom to succeed in unorthodox ways, but also to fail. Doing things your own way works better, but still requires work!

FOR MY SON

When my oldest was considering whether or not to drop into high school at fourteen years of age, we spent many hours discussing pros and cons. At one point I sat down and wrote out for him the benefits of remaining with homeschooling as I saw them applied to his future. Here, maybe for you to share, too, are the top twenty.

1. You won't be motivated by the "crowd."
2. You'll question opinions presented as facts.
3. You'll enjoy learning throughout life.
4. You'll grow into the person you are, not become someone somebody or something else wants you to be.
5. You'll stand up for that which you know is right.
6. You'll listen to and try to understand "the other guy."
7. You'll welcome differences in people, cultures, and circumstances.
8. You'll be comfortable with people both older and younger than yourself.
9. You'll find that time spent in quiet and solitude is time well spent.
10. You'll know that thinking is but one of several faculties at your command.
11. You'll make decisions based on your thoughts and feelings, not those of others.
12. You'll know how to find out anything you may need to know.

13. You'll be confident that choices you make and actions you take are the best for you.
14. You'll understand that doing something for others is more rewarding than doing something for yourself.
15. You'll discover that many things are not black and white/right and wrong.
16. You'll know about the world in which you are growing up, and in which you'll spend your adult life.
17. You'll realize that life is precious and is the true school you were intended to attend.
18. You'll know nobody but you can decide how and when it is best to learn something.
19. You'll be able to find the best in others because you will have found it in yourself.
20. You'll learn how to make choices that serve you and truth well.

My son stayed home, at least until he was sixteen and tested the community college waters. It's five years later now, and he's already seen enough challenges to put this list to a good test. Watching him deal with the many aspects of his independent life—friends, family, work, and community activities—is proving the list quite accurate.

CHAPTER TEN

The Home in Homeschool

"HOMESCHOOLING" IS SUCH a misnomer that I often wish the word had never been invented. It implies a mere link of home and school when, in reality, it is much, much more. But because this is the name now popularized in the mainstream, and it's the name most people associate with what we do, I'm afraid we're stuck with it for a long time to come.

Because of this name, and because this lifestyle frequently begins with an educational decision, all too often the "home" in homeschool disappears. Conversations, news reports, and local school authorities focus on the "school" in homeschool. But as even this misnomer implies, both home and learning are equally important parts of the whole. They cannot be separated. Since you've read much of this book at this point, I'm sure you're beginning to realize this.

So now it's time to give the "home" in homeschool its due, because there will always be those days when it's just as challenging to figure out how you're going to get the laundry done as it is to figure out those algebra problems! Home is much more than housekeeping, though, so we'll also find out what to do about relatives who don't like a decision to homeschool. And where fathers fit into home education.

Now it's time to give the "home" in homeschool its due, because there will always be those days when it's just as challenging to figure out how you're going to get the laundry done as it is to figure out those algebra problems!

We also don't want to be left out of the increasing national fervor about family values. Lawyers, legislators, ministers, governors, and school administrators spend an awful lot of time talking about missing family values. Here we'd like to share what just may be the very best idea on the planet to find them again. It's simple, really. When you put the "home" in homeschool, it grows easier to find the "home" in everything else we do with our children. And home is where the heart—and the values—are.

72

How do I take care of housekeeping when the children are home all day?

BILLY AND NANCY GREER Well, we have to admit that housekeeping is one of our lower priorities. Since we also have a home business, and lots of other activities, having an immaculate house isn't one of our most important concerns.

Nancy and Billy Greer

The level of housekeeping you do is up to you. It is important to us that our children participate in the upkeep of the house, so they help with certain cleaning tasks. This can be a challenge at times, but it is something that they will have to face when living on their own.

JANIE LEVINE HELLYER The parent at home is often busy from daybreak to sunset, and the thought of having our children home all day and doing all we need to do can seem overwhelming. Instead of thinking of homeschooling as "one more job" to do during the day, begin to consider creating an environment where everyone can pitch in and help. This way everyone has more time to pursue interests and no one individual is left feeling like the family housekeeper.

When we begin introducing our children to housekeeping, it sometimes takes more time than it would to do it ourselves. Take enough time so that your child doesn't feel rushed, laugh a little, and have some fun. Believe it or not, this is the stuff that fond memories are made of. Even the youngest child can help sort laundry, match socks, and dust. School-aged children often enjoy running the washing machine, hanging out clothes in the sun to dry, and vacuuming the floors. When we have a positive attitude about house-keeping, children naturally want to participate. They feel like they are making important contributions to our homes and families—and they are!

One of my sons thought that cleaning the bathroom was so much fun, no one else could do that job for years. I finally figured out why one day when I passed by the downstairs bathroom while he was cleaning. There he was drawing a huge picture on the tub surround with a soapy cleanser. No other job in the house offered him the opportunity to draw life-sized pictures, so bathroom detail was actually a treat for him.

Think about why we do housework. Most of us do it because it makes our homes pleasant places for our families to be. Don't think of housework as a negative, something unpleasant that has to be done. Instead, put on some music and include the kids. Doing our work at home can be a wonderful opportunity to spend time doing things with our children, enjoying their company, introducing them to some real life skills, and

> There he was drawing a huge picture on the tub surround with a soapy cleanser. No other job in the house offered him the opportunity to draw life-sized pictures, so bathroom detail was actually a treat for him.

having some real fun in the process. Who knows, you might actually find that you have more time to pursue your own interests than you did before.

DONNA NICHOLS-WHITE Ha ha ha ha ha ha!

Okay. Now that I've finished laughing, I'll offer some helpful suggestions. These I've gleaned from the expertise of those whose homes are a lot cleaner than mine.

First of all, since you aren't the only one who uses your home and creates the messes, you shouldn't be the only one cleaning it up. You have a cleaning crew built-in. One of the best ways to develop cooperation and life skills in your children is to always include them in homemaking activities. This includes toddlers. As soon as they show an interest in the toilet bowl brush, hand them one and show them how to clean with it.

What about cooking? What toddler can resist pulling up a chair to the stove while mom or dad cooks? Let them work right alongside you as soon as they are willing. I've let my children cut vegetables with real knives as early as the age of two or whenever they showed an interest in food preparation. My relatives and friends have screamed over the sight of a three year old chopping carrots, and have even gone as far as to chastise the children for using these utensils. (And wouldn't you know it? The kids only hurt themselves when these folks scream.) I firmly believe that if allowed to use a tool properly, a child will work responsibly.

Some families devote one full day per week to overhauling the house. My personal favorite is decluttering. I love going through closets, the garage, bedrooms, and cabinets and weeding out anything we haven't used within the past eighteen months. I ship most of these items off to charity. (If you like garage sales here's your opportunity!)

Realize you are not like the neighbors, friends, and relatives whose children attend school all day. You don't have six-plus child-free hours each day. Breakfast, lunch, dinner, and snacks are served in your home everyday.

If push comes to shove, tell yourself that cleaning fanatics are control freaks! (Now I'm going to have to apologize to all of my friends who have spotless homes.)

When I get the mid-winter blues I find it's because the house looks bad. That's when I'll assign the family on a major work detail such as window cleaning or wall washing. A couple of days of intense housework exhausts me to the point where I can rest and enjoy the new look. It also convinces me that the rest of the house doesn't look so bad after all.

Don't expect to have a home that looks child-free. We're homeschooling parents. Our children are home with us for good reasons. One important reason is to enjoy their childhoods. Set your standards and have them work alongside you to create a home your family enjoys.

73

How do I handle relatives, friends, or neighbors who don't think homeschooling is a good idea?

MARY GRIFFITH The best way to handle skeptics is to let them see for themselves what your kids are like, how they spend their time, what interests them, what sort of people they are becoming. Unfortunately, this usually takes years to be effective.

Mary Griffith

In the meantime it helps to know what about homeschooling your skeptics particularly object to so you can address those issues directly. What's tricky about dealing with relatives and friends—people you have continuing relationships with, as opposed to the store clerk who

THE TEMPORAL NATURE OF MESSES

When our oldest son first moved out of the house, we wound up rearranging everyone's sleeping quarters to create space for a much-needed office. On the appointed day, the bed and dresser were moving out (look at all those crayons back there!), the desk was coming in from the garage (yuk!), the tangle of computer wires was becoming frustrating, and the piles of papers and files rescued from their various storage spaces were growing higher in the middle of the office floor when the phone rang. It was an invitation to present a couple of workshops at a large homeschooling conference.

"We'd like you to present your homeschool advocacy workshop. And could you do one on 'scheduling and organizing your day?'" I could hardly answer I was laughing so hard. If the caller had been able to see our home at that moment (I will never have a video telephone!), he *never* would have asked!

I was, of course, able to do the workshop. The chaos that was home at that moment was only temporary.

Our time to share homeschooling with our children is temporary, too, and all too soon the Play-Doh messes, scattered Legos, and daily works of art for the refrigerator disappear. Currently, in my home, these have been replaced by paint messes, huge jigsaw puzzles, and scattered science experiments. But I know well that these, too, will fade away in what seems the blink of an eye.

To some it may look like a messy house. To those who know the secret, though, it's the hallmark of a home filled with love, life, and learning.

remarks casually that homeschooling seems kind of odd to her—is that their expressed objections may not be what really bothers them about homeschooling. Your best friend may not be so much upset about your children's socialization as she is that you're doing something entirely differ-

> **Y**our best friend may not be so much upset about your children's socialization as she is that you're doing something entirely different from the norm, and she may feel an implied criticism in the very fact of your homeschooling.

ent from the norm, and she may feel an implied criticism in the very fact of your homeschooling. Your neighbor may simply fear that your children will eventually trample her prize azaleas. Your mom may still think of you as that gawky kid who kept forgetting to turn in her milk money and had a hard time with algebra, and fear that you'll never be able to keep up with your children and their needs.

Whatever the situation, what you need above all is confidence in what you are doing. *You* have to know that you are doing what you believe is the best thing for your children. If you can develop that confidence and faith in your own judgment and in your children, you'll be able to keep those niggling questions and comments in perspective. They'll become the breaches of etiquette, the intrusions into your privacy, the hypothetical commentary they really are.

Which brings us right back to that little matter of time. We all need time to develop that confidence in our homeschooling lifestyle, to learn how our children learn and how we can best help them. Most of us seem to manage this within a year or two. (If we don't, we perhaps need to figure out what secret doubts about homeschooling we're still harboring within ourselves.)

Meanwhile just keep answering those skeptics' questions as best you can, and know that—eventually—time will tell.

Susan Evans Nonsupportive family members and friends can be one of the most frustrating aspects to homeschooling. I've found it helpful to sort out those whose opinions matter, from those whose don't.

It can lessen your internal conflict to assume that most people are acting out of love for your children and concern for their future. So perhaps they'll simply need more information in order to see the wisdom of your actions and will then move from being critics to being your strongest supporters.

In the end, though, consider where your obligations lie. Are you obliged to keep the neighbors and relatives stress-free, or to raise your children the best way you know?

If the situation is hostile, surround yourself with support: people you admire who respect and support your decision, books that speak to your heart and sustain your faith in your decision to homeschool, periodicals that bring a new round of helpful ideas on a regular basis. Mostly, look to your children. Their growth and progress, even through rocky times, will buoy your spirits and remind you that you've made a good choice.

If all else fails, give yourself permission to tune out negative people, even if they're close friends or relatives. You alone are responsible for decisions on what is best for your family. No doubt you will be reexamining and reevaluating your decision to homeschool on a regular basis. You don't have an obligation to other people to constantly second guess yourself.

74

If our religion is a main reason for choosing to homeschool, how can I find others who share my religious values?

DR. RAYMOND MOORE AND DOROTHY MOORE
We sympathize with your desire to associate with those of like faith. Why don't you ask of local churches, synagogues, or other places of worship? Home education is now widely accepted, so don't be shy. We can give you names of state groups if you send a self-addressed, stamped envelope to Box 1, Camas, WA 98607.

For your children's sake, be sure their associates model good character and behavior. The associates' examples may be more important than their religion. Church members often don't live by their principles.

Dorothy and Ray Moore

But we have a question for you! What do you think of Christ's teaching and example about reaching out to others not of your faith or race? In his associations, he didn't first ask about their faith. Take, for example, Cornelius the centurion, Zaccheus the publican, Mary Magdalene, and the Samaritan woman.

We think of the Tetzlaffs in the early 1980s. Their son, Josh, did not mesh well with the Iowa schools. He was too advanced. "About this time," writes his mother, Barb, "I saw Dr. Moore on the *Phil Donahue Show* and knew that homeschool had to be our solution. I kept my husband, Wayne, up into the wee hours of the night convincing him of this new idea."

When she encountered a belligerent school superintendent, she called for our help. Before the days of good laws, if the issue hadn't reached court-case status, our phone call seemed always to make court unnecessary. When new homeschoolers felt very alone, we supplied information on other homeschoolers in their area and suggested they get together, inviting all homeschoolers or others who were interested. This resulted in a room full of families who formed the "O! KIDS" support group.

In those days nobody said anything about religion, even though many were Christians. They were so glad to find a common ground in homeschooling they banded together *equally* to work for parental rights as their concern. Although the Tetzlaffs were not Christians, they liked what they saw and ultimately became Christians. This was before several Christian leaders began to exclude those not of their faith and divided state groups that won good laws in the early years of the movement. The Tetzlaffs express gratitude that they weren't caught by this exclusion.

Why do Christians exclude when Christ did otherwise? The Christian leader who started exclusion needed a constituency, and this was his method. He misinterpreted two Bible texts: 1 Corinthians 5:9–11 and 2 Corinthians 6:14 KJV. Here, St. Paul was warning about associating with "brothers," meaning Christians who are greedy, adulterous, and so on. If St. Paul were warning to stay away from worldly people, he would have to leave this world. Homeschool groups are not "unequal" in preserving the movement.

Homeschool support meetings aren't church services, nor do they need to be unilaterally dominated by a single belief. Even the U.S. Senate allows prayer. If we practice the Golden Rule, families can learn with the counsel of experienced home educators from whom they are now excluded, and in unity the movement could lead the world.

> **I**f we practice the Golden Rule, families can learn with the counsel of experienced home educators from whom they are now excluded, and in unity the movement could lead the world.

75

How can homeschooling contribute to encouraging our family values with our children?

CINDY WADE Homeschooling provides a family with some very important benefits. One of these is *freedom*, the freedom to choose with whom your children will learn, what your children will learn, where your children will learn, and when your children will learn. Freedom to create a custom curriculum for your children or the freedom to use no curriculum at all. Freedom to make mistakes and the freedom to learn from those mistakes.

Another benefit is *time*. Time to rise up in the morning all rested, enjoy a leisurely breakfast in the company of your children while talking to them about *their* goals, *their* hopes, and *their* daydreams. Time to get to know your children. Every day is Saturday when you homeschool.

With time on your side you also get your children at their best—in the morning, when they are clean, rested, fed, and raring-to-go. With schooling, children are sent away from home and certified strangers have them when they're at their best. Parents get them back at the end of the day when they're tired, dirty, and hungry. With schooling, there's the added stress of peer pressure, doing homework, after-school activities, and often no supervision at all until parents arrive home from work. Not a healthy situation for anyone. Encouraging and supporting homeschooling could mean a significant decrease in the amount of child neglect in this country.

Still another benefit is *healthy socialization*. Education doesn't take place in a vacuum, but schooling does. Homeschoolers are out in the real world living real lives. You can instill *your* values and

set examples for your children. Homeschooled children live and socialize in a more natural setting by being with parents, siblings, grandparents, relatives, neighbors, and other acquaintances. They learn to live within their communities as they shop at local stores, go to the library, help with a home business or in their parent's shop, campaign for a candidate, open a savings account, perform in community or professional plays, or volunteer at local events. The list goes on and on.

Homeschooling also gives you *choice*. You decide the curriculum and budget. You set the rules and the pace. You can't get that kind of parental involvement and, therefore, values, by letting government school raise your child.

It's difficult to fathom that some educators and politicians seriously believe parents will damage their children by homeschooling them. Do they honestly think your intention is to purposely harm your children by providing them with an alternative to government run public schools? I have yet to meet a homeschooling parent whose intent was to shelter, corrupt, or damage her child by choosing to homeschool.

Homeschoolers are like wise gardeners. They know better than to plant a tomato seed directly in the garden in the month of May. You raise tomatoes by starting the seed inside a warm and safe environment. You grow it until it can stand alone outside—and even then you must still protect it from certain elements from time to time.

Finally, there is *love*. No one loves your child more than you do. You know what's best for your child. Parents have instincts. If your instincts tell you something is or isn't right for your children then you have every natural and God-given right in the world to act upon those instincts.

You know your children best and you have the right to raise them in your own way with your values. The state and federal governments have no business or right to tell you otherwise.

MICHELLE BARONE The term "family values" has lately become a weapon in political debates, swinging from left-wing liberal rhetoric over into fundamentalist right-wing intolerance. But everyone was raised in a family, and every family has certain values, principles, and beliefs formed from observation, experience, modeling, and maturity.

Family values simply mean what we, as parents, want our children to cherish, principles such as honesty, integrity, hard work, generosity, faithfulness.

Though some will deny it, we all have values. Schools, in particular, struggle to promote value-free education, but this is always going to be a losing game. Teachers and other adults who work with children are, by their very presence, modeling values; and most of these are good ones, although perhaps not the same as a family's. This can be a good thing, exposing children to different ideas. But large numbers of same-age peers also influence a child's growing sense of values. Ruthless competition,

---

THE QUALITIES OF HOMESCHOOLING THAT ENCOURAGE FAMILY VALUES

Freedom	Choice
Time	Love
Healthy socialization	

---

bullying, blind consumerism, distorted body concepts, cruel teasing of younger or weaker children, and racism may not be the pro-social values we would like our children to absorb. With a loving and concerned adult to guide them, children are able to put these influences into a perspective that will guide them throughout their lives.

In order to ensure our children develop values our family sees as important, it is essential our children spend time with us, lots of time. The more time we spend with our children, the more positive influence we will have on them.

When the clerk in the grocery store forgets to charge you for the magazine you are holding, do you return and pay for it? Do you clean up your dog's mess from the neighbor's lawn without hesitation? Do you discuss propositions and candidates with others, and then vote? When you homeschool, and have your children with you, they are watching. They are learning your family values, in context, not adrift or in the abstract.

SHARI HENRY Homeschooling, for us, was a natural extension of the way Tim and I were parenting our children. Because of how much we value our children and the way in which we value them (in addition to our hopes and dreams for them and the kind of family

we want to be), homeschooling was the obvious choice for educating them. When people ask me why we homeschool, my most frequent answer is, "I love being with the children!" or "I can't imagine what life would be like if they were gone all day." On the surface, these comments may either sound selfish or like false martyrdom, but they're true. We all really like being around one another. We like learning on our own terms. We like going to Disney World off season, heading to grandma's and grandpa's on the spur of the moment, and diving into projects with complete abandon without being constrained by a school calendar. To be honest, when I think of everything I appreciate about homeschooling and the way I see it at work in our family, I find it almost impossible to understand why people wouldn't want to do it!

The two things that strike me the most are the maturity level of my children and how, despite their age differences, they are very interested in one another's lives and enjoy doing things together. Generally speaking, they get along splendidly. TJ, at twelve, will often round up the girls to play roller hockey or head out to work on a big fort in our yard. The two older children will help Phoebe make towers for her toys or design intricate raceways for her marbles.

If I'm cleaning, Bekah, age nine, will snuggle with her little sister and read endlessly. When the two older children and I were in Nashville for a weekend, it even surprised me to see how much they missed their little sister and vice versa. We remind the kids that friends will come and go, but their family is forever. The things they do now, the way they treat one another, lay a foundation for a lifetime relationship.

We enjoy being great friends as well as family and, for the most part, choose to spend our time together much more often than we choose to spend it apart. We realize we think very differently than schooling families in this regard. TJ, for example, likes doing occasional activities with his youth group at church, but recently commented that he'd rather have watched a movie with us than gone with the group. He didn't like that we couldn't all share the things he liked about it. People are either dependent on friends outside the family or within the family. We choose to lean on each other, to share our lives and memories with each other. While other families look for that one more "quality time" activity for their children, we're forever

> We're driven by a fundamental belief that strong families make for strong societies. We act on a sense of responsibility to help create that kind of strong society, the best way we know how.

trying to figure out how to integrate our diverse interests into family life. It may mean that the girls attend more hockey games than they would necessarily like to, or that TJ goes to more dance recitals than he would otherwise; but the choice is missing out— and so there really isn't a choice at all. We work together, play together, hang out together. Or sometimes we all are doing our own thing. Right now, for example, one is coloring, one is writing a report, one is memorizing a poem; but we will all stop to admire the picture, help spell a word for the report, or listen to the poem.

It's the day-in-and-day-out stuff that adds up. We're driven by a fundamental belief that strong families make for strong societies. We act on a sense of responsibility to help create that kind of strong society, the best way we know how.

76

What is the father's role in home education?

WILL SHAW I admit it: My wife Margaret does the vast majority of our homeschooling. Planning, assessing curricula, instructing and explaining, reading aloud, and so on—she does virtually all of it. I admire the men who, with a full-time job outside the home and maybe additional church or other responsibilities, somehow find the time to actively and reliably participate in the day-to-day teaching. I know some. Many dads assume a role more closely resembling principal or special resource teacher. I do lead and participate in some field trips, I handle our children's science fair projects, and Margaret and I go to curriculum fairs together.

CHRIS CARDIFF There is no set, predefined, optimal role for fathers in home education. The father's role can vary broadly from family to family, ranging from the traditional breadwinner to the stay-at-home dad who is the primary teacher. Flexibility and freedom are hallmarks of homeschooling. Families taking advantage of them will all make different choices, including the different roles individual family members will play at different times and in different circumstances.

Even the most conventional roles of student and teacher get reversed in homeschooling. For example, my girls know much more about music than I do.

When my middle daughter started learning piano at the age of six, she would follow up her lessons in the afternoon by sitting me down in the evening and teaching me what she learned. We both loved our roles as student and teacher. She would be boiling over with excitement about "teaching daddy," and I enjoyed learning and sharing her infectious enthusiasm.

Despite this flexibility, there is still the need to earn a living. In a majority of homeschooling families, the father takes on the traditional role of breadwinner while the mother is the primary teacher, coach, facilitator, educator, chauffeur, organizer, helper, coordinator, and drill instructor.

Assuming the desire to participate, getting the father involved in this situation is largely one of time management. In a single-income household with the father away from the family forty to sixty hours a week, there isn't as much time available for the father to participate in homeschooling.

In our family, which fits this model, we've discovered a few things that work for us. First and foremost is my responsibility to provide emotional support to the primary teacher. This support may come in the form of affirming the family's decision to homeschool when criticized by friends and relatives—facing these as a united front makes a big difference in these situations.

Sometimes the support is just verbal encouragement—an "attagirl" at the end of the day. At other times, it's playing the role of teacher's aide and helping to sort through the occasional homeschooling chaos by taking care of some mundane homeschooling chores (like chauffeur duty).

On a more practical level, we take advantage of the flexibility of homeschooling to let our girls sleep in a little later than kids going to traditional schools. This allows them to stay up later at night when I'm home from work. To take advantage of this we schedule some homeschooling activities during the evenings and weekends when I'm available. For example, I coach a Math Olympiad team for homeschoolers on Wednesday evenings and get a significant turnout of participating fathers. The same is true of our Geography/Culture group, which meets on weekends.

At the end of the day, homeschooling allows families to choose the educational options and arrangements that work best for them as a family. There is no magic formula that works for everyone and one of the joys of homeschooling is working together as a family to find what works for you.

MARK HEGENER It's simple: All you have to do is display unwavering faith, trust, hope, love, and courage. These are the things that help bind families together, the important things that make families work. Getting to this point has taken me over twenty years plus lots and lots of patience, love, and understanding from my own family.

Along the way it would have been easier, and probably more financially profitable, to become isolated from my family, to lose track of my place and let the family drift apart. Perhaps not physically drift apart, but to drift emotionally, to lose the daily experience of simply living together and the perspective it has developed within each of us.

HELEN HEGENER Because Mark and I have homeschooled our five children while building a business that allows us both to work from home, we've been able to build a family

> **I**t's simple: All you have to do is display unwavering faith, trust, hope, love, and courage. These are the things that help bind families together, the important things that make families work.

closeness and unity that might be unusual in today's fractured and compartmentalized world. And yet our five children are incredibly independent individuals, as comfortable away from the family as within it. This seems like the primary role of any parent, father or mother: to provide his or her children with a sense of safety and security from which to confidently explore the world.

I know my own parents placed this concern for their children foremost in their lives. It gave me a sense that I could be responsible for what happened in my life with the security that no matter what I did, no matter how badly I blew it, my parents would still be there for me, and would still love me unconditionally. They gave me the courage and the freedom to challenge assumptions, to ask questions fearlessly, to search for new answers. My greatest reward as a parent is watching their grandchildren continue the search.

CHAPTER ELEVEN

Personally Speaking

T HE PHONE RINGS. It's a complete stranger asking if you have a few minutes to speak with her about homeschooling. Experience has taught you to turn off the oven and sit down. This is going to take more than a few minutes.

Mostly, you listen. You listen to a variation of a story you've heard umpteen times before. She tells you about herself, her children, her children's school experiences, and anything else she can think of now that someone who understands is listening—finally. Bottom line? The stranger is searching for a different way—a better way—for her children to go about the process of receiving an education. And within a very short time, she is not a stranger anymore.

She's not a stranger anymore because she has opened up to you and, in answering her many questions, you, too, have shared a large piece of your life and lifestyle with her. She may come to your local support group's meetings where homeschoolers gather and, in a refreshing, honest, and open way, others will also listen to her story and share their own.

In a very real sense, this whole book could be called "Personally Speaking": It's filled with the same honest and open sharing that has helped countless new homeschoolers get off to a good start in meetings and get-togethers throughout the country. But the title's been saved for this chapter, the one containing the most personal half-dozen questions asked and answered. They're questions you may often have thought about but were afraid to ask.

New homeschoolers are often filled with self-doubt; you question whether you've got "the right stuff" for homeschooling, and wonder where those who pursue this path find the courage to go about it. Will your children be forever tied to your apron strings if you homeschool, or can they really learn how to think for themselves? The answers, I think, will please you.

If you really want to get a gathering of homeschoolers buzzing, just bring up the subject of television, our consumer culture's two-edged sword. The answers to the "boob tube" question here are just as lively as at any meeting as homeschoolers share their feelings about whether you really should *kill* your television.

Don't worry if you've been living this lifestyle for a while; you haven't been left out of this heart-to-heart. Have you ever wondered if you're the only one in the world who stresses out about some aspect of homeschooling? Are there ways around (or through or under or over) your stress? Oh, and speaking of stress, we're even going to question whether it's possible to share news of homeschooling without coming across as a "homeschool snob."

Even if you've been afraid to ask these questions, thankfully, our contributors were not afraid to answer.

77
How do I know if I'm cut out for homeschooling?

Susan Evans Are you a parent?

Do you enjoy your children most of the time? Some of the time?

Are you curious about all those interesting nooks and crannies in the world that you didn't get to explore when you were in school?

Do you find manufactured stresses and crises (school projects, tests, teacher conferences) annoying? Would you rather not have a parade of strangers telling you who your children are and what you should be making them do?

Do you plan to have a good, solid, close relationship with your children when they're grown? Do you want to lay the solid groundwork for that now?

Are your children some of your closest friends? Would you like them to be?

If you answered, "Yes!" to any of these questions, you have what it takes!

REBECCA KOCHENDERFER Families homeschool in a variety of ways. Some families set up school-at-home. They study the same subjects as the public school, take tests, and issue grades. Other homeschoolers unschool their children. With this approach, children are free to set their own goals and evaluate their own progress.

Parents choose homeschooling for a variety of reasons. Some homeschool for religious reasons. These parents want to combine their children's academic education with their religious education. They want to pass along their family's morals and values. Some parents homeschool for educational reasons. These parents believe that their children will be able to receive a better, more thoughtful education at home rather than at school. Some parents homeschool because they do not want their children to spend their formative years in age-segregated institutions, learning what someone else thinks is important. Still others homeschool because they live overseas or because they live too far from school.

What are *your* reasons for homeschooling? The question of whether or not you are cut out for homeschooling depends a lot on your reasons for choosing homeschooling in the first place. If it's a good fit for you and your family, homeschooling will probably work out well for you. If you are forcing yourself to homeschool against your better instincts, it may not turn out as well for you. I would advise you to explore all of the educational alternatives available. Just because homeschooling is right for me and mine doesn't mean that it is right for everyone. Find out what's available, think about what you want, and go with what feels right.

CAFI COHEN Such a wide range of people homeschool today. Our ranks include the poor, the middle class, and the wealthy; Republicans, Democrats, and Independents; Christians, Muslims, Jews, Pagans, agnostics, and atheists; city dwellers, suburbanites, and country folk; traditional and single-parent families. Occupations of homeschooling parents? Count all of the following: college professors, small business owners, physicians, farm laborers, military officers, artists, bank presidents, and government workers. Even government school teachers find home education attractive, although some teachers—having to overcome years of conditioning about The One Right Way to educate—have a difficult time understanding the possibilities afforded by homeschooling.

Whatever their backgrounds, there are three attributes that successful homeschooling parents share:

- *Desire* to homeschool
- Ability to *read*
- *Time* to spend with their children

That's it. Desire, reading ability, and time. If you have these, a wide range of homeschooling families have proven that you can and will succeed. Desire is the most important. Desire will motivate you to learn about homeschooling approaches and resources. Desire will make you a networker, a person who talks to others to learn about homeschooling and find community educational opportunities.

Reading will help you learn what you need to know. Never taught a child math facts before? No problem. There are dozens of programs available, some free at your public library. If you can read, you can follow the instructions in these programs, some of which take you by the hand, figuratively, and tell you every word to say to the child. Ditto for almost any other elementary subject.

> **D**esire, reading ability, and time. If you have these, a wide range of homeschooling families have proven that you can and will succeed.

How about chemistry and French for your high schooler? Again, no problem—because you can read. You don't have to relearn chemistry or French, but you will want to peruse catalogs and compare various programs. The many excellent self-instructional materials available reduce the parents' job to researching resources and, sometimes, writing checks.

Time. How much time? Figure at least one to two hours of one-on-one each day if using traditional instructional materials. If your approach is more relaxed, your children will appreciate your feedback and your company for as many hours as you can give them. Note that homeschooling can happen anytime. Some families homeschool in the evening and on weekends and make child-care arrangements for their working hours.

Finally, notice what is *not* on the essentials list for a homeschooling parent. You do not need a teaching credential or a college degree. You do not need lots of cash. You do not need confidence to teach or expertise in biology or algebra or American government. You do not need special equipment or facilities. You can network for all of these if you have the desire, reading ability, and time.

78

Where does one find the courage to pursue an education so different as homeschooling?

DORIS HOHENSEE The courage comes from the understanding of what would happen to my child's natural curiosity if I give up homeschooling. I didn't start out with the goal of homeschooling my children. It was something that just happened naturally.

As I taught my oldest child at home from birth, I quickly realized he wouldn't fit into a normal classroom. It wasn't simply because he could read before entering kindergarten. The more important question was, Who would be available to answer all his questions in school? I had little reassurance that his natural spontaneity and enthusiasm would survive an institutional setting. So we simply continued at home.

There's a certain sense of being isolated from the rest of the school-oriented community. But it never outweighed the benefits of watching my children growing and learning in a relaxed environment.

NED VARE The false idea is that going to school gives us an education. It takes common sense, not courage, to realize that. Trust your own, and your children's, intelligence.

Continuity of our culture and society *depends* on the passing along of its collective world view. That is not something to be ashamed of or to deny our children. It is as necessary and inevitable as night following day.

The danger that is being caused by the public schools today, at the insistence of the few in charge of the federal department of education, is that the continuity of culture and society is being broken, on purpose, in order to promote a global government and society. Schools are being changed from their traditional educational purposes and turned into job training centers where children are trained and adjusted for attitudes, opinions, and adaptability to become workers—human resources—for the "global economy" comprised of the businesses that have the ear of political leaders. It is a fraud. As

> The false idea is that going to school gives us an education. It takes common sense, not courage, to realize that. Trust your own, and your children's, intelligence.

Eda LeShan said to her mother, "Let me be how I grow."

MARY GRIFFITH Sending my children to school and watching them learn to tolerate mediocrity and boredom would take courage. Sending my kids to school and letting them believe history is what's contained in textbooks would take courage. Letting my children eat up hours each day waiting for the next event, waiting for the "later" to delve into the things that really interest them would take courage. Teaching my children that I think the most important thing in their lives is to achieve higher test scores than their peers would take courage. Teaching my children they shouldn't trust in their own values and judgment would take courage.

Homeschooling doesn't take courage. Choosing homeschooling is easy.

79

Parents must get stressed out over homeschooling sometimes. How do I cope?

MICHELLE BARONE I have never met a homeschooling parent who has not had doubts or seriously wondered just what she has gotten herself into. There are days when you feel absolutely wonderful about your life and children, and every-

thing is going well. Then it rains for a week nonstop, your car is in the shop, the kids have been fighting since Tuesday, and sending them to school not only looks good, boarding school looks even better!

Your most powerful weapon in times like these is friends. Know that everyone gets stressed out, has doubts and bad days. Find someone to talk to. Throw your fears and questions out at your support group and you will be surprised at the love and caring that come your way. Reread some back issues of magazines and books that got you started in homeschooling. Go for a walk. Look at pictures of your children when they were babies and remember how far you all have come. But be warned! This is not the time to talk with people who have questioned your decision to homeschool.

One of the beauties of homeschooling is setting the pace of family life. Remember, you can always pull back and take "time off" when you or your children are feeling stressed. This is a good time to pay attention to what is going on in your life that is causing stress and begin to reevaluate and make changes.

Often when we feel stressed about "schooling," it is because we have let academics become the only focus of our time with our children. We have narrowed our communication to what they have or haven't done about "school work." This puts tremendous pressure on the entire family. We have to remember the wonderful opportunity we have to enjoy ourselves and our children without the constraints of a rigid agenda. One way I have of centering myself on the truly important is to ask: Will what I am stressing about now matter next week, in one year, in five years? If I were to stop right now and have a cup of tea, read a book, play a game, or read to the kids, would something terrible happen? If not, then that is exactly what I do.

When your family is caught in stressful life situations not so easily remedied by a cup of tea, a phone call, or a hug, then try to approach it as an opportunity for your children to see how you handle crises, and how you deal with "Real Life." All the truly important life lessons can only be learned by personal experience. This is how we grow as people.

DR. RAYMOND MOORE AND DOROTHY MOORE Though some don't want to admit that it's so, burnout is fairly common in homeschooling. The most frequent problem we encounter is caused by conventional "packaged" curricula, keeping the mother and children tied to books six to eight hours or more a day. We have helped literally thousands of families solve this dilemma, many by simply reading *The Successful Homeschooling Family Handbook*. This provides experienced practical, realistic solutions they need in lifestyle, attitudes, methods, curriculum, or understandings. Others who need more help enroll in the Moore Academy for a year or so to learn firsthand how to take the pressure off themselves and their children.

One mother who has been homeschooling for twelve years wrote the best analysis we have yet seen. Now that her oldest is handling college successfully, and her next one is taking much of the responsibility for his own learning, she realizes that many mothers are like she was. They somehow have a hard time understanding that what they are doing, even though imperfect, will bear fruit in future years. She freely admits that everyone has "bad" days or at least days when they don't feel particularly productive.

She says,

> Over the years I have certainly learned that we worry more than we need to (lack of faith in ourselves) and we don't give

Throw your fears and questions out at your support group and you will be surprised at the love and caring that come your way.

enough credit to our child's abilities (lack of faith in our children). Twelve years ago I felt very inadequate as a "teacher" but very convinced as a parent that homeschooling was a must for our family. There was no way out, and the children learned and grew in spite of my mistakes. I've spent many evenings in tears because I didn't have enough patience, time, strength, or intelligence, only to realize it was sleep, exercise, and trust that I didn't have enough of! For me, that is trust in God.

Often I didn't have any plans past the current interest, couldn't keep a journal going, hated grade books, and keeping attendance seemed ridiculous because we were always home. I struggled between Moore Formula "homeschooling" and conventional "school at home." Group field trips were generally more trouble than they were worth, and support groups meant more activities and planning. I liked being at home and having a simple routine.

One thing I learned is that success isn't measured by what others are accomplishing. Rather our success is being together as a family, sharing time, talents and trials. Helping my children to form values and balance work, study and service is my calling.

After we enrolled in the Moore Foundation Academy, doing the reports and receiving evaluations [feedback from her educational counselor] when I needed it, it helped me be more organized and also made me realize just how much we were doing or accomplishing. They serve as good records, too. Thanks for keeping it simple!

Please let us know if you have a better idea.

LILLIAN JONES It's a rare beginning homeschooling parent who doesn't go through some stress. There can be a real disequilibrium over leaving the known for the unknown, staggering under the heavy weight of the responsibility for your child's future.

Lillian Jones

Reading books like this one by seasoned homeschoolers is a great help in coping with that particular stress. Also, make sure you're getting this kind of support from beyond just your local support group. People often become involved in activities with their support groups in a busy way that doesn't include discussing their anxieties about homeschooling. Homeschoolers do tend to love to talk about homeschooling, though, so asking questions can get some great discussions going. You'll find that others are sometimes needing the same kind of support.

A steady source of support can also be newsletters and magazines, as well as online homeschooling forums if you have access to a computer. *Home Education Magazine* and *Growing Without Schooling* are wonderful supports to have arriving in your mailbox on a regular basis. The *Family Learning Exchange* is another good one, and it offers an online e-mail support group. These resources can sometimes feel like a warm hug on a cold and bitter day.

The best homeschool experiences come with no attempt to re-create school at home, and re-creating school at home is the single most stressful force against successful homeschooling. This message is hard to grasp sometimes, but it is vital one. Pay heed.

The best (yet too often overlooked) way for getting through any homeschooling stress is to focus on enjoying your children. If you're not putting school-like stresses on your children, you will see beautifully whole and healthy individuals emerging before your eyes. There will be magical moments when the beauty of the whole situation is so crystalline that you wonder how you ever could have doubted.

Nevertheless, you might occasionally doubt everything you ever believed; times when you suddenly and inexplicably feel you've made a terrible mistake by thinking you could leave the system. That anxiety passes, and it reappears less and less as you see your children growing strong and enthusiastic for life. Make sure you're finding ways of nurturing yourself, too; get exercise and pursue your own interests. Your children don't need you to hover as much as you might think.

> **Anxiety passes, and . . . reappears less and less as you see your children growing strong and enthusiastic for life.**

Don't worry. When you trust your children, you eventually all settle into a place of comfortable self-assurance.

NANCY PLENT Most of us are the authors of our own stress. We want everything to be perfect and go according to schedule, everyone in the family to be happy all the time, we want . . . well, life just doesn't run that smoothly. We need to identify stress as a useful signal that it's time to change something.

When my son was small, I preserved my sanity by getting up at five A.M., taking a predawn bike ride, puttering in the garden, and listening to the birds greet the morning. I'm not a morning person, so the first ten 'minutes were horrible! But the rest of it—the exercise, the solo cup of tea on the back porch afterwards—was good for the soul. The rest of the day I could cope with anything. Other parents have told me they avoided burnout by occasionally tossing out their careful plans for the day and doing something spontaneous that the children suggested. It's too easy to fall into thinking that you have to "do school" for six hours a day, five days a week, even though homeschool doesn't take *nearly* that long!

You know the saying: "If momma ain't happy, ain't nobody happy."

Momma has to be realistic about what she wants her homeschool to be. Make a cup of tea, go for a walk, decide what's really important, and ruthlessly cut out the rest.

80

How will my children develop their own world view if I'm teacher as well as parent?

MARY MCCARTHY Interesting question. I'm not sure we want our children to develop a view too far from our own. Isn't it a parent's responsibility to instill basic values in our children before the world influences them?

Our world view is from a previous generation, theirs has to reflect their generation in their time. I'm afraid we live in a media-drenched world. We catch the headlines on TV—the whole world, live, via satellite—before sitting down to read the paper at breakfast. After a few quick lessons, including such worldly subjects as history and geography, our children can hop on the Internet and communicate with the entire world. I always figure I could never have purchased the education my son obtained on his own from the Internet. Where else can a kid ask a college student a question and get a reasonable answer? Where else can he find out what's

going on in Tokyo? Or know off the top of his head what time it is in Paris? I think as parents we give our children their foundations—then they adapt their views from everything else to create a world view uniquely their own. Besides, who's child ever grows up to be just like his parents? There's a scary thought.

WENDY PRIESNITZ Most homeschooled children are not cocooned at home with a parent. In fact, my experience suggests the opposite; children whose time isn't taken up by schooling have the opportunity to interact with a variety of people within their communities, of many different backgrounds and viewpoints.

In addition, homeschooling parents are not teachers in the traditional sense of the word. In many families, parents act as facilitators, helping their children gain access to the vast and diverse body of information that humankind has amassed over the centuries. This includes exposing their children to many different world views, and discussing those views as part of the educational experience.

Even in situations where parents wish to shield their children from other perspectives, as happens in Amish and Mennonite communities, they find it difficult. We live in the Information Age, and other viewpoints bombard us daily. Instead of needing to broaden their children's horizons, most parents find themselves providing context and perspective to help their children preserve their family's values.

DAVID AND MICKI COLFAX Is the implication here that without contact with an outside-of-the-family teacher the children will not develop an independent "world view?" If so, it raises the more fundamental question of whether or not it is desirable for children to develop world views that are different from their parents. We all know liberal parents who have raised conservative children and conservatives who have raised young liberals. But in most cases the schools have had very little to do with it. Indeed, there is considerable evidence that schools, right on through college, have remarkably little impact on the values that inform the "world views" of young people. Schools may dumb down, teach passivity and conformity, and encourage peer-dependence, but only rarely do they significantly transform the basic value structure or set of assumptions that the child brings from home and family.

> **W**hen we speak of how homeschooling allows more time and opportunities for thinking, reading, working on self-directed projects, and interacting with people of different ages and stations in life, we are talking about the very activities and conditions that nurture the development of independent "world views."

Perhaps this question is better understood as an expression of concern that some homeschooling parents, unlike those who put their children in schools, are able to indoctrinate their children with what some would characterize as narrow and stultifying world views; indeed, that they could be creating intellectual and ideological clones of themselves. According to these critics, bereft of the influence of teachers and the culture of the school, these children have few opportunities to be exposed to values and perspectives that prevail in the society at large—to develop ideas and understandings that extend beyond those which exist within the confines of the family. The school thus viewed does both more and less than educate; "Give us your children and we will *socialize* them" becomes the rallying cry of its advocates.

And while homeschooling parents can be overbearing, overly protective, and yes, even narrow-minded and rigid on occasion, the very *openness and practice* of homeschooling provide children with opportunities to learn and to expand their horizons that are denied their peers who have to cope with the rigidities, inequities, and absurdities of conventional school life. Homeschooling is precisely what the schools claim to be but most emphatically are not: an approach to learning that fosters both intellectual liberation and genuine socialization. When we speak of how homeschooling allows more time and opportunities for thinking, reading, working on self-directed projects, and interacting with people of different ages and stations in life, we are talking about the very activities and conditions that nurture the development of independent "world views." How do we know this?

Talk to the children.

81

Does TV have a place in the homeschooler's home?

MARY McCARTHY Sure, why not? I think it's great that you can turn on the TV and see the world. It opens so many doors, inspires so many interesting topics, and shows you the rest of the world. There are all those diverse viewpoints and lifestyles. Then there are videos, where you can learn about something by just sitting down with a bag of popcorn. Television really expands the possibilities for learning.

SHARI HENRY Well, it sure does in ours! The children each choose thirty minutes of TV programming an afternoon. The girls usually pick PBS shows such as "Arthur" and "The Magic Schoolbus"; TJ likes ESPN. Also, we watch lots of great stuff on CSPAN, Discovery Channel, Animal Network, and History Channel. Television enriches learning, spurs new ideas, and entertains. In moderation, it can be quite useful, though I wouldn't want my children to trade too much of their time exploring in the woods, reading great literature, or baking cookies for staring at the television. More than any single issue, television seems to require that ever-elusive balancing act.

Shari Henry

BILLY AND NANCY GREER Whew! This is a very difficult question to answer. We'd have to defer to the personal preference of parents when making this decision. We personally take the middle ground. While we do not ban television, we do believe that too much television is negative. From our own experience, we think it is an "addictive" medium and time better spent on "real" living is wasted. Our children mostly watch public television (shows such as "Bill Nye," or "Wishbone") or videos. By avoiding commercial television, our children are not exposed to advertising that we'd prefer they not watch.

Some people feel that restricting TV viewing creates a desire for forbidden fruit. We have not seen this with our children. For us, television is such a powerful medium that monitoring its use is akin to preventing them from running in front of a car and getting hit.

Others just toss out the TV, but we have seen benefits to our children watching science and nature programs on public television. They now have such vast reservoirs of animal facts that quite often I've had to go to them for information! Most educational tools have drawbacks and much of what is on television is of little worth, but the same is true of many educational software packages. I find it humorous that many people will limit TV because they don't want their children to be couch potatoes, but they think it is fine for them to spend all day on the computer where they become mouse potatoes.

> For us, television is such a powerful medium that monitoring its use is akin to preventing them from running in front of a car and getting hit.

82

After homeschooling for several years, I've noticed a difference in my children. I want to share this difference with people; but, frankly, it's hard to explain to other parents without risk of them feeling as if I'm criticizing *their* choice to have their children remain in public school. How do homeschoolers who want to share their discoveries overcome this very natural and understandable tendency?

CHRIS CARDIFF It is an unfortunate fact of life that some people feel threatened by other people's choices. You will be unable to overcome some people's defensiveness no matter what you do. For others, however, the right approach will make a huge difference.

It's important to keep in mind that typically the choice to homeschool is more than just an educational choice—it's a lifestyle choice. In that sense it can be as controversial and soul-wrenching as the "mommy wars" between the stay-at-home moms and the go-to-work moms. There is huge potential for implied guilt, with both sides arguing they are doing what's best for their children.

To avoid igniting such a volatile confrontation, I favor a soft-sell approach to homeschooling. There is no reason to shove homeschooling down someone's throat—if you do, they are likely to just spit it back out at you. A better approach is to let them come to you with their questions.

More often than not, your children will be the best (and only) "advertisements" for homeschooling that you will ever need. Adults in particular will notice their social skills and comment on them. This usually provides the opening you need to introduce them to homeschooling and a brief discussion of the corollary benefits (other than academic) your family derives from homeschooling.

In many cases, parents may not even be aware they had an educational option like homeschooling available to them. This will be an eye-opening, mind-expanding, consciouness-raising, revelatory experience for them—the realization that there *are* educational choices for their family.

One key point to make early on is to acknowledge that homeschooling is not for everyone. This lowers defensive barriers by validating their current educational choices.

In many cases, parents may not even be aware they had an educational option like homeschooling available to them. This will be an eye-opening, consciousness-raising, mind-expanding, revelatory experience for them—the realization that there *are* educational choices for their family. This can lead to a wide-ranging discussion on the myriad ways to homeschool.

Take advantage of the positive opportunities you have to share the benefits of homeschooling. A gentle, affirming approach will negate any implied criticism of alternative choices and allow others the freedom to really listen to what you have to say.

CHAPTER TWELVE

Lifeboats:
Final Inspiration

I NEVER SET out to become a homeschool advocate, though that is what I'm often called. As I watched three young hearts and minds blossom in an educational experience antithetical to my own, it was impossible to keep the discovery—the joy, the love, the obvious "naturalness" of the process of learning—to myself. Fourteen years ago it was pretty hard to find more than a handful of people to speak with directly about such a revelation, so I began writing about it. I helped start a support group, and wrote some more. That writing led to invitations to speak, and thus an advocate was born.

While my advocacy began as a desire to share the "good news," it continues today for a different reason. Homeschooling has given me reason and opportunity to ponder, discuss, dissect, and question both what I've been taught and what I've assumed. When educational teachings and assumptions didn't hold up to this scrutiny, there were reason and opportunity to look at other teachings and assumptions related to children and family, the building blocks of a healthy society.

To put it plainly, what I uncovered is appalling. I look around and see my family and I are afloat in a sea of suffering where families and children are concerned. For every one of the increasing number of children reported to end his life, or wind up in jail, or become addicted to drugs, or suffer violence at the hand of another, there is a family, a family whose members' lives are forever changed in a wave of human connection, and the ripples are far-reaching. For each of these children who allow anger and resentment to turn his or her life into a series of conflicts (and isn't that what youth violence really is?), a mother fears, a brother hopes, an uncle mourns, a friendship dies.

In the midst of this sea of despair, I feel compelled to offer homeschooling as a lifeboat. Yet I can only offer the boat. Each family must work together to fill it with their own breath of life and love, hope and commitment. Only *they* can rescue themselves.

I know there will be many whose politics, personal or governmental, won't allow them even to consider an approach to education that contradicts the *one* method chosen for the masses and practiced in the monopoly public school system. Others may desperately want a lifeboat, but they spend so much time and energy simply staying afloat in the sea of suffering it seems impossible to find more time and energy to inflate the boat.

If you don't have much practice thinking alternatively or cooperatively, commonsense solutions may sometimes slip by you. But consider this: If just a few of those safely on their lifeboats gladly keep others afloat as they blow up their boats, soon all would be rescued. The community of the drowning would save itself.

Every contributor to this book has offered that help so selflessly, so joyfully, their kindness will live in my heart forever. They offered up their time, their devotion, their combined 500-plus years of experience in an unprecedented effort to keep members of our society afloat long enough to gather their life and love, hope and commitment. One family at a time. Doing it for themselves.

If there is another lifeboat in addition to home education that can so profoundly enrich parents' and children's lives together, I have yet to find it. And I have looked hard. Homeschooling has been so uplifting it's only appropriate to leave you readers on a note of inspiration, and to offer you your very own, personal lifeboat.

83

All I ever read about in the newspaper is exceptional kids doing exceptional things. Are there any normal homeschoolers?

SUSANNAH SHEFFER They're all normal—and they're all amazing. Does that sound like I'm dodging the question? All homeschoolers do seem normal to me: They're regular kids, with ups and downs and immaturities and bad days, just like everyone else's kids. And all homeschoolers do seem amazing to me: They've each got something special that homeschooling, more often than not, allows to flourish.

It's worth remembering that newspapers cover what they consider newsworthy—in other words, what seems out of the ordinary. The first homeschoolers to be accepted by Ivy League universities got intensive media coverage. Now that homeschoolers are routinely accepted to selective colleges, it's less common for any individual acceptance to make the news. It's also true that with so many skeptics questioning whether homeschooling works, people within the homeschooling community will sometimes want to hold up examples of obvious success in order to counter criticisms. People are understandably proud when a young person not only does something great, but attributes her success to her homeschooling background.

Nonetheless, a newspaper is unlikely to write about the fact that eight-year-old Jane sat with her dolls all day long in a wonderful luxury of fantasy play; or that twelve-year-old Jonathan woke up eagerly, with many things he wanted to do that day, whereas last year his mother could hardly coax him out of bed to get to school on time. Yet these sorts of things may be what the families themselves are thrilled to observe. Years ago a homeschooling mother wrote to *Growing Without Schooling* magazine, "It's okay to be ordinary, living your days out well and happily without newsworthy accomplishments, just everyday going forward, living and learning." That's a sentiment many homeschoolers would heartily endorse. At the same time, with so many skeptics out there—not just about homeschooling, but about children in general—news of good things young people do challenges negative stereotypes and benefits us all. The key, it seems to me, is to make a point of talking about what went into the accomplishment or what was behind it: what steps were involved, what kind of support and help were necessary, how challenges were faced and handled along the way. In thinking about education, what we want to understand is what's possible for human beings and then what helps make it possible. That way, we can learn from others' success and try to offer similar opportunities to all children.

MICHELLE BARONE Yes, most homeschoolers are "normal." Because television, newspapers, and magazines are in the entertainment business, they tend to highlight the "unusual" as a way of selling soap. Our society would consider a child prodigy who had never attended school exceptional enough to create a spectacle—and sell soap.

But I believe all children are exceptional in their own unique way. And, given a nurturing, loving environment where they learn what they want, in their own way, at their own pace, they often look and act exceptional. Not all homeschooled children are composing music, running home businesses, or going to college at age ten. We have bought into a myth that learning has to be hard, and most children have to be coerced to learn. When a child excels at something, say a national spelling bee, without being bribed or graded or rewarded, it is big news. But if one factor could define us as human beings, it would have to be that we are driven to learn. Just look at a two year old putting water into a cup over and over with

Donn Reed

such intense concentration, and with such delight of discovery. This two year old is a genius at what he is doing! He is discovering the physical world in a way that no other animal has ever been able to do.

One of my children is quite creative, always drawing, playing music, and imagining a variety of things. I was worried about his math, his geography, his "academic" progress. So there I was at a homeschooling conference, looking at a math program because I felt he needed some structured instruction. I asked Donna Nichols-White for some suggestions, and the first thing she asked me was, "What does he like to do?" I said, "Play music, draw, create things, which is great, but, well, not going to help him balance his checkbook." Donna said, "He is artistically gifted." "Well, I don't think he's gifted, exactly, it's just that he has always done these things."

We talked some more and she helped me realize not all children do these things. She also told me that artistically gifted children need a lot of creativity with their "academics." I had provided a loving, nurturing environment for my son; and by honoring his creativity, the academics would happen.

This was a great revelation and comfort to me. "Normal" for my child was a life of creativity and imagination. Other children may be exceptional in their math skills, their physical powers, or their social skills. As parents we need to see our children not as ciphers or statistics, but as the wonderful, unique, "exceptional" creatures they all are.

JEAN REED Normal! What's normal? Who is normal? Are you normal?

Exceptional people will make the headlines. Exceptional kids will make bigger headlines. Homeschooled children are essentially no different than children in public schools. Like people everywhere, we all have our strengths and weaknesses. If there are any differences it's because homeschooling can allow all children, gifted or not, to grow more freely

and pursue an interest to the point of excellence.

Our four children may resent me for calling them "average, normal kids" but that's what they are. They are not geniuses, yet they have done some exceptional things because they had the freedom to investigate and follow their special interests. Average children can do exceptional things when interested and encouraged. Susan, who never considered herself to be a great, or even good, writer, won a provincial writing contest. Cathy spent hours studying dinosaurs in third grade and acquired an exceptional knowledge of the subject. Derek got hooked on sharks in about fourth grade and read everything we could find for him. He read through everything in the provincial library and we had to go to the Library of Canada and enlist the aid of friends and relatives to find resources to help satisfy his insatiable curiosity.

He began reading on high school and college levels because he really cared about what he was learning. Karen finished her entire high school studies in two years, tackling every subject in *High School Subjects Self-Taught*, including some advanced courses we tried to dissuade her from

> **T**he point of homeschooling is not to compete for headlines, but to give our children as much freedom and enjoyment as possible in their learning and to help them prepare themselves for their own future.

doing. We couldn't see that she would need them. We were wrong, of course. She's used what she learned and been glad she did it all.

Our kids were just like kids all around the world. They argued, fought, played, failed at some things, and have done some outstandingly great things.

Not every one goes to Harvard, or wants to. Not everyone can write a symphony at age eleven, win a national spelling bee, or be outstanding in some field. Most adults don't make headlines. It's the exceptions who do. If we don't have exceptional kids, that's all right. The point of homeschooling is not to compete for headlines, but to give our children as much freedom and enjoyment as possible in their learning and to help them prepare themselves for their own future.

84

How can I find out where and when homeschooling conferences and curriculum fairs will be in my neighborhood?

NANCY PLENT Here are the four top ways to locate those invisible homeschoolers in your neighborhood:

- Find a book about homeschooling in the library (like this one!), and call a group listed in appendix A.

- Talk to your librarian. She probably knows local families because she's helped them find materials.
- Ask for names at roller rinks, park programs, any fun or educational place. Local homeschool groups probably go there.
- Call your local newspaper and ask for the last reporter who wrote about homeschooling. He or she will have family names in his file.

Notice I didn't suggest you call the local school. They often tell you they don't *have* homeschoolers in their district. Or can't give out the names.

If you follow up every connection you can think of and network until your eyes glaze over a bit, you'll be rewarded by finding an amazing network of homeschoolers who can fill you in on local and statewide events.

SANDRA DODD Join local and state organizations to receive local information. Subscribe to national magazines to get information on regional conferences.

SUSAN EVANS Conferences may be among the best sources of support, information, and refueling for homeschooling families. Finding one in your neighborhood isn't difficult, but it depends on what you consider your neighborhood . . .

Find out about local conferences through local and statewide networks. It doesn't hurt to be in touch with two or three networks if your state has them. (If it doesn't, you might want to start some!) Conferences will be listed in newsletters, or announcements may be sent out in special mailings to publicize the events. Try going to gatherings sponsored by networks you don't usually participate in. The difference in perspective can be eye-opening. The dialogs one-on-one between diverse homeschooling families are extremely valuable in strengthening the homeschooling community.

If you subscribe to any of the fine national homeschooling periodicals like *Home Education Magazine* or *Growing Without Schooling,* you'll find announcements of upcoming conferences, seminars, book fairs, and curriculum fairs. If you have access to the Internet, either through a computer in your home or at your local library, you can find listings of future conferences in your state and across the country.

There are publications that list conferences, vendors, and speakers on an annual or semiannual basis. Look for marketing guides like Jane Williams's *Home School Market Guide* or Ted Wade's

> **C**onferences may be among the best sources of support, information, and refueling for homeschooling families. Finding one in your neighborhood isn't difficult, but it depends on what you consider your neighborhood . . .

Home School Manual. Perhaps your library or local support group can purchase a copy of these titles as reference books available to all interested homeschoolers.

If none of these avenues result in you finding a conference, chances are your neighborhood would benefit from having you (and a few stout-hearted friends) arrange to sponsor a conference or one-day seminar. Don't faint! That's how most big homeschool conferences started once upon a time. The plans don't need to be elaborate—a meeting space for the day, a couple of interesting people who have some experience homeschooling and a willingness to share what they've learned. Attendees can enjoy brown-bag lunches or a pot luck. Such a day can be wonderfully renewing, without burning out volunteers or destroying any family budgets.

85

How do I find a homeschooling support group in my neighborhood? How do I start a support group?

LILLIAN JONES You can get a list of state organizations and local support groups from both *Home Education Magazine* and *Growing Without Schooling.* There are regular listings in the former and an annual Directory Issue from the latter. If you don't find a listing for a local support group, you can usually get lists from the state organizations. Don't be discouraged if all you find at first are groups that don't fit your needs. There really are a variety of homeschoolers out there.

If you have online access, you can post messages in homeschooling forums of electronic bulletin boards like AOL or Prodigy, and on the Internet. Computers with online access, by the way, are becoming increasingly available in libraries and cyber-cafes.

Sometimes local groups are a little challenging to find. If you have no luck locating one through the magazines or state groups, you can explore the territory where homeschoolers take their children during the hours when other children are in school; playgrounds, museums, libraries, educational supply stores, book stores, parks, and amusement attractions. Keep your eyes open for people who might look like they're homeschooling, and go ahead and approach them. They usually love to meet new people. Ask librarians about homeschoolers, especially children's librarians, and leave your name and number, or a card, with them.

Scan bulletin boards at places you think homeschoolers are likely to frequent. Don't forget natural food stores, because homeschooling is one of those "natural" things. If you don't find a no-tice, put one up yourself, and say you're looking for other homeschoolers. The local La Leche League will undoubtedly have members who homeschool—it's a natural outgrowth from another natural practice, nursing babies. Look around at kids' classes like gymnastics or dance. Ask at skating rinks if there are homeschooling groups that have regular get-togethers there.

Check the free parent/family newspapers that are so common these days. Often ads or event notices are placed in there by homeschooling groups. If you don't find one, call the newspaper and ask if they know of any. Also try calling the regular town newspapers. They're often familiar with groups from doing research for articles. They might even have an education editor who keeps track of groups or individuals.

Find out what opportunities the state groups have for getting together with other homeschoolers. Some sponsor large annual conferences and hold wonderful family camp outs. Getting to know homeschoolers from all over the state is great fun for the whole family.

KATHARINE HOUK Independent, marching to a different drummer, following their hearts and minds, people who have chosen to educate their children at home and in the wider world tend toward self-sufficiency. Some people feel they don't need or want to get together with other homeschoolers on a regular basis, but as social beings there is much we can gain from associating with one another. None of us is as smart as all of us.

Support groups for home educators are everywhere and they are enormously diverse. What varies? Many things, including the philosophies they espouse, the activities they undertake, the services they provide, the structure and frequency of meetings, the extent of political activity, the number and ages of people attending, the means of communication with the group, and more. Because groups are diverse, you may need to shop around to find one that feels right for your family.

In my experience, support groups offer:

- Guidance in getting started with homeschooling.
- Accurate up-to-the-minute information about home instruction laws and regulations, which vary from state to state.
- A way to have a voice in creating or changing those laws or regulations.
- A means of organizing enriching events for both adults and children—

> **S**ome people feel they don't need or want to get together with other homeschoolers on a regular basis, but as social beings there is much we can gain from associating with one another. None of us is as smart as all of us.

workshops, field trips, classes, volunteer work, and other learning adventures.
- Communication—through meetings, newsletters, calendars of events, online bulletin boards, phone trees.
- A place to share information about which learning experiences and resources have been helpful.
- An environment where children (and adults) feel they "belong" and are accepted.
- A jumping-off point for the creation of a learning center or parent cooperative, to provide frequent and ongoing learning experiences throughout the year.
- Support! There are occasions when we need the encouragement and good company of one another, especially in times of conflict with school officials or other people, or within our families or ourselves.

So how does a beginner find one of these groups? Even if you are in a rural area, you should be able to find one within a reasonable distance. Start with your state homeschooling organization. National homeschooling organizations often have lists too. Check online—

more and more listings and discussion groups related to homeschooling are appearing on the Internet.

Because homeschoolers tend to frequent their public libraries, a librarian may be able to help you connect with local homeschoolers. You have the option of posting a message on a library or community center bulletin board. Your church may be a good place to start, or if you are involved in La Leche League, a food co-op, or community-supported agriculture you will find alternative-minded people who may know of homeschooling families or groups. Sometimes an ad in the newspaper is a way of finding others.

Those of us who have been involved in homeschooling for many years have created ongoing supportive communities through our groups, learning and resource centers, and conferences. You, too, can reap the benefits by finding and becoming involved in a support group or learning center in your area.

DORIS HOHENSEE The quickest way to start a homeschooling support group is to post a note on the public library bulletin board. Most homeschoolers use their libraries frequently, so it will get noticed. You might arrange to meet in a local park if the weather's appropriate. From there you might set up an outing or two, depending on your interests.

To prevent overloading any one individual, you might suggest that everyone takes responsibility for organizing one outing a year. The goal is to keep things simple so everyone has an enjoyable time.

KATHARINE HOUK I live in a rural area. When our family first took our daughter out of school, there were no support groups for homeschoolers. In fact, we were the only homeschoolers in our district. Nevertheless, I rounded up three or four families who were interested in the homeschooling idea even though their children were not yet school age, and Homeschoolers' Exchange was born. After eight years this group evolved into the Alternative Learning Center, a thriving parent-cooperative resource program for homeschooling families that has been providing workshops, activities, field trips, and classes for children for the past six years.

If you do some research and find that there is no group in your area, or the available group doesn't meet your needs, you, too, may wish to start a group. It can be as simple as getting together with one or two others who are interested in the idea; or, if you don't know anyone, you could advertise in your state homeschooling newsletter or a local newspaper. With those who respond, you can consider what you need from a group— your reasons for getting together, what you hope to learn, what activities would be involved in this learning, and what resources you have to share with one another.

Who do you wish to reach and include in this group?

- All interested people
- Homeschooling families only
- Adults
- Families with children within a certain age range
- Only the families from your church group, or co-op, and so on

What size group do you envision?

- Something small and informal
- A large and diverse group
- Something in between

What would be the purpose of the group?

- Activities, socialization, and learning experiences for the children
- Support and homeschooling ideas for parents
- Help and guidance with regard to the state laws or regulations

- Spread the good news about homeschooling through a newsletter, media contacts, or other methods
- Improvement of state laws and regulations
- Provide guest speakers or workshops on topics related to education
- Make available books, tapes, lab equipment, sports equipment, and other resources through an exchange or lending library

As your group grows, there will be other things to consider: Does the group need a name? Will there be members and dues, and if so, will you open a bank account? How can the group reach out to the community? How can you get input from the children about what *they* hope for from the group? How often should the group meet, and where? Should meetings include adults and children? If conflict arises in the group, how will it be handled? Should you start a lending library or book exchange? What about a newsletter, calendar of events, or Web site? Who will take on which responsibilities, and how can they be rotated? Should you become politically involved in improving the climate or laws concerning homeschooling in your state? What are the advantages of drafting bylaws and becoming incorporated?

There is no one best way in home-schooling, so a good group provides a way to explore diverse needs and helps parents build confidence by finding out what works best for them. Many of the above questions will be answered as those in your group communicate and grow, and all involved will benefit from the camaraderie and support that results.

JANIE LEVINE HELLYER The creation of a new support group or network is something many of us face at one time or another. If you know other families with

the same needs as your own, get together and discuss what type of group would best serve you. Are you looking for an informal group in which families can

Janie Levine Hellyer

get together, a parent network, or a group that focuses on children or teens? Whether you are working with others or on your own, the first task is to define what it is that would best serve your family.

Personally, I prefer informal groups where families can get together. Kids can play and visit, while parents can discuss issues in a relaxed and informal setting. Some people prefer a parent network—an opportunity to sit down with other parents away from the dis-

tractions children might create. Still others feel that the most important aspect of a homeschool support group is to provide positive social activities and experiences for children. It's important to define what you want and need and realize that you can't start out doing everything. Setting priorities allows us to focus on what is most important, then if we choose, add other dimensions.

Talk to others who have organized support groups in your state. Often these people will be very helpful. Your state support group will most likely have lists of local groups, and can refer families to you. Also, they might have names of people in your area who have contacted them in the past, helping you connect with others interested in creating a group.

Once this is done, you can set about getting the word out to others. A good place to start is with your local public library. Most librarians are more than happy to set out fliers, and you might find that your librarian knows of families who might be interested in your new group. Local newspapers often have a section devoted to community activities, and accept press releases from local community groups. If your local television station or cable company has a community calendar, you might also send them the information. Fliers can also be placed at places other home-schoolers might frequent: museums, bookstores, and specialty shops. Often local school districts are also happy to give a flier to homeschooling families contacting them.

Probably the most important thing to keep in mind when organizing a support group is this: Do not try to do everything yourself. Work with others, learn to delegate responsibilities, and make it a group effort. Too often, a support group organizer or leader has so much responsibility that it interferes with family responsibilities, leading to burnout. Don't be afraid to ask others to help! Often, people are standing back just waiting to be asked.

86

Is there anything today's legislators can do to ensure this educational approach remains a choice for families in the future?

DORIS HOHENSEE Unless a legislator has homeschooled his own children, it is very unlikely that he would understand how best to protect homeschooling freedom. Many legislators think they can impose "compulsory education" on homeschoolers, avoiding the fact that no one can define what "education" is. They don't quite understand that public and private school students have only to satisfy a "compulsory attendance" requirement. Although it may not seem like much, this is inequitable treatment. What's more, the difference between compulsory attendance and compulsory education is significant. Whereas homeschoolers in many states must demonstrate educational mastery, these other students need only locate and enter their school building in order to be in compliance with the law.

Whatever happened to "equal treatment before the law?" It's not fair to separate out any segment of the population and discriminate against them. That's what's been happening in many states.

The task of protecting our freedom is far too important to delegate to anyone but ourselves. Many homeschoolers have tried to give away this individual responsibility by hiring "experts" and joining a legal defense association to protect their freedoms. This has backfired on homeschoolers and the homeschooling community at large causing problems. Not only do some of these parents get far less "protection" than they had expected, but this organization has repeatedly lobbied state legislatures, compromising away our rights and increasing the amount of regulation required to legally homeschool. The reason this method failed is that homeschoolers haven't carefully watched what sort of "protection" is actually being provided for their membership fees.

If parents want the job done right, they must do it themselves. Just as they decided to assume responsibility for the education of their children, they must also assume the responsibility to educate themselves regarding their state's political situation. Parents need to read a copy of the law, which can be found in most public libraries. Only then will they be able to tell exactly what is expected of them and what exceeds the requirements of the law. Only then can they begin to decide whether or not these requirements are reasonable.

Many homeschoolers cannot in good conscience comply with certain state laws, myself included. Some quietly refuse to comply, others are quite vocal in their opposition. It would appear that the very act of complying with such a law relinquishes your rights and grants the state control over your home education program. Those who refuse outright retain these rights and frequently have had far less problems with the state.

> **If parents want the job done right, they must do it themselves. Just as they decided to assume responsibility for the education of their children they must also assume the responsibility to educate themselves regarding their state's political situation.**

All of these issues and risks need to be understood and evaluated before proceeding, as the precedent set in the first year of homeschooling is crucial. Parents can't comply with a law and then later claim that doing so is a violation of their rights.

CHRIS CARDIFF You bet! But the answer may surprise you . . .

Unfortunately, many people have been trained to turn to government to solve their problems for them. "There oughtta be a law" is a familiar refrain that is now ingrained in people. Special interest groups across society turn to legislators at all levels of government to pass laws and ordinances that favor them. One of the worst things that could happen to the homeschooling movement is for it to become just another special interest group petitioning legislators for benefits, privileges, exemptions, and regulations.

The only way to ensure the continued viability of homeschooling as an educational option is the gradual restoration of *total educational freedom for all families.* We don't need legislators passing new laws giving us permission to homeschool and telling us how and when we can do so. What we need to do is remove education from the political process and return it to families where it belongs. Today's legislators can restore educational freedom to us not by passing new laws, but by *repealing* old laws concerning:

- Compulsory attendance
- Mandatory curricula
- Mandatory testing
- Education and credentialing requirements for teachers
- Compulsory funding

While each state has its own set of laws and regulations for education in general and homeschooling in particular, they all impose the core compulsions listed above in one form or another. Underlying these compulsions is the fundamental principle that government is responsible for what children know and learn. Embodied as laws, the further implication is that government is fully within its rights to use the full force and power at its disposal to achieve this goal.

The linchpin of government control of education is compulsory funding. Spending over $350 billion a year for kindergarten to twelfth grade, our educational system is the second largest income transfer and entitlement program in the world. This enormous amount of money attracts powerful special interest groups who need to force children into the system to help justify the continued flow of money. Breaking this financial link would eliminate much of the political resistance to repealing the rest of the state's educational framework.

The $350 billion in compulsory funding must be returned to families so they can spend it on the educational options appropriate for their family. This, more than anything else, will ensure educational freedom for all families. Educational providers will be forced to compete to provide educational services to families rather than organize politically and force families to pay them through compulsory taxation. Rather than being at the mercy of the latest educational fad, education consumers—families—will be free to choose from a smorgasbord of educational options.

The freedom to homeschool is only a special instance of a general problem. You can't ensure your freedom to homeschool unless you solve the broader issue of total educational freedom. As long as education is embedded in the political process, families will be subject to the political winds of the majority (or a special interest minority) and the educational whims of an unconstrained bureaucracy.

The Kasemans answered this question from their perspective as political writers intent on preserving and protecting our freedom to homeschool in this nation. Their answer, therefore, focuses on what we as homeschoolers can do.

SUSAN AND LARRY KASEMAN It is unlikely that homeschooling will be outlawed in the foreseeable future. However, pressure to increase government regulation of homeschooling and to require that homeschools become more like public schools will undoubtedly continue. Many school officials (some of whom are well-intentioned) and some members of the general public have the mistaken idea that homeschoolers would benefit from guidance from experienced professional educators. Despite all the evidence that homeschooling works, some public officials are not yet convinced that homeschooling parents can be trusted. In addition, new state and federal standards in education and greater emphasis on state and national testing are increasing government control of education and making public schools more standardized. Homeschooling parents will increasingly be expected to meet these standards, and perhaps even administer state-mandated tests. These and other developments would reduce homeschoolers' opportu-nities to decide how they will home-school.

Therefore, if we homeschoolers are going to maintain the right and freedom to homeschool without unnecessary and increasingly restrictive government regulation, we need to act. We are in the best position to do this, because we have the strongest motivation and we understand the importance of homeschooling. If we don't work to maintain our freedom, no one else will do it for us. Among the things we can do are the following.

- As we are planning our homeschooling, we can budget some money, time, and energy to spend working to maintain our freedoms in some of the ways listed below.
- We can read and interpret homeschooling laws ourselves and refuse to do more than the minimum required by law. (See Question 2.)
- We can understand the basic foundations of our homeschooling rights and freedoms, including the difference between compulsory attendance and compulsory education. (See Question 5.)
- We can work with other homeschoolers through inclusive grassroots homeschooling organizations when they exist or start them ourselves, if

necessary. (See our book *Taking Charge Through Homeschooling: Personal and Political Empowerment,* pages 149–164.)

- We can work to increase public support, or at least acceptance, by sharing our homeschooling experiences with friends, relatives, and acquaintances; getting positive homeschooling reports into the media; countering negative press; and so on. Linda Dobson's "News Watch" column in *Home Education Magazine* offers excellent information about homeschooling in the media.

- We can counter individuals and organizations that threaten to decrease our homeschooling freedoms through carelessness, lack of understanding, or willingness to sacrifice homeschooling freedoms for the benefit of some other agenda.

- Most important, we can enjoy living and learning with our children, activities that will be much more difficult to do if our homeschooling freedoms are reduced.

87

Who are the homeschool experts?

CAFI COHEN The short answer? Other homeschooling parents and you.

When I speak at homeschooling conferences, I always include a question and answer period with each presentation. It is my opportunity to learn from the audience. Not uncommonly, one or more audience members' questions and comments reveal that they could have given a better presentation than I did. The only thing that differentiates me from these other experienced homeschooling parents is that I wrote a book on one aspect of home education and, consequently, someone asked me to speak.

Experienced homeschoolers are the experts on homeschooling. If you are new and looking for advice, these experts are all around you, in your communities, in your local support groups. Do you want to know how to involve your child in sports? Ask these people. What about dealing with a late reader or a math-phobic child? Check out the homeschoolers' answers on computer bulletin boards. Questions on a particular curriculum or diploma program? Ask homeschoolers who have used the materials.

In addition, hundreds of books and magazines now exist to guide your homeschooling efforts. Many of these have been written by homeschooling parents. Others were penned by individuals interested in alternative education

---

PEOPLE WHOSE OPINIONS OF HOMESCHOOLING I DISTRUST

CAFI COHEN

- Professional educators furthering a public school agenda
- Some politicians, especially those who support national testing, outcome-based education, the new-new math, and other quick fixes
- Nationally syndicated columnists and talk show hosts—and all others—who make no effort to research homeschooling before commenting on it
- Extended family members who also fail to do their research
- Anyone who insists a Scope and Sequence (a list of who learns what and when) matters more than honoring a child's curiosity
- Homeschooling vendors who claim that their approach is The One Right Way to Homeschool or that their program will solve all your problems

---

and the possibilities of home education. I encourage you to go to conferences and meet these people, hear them speak. Do it. Read as much as you can. Hear as much as you can. Discuss, discuss, discuss.

Weigh everything you read and hear: "That sounds good. That idea is ridiculous. That might work later." *Take what you can use and leave the rest.* Do not try to exactly follow anyone's blueprint for homeschooling. Why? Because you will not be as successful as if *you* had made your own plans for your children and your family.

Homeschooling advice is like a buffet. There is something for everyone, but only you can fill your dinner plate. If you dish up exactly what your neighbor prefers, you will enjoy some of it, ignore some of it, spit out some. Similarly, if you homeschool exactly like a more experienced homeschooling family (recognized or not), you will best address your children's needs by picking from among many approaches and resources.

WILL SHAW This depends on the aspect of homeschooling and what you mean by expert. People who have home-schooled for a while can say what they have done and what appears to have worked, and maybe why—for them. But being experienced doesn't make you an expert. Some individuals have tried hard to learn what's happening,

Will Shaw

what's available, who's doing what, what's new. Some may possess more knowledge on a given subject. They can give their perspective, which can have value. But homeschoolers need to rely on themselves. They should gather information from many sources and use their own judgment on methods, resources, and issues. There are a wealth of books about home education. Look at various books, and read new ones as they're published. Associate with local homeschool groups or networks, and join a statewide homeschool organization (or at least subscribe to its newsletter). You should also read national homeschool magazines. Stay informed so you can wisely think for yourself about your educational choices, your rights and responsibilities. If you never go to curriculum fairs or conventions, don't get state organization newsletters, and so on, you will be clueless when a fantastic homeschool resource appears or if the homeschool laws in your state are about to be fundamentally changed.

Some *think* they are informed, but aren't. They may belong to a local homeschool organization that is connected with a certain state organization that is associated with a certain national organization that is connected with a certain national homeschool magazine, and they all hear and read the same homeschool viewpoints and spokespersons. So some homeschoolers really only get one perspective and don't realize it.

Make the connections, get the newsletters and magazines, but be sure they represent a true variety of sources and resources.

MICHELLE BARONE Our culture really likes experts. It is comforting to be told what to do and how to do it. That way, when things go wrong, we can abdicate responsibility and point a finger somewhere else. Homeschooling is an entire movement based on the principle of accepting responsibility for our children's education, and still we seem unable to shake the notion that someone else knows more about our children and their needs then we do. Those of us who have been homeschooling for a few years may have many wonderful ideas and suggestions to share. We may have read lots of books, gone to conferences, field trips, and lectures. Talking to us can be helpful when you are new to home-schooling and uncertain of your path.

Remember when you were pregnant the first time and it seemed as though every woman you met could not stop herself from telling you her story—in all the gory detail? But you went to classes, read all you could, talked to doctors, mid-wives, experienced moms. When the day came and you gave birth, it was in your own unique way. The same is true of homeschooling: You will do it your way, the unique way that fits your family.

There are many wonderful, bright, interesting, motivating people who are

> I would venture to guess all these experienced homeschoolers would be the first to encourage you to take your own path, let in all the information that works for your family, let the rest go.

writing and lecturing about homeschooling. Here you are, reading a book full of "experts." But I would venture to guess all these experienced homeschoolers would be the first to encourage you to take your own path, let in all the information that works for your family, let the rest go. Truly, you are the homeschooling expert for your children.

88

What have homeschooling parents learned from this experience?

MARY GRIFFITH I've learned that my children are just as curious as I am, that

---

NO MATTER THEIR AGE, EACH DAY PROVIDE YOUR CHILDREN WITH A MINIMUM OF AT LEAST ONE

- Kiss
- Hug
- Compliment
- Chance to share
- Opportunity to teach something
- Reason for learning something new

they want to know how their world works, and that they're capable of learning far more than I am capable of teaching them. I've learned that my children are essential members of this family, that they often find solutions I've missed for problems we've faced. I've learned (and keep learning, over and over again!) that my children are the best judges of how and when and what they need to learn. I've learned that my children, like me, learn most from doing real, useful work rather than from make-believe projects. I've learned that learning is the best part of life, that learning is something I will do until the day I die. And I've learned that my children already know all this. They won't need to be thirty-five years old before they finally figure it out.

HELEN AND MARK HEGENER We've learned to trust our children and ourselves. Trust is not easy to come by, and it's made even harder by schooling which teaches us not to trust ourselves, or our own instincts and feelings, but to rely on expertise and authority instead. Schooling utilizes a top-down chain of command, a hierarchical student-teacher relationship, but homeschooling doesn't need to replicate this hurtful pattern. Homeschooling encourages the development of a loving relationship based on caring and trust between parent and child, and

this is the best possible environment for real learning to take place. Real learning, like how to talk to other people about minor and major things, how to determine what needs doing and the best way in which to get it done, how to find one's rightful place in a confusing and complex world, how to truly live a life filled with goodness and worthiness and love.

While this learning is happening to our children, similar learning is happening to us as parents. We begin to question long-held assumptions about children and learning and our own place in the puzzle. We begin to see that what we were told about certain things like education and earning a living and what's worth doing with our lives is not necessarily true, and we find ourselves searching for answers to questions we thought we already knew the answers to.

As parents for over twenty years now, we've learned that we don't have all the answers. Sometimes our children have better answers than we do, especially as they've grown older. We've taught them to think carefully, and to consider several angles and approaches to a situation when necessary, but we're not as good at it as they are now. We've learned that being open to new ideas, new ways of looking at things, is a valuable approach in life, but old habits and old ways of doing things can be difficult to let go. Our children are helping us learn to let go and embrace new ways of seeing, hearing, feeling.

We've often quoted an old saying, whose author we've long forgotten, that goes something like this: "We can teach our children to have courage, faith and endurance; they can teach us to laugh, to sing, and to love." In the final analysis, these lessons are probably the most important ones.

BECKY RUPP Each homeschooling family doubtless has its own list of unexpected revelations. What Randy and I have learned from our homeschooling experiences could fill a book. Homeschooling has been much more than we ever expected. In a way, it's like those little sponge capsules about the size of a vitamin pill—the kind you drop in water and suddenly it swells to the size of a pancake and turns into an octopus.

We've learned, from hands-on experience, that a true education is something that each person does for him or herself. It's not what we teach that makes an education; it's what they learn. This may not sound like much: these

> **As parents for over twenty years now, we've learned that we don't have all the answers. Sometimes our children have better answers than we do, especially as they've grown older. We've taught them to think carefully, and to consider several angles and approaches to a situation when necessary, but we're not as good at it as they are now.**

days it's accepted homeschool dogma. Observing it in practice, however, in our very own living room, was something else again. I hadn't realized that "pursuing their own interests in their own way" was going to be so emphatically individual. Each of our sons assimilated something different from his homeschool experience and used it to build a unique education—and the outcomes, in each case, are not necessarily the educations we would have chosen for them. Instead, these are the educations they chose for themselves.

When we decided to homeschool our boys, starting some eleven years ago when our oldest was just reaching kindergarten age, we had a number of goals in mind. We wanted to raise children who could think for themselves, undeterred by peer pressure. We wanted the boys to develop as individuals, with the confidence to march to the beats of their own—perhaps very different—drummers. We wanted the boys to have time and freedom to pursue their own interests and set their own goals.

There's an old saying: "Be careful what you wish for, because you just might get it." Homeschooling gave us just what we wished for: it turned out three unconventional and independent thinkers. This means that our sons don't always think like we do and it means that we don't always agree with each other. It's not quite what we expected. But we wouldn't trade it for anything.

LINDA DOBSON I wish I'd had the opportunity to learn what I've realized through homeschooling much earlier in life. That's probably why I look at homeschooled children, including my own, with awe and respect and optimism. I emerged from high school confused and unsure, told to jump into a new world when I didn't know if or where it had a place for me. These children generally finish homeschooling comfortable and confident, moving gracefully through growing independence into a world where their place is well established through years and exposure.

What was the vital difference between my experience and theirs? The answer is as clear as the stars on an Adirondack winter night. You see, the homeschooled children were never forced away from the world in the first place. And this has made all the difference.

Homeschooled children have experienced educational freedom in as many forms as the term freedom implies. Educational freedom means children's minds, hearts, and hands are delivered from restriction, schedule, and agenda externally imposed. Thus freed, the children have room—lots of space and time—to discover self. This discovery is a necessary foundation, an essential first step before any learning can possibly become meaningful and significant.

This step leads to the ability of self-determination. It's the self-determination of which Thomas Jefferson spoke so eloquently when he imagined an educated populace charged with electing forthright government representatives, the same self-determination implied in the phrase "life, liberty, and the pursuit of happiness." Yet self-knowledge and self-determination are made impossible by the very nature of any educational "system," most notably one that locks children away from the world.

This, I believe, is the most important of a long list of homeschooling lessons I've learned. When an educational system is set up to discourage self-determination from the start, and when I must financially support this discouragement of self-determination under threat of losing my home, then connections to life, liberty, and pursuit of happiness have been severed. A system like this must be a vehicle for something else. The evidence, too plentiful to include in this short piece, points to a "systematic" replacement of self-determination with dependence. The system serves up a curriculum—no, a lifestyle—that readies children for dependence on government for, just to name a few, increased police protection, health care, child care, jobs, housing, and food; in short, survival.

Did you notice the common thread running through all three of the other answers to this question?

Mary Griffith wrote: "[My children] often find solutions I've missed for problems we've faced."

The Hegeners wrote: "Sometimes our children have better answers than we do."

Becky Rupp wrote: "Our sons don't always think like we do."

This is anecdotal evidence of homeschooling children's self-determination—from three out of three families. These children are not being educated for dependence on government or anything or anyone else. If you prefer scientific evidence, I know of only one formal study of adult homeschoolers, which was undertaken by J. Gary Knowles and reported in 1991. None of the adults who were homeschooled as children that Mr. Knowles surveyed were unemployed (a large percentage had their own businesses), and none were on *any* form of welfare assistance.

The lesson is elementary: An education that starts with self-determination will finish with self-determination. Homeschooling parents and children alike are pressing the concept of educational freedom against its boundaries—and beyond—and reclaiming our ancestors' promises.

The value of educational freedom is a lesson too important to keep to ourselves. Throughout this book we have freely shared it with you. If you appreciate your home, you may be forced to keep supporting the system with your money, but you don't have to support the system by feeding it your children. You *can* choose to allow them to remain in the world.

And this will make all the difference.

Resources: Terribly Incomplete, But More Than Enough to Get You Started

I N MANY WAYS the search for resources was a lot easier for beginning homeschoolers ten years ago: What you wanted was either available from a limited number of suppliers or you went about creating it yourself! In one sitting I could quickly put together a resource list that covered most of the territory. But with homeschooling's growing popularity and acceptance, putting together a *complete* resource list has become a monumental task, and the quantity of suppliers fills many books devoted specifically to that task.

This list is not an attempt to duplicate those heroic efforts; it's just a way to get you off and running to collect the information and materials you may feel you need to get started—a little of this and a little of that. As you read books, subscribe to periodicals, and start sending away for information, ever more resources will come to your attention. Look at it like a treasure hunt: You'll dig in a lot of places in order to uncover those few gems that fit your unique needs.

Throughout this book experienced homeschoolers have echoed a similar refrain. Despite our learned thinking to the contrary, you don't need to spend a lot of money and buy a lot of "stuff" to provide a quality education for your children. Like most of the contributors to this book, I remember all too well spending money on materials I initially felt were essential, only to watch them sit on shelves collecting dust and wishing I had back just *half* of the money spent to do it over again.

At the same time, I encourage everyone to check out every resource that looks even remotely interesting to your children. Materials are as diverse as the people you've met in this book who use (or don't use) them. You never know when a book, a story, a documentary, a game, a movie, or a little-known occupation will ignite an imagination and set a child off on a life-influencing exploration.

One caveat: *Take it easy!* There's a lot of great "stuff" out there, but you don't need it all and you certainly don't need it all at once. Homeschooling doesn't have to be a "budget buster." In fact, when education is seamlessly integrated into living life, the ordinary becomes educational. "Educational" toys, books, games, videos, audio tapes and more are gifts happily welcomed by youngsters' as birthday and Christmas presents. While it felt a bit "tacky," I would always compile a list of all those neat things I saw in catalogs throughout the year, then provide Grandma and Grandpa, aunts and uncles, with the list and catalog ordering information when holidays rolled around. Ordering information was necessary because many of these great resources just aren't available on local store shelves; and since many of the suppliers are home educators with home businesses, I want to support their efforts.

After reading this book, you also realize that homeschooling frees our minds from the compartmentalization of subject matter, so many of the available resources defy strict categorization. A good child's magazine may focus on history, for example, yet provide your son with knowledge of geography, science, and throw in a few great art projects for good measure. For the sake of making the following list as easy to use as possible, it has been broken down into categories, so just remember the lines between those categories are thin and flexible.

Since this is an incomplete list, please keep in mind that just because a resource *isn't* included, that doesn't mean it's not a good one. Any lack of inclusion simply means *we're out of room, folks!*

I leave you with many best wishes for an enjoyable, enlightening romp through learning at home with your children. Happy learning . . . always.

SUPPORT GROUPS

Homeschool support groups come in all shapes and sizes. They may focus on serving home-schoolers around the nation, or simply around the neighborhood. Most, regardless of scope, work on shoestring budgets, so including a stamped, self-addressed envelope is always greatly appreciated.

National Homeschool Groups and Allies

Most of the following organizations focus on special areas of homeschooling. Others address home education in the broader areas of alternative education, legal issues, and parental involvement in education.

The Adventist Home Educator
PO Box 836
Camino, CA 95709
916-647-2110

Alliance for Parental Involvement in
    Education
PO Box 59
East Chatham, NY 12060-0059
518-392-6900
E-mail: allpie@taconic.net

Alternative Education Resource Organization
417 Roslyn Road
Roslyn Heights, NY 11577
516-621-2195
Fax: 516-625-3257
Web site:http://www.speakeasy.org/~aero

American Homeschool Association
PO Box 3142
Palmer, AK 99645-3142
907-746-1336
Fax: 907-746-1335
E-mail: AHA@home-ed-magazine.com
Web site: http://www.home-ed-magazine.com/
    AHA/aha.html

The Association of Canadian Home-Based
    Education
E-mail: Jillcampbell@xpressnet.com

Canadian Alliance of Homeschoolers
272 Highway 5, RR 1
St. George, Ontario N0E 1N0
Canada
Wendy Priesnitz: 519-448-4001

Catholic Homeschool Network of America
PO Box 6343
River Forest, IL 60305-6343
Fax: 330-652-5322, 708-386-3380,
    608-592-5893

Family Unschoolers Network
1688 Belhaven Woods Court
Pasadena, MD 21122-3727
Voice Mail/Fax 410-360-7330
E-mail: FUNNews@MCImail.com

Future of Freedom Foundation
11350 Random Hills Road, Suite 800
Fairfax, VA 22030
703-934-6101

Homeschoolers for Peace
PO Box 74
Midpines, CA 95345

Homeschooling Unitarian Universalists and
    Humanists and Learning Happens!
3135 Lakeland Drive
Nashville, TN 37214
Jacki Willard 615-889-4938
E-mail: lrnghppn@bellsouth.net
Web site: http://members.aol.com/
    lrnghppns/index.html

Islamic Homeschool Association of North
    America
1312 Plymouth Court
Raleigh, NC 27610

Jewish Home Educator's Network
1295 Marshall Drive SE
Salem, OR 97302
Marilyn Lowe: 503-362-1203
E-mail: marilyn.lowe@chemek.com

Moore Foundation
PO Box 1
Camas, WA 98607

Muslim Home School Network and Resources
PO Box 803
Attleboro, MA 02703
E-mail: MHSNR@aol.com
Web site: http://www.ici.net/cust_pages/
    taadah/taadah.html

National Association for the Legal Support of
    Alternative Schools
PO Box 2823
Santa Fe, NM 87501
505-471-6928

National Association for Mormon Home
    Educators
2770 S 1000 W
Perry, UT 84302

National Association of Catholic Home
    Educators
PO Box 787
Montrose, AL 36559
Web site: http://www.nache.com

National Center for Fair and Open Testing
342 Broadway
Cambridge, MA 02139
617-864-4810

National Coalition of Alternative Community
    Schools
PO Box 15036
Santa Fe, NM 87501
505-474-4312

National Handicapped Homeschoolers
    Association
5383 Alpine Road SE
Olalla, WA 98359
Tom and Sherry Bushnell: 206-857-4257

National Homeschool Association
PO Box 290
Hartland, MI 48353-0290
Voice mail: 513-772-9580
Web site: http://www.alumni.caltech.edu/
    ~casner/nha.html

Native American Home School Association
PO Box 979
Fries, VA 24330
Web site: http://expage.com/page/
    nahomeschool

Pacific Justice Institute
916-646-6232
www.pacificjustice.org

Resource Center for Redesigning Education
PO Box 298
Brandon, VT 05733-0298
800-639-4122 (802-247-8312)
Web site: http://www.sover.net.~holistic

Rutherford Institute
PO Box 7482
Charlottesville, VA 22906
804-978-3888

Separation of School and State Alliance
4578 N First #310
Fresno, CA 93726
209-292-1776
Web site: http://www.sepschool.org

Single Parents Educating Children in
    Alternative Learning
2 Pineview Drive #5
Amelia, OH 45102

State and Local Support Groups

Local, regional, and state support groups may be one of the most important contributors to homeschooling's success. Sources of information, inspiration, activities, and lasting friendships, these backbones of the homeschooling movement are overwhelmingly started and maintained by volunteers doing what they love, and sharing what they do.

Because of the voluntary nature of these groups, contact information is ever-changing. As careful as I've been to provide the most accurate way to get in touch with a support group near you, chances are very good that *somewhere,* on the day after I put the information on paper, someone "retired" or moved or served her term and handed over the reins to another volunteer.

The good news is that a former volunteer can lead you quickly to the person you need. If this fails, you can always use any of the terrific ideas the writers in this book provided about how to contact a local support group. And remember, if all else fails, you can always start your own.

Good luck, and happy meetings!*

Canada

London Educational Alternatives Program
(Ontario)
E-mail: womble@zap.wwdc.com

Montreal Metropolitan Support Group for
Home-based Education
PO Box 663
Victoria Station
Westmount, QC H3Z 2Y7
Marguerite: 514-284-2187
Web site: http://www.angelfire.com/mn/
nevenfamily

Ontario Federation of Teaching Parents
145 Taylor Road W
Gananoque, Ontario K7G 2V3
Gayle Remisch: 613-382-4947
E-mail: oftp@kingston.net

Yukon Home Educators Society
PO Box 4993
Whitehorse, Yukon Y1A 4S2

Alabama

AL Home Educators Network (AHEN)
3015 Thurman Road
Huntsville, AL 35805
Lisa Bugg: 205-534-6401
E-mail: KaeKaeB@aol.com

AL Home Educators
PO Box 16091
Mobile, AL 36116

Alaska

AK Homeschool Network
PO Box 3142
Palmer, AK 99645
907-745-1323
E-mail: OldAlaskan@aol.com

AK Homeschoolers Association
PO Box 230973
Anchorage, AK 99504-3527

Anchorage Home Spun Educators
PO Box 798
Girdwood, AK 99587
E-mail: HomeSpuned@aol.com

Homeschoolers Unlimited
7390 J Street #B
Elmendorf AFB, AK 99506
Sue Patterson
E-mail: Pattrson5@aol.com

*Most of this collection is courtesy of the efforts of *Home Education Magazine.* Please remember that addresses, phone numbers, and e-mail addresses change frequently.

Sitka Home Education Association
506 Verstovia Street
Sitka, AK 99835
Molly Jacobson: 907-747-1483

Arizona
Apache Junction Unschooler
PO Box 6341
Apache Junction, AZ 85278
E-mail: ajunschl@aol.com
Web site: http://members.aol.com/ajunschl

AZ Families for Home Education
PO Box 4661
Scottsdale, AZ 85261-4661
800-929-3927

Phoenix Learning Alternative
    Network
Nancy Sherr: 602-483-3381

SPICE
10414 W Mulberry Drive
Avondale, AZ 85323
Susan Taniguchi: 602-877-3642
E-mail: pompey@juno.com

TELAO Home Educators
4700 North Tonalea Trail
Tucson, AZ 85749
520-749-4757

Arkansas
Coalition of AR Parents (CAP)
PO Box 192455
Little Rock, AR 72219

Home Educators of AR Voicing Excellence
    Now (HEAVEN)
8 Glenbrook Place
Sherwood, AR 72120

California
All Ways Learning of San Jose
Faye: 408-226-1518

Antelope Valley Homeschoolers
Jara Foreman-Self: 805-947-3674

Bayshore Homeschoolers
PO Box 13038
Long Beach, CA 90803
Lenore Hayes: 310-434-3940
E-mail: BayShSch@aol.com

Butte Homeschool Network
Christina Dyer: 916-877-3543
E-mail: CedarMt@aol.com

CA Hi-Desert Home Education
    Association
15185 Cactus Street
Hesperia, CA 92345
Sue Roper: 619-949-9725

CA Homeschool Network
PO Box 44
Vineberg, CA 95487
800-327-5339
E-mail: CHNMail@aol.com
Web site: http://www.comenius.org/
    chnpage.htm

Campbell Vicinity Homeschoolers
Carolyn Hammond: 408-866-0426
E-mail: Boonemas@aol.com

Central CA Homeschoolers
7600 Marchant Avenue
Atascadero, CA 93422
Barbara Alward: 805-462-0726

Conejo Valley Homeschoolers
Sandra: 805-373-8588
Jennifer: 805-499-2475

East Bay Family Educators
1090 Mariposa Avenue
Berkeley, CA 94707
Jane Ahrens: 510-524-1224

Excellence in Education (Monrovia)
Carolyn: 818-357-4443

Family Centered Education of
    Los Angeles
Marsha Lenox: 818-766-8914

High Desert Homeschoolers
Karen Taylor: 760-956-1588
E-mail: taylors@ctainforms.com

Home Education League of Parents
    (HELP-LA)
3208 Cahuenga Boulevard W, Suite 131
Los Angeles, CA 90068

Homeschool Association of CA
PO Box 2442
Atascadero, CA 93423
Barbara Alward: 888-472-4440
E-mail: info@hsc.org
Web site: http://www.hsc.org

Homeschooling Co-op of Sacramento
15 Moses Court
Sacramento, CA 95823

Humboldt Homeschoolers
PO Box 2125
Trinidad, CA 95570
Paige Smith: 707-677-3290
E-mail: psmith@humboldt1.com

Independent Homeschoolers
Martine: 310-788-9788

Inland Empire Homelearners (Rancho
    Cucamonga)
909-946-5251

Lompoc Valley Home Educators
Chris Tykeson: 805-733-2710

Los Angeles Homeschoolers
PO Box 1166
Malibu, CA 90265
310-456-5447

Marin Homeschoolers
905 Tiburon Boulevard
Tiburon, CA 94920
415-435-0768

Monterey Bay Christian Home Schoolers
1558 Flores Street
Seaside, CA 93955
Diane Moss: 408-394-9504
Web site: http://www.redshift.com/~mizmooz

North Bay HomeScholars
PO Box 621
Vineburg, CA 95487
Cyndie Moi: 707-939-9525
E-mail: CynMoi@metro.net

Oakleaf Homeschoolers (1000 Oaks)
Leslie: 805-498-1999

Riverside Area Home Learners
731 Mt. Whitney Circle
Corona, CA 91719
Charlie Miles-Prystowsky: 909-279-4026

Rose Rock Homeschool Support Group of
    Southern CA
1752 East Avenue J, Suite 115
Lancaster, CA 93535
E-mail: roserock@geocities.com
Web site: http://www.geocities.com/Athens/
    Parthenon/8503

San Diego Home Educators
JoAnn Basnino Kelly: 619-560-8866

San Francisco Homeschoolers
3639 Webster Street
San Francisco, CA 94123
Franceasca Pera: 415-673-8092

Sonoma County Home Schoolers Association
PO Box 431
Petaluma, CA 94953
Lillian Jones: 707-874-2740
Toll-free: 888-HSC-4440
E-mail: wrensong@aol.com

South Valley Homeschoolers Association
7500 Chestnut Street
Gilroy, CA 95020
Mary Drummond: 408-847-2017 (after 1 P.M.)

SPICE (Sacramento Valley)
PO Box 282
Wilton, CA 95693
Bonnie: 916-687-7053
E-mail: spice-sacramento@juno.com

1000 Oaks Homeschool Group
Holly: 805-499-9429

Tri-City Homeschoolers
Newark, CA
Bry Conley: 510-796-3806
Catherine Dorman: 510-790-3871

West San Fernando Valley Playgroup
20555 Dumont Street
Woodland Hills, CA 91364
Sara Brecht: 818-888-2480

Whittier Homeschoolers
7432 Duchess Drive
Whittier, CA 90606
Rita Poncedeleon-Smith

Yolo County Homeschoolers
Katje Sabin-Newmiller: 916-758-8459
E-mail: klsabin@wheel.dcn.davis.ca.us

Yosemite Area Homeschoolers
PO Box 74
Midpines, CA 95345
Pam Gingold: 209-742-6802

Colorado

Boulder County Home Educators
Boulder, CO 80304
Valerie Berg: 303-449-5916

CO Home Educator's Association
3043 S Laredo Circle
Aurora, CO 80013
303-441-9938
E-mail: pinewood@dash.com

CO Home Schooling Network
1247 Harrison Street
Denver, CO 80206
303-369-9541

Concerned Parents of Colorado
PO Box 547
Florissant, CO 80816
719-748-8360

Independent Network of Creative
  Homeschoolers (INCH)
5984 S Netherland Circle
Aurora, CO 80015
303-766-7882

Mesa Verde Homeschoolers
PO Box 134
Mancos, CO 81328
The MacLaren Family: 970-892-7802

Rocky Mountain Education Connection
20774 E Buchanan Drive
Aurora, CO 80011
303-341-2242
E-mail: connect@ecentral.com

West River Unschoolers
2420 N 1st Street
Grand Junction, CO 81501
Peggy Nishikawa: 970-241-4137

Connecticut

CT Home Educators Association
80 Coppermine Road
Oxford, CT 06478
Mary Beth Nelson: 203-732-0102

CT's CURE (CT's Citizens to Uphold the
   Right to Educate)
PO Box 597
Sherman, CT 06784
Alison Brion: 203-355-4724

The Education Association of Christian
   Homeschoolers (TEACH)
25 Field Stone Run
Farmington, CT 06032
800-205-8744

Unschoolers Support
22 Wildrose Avenue
Guilford, CT 06437
Luz Shosie 203-458-7402

Delaware
DE Home Education Association
Box 1003
Dover, DE 19903

Tri-State Home School Network
PO Box 7193
Newark, DE 19714-7193
302-234-0516

Florida
The Family Learning Exchange
2020 Turpentine Road
Mims, FL 32754
407-268-8833

FPEA
PO Box 371
Melbourne, FL 32902
407-722-0895
E-mail: office@fpea.com
Web site: http://www.fpea.com

Home Education Resources and Information
711 St. Johns Bluff Road
Jacksonville, FL 32225
904-565-9121
E-mail: herijax@juno.com

Home Educators Assistance League
3343 Shoal Creek Cove
Crestview, FL 32539
Carrie Bundy: 904-682-2422

Home Educators Lending Parents Support
5941 NW 14 Court
Sunrise, FL 33313
Susie Capraro: 954-791-9733
E-mail: Scapraro-helps@juno.com

The Homeschool Network
PO Box 940402
Maitland, FL 32794
Lyn Milum: 407-889-4632
E-mail: forest5@gdi.net

Parkland Home Educators
517 Roughbeard Road
Winter Park, FL 32792
407-657-7560

SOAR
Holly Palermo: 407-997-9874

Georgia
Atlanta Alternative Education Network
1586 Rainier Falls Drive
Atlanta, GA 30329
404-636-6348
E-mail: mickaels@mindspring.com
Web site: http://www.mindspring.com/
   ~lei/aaen

Catholic Family Educators of GA
770-516-2624

Douglas County Home Educators
3855 Jims Court
Douglasville, GA 30135
Lucas and Kaycee Mancas: 770-949-3297

Family Education for Christ
PO Box 16619
Savannah, GA 31416
Becky Gianino: 912-354-5204

Free to Learn at Home
4439 Lake Forest Drive
Oakwood, GA 30566
Chris Bishop: 770-536-8077

Georgians for Freedom in Education
7180 Cane Leaf Drive
Fairburn, GA 30213
Billie Jean Bryant: 770-463-1563

LIGHT
PO Box 2724
Columbus, GA 31902
706-324-3714

Robins Air Force Base Homeschool Network
607 Langley Street
Robins Air Force Base, GA 31098
Barbara Frederick
E-mail: barbfred@aol.com

Hawaii

Christian Homeschoolers of Hawaii
91-824 Oama Street
Ewa Beach, HI 96706
808-689-6398

Hawaii Homeschool Association
PO Box 3476
Mililani, HI 96789
E-mail: TGthrngPlc@aol.com

Kauai Home Educators Association
Jeanne Ferrari Amas: 808-245-7867
E-mail: jeanne@aloha.net

Idaho

Family Unschoolers Network
1809 North 7th Street
Boise, ID 83702
208-345-2703

ID Home Educator's Network
Rosalind: 208-782-8305

Palouse Home Learning Alternatives
802 White Avenue
Moscow, ID 83843
Peg Harvey: 208-882-1593

Illinois

Homeschooling Answers
806 Oakton
Evanston, IL 60202
Anne Wasserman: 847-328-7129
E-mail: RichardW@tezcat.com

HOUSE
2508 E 22nd Place
Sauk Village, IL 60411
Teresa Sneade: 708-758-7374

IL Christian Home Educators
PO Box 261
Zion, IL 60099
708-662-1909

Islamic Homeschooling Education Network
    of IL
241 Meadowbrook Drive
Bolingbrook, IL 60440
A. Zaakiya Abdul-Ra'ees Arshad
E-mail: ILYASAH@aol.com

Round Lake Area Homeschoolers
Sissy Cossarek: 847-740-8136
E-mail: jsc@iconnect.net

Spectrum Homeschoolers
10859 S Longwood Drive
Chicago, IL 60643-3312
Karolyn Kuchner: 773-779-7608

Unschoolers Network
736 N Mitchell Avenue
Arlington Heights, IL 60004
Pattie Donahue-Krueger: 847-253-8902
E-mail: PJADK@aol.com

Indiana

Families Learning Together
1714 E 51st Street
Indianapolis, IN 46205
Jill: 317-255-9298
E-mail: whelan.mullen@juno.com

Homefront
1120 W Whiskey Run Road
New Salisbury, IN 47161
Donnell and Teresa Royer: 812-347-2931

IN Association of Home Educators
1000 North Madison #S2
Greenwood, IN 46142
317-638-9633

L.E.A.R.N.
9577 E State Road 45
Unionville, IN 47468
Barbara Benson: 812-336-8028

Wabash Valley Homeschool Association
PO Box 3865
Terre Haute, IN 47803
E-mail: WVHA@aol.com

Iowa

IA Home Educators' Association
PO Box 213
Des Moines, IA 50301

Rebecca Leach
2301 S Henry Street
Sioux City, IA 51106
712-274-0472
E-mail: Beckyleach@aol.com

Network of IA Christian Home Educators
Box 158
Dexter, IA 50070

Kansas

Circle of Homeschoolers and Unschoolers in
    Central Kansas
RR 1, Box 28A
Rush Center, KS 67575
Susan Peach: 913-372-4457

Heartland Area Homeschoolers' Association
823 West Street
Emporia, KS 66801
Shiuvaun Sowder: 316-343-3696

Konza Homeschoolers Association
319 Knoxberry Drive
Manhattan, KS 66502
Mary Levin: 913-587-8280 (Manhattan)
Martha Hackney: 913-494-2884 (St. George)

Lawrence Area Unaffiliated Group
    of Homeschoolers
RR 1, Box 496
Perry, KS 66073
Barbara Michener: 913-597-5579

Teaching Parents Association
PO Box 3968
Wichita, KS 67201
316-945-0810

Kentucky

Bluegrass Home Educators
600 Shake Rag Road
Waynesburg, KY 40489
Cherie Carroll: 606-365-8568
E-mail: KyHomeEd@mis.net
Web site: http://www.BluegrassHmEd.nvo.com

KY Home Education Association
PO Box 81
Winchester, KY 40392-0081

KY Independent Learners Network
PO Box 275
Somerset, KY 42501
Meg McClory: 606-678-2527

Louisiana
Homeschoolers Learning from Mother Earth
14189 Ridge Road
Prairieville, LA 70769
Roxann Phillips

LA Citizens for Home Education
3404 Van Buren
Baker, LA 70714

Wild Azalea Unschoolers
6055 General Meyer Avenue
New Orleans, LA 70131
Tracey Sherry: 504-392-5647
E-mail: tws@gnofn.org

Maine
Homeschoolers of Maine
HC 62, Box 24
Hope, ME 04847
207-763-4251

ME Home Education Association
PO Box 421
Popsham, ME 04086
800-520-0577

Southern ME Home Education
    Support Network
76 Beech Ridge Road
Scarborough, ME 04074
Eileen Yoder: 207-883-9621

Maryland
Educating Our Own
686 Geneva Drive
Westminster, MD 21157
410-857-0168 or 410-848-3390

Live and Learn Home Educators
Harford County, MD
E-mail: nelmod@erols.com

MD Home Education Association
9085 Flamepool Way
Columbia, MD 21045
Manfred W. Smith: 410-730-0073

Montgomery Homeschool Resource Group
306 Hannes Street
Silver Spring, MD 20901
Martine Palmiter: 301-871-6431

North County Home Educators
    (Anne Arundel)
1688 Bellhaven Woods Court
Pasadena, MD 21122
Nancy or Billy Greer: 410-437-5109
E-mail: FUNNews@MCImail.com

Massachusetts
The Family Resource Center
PO Box 308
Salem, MA 01970
Tammy and Rick Rosenblatt: 508-741-7449
E-mail: BigBear001@aol.com

Franklin County Homelearning Families
72 Prospect Street
Greenfield, MA 01301
Jean Johnson: 413-773-9280

Homeschooling Together
24 Avon Place
Arlington, MA 02174
E-mail: ses@world.std.com

Jewish Homeschoolers of MA
E-mail: FernReiss@aol.com

MA Home Learning Association
PO Box 1558
Marstons Mills, MA 02648

Loretta Heuer: 508-429-1436
E-mail: LorettaMCH@aol.com
Kathy Smith: 508-249-9056
E-mail: Lisawood@aol.com

MA Homeschoolers Organization of
    Parent Educators
15 Ohio Street
Wilmington, MA 01887
508-658-8970

Merrimack Valley Homelearners Group
13 Ashdale Road
N Billerica, MA 01862
Alysa Dudley: 508-663-2755
E-mail: garyd@chelmsford.com

Michigan

Celebrating Home Under Rome—
    Catholic Homeschoolers
Rachel Mackson: 517-349-6389
E-mail: RWittLans@aol.com

Families Learning and Schooling at Home
21671B Drive North
Marshall, MI 49068
Natalie Valle: 616-781-1069

HELP Michigan
125 E Lincoln
Negaunee, MI 49866
906-475-5508
E-mail: up4hmsklrs@aol.com

Heritage Home Educators
13339 Firestone Court
Fenton, MI 48430
Lisa Hodge-Kander

Hillsdale Area Homeschoolers
5151 Barker Road
Jonesville, MI 49250
Linda Kline: 517-287-5565

Home Educator's Circle
1280 John Hix Street
Westland, MI 48186
313-326-5406

Older Homeschoolers' Group
9120 Dwight Drive
Detroit, MI 48214
Lynn Family: 313-331-8406

Minnesota

MN Association of Roman Catholic
    Home Educators
7211 Sherwood Echo
Woodbury, MN 55125
Kaye Harker-Hansen: 612-730-8101

MN Homeschoolers Alliance
PO Box 23072
Richfield, MN 55423
612-491-2828

Mississippi

Coast Military Home Educators
9212A Givens Circle
Biloxi, MS 39531
Lori and John Hudson: 601-388-4522

Home Educators of Central MS
535 Luling Street
Pearl, MS 39208
John and Dawn Bynum

MS Home Educators Association
RR 9, Box 350
Laurel, MS 39440-8720

Missouri

Families for Home Education
400 East High Point Lane
Columbia, MO 65203
816-826-9302

LEARN
PO Box 10105
Kansas City, MO 64171
913-383-7888
E-mail: Kwilson898@aol.com,
    Krissmoose@aol.com

Ozark Lore Society
HC 73, Box 160
Drury, MO 65638
Debra Eisenmann: 417-679-3391

St. Louis Homeschooling Network
4147 Est Pine
St. Louis, MO 63108
Karen Karabel: 314-534-1171

Montana
Independent Homeschoolers Network
    of Bozeman
415 S 9th Avenue
Bozeman, MT 59715
Katie Perry: 406-586-4564

Mid-Mountain Home Education Network
PO Box 2182
Montana City Station, MT 59634
Karen Semple: 406-443-3376

MT Coalition of Home Educators
PO Box 654
Helena, MT 59624
406-443-5826

Nebraska
LEARN
7741 E Avon Lane
Lincoln, NE 68505
Rose Yonekura: 402-488-7741

Nevada
Northern NV Home Schools, Inc.
PO Box 21323
Reno, NV 89515
702-852-6647
E-mail: NNHS@aol.com

New Hampshire
Homeschooling Friends
204 Brackett Road
New Durham, NH 03855
Beverly Behr: 603-332-4146
E-mail: nothome@world-path.net
Web site: http://www.geocities.com/
    Heartland/Plains/9175

NH Alliance for Home Education
17 Preserve Drive
Nashua, NH 03060
Betsy Westgate: 603-880-8629

NH Homeschooling Coalition
PO Box 2224
Concord, NH 03304
Abbey Lawrence: 603-539-7233

New Jersey
Homeschoolers of South New Jersey
1239 Whitaker Avenue
Millville, NJ 08332
Rose: 609-327-1224
E-mail: Tutor@Pulsar.net
Web site: http://www.pulsar.net/~tutor

Unschooler's Network
2 Smith Street
Farmingdale, NJ 07727
Nancy Plent: 732-938-2473

Unschooling Families Support Group
of Central NJ
150 Falwell Station Road
Jobstown, NJ 08041
Karen Mende-Fridkis: 609-723-1524

New Mexico
Carlsbad Family Educators
22 Comance Drive
Carlsbad, NM 88220
Manuela Ptacek: 505-887-6229

Corpus Christi Catholic Home Educators
150 Valle Chaparral
Cedar Crest, NM 87008
Mary Morse: 505-256-4345

Home Educators of Dona Ana
748 Roualt Avenue
Las Cruces, NM 88005
Dee McLaughlin: 505-647-0952

Home Educators of Santa Fe
21 Frasco Road
Santa Fe, NM 87505
Darla McCloud: 505-466-4462

Homeschooling PACT
PO Box 961
Portales, NM 88130
Barbara Klapperich Senn: 505-359-1618

NM Family Educators
PO Box 92276
Albuquerque, NM 87199
505-275-7053

Socorro Association of Family Educators
1208 Drake NW
Socorro, NM 87801
Titia Barham: 505-835-0497

Unschoolers of Albuquerque
8505 Bellrose NE
Albuquerque, NM 87111
Barbara Dawson: 505-275-0422
Sandra Dodd: 505-299-2476
E-mail: SandraDodd@aol.com

New York
Columbia County Homeschooling
Mothers' Group
29 Kinderhook Street
Chatham, NY 12037
Katharine Houk: 518-392-4277

Families for Home Education
3219 Coulter Road
Cazenovia, NY 13035
Peg Moore: 315-655-2574

Fingerlakes Unschoolers Network
201 Elm Street
Ithaca, NY 14850
Clare Grady: 607-273-6257
E-mail: Laundress@aol.com

Independent Home Educators of the
Hudson Valley
904 Route 9
Staatsburg, NY 12580
Heidi: 914-889-4682

Kids' Place of Choice (Freeport, LI, NY) South
Nassau Home Educators' Resource Room
516-868-5766
E-mail: Devww@aol.com

New York City Home Educators Alliance
8 East 2nd Street
New York, NY 10003
212-505-9884
E-mail: RTricamo@aol.com

NYS Home Education News
PO Box 59
East Chatham, NY 12060
Seth Rockmuller/Katharine Houk:
    518-392-6900
E-mail: allpie@taconic.net

Oneida Lake Area Home Educators
PO Box 24
Sylvan Beach, NY 13157
Chris Wheeler: 315-762-5166

Oneonta Area Sharing in Homeschooling
PO Box 48
Gilbertsville, NY 13776
Darlene Abajian: 607-783-2271

Rochester Area Homeschoolers Association
275 Yarmouth Road
Rochester, NY 14610
Voice mail: 716-234-0298

Tri-County Homeschoolers
PO Box 190
Ossining, NY 10562
Chris and Andy Hofer: 914-941-5607
E-mail: chofer@croton.com
Web site: http://www.croton.com/home-ed

Tri-Lake Community Home Educators
PO Box 270
Ray Brook, NY 12977
Lynn Waickman: 518-891-5657

Ulster County Home Ed Resource Person
94 Plains Road
New Paltz, NY 12561
914-256-0464
E-mail: KimSquared@aol.com

Western New York Homeschoolers
18 Maple Avenue
Portville, NY 14770
Gloria Zemer: 716-933-8669

North Carolina

Families Learning Together
Route 1, Box 219
Chocowinity, NC 27817

North Carolinians for Home Education
419 N Boylan Avenue
Raleigh, NC 27603-1211
Susan Van Dyke: 919-834-6243

North Dakota

ND Home School Association
4007 North State Street
Bismarck, ND 58501
701-223-4080

Ohio

Association of Ohio Homeschoolers
3636 Paris Boulevard
Westerville, OH 43081

Families Unschooling in the Neighborhood
4132 Spring Flower Court
Gahanna, OH 43230
614-794-2171
E-mail: roy@qn.net

Families Unschooling in the Neighborhood—
    Mid Ohio
5668 Township Road 105
Mount Gilead, OH 43338
419-947-6351
E-mail: laurie@redbird.net

HEART
7979 Greenwich Road
Lodi, OH 44254
Naome Carter: 216-948-2941

HELP—Central OH
4132 Spring Flower Court
Gahanna, OH 43230
614-759-7553
E-mail: help.columbus@pobox.com

Web site: http://www.help.columbus@
  pobox.com/~help.columbus

HELP—Miami Valley
1340 Rice Road
Yellow Springs, OH 45387
Leslie Baynes: 513-767-2346

HELP—Northern OH
10915 Pyle—S Amherst Road
Oberlin, OH 44074
Gina McKay Lodge: 216-774-2720

HELP—NW OH
PO Box 98
Perrysburg, OH 43552-0098
419-478-9729 or 419-476-1088

HELP for Homeschooling Parents
PO Box 93
Ashland, OH 44805
Ashland Co.—Judy Stanton: 419-281-9373
Richland Co.—Cyndde DeWeese:
  419-883-3694

Home Education Resource Organization
170 W Main Street
Norwalk, OH 44857
Rob and Donna King: 419-663-1064

Home Educators Advocacy League
26140 Yearsley Road
Raymond, OH 43067
Charles and Patricia Tonkin-Lentz:
  513-358-2450

Home Educators Advocacy League
348 Cobblestone Drive
Delaware, OH 43015
Sandy Rieske: 614-369-4706

Homeschool Network of Greater Cincinnati
3470 Greenfield Court
Maineville, OH 45039
Susan Duncan: 513-683-1279

Newark Area Unschoolers
Cassie Holderman: 614-787-2947
E-mail: BPImages@aol.com

OH Home Educators Network
PO Box 23054
Chagrin Falls, OH 44023-0054
Debra: 330-278-2540
E-mail: buresmom@aol.com
Barbara: 330-274-0542

Parents and Children Together
8944 Weiss Road
Union City, OH 45390
937-692-5680, 937-968-4942

Oklahoma
Cornerstone
PO Box 459
Sperry, OK 74073
918-425-4162

Green Country Home Education
  Resource Organization
183 Fox Run Circle
Jenks, OK 74037

Home Educators Resource Organization
4401 Quail Run Avenue
Skiatook, OK 74070
Leslie Moyer: 918-396-0108
E-mail: moyerles@wiltel.net
Web site: http://www.geocities.com/Athens/
  Forum/3236

Oregon
Homeschool Information and Service Network
1044 Bismark
Klamath Falls, OR 97601

Greater Portland Homeschoolers
PO Box 82415
Portland, OR 97282
Voice mail: 503-241-5350

Jewish Home Education Network (Salem)
503-362-1203

OR Christian Home Education Association
2515 NE 37th Avenue
Portland, OR 97212

OR Home Education Network
4470 SW Hall Boulevard #286
Beaverton OR 97005
Jeanne Biggerstaff: 503-321-5166
E-mail: sassenak@msn.com

Pennsylvania
Blue Mountain Homeschoolers
636 Almond Road
Walnutport, PA 18088
Peggy Kreider

Catholic Homeschoolers of Scranton
1317 St. Ann Street
Scranton, PA 18504
Michele Fitzgerald: 717-344-8866

Center City Homeschoolers
2203 Spruce Street
Philadelphia, PA 19103
Marion Cohen: 215-732-7723
Kitty Anderson: 215-482-7933

Diversity—United in Homeschooling
233 Blue Bell Avenue
Langhorne, PA 19407
Pat Porter: 215-428-2865

McKeesport Area Homeschoolers
404 Owens Avenue
Liberty Borough, PA
Jan Conrad: 412-672-7056

MD/PA Home Educators (Mason-Dixon area)
PO Box 67
Shrewsbury, PA 17361
717-993-3603

PA Home Education Network
285 Allegheny Street
Meadville, PA 16335
Kathy Terleski: 412-561-5288

PA Homeschoolers
RD 2, Box 117
Kittanning, PA 16201

People Always Learning Something
105 Marie Drive
Pittsburgh, PA 15237
Christina Barry: 412-367-6240

Rolling Green Home Education
    Resource Room
2725 Aquetong Road
New Hope, PA 18938
215-862-2968

Southwestern PA Home Education Network
429 Union Avenue
Pittsburgh, PA 15205
Gloria Molek: 412-922-8344

Valley Unschoolers Network
4458 Coffeetown Road
Schneckville, PA 18078
Kiernan Family: 610-799-2742

Rhode Island
Parent Educators of Rhode Island
PO Box 782
Glendale, RI 02826

RI Guild of Home Teachers
PO Box 11
Hope, RI 02831
401-821-7700

South County Homeschoolers
500 Carolina Back Road
Charleston, RI 02813
Beth Richardson

South Carolina

Home Organization of Parent Educators
1697 Dotterer's Run
Charleston, SC 29414
803-763-7833
E-mail: epeeler@awod.com

SC Association of Independent Home Schools
PO Box 2104
Irmo, SC 29063-2104

SC Home Educators Association
PO Box 612
Lexington, SC 29071

SC Homeschool Alliance
1679 Memorial Park Road, Suite 179
Lancaster, SC 29720
E-mail: ConnectSC@aol.com
Web site: http://members.aol.com/connectsc

Teacher's Ink
PO Box 13386
Charleston, SC 29422
Deborah Todus White: 803-795-9982
E-mail: pfmsuper@worldnet.att.net

South Dakota

SD Home School Association
PO Box 882
Sioux Falls, SD 57101
Kim Liedtke: 605-338-9689

Tennessee

State of Franklin Homeschoolers
494 Mill Creek Road
Kingsport, TN 37664
423-349-6125
E-mail: kramerbg@mounet.com

TN Homeschooling Families
214 Park Lane
Oliver Springs, TN 37840
Lin Kemper Wallace: 615-435-4375

Unschoolers of Memphis
Margaret Meyer: 901-757-9859

Wednesdays Homeschool Park Group
Jackie: 615-889-4938

Texas

Austin Area Homeschoolers
510 Park Boulevard
Austin, TX 78751

Community Institute
3 Stargazer Place
The Woodlands, TX 77381
Kim Rodeffer Runk: 409-321-3982

Heart of TX Home Schoolers
1710 Vincent
Brownwood, TX 76801
Charlotte Laughlin: 915-643-1182
E-mail: charlotte@gte.net

Highland Lake Area Homeschoolers
Rt. 1, Box 239
Burnet, TX 78611
Melissa Tolliver: 512-756-2982
E-mail: tolliver@tstar.net

Houston Alternative Education Alliance
14222 Ridgewood Lake Court
Houston, TX 77062
Claire Bacani: 713-667-7837

Houston Unschoolers Group
9625 Exeter Road
Houston, TX 77093
Holly Furgason: 713-695-4888
E-mail: furgason@swbell.net

Learning and Education Alternatives
  Resource Network
PO Box 176
Arlington, TX 76004-0176
E-mail: deblewis@fastlane.net

North TX Self Educators
150 Forest Lane
Double Oak/Lewisville, TX 75067
Sarah Jordan: 817-430-4835

Northwest CHILD
7906 Split Oak Drive
Houston, TX 77040
Kerry Faler: 713-849-3963

South Fort Worth Christian Home Educators
PO Box 16573
Fort Worth, TX 76133
817-249-1975
E-mail: robbjh@flash.net

South Texas Self-Learners
1005 Delta Drive
Corpus Christi, TX 78412
Becky Davis: 512-992-7549

SW Dallas Home School Association
PO Box 1104
Cedar Hill, TX 75106
E-mail: StoryLadee@aol.com

Tarrant Home Educators Association
6080 Hulen Drive, Suite 360-109
Fort Worth, TX 76132
817-421-1761

TX Advocates for Freedom in Education
13635 Greenridge Street
Sugar Land, TX 77478
Beth Jackson: 713-242-7994

Wharton County Christian Homeschool
    Organization
PO Box 1411
El Campo, TX 77437
Colleen Reid: 409-543-1999
E-mail: car@wcnet.net

Woodlands Innovative Scholastic Environments
130 N Rushwing Circle
The Woodlands, TX 77381
Robin Caldwell: 713-364-7084

Utah
HELP-Four Corners
Castle Valley Star Route, Box 1901
Moab, UT 84532
Ann Cummings: 801-259-6968

Latter-day Saint Home Educators' Association
2770 S 1000 W
Perry, UT 84302
Joyce Kinmont: 801-723-5355

Salt Lake Home Educators
Holly Godard: 801-562-9169
E-mail: shark@xmission.com

Utah Home Education Association
PO Box 167
Roy, UT 84067
888-887-UHEA
Web site: http://www.itsnet.com/~uhea

Vermont
Christian Home Educators of VT
214 N Prospect #105
Burlington, VT 05401
802-658-4561
E-mail: GESA97@aol.com

The Resource Center for Homeschooling
RR 2, Box 289-C
St. Albans, VT 05478
Deb Shell: 802-524-9645
E-mail: shell@together.net

Right at Home
RR 2, Box 145
E Wallingford, VT 05742
Cindy Wade: 802-259-3493
E-mail: cwade@vermontel.com

VT Homeshoolers' Association
RR 2, Box 4440
Bristol, VT 05443
802-453-5460

Virginia

Blue Ridge Area Network for Congenial
    Homeschoolers
3131 Hamm Road
Barboursville, VA 22903
540-832-2018

Children's Circle
RR 1, Box 132A
Mouth of Wilson, VA 24363
Deborah Greif: 703-579-4252

Community of Independent Learners
PO Box 16029
Alexandria, VA 22302

Fauquier Unschoolers Living Classroom
PO Box 51
Goldvein, VA 22720
Rene Pleasant: 540-752-2478

Home Educators Assisting, Reaching
    and Teaching
101 William Claiborne
Williamsburg, VA 23185
Donna McEvoy: 757-220-2052
E-mail: BIZIMOM807@aol.com

Home Educators Association of VA
PO Box 1810
Front Royal, VA 22630
703-635-9322

LEARN (Northern VA Homeschoolers)
1111 Waynewood Boulevard
Alexandria, VA 22308
Ann Vernon

Learning in a Family Environment
40672 Tankerville Road
Lovettsville, VA 20180
E-mail: EBarkan@aol.com

Lifespan Education and Resource Network
3703 Merrimac Trail
Annandale, VA 22003
Deborah Secrist: 703-569-3264
E-mail: DramaDeb@aol.com

Richmond Educational Alternatives for
    Children at Home
PO Box 36174
Richmond, VA 23235-8003
804-795-7624
E-mail: carmel@compuserve.com
Web site: http://www.geocities.com/
    Heartland/Plains/7440

VA Home Education Association
1612 Columbia Road
Gordonsville, VA 22942
540-832-3578
E-mail: vhea@virginia.edu
Web site: http://poe.acc.virginia.edu/
    ~pm6f/vhea/html

We Home Educate and Train
13162 Putnam Circle
Woodbridge, VA 22191

WELCOME
108 Fardale Street SE
Vienna, VA 22180
Lori Markoff: 703-573-7121
E-mail: Markoff@dcnet.com

Washington

Family Learning Organization
PO Box 7247
Spokane, WA 99207
Kathleen McCurdy: 509-924-3760

Homeschoolers Support Association
PO Box 413
Maple Valley, WA 98038
Teresa Sparling: 206-746-5047

Kittitas Valley Homeschool Association
Ellenburg, WA 98926
Debbie: 509-925-4033

Military Homeschool F.A.M.I.L.I.E.S.
    of Kitsap County
3043 Albacore Circle #D10
Silverdale, WA 98315
E-mail: kepola@silverlink.net

Network of Vancouver Area Homeschoolers
162 Krogstad Road
Washougal, WA 98671
Lori Loranger: 360-837-3760
E-mail: 71230.66@compuserve.com

North Central, WA Homeschool Co-op
PO Box 147
Curlew, WA 99118

Palouse Home Learning Alternatives
SE 405 Hill
Pullman, WA 99163
Susan McMinn Seefelt: 509-332-8127

St. Thomas More Home Education
3853 76th Avenue SE
Mercer Island, WA 98040
Judi Crow: 206-232-2680

Seattle Homeschool Group
819 NE 84th
Seattle, WA 98115
Julie Scandora: 206-525-8359

Teaching Parents Association
PO Box 1934
Woodinville, WA 98072
Meriann Roberts: 206-788-5272
Janice Kugler: 206-821-2753

Valley Home Educators
1413 Easthills Terrace
E Wenatchee, WA 98802
Emilie Fogle: 509-884-1237

WA Homeschool Organization
18130 Midvale Avenue N, Suite C
Seattle, WA 98133
206-298-8942

Washington, D.C.
Bolling Area Home Educators
202-574-1217
E-mail: Tjensen718@aol.com

West Virginia
WV Home Educators Association
PO Box 3707
Charleston, WV 25337
800-736-9843

Wisconsin
HOME
5745 Bittersweet Place
Madison, WI 53705
Alison McKee: 68-238-3302
E-mail: amckee73@hotmail.com

La Crosse Educational Alternative
    Resource Network
W 6442 Schilling Road
Onalaska, WI 54650

Milwaukee Area Home Learners
W260 N7751 Jay Lane
Sussex, WI 53089
Erich Moraine: 414-246-3604

Ozaukee Explorers
4410 Bittersweet Lane
Cedarburg, WI 53210
Kathy Flaherty: 414-377-7734
E-mail: PIPPENN@aol.com

Sheboygan County Homeschoolers
W5607 Highway W
Adell, WI 53001
Darcy Zwier
E-mail: dmz@mail.tcbi.com

WI Parents Association
PO Box 2502
Madison, WI 53701-2502

Wyoming
Homeschoolers of Wyoming
PO Box 926
Evansville, WY 82636

Unschoolers of Wyoming/Laramie Home
    Education Network
429 Hwy. 230, #20
Laramie, WY 82010
Chris Anderson-Sprecher

RESOURCES, RESOURCES, AND MORE RESOURCES

The title of this section says it all!

Books: Just a Bit More to Read About the Homeschooling Lifestyle, Including Books Mentioned Within . . .

The number of books devoted to homeschooling has exploded in the last decade as more and more parents seek useful information. While most of the titles below deal specifically with homeschooling, the others are included because they are recommended by this book's contributors for the information they provide to aid in the homeschooling lifestyle.

Armstrong, Thomas. *Awakening Your Child's Natural Genius: Enhancing Curiosity, Creativity, and Learning Ability.* J. P. Tarcher, 1991.

————. *In Their Own Way.* J. P. Tarcher, 1988.

Bolles, Richard Nelson. *The 1998 What Color is Your Parachute: A Practical Manual for Job-Hunters and Career Changers.* Ten Speed Press, 1997.

Cohen, Cafi. *And What About College? How Homeschooling Leads to Admissions to the Best Colleges and Universities.* Holt Associates, 1997.

Colfax, David and Micki. *Hard Times in Paradise: An American Family's Struggle to Carve Out a Homestead in California's Redwoods.* Warner Books, 1992.

Copelan, Lewis, editor. *High School Subjects Self-Taught.* Halcyon House, 1940 (available through Brook Farm Books).

Dobson, Linda. *The Art of Education: Reclaiming Your Family, Community, and Self.* Holt Associates, 1997.

————. *The Complete Book of Home Education: A Parent's Guide to Education the Natural Way.* Element Books, forthcoming 1999.

Dominguez, Joe and Vicki Robin. *Your Money or Your Life: Transforming Your Relationship with Money and Achieving Financial Independence.* Penguin USA, 1993.

Gelner, Judy. *College Admissions: A Guide for Homeschoolers.* Poppyseed Press, 1988.

Griffith, Mary. *The Homeschooling Handbook.* Prima Publishing, 1997.

————. *The Unschooling Handbook.* Prima Publishing, 1998.

Guterson, David. *Family Matters: Why Homeschooling Makes Sense.* Harcourt Brace Jovanovich, 1992.

Healy, Jane M. *Endangered Minds: Why Our Children Don't Think and What We Can Do About It.* Touchstone Books, 1991.

Hegener, Mark and Helen, eds. *The Homeschool Reader: Perspectives on Homeschooling.* Home Education Press. 1995.

Holt, John. *Teach Your Own: A Hopeful Path for Education.* Delacorte Press, 1989.

————. *How Children Fail.* Addison-Wesley Publishing Co., 1995.

————. *How Children Learn.* Addison-Wesley Publishing Co., 1995.

Illich, Ivan. *Deschooling Society.* HarperCollins, 1983.

Kaseman, Larry and Susan. *Taking Charge Through Homeschooling: Personal and Political Empowerment.* Koshkonong Press, 1990.

Kenyon, Mary Potter. *Home Schooling from Scratch: Simple Living—Super Learning.* Gazelle Publications, 1996.

Liedloff, Jean. *The Continuum Concept: In Search of Happiness Lost.* Addison-Wesley Publishing Co., 1986.

McKee, Alison. *From Homeschool to College and Work: Turning Your Homeschool Experiences into College and Job Portfolios.* Bittersweet House (WI), 1997.

Meighan, Roland. *The Next Learning System: And Why Homeschoolers Are Trailblazers.* Educational Heretics Press, 1997.

————. *Learning from Home-Based Education.* Education Now Publishing Cooperative, 1992.

Moore, Raymond and Dorothy. *The Successful Homeschooling Family Handbook.* Thomas Nelson Publishers, 1994.

————. *Minding Your Own Business.* Wolgemuth & Hyatt Publishing, 1990.

————. *Home Built Discipline.* Thomas Nelson, 1990.

————. *Home Made Health.* Word Books, 1989.

Pearce, Joseph Chilton. *Magical Child.* Dutton, 1974.

————. *Evolution's End: Claiming the Potential of Our Intelligence.* HarperSanFrancisco, 1993.

Rupp, Becky. *Getting Started in Homeschooling.* Crown, 1998.

Sheffer, Susannah. *A Sense of Self: Listening to Homeschooled Adolescent Girls.* Boynton/Cook Heinemann, 1995.

Williams, Jane. *Home School Market Guide.* (Annual.) Bluestocking Press, 1998.

. . . And Books Teeming with Resources!

Buy these books, or check them out from your library, and you will *never* wonder where to get resources again!

Hubb, Don. *Home Education Resource Guide.* Blue Bird Publishing, 1994.

Pride, Mary. *The Big Book of Home Learning.* (Series.) Crossway, 1990.

Reed, Donn. *The Home School Source Book.* Brook Farm Books, 1994.

Rupp, Becky. *Good Stuff: Learning Tools for All Ages.* Holt Associates, 1997.

————. *Home Learning Source Book.* Crown, 1998.

Wade, Theodore E., Jr., ed. *The Home School Manual: Plans, Pointers, Reasons and Resources.* Gazelle Publications, 1998.

Peterson's Guides

Don't miss out on these collections of interesting and exciting educational opportunities for older children.

Learning Adventures Around the World 1998 (Peter S. Greenberg, editor).

Peterson's Internships 1998: More Than 40,000 Opportunities to Get an Edge in Today's Competitive Job Market (18th Edition), 1997.

Peterson's Summer Opportunities for Kids and Teenagers 1998 (15th Edition), 1997.

Summer Opportunities for Kids and Teenagers 1998 (15th Edition), 1997.

Homeschool Periodicals

Subscribing to homeschooling magazines is like insuring you'll receive a periodic booster shot of encouragement, inspiration, news, and practical advice. Go ahead, build another bookcase!

The Catholic Home Educator
PO Box 420225
San Diego, CA 92142

The Drinking Gourd Magazine
PO Box 2557
Redmond, WA 98073
206-836-0336
E-mail: TDrnkngGrd@aol.com

F.U.N. News
1688 Belhaven Woods Court
Pasadena, MD 21122-3727
Voice mail/fax: 410-360-7330
E-mail: FUNNews@MCImail.com
Web site: http://members.aol.com/funnews

Growing Without Schooling
2269 Massachusetts Avenue
Cambridge, MA 02140
617-864-3100
Fax: 617-864-9235
E-mail: HoltGWS@aol.com
Web site: http://www.holtgws.com

Home Education Magazine
PO Box 3142
Palmer, AK 99645-3142
907-746-1336
Fax: 907-746-1335
Orders: 800-236-3278
E-mail: HEM@home-ed-magazine.com
Web site: http://www.home-ed-magazine.com

Homefires (Homeschool Resource
    Network)
180 El Camino Real, Suite 10
Millbrae, CA 94030
888-4-HOME-ED
E-mail: Editor@Homefires.com
Web site: http://www.Homefires.com

HomeSchool Dad Magazine
609 Starlight Drive
Grand Junction, CO 81504
E-mail: hsd@acsol.net
Web site: http://www.acsol.net/hsd

Homeschooling Today
PO Box 1425
Melrose, FL 32666
904-475-3088

The Link
587 N Ventu Park Road
Suite F-911
Newbury Park, CA 91320
805-492-1373
Fax: 805-493-9216
E-mail: hompaper@gte.net
Web site: http://www.conejovalley.com/thelink

Moore Report International
Box 1
Camas, WA 98607
360-835-2736
Fax: 360-835-5392
E-mail: moorefnd@pacifier.com

National Homeschool Journal
PO Box 1372
Camano Island, WA 98292

Practical Homeschooling
PO Box 1250
Fenton, MO 63026
800-346-6322

Useful Non-Homeschool Periodicals
These periodicals address additional lifestyle aspects that may help you "tweak" your current circumstances enough to make room and opportunity for homeschooling. Most deal with the philosophy of simplifying, living a natural lifestyle, and parents at home.

Back Home Magazine
PO Box 70
Hendersonville, NC 28793
800-992-2546
E-mail: backhome@ioa.com
Web site: http://www.ioa.com/home/
    backhome

Full-Time Dads
PO Box 12773
St. Paul, MN 55112
612-633-7424

Holistic Education Review
PO Box 298
Brandon, VT 05733-0298
800-639-4122 (802-247-8312)
E-mail: holistic@sover.net
Web site: http://www.sover.net/~holistic

Liedloff Continuum Network Newsletter
PO Box 1634
Sausalito, CA 94966

Living Gently Quarterly
PO Box 8302
Victoria, British Columbia
V8W 3K9 Canada
250-388-7847
E-mail: see@islandnet.com
Web site: http://www.islandnet.com/
    ~see/living.htm

Mothering
PO Box 1690
Santa Fe, NM 87504
505-984-8116

Mother Tongue
PO Box 640
Candler, NC 28715
704-665-4572

Natural Life Magazine
RR 1
St. George, Ontario
N0E 1N0 Canada
E-mail: altpress@netroute.net
Web site: http://www.life.ca

Parents' Choice
Box 185
Waban, MA 02168
617-965-5913

Parents Resource Connection
5102 Deerwood Lane, NE
Bemidji, MN 56601
218-751-3136

*Simple Living—The Journal of
    Voluntary Simplicity*
2319 N 45th Street
Box 149
Seattle, WA 98103

Simple Living Network
available online at Web site:
    http://slnet.com/hot.htm

SKOLE: The Journal of Alternative Education
72 Philip Street
Albany, NY 12202
518-432-1578

Staying Home
812 Magnolia Ext. #5
Johnson City, TN 37604
E-mail: athome9754@aol.com

Welcome Home
Mothers at Home
8310-A Old Courthouse Road
Vienna, VA 22182
800-783-4666

Periodicals for Your Children

Children love to receive mail, and getting any of these magazines is sure to put a smile on their faces as you bring fun, up-to-the-minute learning materials into your home. Don't forget to search for magazines that cover any of their favorite hobbies and activities.

3-2-1 Contact
212-595-3456

Classical Beginnings
PO Box 300
Simi Valley, CA 93062
805-522-9800

Cobblestone/Faces/Odyssey/Calliope
7 School Street
Peterborough, NH 03458
800-821-0115

GAMES Magazine
PO Box 10147
Des Moines, IA 50347-0147

International Kids' News (by and for kids)
1926 W Beaver Lake Drive SE
Issaquah, WA 98029

KidsArt News
PO Box 274
Mt. Shasta, CA 96067
916-926-5076

Kids at Home (by and for kids)
PO Box 363
Astoria, OR 97103
E-mail: kidshome@transport.com
Web site: http://www.transport.com/
   ~kidshome/kah.html

Kids Discover
212-242-5133

Muse (from *Smithsonian*)
800-827-0227

National Geographic World
800-638-4077

Old News
400 Stackstown Road
Marietta, PA 17547
717-426-2212
Web site: http://www.ourworld.compuserve.
   com/homepages/oldnews

Ranger Rick/Your Big Backyard
8925 Leesburg Pike
Vienna, VA 22184
800-588-1650

Skipping Stones (by and for kids)
PO Box 3939
Eugene, OR 97403
541-342-4956

Stone Soup (by and for kids)
PO Box 83
Santa Cruz, CA 95063
800-447-4569
E-mail: editors@stonesoup.com
Web site: http://www.stonesoup.com

Tomorrow's Morning
125 S Barrington Place
Los Angeles, CA 90049
888-322-READ

Zoobooks
800-992-5034

CURRICULUM SOURCES/CORRESPONDENCE SCHOOLS/POTENTIAL DIPLOMAS

There is a wide variety in cost, services, and expectations among the various providers.

Thorough research into many options is recommended in order to decide whether or not you need a program. If you find that you do, your research will help you and your child decide which one best fits your needs.

Calvert School
105 Tuscany Road
Baltimore, MD 21210
410-243-6030
Fax: 410-366-0674
Web site: http://www.calvertschool.org

Cambridge Academy
3300 SW 34th Avenue #102
Ocala, FL 34474
800-252-3777

Clonlara School
1289 Jewett
Ann Arbor, MI 48104
313-769-4515
Fax: 313-769-9629
E-mail: clonlara@delphi.com
Web site: http://www.grfn.org/education/
    clonlara

Curriculum Resource Center
PO Box 241
Dublin, NH 03444
888-899-0188

HCL Boston School
PO Box 2920
Big Bear City, CA 92314
909-585-7188

Home Study International
12501 Old Columbia Pike
Silver Spring, MD 20904
800-782-4769

Indiana University Independent Study
800-334-1011

Keystone National High School
School House Station
420 West 5th Street
Bloomsburg, PA 17815
800-255-4937
E-mail: info@keystonehighschool.com
Web site: http://www.keystonehighschool.com

Laurel Springs School
1002 E. Ojai Avenue
PO Box 1440
Ojai, CA 93024
805-646-2473
Web site: http://www.laurelsprings.com

Oak Meadow School
PO Box 740
Putney, VT 05346
802-387-2021
E-mail: oms@oakmeadow.com
Web site: http://www.oakmeadow.com

Seton Home Study School
1350 Progress Drive
Front Royal, VA 22630

Sonlight Curriculum, Ltd.
8185 South Grant Way
Littleton, CO 80127

The Sycamore Tree Center for
    Home Education
2179 Meyer Place
Costa Mesa, CA 92627
Order: 800-779-6750
Information: 714-650-4466
E-mail: 75767.1417@compuserv.com

University of Nebraska at Lincoln
Independent Study High School
33rd and Holdrege Street
Lincoln, NE 68653-0900
402-472-4321

University of Wisconsin—Extension
800-442-6460
Web site: http://www.uwex edu/ilearn

Unschoolers Network
2 Smith Street
Farmingdale, NJ 07727

Vanguard Academy
508-529-6630
E-mail: vanguard@schoolmail.com

West River Academy
2420 North First Street
Grand Junction, CO 81501
970-241-4137
E-mail: WRU2420@aol.com

THE THREE R'S, AND MORE

Any resource worth its salt will cover more than one "subject" area as your child learns. Such is the case with the resources contained in this section. Typical subject headings are used to serve as a rough guide as you discover what is available.

Reading

Reading opens up the world for children. Here are resources that will let them see the possibilities from the very first word.

Ball-Stick-Bird Publications (Learn to read)
PO Box 13
Colebrook, CT 06021
806-738-8871

Book Links (Bimonthly information on books by themes)
434 W Downer Place
Aurora, IL 60506-9954
630-892-7465
Web site: http://www.ala.org/BookLinks

Chinaberry Book Service (Great books by reading level)
2780 Via Orange Way Suite B
Spring Valley, CA 91978

EDC Publishing (U.S. source of Usborne books)
PO Box 470663
Tulsa, OK 74147-0663
800-475-4522

Harper Trophy (Children's paperbacks)
10 E 53rd Street
New York, NY 10022
800-242-7737

Lost Classics
PO Box 3429
Lake Wales, FL 33859-3429
888-676-2665
E-mail: lcbc@gte.net

The Prairie Primer
Cadron Creek Christian Curriculum
(Literature-based unit study grades
3 through 6 on *The Little House* series)
4329 Pinos Altos Road
Silver City, NM 88061
505-534-1496

Mathematics

Child(ren) + homeschooling = ? A family that discovers math together can embark on a very interesting journey!

Academy for Economic Education
125 Nationsbank Center
Richmond, VA 23277
804-643-0071

Books by Marilyn Burns: *The I Hate Mathematics! Book; Math for Smarty Pants; This Book Is About Time; The Book of Think (Or How to Solve a Problem Twice Your Size)*

Cuisenaire Company of America
PO Box 5026
White Plains, NY 10602-5026
800-237-3142

Family Math
Lawrence Hall of Science
University of California
Berkeley, CA 94720
415-642-1016

Hands-On Equations
Borenson & Associates
PO Box 3328
Allentown, PA 18108
215-820-5575

Miquon Math materials
Key Curriculum Press
PO Box 2304
Berkeley, CA 94702
800-338-7638 (510-548-2304)

Saxon Math
Saxon Publishers
1300 McGee #100
Norman, OK 73072

Writing

Here are some resources that cover the physical act of writing, and others that explore the proper usage of the written word.

AccuWrite (correspondence course ages 8 to18)
4536 SW 14 Avenue
Cape Coral, FL 33914
941-549-4400

Grammar Songs
Audio Memory Publishing
2060 Raymond Avenue
Signal Hill, CA 90806
310-494-8822

Italic Handwriting Series
Portland State University
Division of Continuing Education
Box 1394
Portland, OR 97207
503-725-4846

National Writing Institute
7946 Wright Road
Niles, MI 49120
616-684-5375

Zaner-Bloser (workbooks)
2200 W Fifth Avenue
PO Box 16764
Columbus, OH 43216-6764
800-421-3018

Science

Did you know Thomas Edison was a home-schooler? With all these great science resources, you'll never know what your children will invent to join him in the history books!

Carolina Biological Supply Co.
2700 York Road
Burlington, NC 27215
910-584-0381
E-mail: carolina@carolina.com
Web site: http://www.carolina.com

Edmund Scientific Co.
101 E Gloucester Pike
Barrington, NJ 08007
800-728-6999
E-mail: scientifics@edsci.com

Home Training Tools
2827 Buffalo Horn Drive
Laurel, MT 59044
800-860-6272

Science By Mail
800-729-3300

The Science Education Company
4850 A1A South
St. Augustine, FL 32084
904-471-45948
E-mail: Krampf@aol.com
Web site: http://members.aol.com/ kra
   mpf/home.html

Science Is Elementary (quarterly journal)
MITS/SIE
79 Milk Street Suite 210
Boston, MA 02109-3903
617-695-9771

Tobin's Lab
PO Box 6503
Glendale, AZ 85312-6503
800-522-4776 (602-843-4265)
E-mail: mike@tobinlab.com
Web site: http://www.tobinlab.com

TOPS Learning Systems
10970 S Mulino Road
Canby, OR 97013
503-263-2040
E-mail: tops@canby.com

World's Most Unusual Science Catalog
c/o WREN Enterprises
3145 W Monmouth Avenue
Englewood, CO 80110
303-798-2778

History and Social Studies
The world's a big place. Bring it home, study its past, and build hope for its future.

Bluestocking Press
PO Box 2030
Shingle Springs, CA 95682-2030
800-959-8586

Books by Jean Fritz, including: *Where Do You Think You're Going, Chris Columbus?; Can't You Make Them Behave, King George?; And Then What Happened, Paul Revere?; Shh! We're Writing the Constitution!; The Double Life of Pocahontas; Traitor; The Great Little Madison.*

Clarion Books
215 Park Avenue South
New York, NY 10003
800-225-3362
Fax: 800-634-7568
(MA, call collect 617-272-1500)

Dover Children's Books
31 E 2nd Street
Mineola, NY 11501

The Explorer's Club
PO Box 852
Goshen, IN 46737-0852

Hear & Learn Publications
603 SE Morrison Road
Vancouver, WA 98664-1545

Smithsonian Institution Museum Shop
Dept. 0006
Washington, D.C. 29973-0006
202-357-1826

Wide World Books and Maps
1911 N 45th Street
Seattle, WA 98103-6804

Foreign Language
In how many languages can you say "Yes!" to homeschooling?

Audio Forum
96 Broad Street
Guilford, CT 06437-2635
800-243-1234

Bolchazy-Carducci Publishers, Inc. (Latin)
1000 Brown Street
Wauconda, IL 60084
847-526-4344
E-mail: latin@bolchazy.com
Web site: http://www.bolchazy.com

French Kid Stuff
E-mail: French4kdz@aol.com

International Linguistics Corporation
3505 East Red Bridge
Kansas City, MO 64137
800-237-1830 (816-765-8855)

Living Language
Outlet Book Co.
40 Englehard Avenue
Avenel, NJ 07001
908-827-2700

Art

Start thinking about where you're going to display all the soon-to-be works of art your children will present to you. Don't forget, they make great gifts too.

1001 Crafts by J & A
J & A Handy-Crafts, Inc.
165 S Pennsylvania Avenue
Lindenhurst, NY 11757-5058
516-226-2400
Fax: 516-226-2564

Blitz Art Products, Inc.
PO Box 8022
Cherry Hill, NJ 08002

Curiosity Kits, Inc.
PO Box 811
Cockeysville, MD 21030
410-584-2605

Dick Blick Art Materials
PO Box 1267
Galesburg, IL 61402-1267
800-828-4548
Fax: 800-621-8293

RB Walter Art and Craft Materials
PO Box 6231
Arlington, TX 76005
800-447-8787

Music

Music can be appreciated on so many levels, whether your child plays an instrument or not. And with the wide variety of sources of instruments and methods for learning how to play, it's easy to fill your home with the sound of music.

Harps of Lorien
610 North Star Rte. GS
Questa, NM 87556
505-586-1307

Homespun Music Tapes
Box 694
Woodstock, NY 12498

Lark in the Morning
Box 1176
Mendocino, CA 95460
707-964-5569

Making Music Video Series
510-452-9334
E-mail: sfbayrevels@earthlink.net

Suzuki Musical Instruments
800-854-1594

EVEN MORE WAYS TO LEARN

Stretch your thinking about education and see how many ways there are to learn with resources your children will think are just plain fun.

Audio Tapes

Pop one of these companies' tapes into the car tape player, and the trip becomes more interesting than the destination!

A Gentle Wind
Box 3013
Albany, NY 12203

Blackstone Audiobooks
PO Box 969
Ashland, OR 97520
800-729-2665

Bodkin, Odds
Rivertree Publications
PO Box 410
Bradford, NH 03221

Boomerang!
The Children's Audiomagazine About Big Ideas
Box 261
La Honda, CA 94020
800-333-7858

Family Classics Library
Newport Publishers
100 North Lake Avenue #203
Pasadena, CA 91101-1885
800-579-5532

Greathall Productions (Jim Weiss)
PO Box 813
Benicia, CA 94510
Orders: 800-477-6234

The Growler Tapes Audio Adventures
800-GROWLER

Music for Little People
1144 Redway Road
Redway, CA 95560
800-346-4445

O'Callahan, Jay
Box 1054
Marshfield, MA 02050
800-626-5356

Yellow Moon Press
800-497-4385

Games and Puzzles

Countless homeschoolers have found games and puzzles enlightening, fun ways to spend time together as families, learning as they play.

Ampersand Press
750 Lake Street
Port Townsend, WA 98368
800-624-4263
Fax: 360-379-0324

Animal Town Game Company
PO Box 485
Healdsburg, CA 95448
800-445-8642

Aristoplay
PO Box 7028
Ann Arbor, MI 48107

Bits and Pieces
One Puzzle Place
Stevens Point, WI 54481-7199
800-JIGSAWS

Chatham Hill Games
Ray Toelke Associates
PO Box 253
Chatham, NY 12037

Family Pastimes
RR 4
Perth, Ontario
Canada K7H 3C6
613-267-4819
Fax: 613-264-0696
E-mail: fp@superaje.com

HearthSong
PO Box B
Sebastopol, CA 95473-0601
707-578-4215

MindWare
2720 Patton Road
Roseville, MN 55113
800-999-0398
Fax: 888-299-9273

Rex Games, Inc.
530 Howard Street #100
San Francisco, CA 94015-3007
800-542-6375
E-mail: rexgames@rexgames.com
Web site: http://www.rexgames.com

Rosie Hipp's Wooden Toys and Games
800-385-2620

Software

The Information Age has arrived, and with it a virtual cornucopia of computer software to help children learn. Regardless of age, sex, or interests and needs, today there is something available for everyone.

The Edutainment Catalog
PO Box 21210
Boulder, CO 80308
800-338-3844
Web site: http://www.edutainco.com

Homeschool Software Catalog
800-446-2089

I.Q. Smart Educational Software
888-612-4222

Zane Publishing
800-460-8923

TEXTS

Despite our warnings about text books, you may not feel comfortable unless you have a few on your shelves. This section is an attempt to at least keep your spending to a minimum by guiding you to sources of used books!

The Book Cellar (used available)
189 Elm Street
Milford, NH 03055
800-338-4257 (603-672-4333)
E-mail: bookcellar@juno.com

BUDGETexT Home Education
PO Box 1487
Fayetteville, AR 72702-1487
888-888-2272
Fax: 800-642-2665
E-mail: sales@homeschoolmall.com

Educators Exchange (used available)
10755 Midlothian Tpk.
Richmond, VA 23235
804-794-6994
E-mail: jscgec@aol.com

Follett Home Education (used available)
800-554-5754

Homeschool Exchange (used from other homeschoolers; business for sale at time of editing)
PO Box 1378
Boerne, TX 78006
800-894-8247 (210-336-2021)
E-mail: HSXchange@aol.com

Laurelwood Publications (used available)
Rte. 1, Box 87
Bluemont, VA 20135
540-554-2500, 1 to 5 P.M. EST
E-mail: Laurelwd01@aol.com

Wilcox & Follet Book Co. (used available)
1000 W Washington Boulevard
Chicago, IL 60607
800-621-4272

Special Needs

If you would like to homeschool but your child has special needs, you don't have to feel alone. These organizations are there to offer help, advice, and encouragement. If you need leads to more help, these are the folks who can help point the way.

At Our Own Pace
Jean Kulczyk
102 Willow Drive
Waukegan, IL 60087

Gallaudet University Bookstore (American Sign
　　Language material and more)
800 Florida Avenue NE
Washington, D.C. 20002-3695
202-651-5380

Hadley School for the Blind
PO Box 299
Winnetka, IL 60093
312-323-4238

National Association for the Deaf
814 Thayer Avenue
Silver Spring, MD 20910

NATTHAN
5383 Alpine Road
SE Olalla, WA 98359
253-857-4257
E-mail: Nathanews@aol.com

Science Research Association
800-843-8855

Utgnet: Uniqueness, Twice-Gifted & Gifted
　　Network (Support network for parents and
　　home educators of exceptional students—
　　special needs to gifted)

Uni-Gift (Margaret Bradley-Simard)
10831 W Broad Street #231
Glen Allen, VA 23060
804-883-6757, mailbox #2
E-mail: UniGift@aol.com

Catalogs with a Little of This and That

As mentioned before, homeschooling resources don't always fit into neat little categories, and neither do the many catalogs that serve up a buffet of items for different subjects and ages. These catalogs offer wonderful examples of the choices that await you.

The Book Peddler
PO Box 1960
Elyria, OH 44036-1960
800-928-1760
E-mail: TheBookPeddler@juno.com

The Education Connection
Box 1417
Tehachapi, CA 93581
800-863-3828

Creative Home Teaching
PO Box 152581
San Diego, CA 92195
619-263-8633

The Elijah Company
Rte. 2, Box 100-B
Crossville, TN 38555
615-456-6284

F.U.N. Books
1688 Belhaven Woods Court
Pasadena, MD 21122-3727
Voice mail/fax: 410-360-7330
E-mail: FUNNews@MCImail.com
Web site: http://members.aol.com/FUNNews

The Genius Tribe
Box 1014
Eugene, OR 97440

John Holt Book and Music Store
2269 Massachusetts Avenue
Cambridge, MA 02140
617-864-3100

Latter Day Family Resources
242 E Southfield Road
Spanish Fork, UT 84660
800-290-2283

Learning Home, Inc.
5573 Ashbourne Road
Baltimore, MD 21227-2813
410-536-5990
Web site: http://members.aol.com/learnghome

Rainbow Re-Source Center
8227 Ulah Road
Cambridge, IL 61238
888-841-3456
Voice mail: 800-705-8809

Skekinah Curriculum Cellar
101 Meador Road
Kilgore, TX 75662
903-643-2760

For Teens

Homeschooled teens face increased freedom and choices on their trip toward adulthood as the world continues to open up to them. Here are just a few of the many opportunities available to them, along with sources of inspiration to create even more.

A Guide to Unconventional Colleges
Sara Campbell
38th Street
Astoria, OR 97103
Web site: http://www.pacifier.com/~vcampbe

AFS International Exchange Program
     (Be or host an exchange student)
313 E 43rd Street
New York, NY 10017
800-AFS-INFO

Apprenticeship Alliance (Be or take on an
     apprentice)
151 Potrero Avenue
San Francisco, CA 94103
415-863-8661

Center for INTERIM Programs
PO Box 2347
Cambridge, MA 02238
617-547-0980
E-mail: InterimCIP@aol.com

Invest Yourself (A guide to volunteering
     in North America)
Commission on Voluntary Service
     and Action
PO Box 117
New York, NY 10009
800-444-2524

Student Conservation Association, Inc.
     (Five weeks of work in nature for
     sixteen to nineteen year olds)
689 River Road
PO Box 550
Charlestown, NH 03603-0550
603-543-1700
E-mail: www.sca-inc.org

*The Teenage Liberation Handbook: How to
     Quit School and Get a Real Life and Educa-
     tion,* by Grace Llewellyn (International edi-
     tion available from Element Books in a
     bookstore near you)
Available from Genius Tribe catalog

PRETTY NEAT ODDS AND ENDS

Even more opportunities for your children that defy even the loose categories we've already established. Enjoy!

Amateur Athletic Union (an alternative to government school sports)
800-AAU-4USA
Web site: http://www.aausports.org

Barnes and Noble
Homeschoolers' discount—check local store for details

Harrisville Designs (children's weaving products)
PO Box 806
Harrisville, NH 03450
800-338-9415
Web site: http://www.harrisville.com

Home Again
888-666-0721

Home Education Magazine's Information and Resource Guide (free)
PO Box 3142
Palmer, AK 99645-3142
907-746-1336

Kits 'n Kaboodles
35819 Ramada Lane
Yucalpa, CA 92399
888-338-5487

National Geographic Awareness Week (November)
National Geographic Society
PO Box 98190
Washington, D.C. 20090-8190

National Homeschool Association Travel Directory (for $5 find homeschoolers looking for/offering hosts)

PO Box 290
Hartland, MI 48353
Voice mail: 513-772-9580

Newsweek Education Program (Mention you're a homeschooler and get special rate: 57 cents per issue for 52 issues, plus a 176-page resource of articles from 1933 to1993, and "teaching strategies and activities.")
PO Box 59937
Boulder, CO 80322-9937
800-526-2595

People to People Student Ambassador Program (Two- to three-week adventures for high school and college age)
800-669-7882
E-mail: info@studentambassadors.org
Web site: http://www.studentambassadors.org

Pizza Hut's Book It! Reading Program
800-426-6548

Publish-A-Story Contest (Ages seven through eighteen write a story about how they tackled a difficult situation in their lives. Must be true. February 1 deadline, first prize $1,000.)

Fairview Press
2450 Riverside Avenue S
Minneapolis, MN 55454
Jessica Thoreson 612-672-4311

Toshiba/NSTA Explore Vision Awards
(World's largest K through 12 student science competition for teams of three to four. Prizes to $10,000.)

National Science Teachers Association
1840 Wilson Boulevard
Arlington, VA 22201

(cont.)
800-EXPLOR-9
E-mail: exploravision@nsta.org
Web site: http://www.org/programs/
    exploravision.html

U. S. Chess Federation
3054 NYS Route 9W
New Windsor, NY 12553
800-388-5464
Web site: http://www.uschess.org

World of Science
Homeschoolers' discount—check local
    store for details

Young Astronauts Council
PO Box 65432
Washington, D.C. 20036

INTERNET

Whether you're looking for more books, a support group, legal information, learning ideas, or chats with other homeschoolers, you'll find it— and much, much more.

Homeschool Web Sites

No question, homeschooling has found a home on the Internet. Sites related to teaching your children at home multiply faster than the rabbits in your hutch!

American Homeschool Association
Web site: http://www.home-ed-
    press.com/AHA/aha.html

Catholic Homeschoolers of Texas
Web site: http://www.geocities.com/athens/
    delphi/5329/Index2.html

Discussion Board for Home Educators
    (Kaleidoscapes)
Web site: http://www.kaleidoscapes.com/wwboard

The Education Source
Web site: http://www.edusource.com/ home/html

Exploring Homeschooling with Ann Lahrson
    Fisher
Web site: http://www.teleport.com/~annl/index.shtml

F.U.N. Books
Web site: http://www.iqcweb.com/fun

Home Education Magazine
Web site: http://www.home-ed-press.com

Homeschool Conferences by State (not an extremely complete list but growing)
Web site: http://www.sound.net/~ejcol/
    confer.html

Homeschool Connection
Web site: http://members.aol.com/hsconnect

The Homeschool Connection, Inc.—
    A Professional Consulting Firm
Web site: http://frontpage.inet-
    images.com/hsconnection

Homeschool Headlines
Web site: http://www.homeschoolheadlines.
    com

Homeschool Laws
Web site: http://frontpage.inet-images.com/
    hsconnection/homeschoollaws.htm

Homeschooler's Curriculum Swap
Web site: http://www.theswap.com

Homeschooling on a Shoestring
Web site:
    http://www.geocities.com/Athens/4663/

Homeschooling Today Magazine
Web site: http://www.ebicom.net/
    ~rileyafr/hometoda.htm

Homeschooling Unitarian Universalists and
    Humanists
Web site: http://members.aol.com/
    lrnghppns/index.html

Homeschooling Zone
Web site: http://www.caro.net/~joespa/ guestbk.htm

Home School Headlines
Web site: http://www.homeschoolheadlines.com

Home School Village
Web site: http://www.home-school-village.com

Homeschoolers of Colour Connection
(Canadian, but encourages worldwide
participation)
Web site: http://www3.sympatico.ca/cher

(Cindy Duckert's) Homeschooling Resources
(support group list)
Web site: http://www.alumni.caltech.edu/
~casner/statelist.html

Integrating Scout badge requirements into
homeschooling
Web site: http://www.geocities.com/
Heartland/Plains/7038/ScoutSchool.html

Jon's Homeschool Resource Page
Web site: http://www.midnightbeach.com/hs

The Mining Company's Homeschooling Page
Web site: http://homeschooling.miningco.com

Muslim Homeschool Association
Web site: http://www.ici.net/cust_pages/taadah/
taadah.html

National Homeschool Association
Web site: http://www.alumni.caltech.edu/
~casner/nha.html

Prodigy Home School Resource Guide
Web site: http://pages.prodigy.com/
ct_homeschool/guide.htm

School Is Dead, Learn in Freedom
Web site: http://learninfreedom.org

(Charlene Smith's) Texas Homeschoolers' Alert
and Action Page
Web site: http://www.n-
link.com/~csmith/alert1.htm

Upattinas School and Resource Center
Web site: http://www.chesco.com/
upattinas

The Unschooling Homeschooler
Web site: http://www.islandnet.com/~bedford/
home_lrn.html

Web Sources for the Home-Based Educator
Web site: http://www.integralink.com/
homeschool.html

General Internet Sites for Parents

These sites are not homeschool specific, but they
contain even more information that will enrich
your family's homeschool experience.

The Children's Book Council
Web site: http://www.cbcbooks.org

Consumer Information Catalog
Web site: http://www.pueblo.gas.gov

The Frugal Living Network
Web site: http://shell.kingston.net/~goju/flo

Frugal Living Resources
Web site: http://www.igc.apc.org/frugal

Julie's Frugal Tips
Web site: http://www.brightok.net/~nei/mayo

LearningWare Reviews (software)
Web site: http://members.aol.com/juline

Natural Learning Rhythms
Web site: http://www.wfv.com

Parent Soup
Web site: http://ww.parentsoup.com

Resources for Parents and Teachers
of Blind Kids
Web site: http://www.az.com/~dday/
blindkds.html

Tight-Wadding with Doris O'Connell
Web site: http://pages.prodigy.com/
Tightwadding-frugal-living

E-Mail Lists and Newsletters

The mailing lists and newsletters you can subscribe to by e-mail are terrific sources of information and connection within the homeschooling community. Some of these lists are quite active, which means they can generate a lot of mail.

Please note: Where < > brackets are used to indicate information you must fill in to subscribe, *do not* use the brackets in your reply.

African American Resources Newsletter (list)
To join: Send note to Kriswms@aol.com

American Homeschool Association (newsletter)
To receive: Send note to AHAonline@aol.com

Aut-2b-Home (list)
To join: Send note to tamglsr@sgi.net

The Education Source (newsletter)
To receive: Send note to editor@edusource.com

Eclectic Homeschoolers of Colorado Loop (list)
To join: Send note to EHCL@aol.com

Family Learning Exchange (newsletter)
To join: Send e-mail to editor@flexonline.org
In subject line: Subscribe FLEx Online

Frugal-ed (list)
To join: listproc@listproc.wsu.edu
In body: subscribe frugal-ed <your full name>

Home Education Magazine (newsletter)
To join: majordomo@home-ed-magazine.com
In body: subscribe hem-online-newsletter <your nameadd<your e-mail address>

Home Education Politics (list)
To join: LISTPROC@mainstream.com
In body: SUBSCRIBE HOME-ED-POLITICS <real name>

Homeschooling Unitarian Universalists and Humanists (list)
To join: listproc@uua.org
In body: subscribe HUUH-L <your name>

Jewish Homeschool Network (list)
To join: Send note to Zimra@aol.com

Maxlife (list)
To join: LISTSERV @BROWNVM. BROWN.EDU
In body: subscribe Maxlife <your full name>

Many Paths Homeschoolers
To join: Send note to Barbooch@aol.com or Harperblue@lvnworth.com

Muslim Educators (list)
To join: majordomo@world.std.com
In body: subscribe holdfast <your e-mail address>

Unschooling Gifted Children (list)
To join: ugc-request@Esosoft.com
In body: subscribe homeschool-autism list

State Mailing Lists

These lists serve the same function as those above, with a focus on homeschooling in a particular state.

Alaska Homeschool Network
To join: OldAlaskan@aol.com
In subject line: subscribe AHN

Alaskan Homeschoolers Mailing List
To join: list@beluga.com
In body: join ah

Eclectic Homeschoolers of Colorado Loop
To join: Send note to EHCL@aol.com

Georgia Homeschoolers
To join: LISTSERV@LISTSERV.AOL. COM
In subject line: Subscribe
In body: SUB GeorgiaHomeschoolers <your name>

New Mexico Loop
To join: E-mail HerbNetMom@aol.com and ask to join

Ohio Unschoolers
To join: unschoolers-ohio-request@kjsl.com
In body: subscribe <your name>

Home Educators Resource Organization
    (Oklahoma)
To join: moyerles@wiltel.net
In subject line: subscribe

Oregon Special Interest Group
To join: Retromom@aol.com
In subject line: Oregon SIG

Penn Homeschooler
To join: hub@xc.org
In body: subscribe pa-hs

South Carolina List
To join: listserv@listserv
In subject line: subscribe
In body: subscribe SCHomeschooling
    @listserv.aol.com <your name>

Tennessee Homeschoolers
To join: majordomo@Mailinglist.net
In body: subscribe tennhomeschoolers

Texas Advocates for Freedom in
    Education
To join: taffie-request@jsoft.com
In subject line: info

Washington Home Education Network
To join: Send note to Gardenfev@aol.com

Site-Seeing for Kids

You're going to have to take a break once in a while from all your Net surfing and e-mail looping. Grab the children and check out these terrific sites they're sure to love. They'll lead you to other sites that will lead you to still more sites . . . you get the idea!

Africa Online
Web site: http://www.africaonline.com

The Concord Review
Web site: http://www.tcr.org

The Electronic Zoo
Web site: http://netvet.ustl.edu/e-zoo.htm

Exploratorium
Web site: http://www.exploratorium.edu

Eyewitness—history through the words
    of witnesses
Web site: http://www.iviscom.com/
    index.html

Franklin Institute of Science
Web site: http://sln.fi.edu

Kids Bank
Web site: http://www.kidsbank.com

Lego Site
Web site: http://www.lego.com

Little Explorers
Web site: http://www.EnchantedLearning.com/
    Dictionary.html

Louvre W3
Web site: http://mistral.culture.fr/louvre/
    louvrea.htm

MEGA Mathematics
Web site: http://www.c3.lanl.gov/mega-math

NASA
Web site: http://www.nasa.gov

PBS OnLine
Web site: http://www.pbs.org/welcome.html

Puppet's Page
Web site: http://fox.nstn.ca/~puppets/
    activity.html

Smithsonian Institute Homepage
Web site: http://www.si.edu

Tales of Wonder
Web site: http://itpubs.ucdavis.edu/richard/tales

State Legislative Web Site Links

One of the best ways to preserve the freedom to homeschool is to *stay informed!* When rumors fly about legislation that could potentially bear on homeschoolers, it's best to go directly to the source. The Internet makes this easier than ever, as most states offer links to this information free for the taking.

Many thanks to Laura Derrick, an active homeschool advocate from Texas, for compiling this list. The links are accurate at the time of submission.

Alabama State Legislature
Web site: http://www.asc.edu/archives/legislat/
   legislat.html

Alaska State Legislature
Web site: http://www.legis.state.ak.us

ALIS Home Page (Arizona)
Web site: http://www.azleg.state.az.us

Arkansas General Assembly
Web site: http://www.arkleg.state.ar.us

Official California Legislative Information
Web site: http://www.leginfo.ca.gov

Colorado State Legislature Information
Web site: http://www.state.co.us/gov_dir/
   stateleg.html

Connecticut Legislative Guide
Web site: http://www.ctstateu.edu/state/
   legislative_guide/legis_guide.html

State of Delaware General Assembly
Web site: http://www.state.de.us/research/
   assembly.htm

Online Sunshine—The Florida Legislature
Web site: http://www.leg.state.fl.us

Georgia General Assembly
Web site: http://www.state.ga.us/Legis

Hawaii LRB Library
Web site: http://www.hawaii.gov/lrb/lib.html

Idaho Legislature
Web site: http://www.state.id.us/legislat/legis-
   lat.html

State of Illinois Legislature
Web site: http://www.state.il.us/legis/
   default/htm

Indiana General Assembly
Web site: http://www.state.in.us/iga/
   index.html

Iowa General Assembly
Web site: http://www.legis.state.ia.us

Kansas Legislative Services
Web site: http://www.ink.org/public/
   legislative

Kentucky Legislative Services
Web site: http://www.lrc.state.ky.us/home.htm

Welcome (Louisiana)
Web site: http://www.senate.state.la.us

State of Maine Legislative Home Page
Web site: http://www.state.me.us/legis

Maryland General Assembly Home Page
Web site: http://mlis.state.md.us

The General Court (Massachusetts)
Web site: http://www.magnet.state.ma.us/legis
   /legis.htm

Minnesota State Legislature
Web site: http://www.leg.state.mn.us

Michigan State Legislature
Web site: http://www.migov.state.mi.us/
   legislature.html

Mississippi State Legislature
Web site: http://www.ls.state.ms.us

Missouri General Assembly
Web site: http://www.moga.state.mo.us

Montana Legislative Branch
Web site: http://www.mt.gov/leg/branch/
branch.htm

Nebraska Legislature
Web site: http://unicaml.lcs.state.ne.us

Nevada State Legislature Home Page
Web site: http://www.leg.state.nv.us

New Hampshire General Court
Web site: http://www.state.nh.us/gencourt/
gencourt.htm

New Jersey State Legislature: Home Page
Web site: http://www.njleg.state.nj.us

New Mexico Legislature: Home Page
Web site: http://www.technet.nm.org/
legislature

New York State Assembly—Welcome Page
Web site: http://assembly.state.ny.us

North Carolina General Assembly
Web site: http://ftp.legislature.state.nc.us

North Dakota Legislative Branch
Web site: http://www.state.nd.us/lr

State Front Page: Legislative Branch (Ohio)
Web site: http://www.ohio.gov/ohio/
legislat.htm

Legislature (Oklahoma)
Web site: http://www.state.ok.us/osfdocs/
leghp.html

Oregon State Legislature
Web site: http://www.leg.state.or.us

Pennsylvania Senate WWW Server
Web site: http://www.pasen.gov

Rhode Island General Assembly
Web site: http://www.rilin.state.ri.us

South Carolina General Assembly
Web site: http://www.lpitr.state.sc.us

South Dakota Legislature
Web site: http://www.state.sd.us/state/legis/
lrc/lawstat/lrcmenu.htm

Welcome to the Tennessee General Assembly
Web site: http://www.legislature.state.tn.us

Texas Legislature Online
Web site: http://www.capitol.state.tx.us

Legislature (Utah)
Web site: http://www.state.ut.us/html/
legislature.htm

Vermont Legislative Home Page
Web site: http://www.leg.state.vt.us

Welcome to the Virginia General Assembly
Web site: http://legis.state.va.us

Washington State Legislature
Web site: http://leginfo.leg.wa.gov

West Virigina State Main Page
Web site: http://www.state.wv.us

Wisconsin State Legislature
Web site: http://www.legis.state.wi.us

Wyoming State Legislature
Web site: http://legisweb.state.wy.us

APPENDIX B

Homeschooling Requirements in the United States*

	Statutory language describing nonschool options	Statutory requirements for the home teacher	Does statute give education officials discretion to judge and disallow program?	Does statute require standardized tests for pupil?	Home School or compulsory education law—citations
Alabama	(1) Instruction by tutor; or (2) Qualify as church school	Certification of tutor under option 1 only	Yes, under option 1 only	No	Alabama Code 16-28-3
Alaska	(1) Tutored by certified teacher; or (2) Enrolled in full-time approved correspondence course; or (3) Educational experience approved by LEA**; or (4) Meet requirements for private or religious schools (current SEA policy)	Teacher certificate under option 1	LEA approval under option 3 only	Yes, for options 2 and 4 only; testing at grades 4, 6, and 8	Alaska Statutes 14-30.010; 14.45-120(a)

*Adapted from Patricia Lines, "Homeschooling: An Overview for Education Policy Makers," Working Paper for the U.S. Department of Education, Office of Educational Research and Improvement (Rev. March 1997).

**Abbreviations: "LEA" means local education agency—either a designated official or board at the local level. "SEA" means state education agency and can mean either the state board or the state school chief. "Parent" includes guardians. "H.S." means high school. "NTE" means National Teachers Examination. The phrase "home can be a school" is consistently used to mean that some administrative or judicial authority in the state has ruled that a home can qualify as a private school under the requirements for private schools in the state. This may also be true in other states, but if there is no formal ruling on the matter, it is not included.

	Statutory language describing nonschool options	Statutory requirements for the home teacher	Does statute give education officials discretion to judge and disallow program?	Does statute require standardized tests for pupil?	Home School or compulsory education law—citations
Arizona	Home instruction by parent or other tutor	None	No	No	Ariz. Rev. Stat. 15-802 through 805; 15-745
Arkansas	Home school	None (except for special needs students)	No (sec. 6-15-503(b): Reports to SEA are for statistical purposes only)	Yes. Children seven and older are to take a standardized test from an SEA list; children at age 14 also must take state's eighth-grade minimal competency test. Remediation required if below standard.	Ark. Stat. Ann. 6-18-201, 6-15-501
California	(1) Instruction by tutor; or (2) Independent study arranged through school; or (3) Submit documents as a private school	Tutor's certificate under option 1	No	No	Calif. Educ. Code sec. 48222; 48224; 51745
Colorado	(1) Instructed by certified teacher; or (2) "Home-based education"; or (3) Enrolled in private school that permits independent study at home (*People in re D.B.*, 767 P.2d 801 (Colo. App. 1988)	Teacher certificate under option 1	No	Option 2 (which is structured as an exemption from compulsory requirements) depends on child testing above 13th percentile, at grades 3, 5, 7, 9, and 11. Child has opportunity for re-	Col. Rev. Stat. 22-33-104 and 104.5

State	Definition	Teacher qualifications	SEA approval	Assessment/evaluation requirements	Statute
Connect-icut	"Equivalent" instruction "elsewhere"	None	No	test before exemption is denied. The SEA guidelines recommend a portfolio review; all LEAs require it	Conn. Gen. Stat. Ann. 10-184
Delaware	"Regular and thorough" instruction "elsewhere"	None	Law authorizes SEA to set approval standards, but it does not do so	Law authorizes SEA to require examinations, but SEA does not do so	Delaware Code 14-2702 through 2703
Florida	"Sequentially progressive instruction . . . by . . . parent"	None	No	Law requires an evaluation. It can be by means of testing, portfolio assessment, evaluation by trained third party, or any valid method authorized by the LEA.	Fla. Stat. Ann. 232.01
Georgia	"Home study"	Parent must have H.S. degree or GED; teacher who is not a parent must have college degree	No	Yes, but law specifies that parents are not required to submit test (§20-2-690[7]); reevaluation required if pupil does not show progress after one year of remediation at home	Official Code of Georgia Ann. 20-2-690
Hawaii	(1) "Appropriate alternate educational program"; or	Under option 3, tutor must have	SEA approval required under option 1 only	Yes; standardized testing in grades	Hawaii Rev. Stat. 298-9

	Statutory language describing nonschool options	Statutory requirements for the home teacher	Does statute give education officials discretion to judge and disallow program?	Does statute require standardized tests for pupil?	Home School or compulsory education law—citations
Hawaii *continued*	(2) "Home school" filing certain papers; or (3) Instruction by tutor	B.A. degree		3, 6, 8, and 10	
Idaho	"Comparably instructed"	None	No	No	Idaho Code 33-202
Illinois	School attendance only, but home can be a school; *People v. Levison*, 404 Ill. 574, 90 N.E. 2d 213 (1950)	None	No	No	Ill. Rev. Stat. ch. 122, par. 26-1
Indiana	"Equivalent" instruction	None	No	No	Ind. Stat. Ann. 20-8.1-3-17 and 20-8.1-3-34
Iowa	"Competent private instruction," which the statute defines as instruction for 37 days per quarter, resulting in student progress	Teacher certificate unless parent enrolls child in a home school assistance program or otherwise offers "competent private instruction"	No	Yes, standardized test or other evaluation, including portfolio review. Must be above 30th percentile or make six months progress in year.	Iowa Code Ann. 299A.1
Kansas	School attendance only, but several unpublished court decisions have ruled that home can be a school	None	No	No	Kan. Stat. Ann. 72-1111 through 72-1113

Kentucky	School attendence only, but state board regs. allow home to be a school	None	No	No	Ky. Rev. Stat. 159-010 through 159.990
Louisiana	"Home study"	None	No, so long as parent certifies that the curriculum is equal in quality to that offered in the public schools	Yes, or evaluation by a certified teacher	LA. Rev. Stat. 17:221(A) and 17.236
Maine	"Equivalent instruction through home instruction"	None	SEA approval. Copy of application must go to LEA, which has opportunity to comment	Yes, or evaluation by a certified teacher, an LEA advisory panel, or a home school panel that includes a certified teacher	Me. Rev. Stat. Ann. 20A-5001A
Maryland	"Otherwise receiving regular, thorough instruction" in subjects usually taught in public school	None	No	No (voluntary testing at local public schools)	Ann. Code of Md., ch. 22, 7-301(a)
Massa-chusetts	"Otherwise instructed in a manner approved in advance by the superinten-dent or school committee"	None	LEA approval	Not by statute, but LEA may do so (several evaluation options available)	Mass. Gen. Laws 76-1
Michigan	Nonstatutory option: Attorney General opinion holds home can be a school. A.G. Op. 5579 9/27/79). New statutory option as of July, 1996: A child is in compliance	None	No	No	S.B. 679, Amendment A, signed into Law Jan. 9, 1996 with effective date of July 1, 1996

	Statutory language describing nonschool options	Statutory requirements for the home teacher	Does statute give education officials discretion to judge and disallow program?	Does statute require standardized tests for pupil?	Home School or compulsory education law—citations
Michigan *continued*	with compulsory education laws if he or she is "being educated by his or her parent . . . at . . . home in an organized educational program that is appropriate" to the child's age and ability, and that covers specified subject areas.				
Minnesota	"Home-school" is included in definition of school	(1) Teacher certificate; or (2) Supervised by certified teacher; or (3) Pass teacher competency exam; or (4) Use of accredited program approved by board; or (5) College degree; or (6) Be a parent teaching a child who complies with pupil testing requirements	No	Yes, option 6 only; children below 30th percentile must be evaluated for learning problems	Minn. Stat. Ann. 120.101 and 127.20
Mississippi	Home instruction	None	No	No	Miss. Code Ann. 37-13-91

State	Term	Requirements	Approval	Testing	Citation
Missouri	"Home school"	None	No	No	Ann. Mo. Stat. 167-031 and 167.042
Montana	"Home school"	None	No	No	Mont. Code Ann. 20-5-102 and 20-5-109
Nebraska	School attendance only, but SEA allows home to qualify as (1) An "approved" private school; or (2) "Exempt" private school where parents have sincere religious objection	(1) Teacher certificate; or (2) Meet board standards for exempt private school	No, but SEA approval required for option 1	Statute gives board discretion to require tests but it does not require them	Neb. Rev. Stat. 79-201, 79-1701, 85-607
Nevada	"Equivalent instruction" at home	(1) Teacher certificate; or (2) Parent must consult with certified teacher (requirement waived after one year of pupil progress); or (3) Use approved correspondence program; or (4) Board waiver	No. Statute requires "satisfactory written evidence" of kind approved by SEA, but SEA regs. leave no discretion if specified information is submitted	Not by statute, but SEA regs. requires testing at grades 2, 3, 4, 7, and 8 for options 1 and 2	Nev. Rev. Stat. 392.070
New Hampshire	"Home education," which consists of "planned and	None	SEA approval (sec. 193A)	Yes; or take a district test; or obtain a	N.H. Rev. Stat. Ann. 193:1

	Statutory language describing nonschool options	Statutory requirements for the home teacher	Does statute give education officials discretion to judge and disallow program?	Does statute require standardized tests for pupil?	Home School or compulsory education law—citations
New Hampshire *continued*	supervised instructional and related educational activities . . ."			teacher evaluation or other valid evaluation of child's portfolio	and 193-A
New Jersey	"Equivalent instruction elsewhere"	None	No. LEA limited to verifying subject matter coverage, *Cf. State v. Massa*, 95 N.J. Super. 382, 231 A.2d 252 (Morris County Ct. Law Div. 1967)	No	N.J. Stat. Ann. 18A.38-25
New Mexico	"A home study program that provides a basic academic educational program" operated by parent	High school diploma or equivalent	No	Yes	N.M. Stat. Ann. 22-1-2 and 21-1-2.1
New York	Attendance "elsewhere" and instruction that is "substantially equivalent" by "competent" teacher	Must be "competent"	LEA has authority to determine equivalency	Not by statute, but SEA requires taking test from list of SEA-approved tests	N.Y. Educ. Law 3204, 3205, 3210, 3212
North Carolina	"Home school" serving children from no more than two families	Must be parent or member of household of one of two families forming home	No	Yes; annually	N.C. Gen. Stat. 115C-378, 115C-547, 115C-563 through 565

336

State	Definition	Teacher Qualifications	Notification/Reporting	Testing	Statute
North Dakota	"Home-based instruction"	Parent must be (1) certified; or (2) Have high school education and be supervised by certified teacher; or (3) Pass national teacher exam / school; and have high school degree or equivalent	Parent reports to LEA; may determine if child is making satisfactory progress for children testing below 30th percentile	Yes	N.D. Cent. Code 15-34.1-03 and 15-34.1-04
Ohio	"Instructed at home by a person qualified to teach the branches on which instruction is required . . ."	(1) H.S. degree or equivalent; or (2) Satisfactory test scores showing H.S. equivalence; or (3) Supervised by person with college degree until child shows proficiency on test	LEA approval, as delimited by State Board Regulations	Yes; or evaluation by a certified teacher; an agreed-upon person, or undergo alternative assessment	Ohio Rev. Code 3301-34-04, 3321.03, and 3321.04
Oklahoma	"Other means of education . . . for the full term the schools of the district are in session"	None	No	No	Okla. Stat. Ann., Title 70 10-105(A) and (B)
Oregon	Instruction by a parent or other qualified person	None	No	Yes. Parents may choose among a list of standardized tests.	Oregon Rev. Stat 339.010, 339.030, and 339.035

	Statutory language describing nonschool options	Statutory requirements for the home teacher	Does statute give education officials discretion to judge and disallow program?	Does statute require standardized tests for pupil?	Home School or compulsory education law—citations
Pennsylvania	(1) "Regular daily instruction . . . by a properly qualified private tutor" and satisfactory to district superintendent; or (2) "home education program"	Certificaton for option 1; H.S. degree or equivalent for option 2	LEA approval	Yes, at grades 3, 5, and 8, plus annual evaluation of portfolio by certified teacher or other specified professional	Pa. Stat. Ann., Title 24, 13-1326 and 13-1327
Rhode Island	"At-home instruction approved by the school committee . . ."	None	LEA approval	No, but SEA gives LEA authority to require an evaluation	R.I. Gen. Laws 16-19-1
South Carolina	Parents "may teach their children at home"; must meet specific requirements listed in statute	H.S. degree or equivalent	Approval by LEA, So. Carolina Ass'n. of Indep. Home Schools, or other association with 50 or more members and meets other requirements in statute (state reviews association standards periodically)	Yes	Code of Laws of S.C. Ann. 59-65-10, 40, 45, and 47
South Dakota	"Alternative instruction for an equivalent period of time . . . in the basic skills"	None	If probable cause exists to believe family is not in compliance, SEA may deny status	Yes. Parents may choose any nationally standardized test.	S.D. Comp. Law 13-27-2, 13-27-3 and 49-6-3001
Tennessee	(1) "Home school" "conducted by parents	H.S. degree or GED required to	No	Yes; at grades 2, 5, 7, and 9. If child is 6	Tenn. Code Ann. 49-6-3001 and

338

State	Definition	Teacher qualifications	Approval	Assessment	Citation
	"... for their own children ...''; or (2) Affiliated with and supervised by church school	teach grades K–8, and college degree for grades 7–12 under option 1; no requirement for option 2. SEA has authority to grant exemptions to requirements.		to 9 months behind in core subjects, parent must work with certified teacher to develop remedial course.	49-6-3050
Texas	School attendance, "which includes home schools"	None	No	No	Tex. Educ. Code 4.25, 21.032 through 21.040
Utah	"Taught at home in the subjects prescribed by the state board ..."	None	LEA approval	No	Utah Code Ann. 53A-11-1012
Vermont	A "home study program"	None	SEA approval	Yes; or other assessment among various options listed in statute	Vt. Stat. Ann. Title 16, 1121; 16(11); 166b
Virginia	(1) "Instruction of children by their parents in their home"; or (2) Child enrolled in approved correspondence course; or (3) Program approved by division superintendent; or (4) Bona fide religious objection to school	For option 1, parent must hold college degree, or qualify as teacher	Yes, under option 4	Yes (must achieve 4th stanine on test) or undergo alternative assessment approved by LEA. Law allows 1 year probation if test results are unsatisfactory.	Va. Code 22.1-254.1

	Statutory language describing nonschool options	Statutory requirements for the home teacher	Does statute give education officials discretion to judge and disallow program?	Does statute require standardized tests for pupil?	Home School or compulsory education law—citations
Virginia *continued*	attendance (§22.1–254.1D); or (5) Use of certified teacher				
Washington	"Home-based" instruction with "planned and supervised activities" and which covers basic skills provided by parent to their own children only	(1) Parent has 45 college credits or completes a course on home instruction at a postsecondary institution or a vocational technical institute; or (2) Parent teaches under supervision of state certified teacher; or (3) LEA deems parent qualified to teach	No	Yes; SEA-approved tests taken annually; or annual assessment by a certified person currently working in education	Wash. Rev. Code 28A.200.200; 28A.225.10
West Virginia	(1) "Instruction . . . in the home" or place approved by the LEA and by a "qualified" person; or (2) File report on home school program	Under option 1, home teacher must be qualified to teach public elementary school. Under option 2, teacher must have a H.S. degree and a) 4 years formal education above the	Yes, under option 1; no, under option 2	Yes. In addition, SEA has authority to adopt guidelines for alternative assessments for special education students.	W. Va. 18-18-1

State	Definition	Teacher Qualification	Approval Required	Testing/Assessment	Statute
		pupil's; or b) achieve acceptable score on NTE.			
Wisconsin	"Homebased educational program provided . . . by the child's parents . . . or by a person designated by the parent . . . ."	None	No	No	Wis. Stat. Ann. 118.15 and 118.165
Wyoming	"Basic academic education program" at home, and approved by LEA	None	Yes	No	Wyo. Stat. 21-4-101

Other Jurisdictions:

Jurisdiction	Definition	Teacher Qualification	Approval Required	Testing/Assessment	Statute
District of Columbia	"Equivalent" instruction	None	Yes	No	D.C. Code 31-401 and 402
American Samoa	No statutory provision	If qualifying as private school, certified teacher required	Yes, if qualifying as private school	No	American Samoa Code 16.0302 through 16.0308
Guam	Home instruction by parent or tutor	None	No, but Guam board rules require approval	No, but Guam board regulations require testing or other assessment	Guam Code Ann. Tit. 17, 6101 through 6109
Virgin Islands	Home instruction by parent	None	Commissioner of Education must approve program and teacher	No, but Dept. of Education meets with parents and children quarterly	V.I. Code Ann. Tit. 17, 81 through 97

341

	Statutory language describing nonschool options	Statutory requirements for the home teacher	Does statute give education officials discretion to judge and disallow program?	Does statute require standardized tests for pupil?	Home School or compulsory education law—citations
Puerto Rico	No statutory provision	None for private schools	None for private schools	No	P.R. laws Ann. Tit. 18, secs. 71–81
Northern Marianas	Home study	To be set by board	Yes	No	Mariana Code 3-1141

Author's Notes on Table

- The table is based on statutory analysis; check with your State Board of Education to verify information or to obtain up-dated information.

- Column three, "Does statute require approval" indicates that approval is needed if the SEA or LEA has authority to do something more than simply verify that the required documents are filed and provide the required information. Note all states except Texas and Oklahoma have mandatory or voluntary filing requirements. Typically, a parent must provide the name, age, grade of child instructed, and often material on the curriculum are part of information reported. Many states identify the form as a "notice of intent to home school."

- The table does not include information applicable to all children, whether in home school or other school, e.g., age of compulsory education, and durational requirements for the school day and school year. Most states mandate the same requirements for all children, regardless of where they are educated.

- The table does not attempt to resolve legal ambiguities. Where a state or local education agency adopts rules that are not specifically authorized by the statute, there is always a question of the extent to which the rules are authorized. The table does not attempt to indicate the situation where the agency is the source of a policy, if only to note the possibility of a legal challenge. Of course, a board with express authority to approve a home program will be in a better position to defend its more stringent requirements.

Index

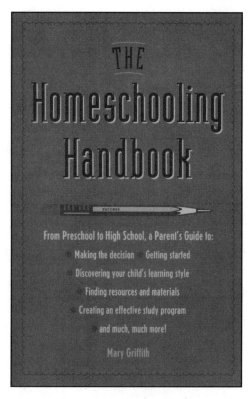